Rising to the Challenge: China's Grand Strategy and International Security

Studies in Asian Security

A SERIES SPONSORED BY THE EAST-WEST CENTER WASHINGTON

Muthiah Alagappa, Chief Editor

The aim of the Asian Security series is to promote analysis, understanding, and explanation of the dynamics of domestic, transnational, and international security challenges in Asia. The peer-reviewed books in this series will analyze contemporary security issues and problems to clarify debates in the scholarly and policy communities, provide new insights and perspectives, and identify new research and policy directions related to conflict management and security in Asia. Security is defined broadly to include the traditional political and military dimensions as well as the non-traditional dimensions that affect the survival and well being of political communities. Asia, too, is defined broadly, to include Northeast, Southeast, South, and Central Asia.

Designed to encourage original and rigorous scholarship, books in the Asian Security series seek to engage scholars, educators, and practitioners. Wide-ranging in scope and method, the series welcomes an extensive array of paradigms, programs, traditions, and methodologies now employed in the social sciences.

*   *   *

The East-West Center, with offices in Honolulu, Hawaii, and in Washington, D.C., is a public, nonprofit educational and research institution established by the U.S. Congress in 1960 to foster understanding and cooperation among the governments and peoples of the Asia-Pacific region, including the United States.

Rising to the Challenge

China's Grand Strategy and International Security

Avery Goldstein

SPONSORED BY THE EAST-WEST CENTER WASHINGTON

Stanford University Press • Stanford, California

Published with the partial support of the
Sasakawa Peace Foundation (USA)

Stanford University Press
Stanford, California

Printed in the United States of America

Library of Congress Cataloging-in-Publication Data

Goldstein, Avery
   Rising to the challenge : China's grand strategy and international security / Avery
Goldstein.
      p. cm. — (Studies in Asian security)
   Includes bibliographical references and index.
   ISBN 0-8047-5138-2 (cloth : alk. paper) — 0-8047-5218-4 (pbk. : alk. paper)
   1. China—Foreign relations—1976-.   I. Title: China's grand strategy and
international security.   II. Title.   III. Series.

DS779.27.G65   2005
355'.033051—dc22   2004030097

This book is printed on acid-free, archival-quality paper.

Original printing 2005

Last figure below indicates year of this printing:
14   13   12   11   10   09   08   07   06

Typeset at Stanford University Press in 10/13 Bembo

For Karen

Acknowledgments

In addition to the publications cited, this book draws on approximately 125 hours of interviews the author conducted in Beijing (85 hours in June–July 1998, March–April and October 2000, and March 2003), Shanghai (15 hours in June–July 2001), Washington, D.C. (10 hours in February 2000), and Tokyo (15 hours in March 1999). I thank all of my interlocutors and their institutions for their hospitality.

The interview subjects, all promised confidentiality, were civilian officials and military officers, as well as advisers and independent analysts. In Tokyo, these included individuals affiliated with the Ministry of Foreign Affairs, the Nomura Institute, the Okazaki Institute, and Japan's self-defense forces, as well as journalists and academics. In Beijing, these included individuals affiliated with the Ministry of Foreign Affairs, the Ministry of National Defense, the PLA's Academy of Military Sciences, the PLA's National Defense University, the China Institute for International Strategic Studies, the China Institute for Contemporary International Relations, the Foundation for International and Strategic Studies, the China Institute of International Studies, the China Society for Strategy and Management Research, four institutes within the Chinese Academy of Social Sciences (the Institute of American Studies, Institute for the Study of World Politics and Economics, Institute for Asia-Pacific Studies, and Institute of East European, Russian, and Central Asian Studies), Beijing University, Qinghua University, and the Foreign Affairs College. In Shanghai, these included individuals at the Shanghai Academy of Social Sciences, the Shanghai Institute for International Studies, the Shanghai Institute for International Strategic Studies, the School of International Relations and Public Affairs and Center for American Studies at Fudan University, the Center for RimPac Strategic and International Studies, and the Pudong Institute for the US Economy.

For helpful comments, criticisms, and suggestions at various stages in this book's development, I thank Muthiah Alagappa, Jean-Marc Blanchard, Tom Christensen, Iain Johnston, Jonathan Kirshner, Ed Mansfield, Pat McDonald, Evan Medeiros, Samantha Ravitch, Alan Romberg, David Rousseau, Michael Swaine, Tang Wei, and several anonymous reviewers. I also thank Tang Wei, Cheng Chen, and Yanbo Wang for their research assistance. Once again, I have had the good fortune to work with Muriel Bell and John Feneron at Stanford University Press. They have provided invaluable editorial assistance and advice. I am especially indebted to Sharron Wood for her masterly copyediting.

I gratefully acknowledge the financial support this project received from the Smith Richardson Foundation, the East West Center, and the Research Foundation and the Center for East Asian Studies at the University of Pennsylvania. Earlier versions of some of the material in this book appeared in articles published in the journals *International Security*, *China Quarterly*, and *Orbis*, and in a chapter of *International Relations Theory and the Asia-Pacific* (Columbia University Press). This material is included here with their permission.

As ever, my work has benefited in immeasurable ways from the support of my family, including my wife, Karen Tulis, our children, Julia and Loren, and our dog, Dreyfus.

Contents

**Rising to the Challenge: China's Grand Strategy
and International Security**

1

Introduction

At the start of the twenty-first century, China and the United States teetered on the brink of a new Cold War. In early 2001 such an outcome seemed nearly inevitable as the two countries found themselves locked in a bitter dispute about the collision of an American reconnaissance aircraft and a Chinese fighter jet that left the Chinese pilot dead and the U.S. crew in Chinese custody. Within weeks, however, the incident that had touched raw nerves on both sides was defused, and within months Sino-American relations showed clear signs of recovery. U.S. trade representative Robert Zoellick visited China and signaled continued American support for China's accession to the World Trade Organization. Secretary of State Colin Powell soon followed to lay the groundwork for a state visit by President Bush that was scheduled for October 2001, coinciding with his participation in the APEC meetings to be held in Shanghai. Although the terrorist attacks against the United States on September 11, 2001, led President Bush to modify his plans so that he met China's leaders only briefly during a short stay at the APEC session, the initiation of the war on terrorism also accelerated the trend toward improving Sino-American relations that had been evident since the early summer.

Yet even as the rhetoric of cooperation replaced that of conflict, both sides in this bilateral relationship clearly remained wary. Unlike the dramatic transformation in an initially cool Russo-American relationship that was begun by meetings between U.S. president Bush and Russia's president Putin during 2001, the tangible changes in Sino-American relations during 2001 were modest, tentative, and provisional. Potentially dangerous disagreements remained unresolved, and mutual suspicion about future capabilities and intentions endured. In short, the prospect of a renewed chill in relations hovered not very far in the background. Though it no longer seemed inevitable, a Sino-American Cold War remained possible.

Perhaps the tenuous nature of this bilateral relationship now seems un-
surprising, yet when the current era of international politics began to emerge
at the end of the 1980s, few anticipated such fragility in Sino-American relations. On the contrary, optimism about an emerging "new world order"
that prevailed as the Cold War was ending, and nearly two decades of basically friendly ties between Beijing and Washington, instead seemed to bode
well for the immediate future. In a sense, however, the strains that quickly
emerged during the 1990s are easy to understand. They reflected changes in
the international situation that accompanied the end of a Soviet-American rivalry that had dominated world affairs for four decades. The bedrock of Sino-
American cooperation since 1972, after all, had been a shared interest in opposing a hostile and threatening U.S.S.R. As diplomacy eased the Soviet
threat to both China and the United States during the 1980s, and especially as
the U.S.S.R. itself collapsed in the early 1990s, the solid military-strategic
foundation of self-interest that had encouraged Sino-American entente crum-
bled. When it did, areas of disagreement once obscured resurfaced. Without a
common strategic purpose binding Beijing and Washington, the remaining
incentives for cooperation were mainly mutual economic interests and shared
perspectives on a few, less pressing, regional and international security concerns (most notably maintaining peace in Korea, fighting transnational crime,
and preventing nuclear proliferation). Though these shared interests were far
from trivial, after 1989 they were not sufficiently compelling in themselves to
offset old differences that had been kept at a relatively low simmer during the
final two decades of the Cold War while both parties focused on the need to
deal with the more parlous threat from Moscow. Nor were remaining common interests sufficiently compelling to offset new differences that emerged at
the end of the Cold War, differences that reflected both China's growing capabilities and the transformed international system. The combination of resurfacing old and newly emerging areas of disagreement provided the back-
drop for a change in the character of the Sino-American relationship that began in the last decade of the twentieth century. The change in the Sino-
American relationship also provided the most important impetus for China to
embrace the grand strategy on which it settled after the mid-1990s and that is
the focus of this book's subsequent chapters.

Old Sino-American Differences Reemerge

Political

In classic realpolitik fashion, during the 1970s and 1980s both Washington
and Beijing had been willing to set aside deep-seated political-ideological dif-

ferences as they faced a common enemy. Washington believed that the strate-gic benefits of cooperation with China justified overlooking the distastefulness of its authoritarian communist partner. Similarly, the Chinese regime (radical-ly socialist during the era of Mao Zedong, economically pragmatic but polit-ically still committed to Leninism under Deng Xiaoping) believed that the need for a military counter to Soviet capabilities it could not parry justified cooperation with the ideologically unappealing champion of capitalist de-mocracy (intermittently lambasted as a hegemonic superpower).

After 1989, however, ideological preferences on both sides were no longer overshadowed by pressing concerns about a common enemy. As differences resurfaced, they weakened the bonds of Sino-American entente. Widespread antigovernment protests in China during April and May 1989, as well as the unfolding collapse of communist regimes in the Soviet empire, induced new fears among the leaders in Beijing. They no longer saw the United States pri-marily as a valuable military counterweight to a powerful and threatening su-perpower neighbor. Instead, in a throwback to rhetoric of the 1950s, they once again saw America as the leading advocate for a strategy of "peaceful evolution" (*heping yanbian*) designed to end communist rule in China as it was being ended elsewhere.[1]

At the same time, Washington's late Cold War view of China as a helpful and hard-working strategic partner against the Soviet menace was decisively transformed when the leaders of the Chinese Communist Party decided to respond to the popular demonstrations in 1989 by declaring martial law in May and then resorting to the use of lethal force on the evening of June 3–4. Overnight, a broadly positive American perception of China—regularly bol-stered by the public relations barrage surrounding successive summits between the two giants of Chinese communism, Mao Zedong and Deng Xiaoping, and American presidents from Nixon through the elder Bush—was de-stroyed.[2] After June's bloody clashes in Beijing, the favorable image that had

---

[1] During the crisis of spring 1989, the conservative leaders who ultimately decided to resort to force to ensure an end to popular protests repeatedly insisted that the dem-onstrations were not only inspired by but also supported by foreign opponents of CCP rule. See Andrew J. Nathan and Perry Link, *The Tiananmen Papers*. China's leaders first discussed the threat of foreign-inspired "peaceful evolution" in the 1950s. See Qiang Zhai, "Mao Zedong and Dulles's 'Peaceful Evolution' Strategy: Revelations from Bo Yibo's Memoirs."

[2] Despite broadly positive Sino-American relations from 1972 to 1989 there were important ups and downs. Domestic politics in each country and unresolved bilateral disagreements repeatedly challenged the leaders on each side, who nonetheless man-aged to preserve and gradually strengthen Sino-American ties. See Robert S. Ross,

helped ensure broad bipartisan support for U.S. China policy was quickly re-placed by the perception that China was an old-style authoritarian communist regime whose brutality could not be overstated. However complex the reality of China in the reform era might be, the widely replayed image of the lone Chinese citizen standing his ground in front of a tank deployed to enforce martial law in Beijing was burned into the conscience of Americans and es-tablished an unfavorable view of the PRC. In the ensuing months this new negative American perception of China hardened as it became clear that the leaders in Beijing were determined to resist the dramatic political changes sweeping most of the rest of the communist world.

Taiwan

Realpolitik concerns about threatening Soviet power during the 1970s and 1980s had also encouraged both Washington and Beijing to contain their long-standing disagreement about the future of Taiwan. The issue dated to President Truman's reversal of his decision, after the failure of the Marshall Mission, to terminate U.S. involvement in China's civil war. When the Ko-rean War erupted in June 1950, the United States recommitted its military in support of Chiang Kai-shek's regime, still claiming to be the Republic of China (ROC) in temporary exile on Taiwan. In what was seen as a global Cold War, containment of the Soviet-led communist bloc entailed also the containment of "Red China." As the United States embraced this new grand strategy in 1950, the ROC, which Washington had recently abandoned as a hopelessly corrupt regime in its death throes, was redefined as a loyal and po-tentially important ally on the Far Eastern front of the international struggle against communism.[3] The U.S. decision to forge new ties to the regime on Taiwan during the first decade of the Cold War established a commitment that became a major obstacle to improving American relations with the PRC even when Beijing and Washington both developed a strong interest in doing so during the late 1960s.

Negotiating Cooperation: The United States and China, 1969–1989; James H. Mann, *About Face: A History of America's Curious Relationship with China, from Nixon to Clinton*; Pat-rick Tyler, *A Great Wall: Six Presidents and China—An Investigative History*.

[3] On the domestic political reasons why it was essential to rely on more or less indis-criminate anti-communist mobilization to ensure support for the burden that Truman believed the United States would have to shoulder in Europe, see Thomas J. Chris-tensen, *Useful Adversaries: Grand Strategy, Domestic Mobilization, and Sino-American Con-flict, 1947–1958*. On the complexities of changing U.S. policy toward China and Tai-wan during this period, see Alan D. Romberg, *Rein in at the Brink of the Precipice: American Policy toward Taiwan and U.S.-PRC Relations*, chapter 1.

Internal deliberations in both capitals after 1969 and then a delicate and highly secretive period of bilateral negotiation did finally enable the United States and China to finesse their differences about Taiwan's status, but the issue remained one on which the parties fundamentally disagreed.[4] Strong parallel strategic interests induced Beijing and Washington to devise artful language addressing the delicate issue in the Shanghai Communiqué that capped President Nixon's pioneering visit to China in February 1972. And over the next decade, determined efforts generated two more communiqués that served as the diplomatic keystones of Sino-American relations. By its nature, however, that artful language actually permitted each side to adhere to its own perspective on the issue. The communiqués enabled each to believe that an interest in cooperating against the Soviets had not required it to abandon its bottom line on Taiwan—for China, that unification would occur; for the United States, that China would not use force to achieve this goal.

Even so, during the period of Sino-American entente that followed Nixon's breakthrough, disagreements about Taiwan were barely contained. Beijing was willing to proclaim its preference for peaceful reunification, but consistently refused to renounce what it claimed was a sovereign right to use force to ensure the nation's territorial integrity. It also repeatedly criticized Washington's continued support for Taiwan (especially the sale of military equipment) as counterproductive interference in China's domestic affairs. And though Washington was willing to proclaim that it accepted the principle that there was only one China and to acknowledge Beijing's position that Taiwan was a part of China (but not to explicitly recognize Beijing's claim),[5] it also

---

[4] For recently declassified documents covering early discussions about Taiwan, see "The Beijing-Washington Back-Channel and Henry Kissinger's Secret Trip to China, September 1970–July 1971."

[5] Rather than explicitly recognizing Beijing's position that "there is only one China and Taiwan is a part of China," the U.S. position set forth in the 1972 Shanghai Communiqué was: "The U.S. side declared: The United States acknowledges that all Chinese on either side of the Taiwan Strait maintain there is but one China and that Taiwan is a part of China. The United States Government does not challenge that position." The Chinese version of that communiqué used "*renshidao*" for "acknowledge," which has a similar meaning. The Chinese version of the 1979 communiqué establishing formal diplomatic relations, however, used the term "*chengren*," which connotes acceptance or recognition, even though the English version stuck with "acknowledge." For a careful parsing of this complex matter, see Romberg, *Rein in at the Brink of the Precipice*, pp. 99–101. For the U.S. versions of the communiqués, see "Joint Communiqué of the United States of America and the People's Republic of China (Shanghai Communiqué)"; "Joint Communiqué on the Establishment of Diplomatic Relations between the People's Republic of China and the United States of America." For

regularly asserted that American policy was nevertheless based on the premise that cross-strait relations would remain peaceful. Thus, while endorsing a diplomatic resolution of tensions, U.S. policy also included varying degrees of military support for Taipei, allegedly to preserve strategic stability that would both reduce the temptation for Beijing to use force against the island and provide incentives for it to search for a negotiated solution. The American stance was formalized in the Taiwan Relations Act of April 1979, which established a basis in U.S. law for continuing arms sales to Taiwan even after Washington switched diplomatic recognition of the government of China from Taipei to Beijing on January 1, 1979.

The creative word choices used in the separate Chinese- and English-language versions of the three communiqués that guided bilateral relations during the period of Sino-American entente partially obscured the salience of continuing disagreements about Taiwan. In the end, however, it was not the creativity of communiqué writers but rather the pressing political-strategic interest in anti-Soviet cooperation that had made it possible to set aside Sino-American differences about a matter whose problematic resolution both were willing to postpone.[6] When the political commitment rooted in shared strategic interests dimmed, the disputes about cross-strait relations reintensified, especially because the Taiwan issue became entwined with broader Chinese and American political and military disagreements in the post–Cold War world.

By the 1990s, Taiwan had been transformed. It was no longer simply the redoubt of the desperate losers in China's Civil War of the mid-twentieth century to whom the United States had once made a Cold War treaty commitment. The island had first become one of Asia's successful "newly industrialized countries" and then one of Asia's remarkable "newly democratized countries." For Beijing, the political implications of democratization on prosperous Taiwan were potentially threatening. When foreign observers touted reforms on the island as proof that democracy and Chinese culture were not

---

the Chinese versions, see "Zhonghua Renmin Gongheguo He Meilijian Hezhongguo Lianhe Gongbao"; "Zhonghua Renmin Gongheguo He Meilijian Hezhongguo Guanyu Jianli Waijiao Guanxi De Lianhe Gongbao." See also Thomas J. Christensen, "New Challenges and Opportunities in the Taiwan Strait: Defining America's Role," p. 7.

[6] The time frame for solving this problem seems to have been different for each side. Mao and Deng spoke in vague terms about solutions being discovered many decades into the future; Henry Kissinger anticipated the possibility that the United States might have to accept Beijing's position on the status of Taiwan within just a few years. See "The Beijing-Washington Back-Channel and Henry Kissinger's Secret Trip to China, September 1970–July 1971."

incompatible, the leaders of the Chinese Communist Party (CCP) saw the invidious comparison with the mainland as another facet in the American post–Cold War strategy of peaceful evolution designed to subvert their regime. Beijing's political concern was compounded by military concerns as American arms sales to Taipei remained robust after the 1980s, contrary to China's expectation that they would gradually decline in quantity and quality according to the terms of the third Sino-American communiqué (August 17, 1982).[7] During the 1990s, Beijing saw such sales as a part of an unfolding strategy to ring the PRC with a network of U.S.-backed allies, complementing the continued forward presence of American military forces in the western Pacific.

For Washington, political reforms on Taiwan during the 1990s rekindled interest in the security of the island as part of the world's enlarging community of democracies. American leaders saw this trend as desirable not merely because it validated the universality of U.S. ideals, but also because it served practical national interests in peace and stability. American leaders in the 1990s had come to embrace the proposition that democracies do not fight wars with one another; consequently, enlarging the community of democracies enlarged the "zone of peace."[8] Perhaps more importantly, as Beijing grew nervous about the prospects for unification and the possibility of a Taiwanese lurch toward independence, it had begun to strengthen its ability to act on the military option that it had never renounced. As will be described in subsequent chapters, such military modernization focused on the Taiwan contingency after the minicrisis of 1995–96, and this in turn aggravated a larger American concern that developed in the mid-1990s about potential military problems an increasingly powerful China might pose for U.S. interests in East Asia.

Lingering disagreements about political ideology and Taiwan served as important triggers for the deterioration of Sino-American relations after the Cold War. U.S. attempts to pressure China to make domestic political changes (promoting democracy and human rights) were threats because Beijing saw them as a challenge to the internal stability the CCP insisted was necessary for the economic growth that would lead to China's modernization. American policy toward Taiwan was viewed as part of a U.S.-led effort to frustrate China's ability to ensure its vital national interest. Ultimately, however, the redefinition and renewed significance of political ideology and the Taiwan problem in Sino-American relations reflected a growing mutual suspicion

[7] See "Joint Communiqué between the People's Republic of China and the United States of America (China-U.S. August 17 Communiqué)."

[8] See chapter 3 for a discussion of the academic debate about interdemocratic peace.

about capabilities and intentions. Within just a few years after the end of the Cold War, the United States had begun to worry that a rising China might challenge the existing security order in the Asia-Pacific that rested on American preponderance and leadership. And China had begun to worry that the preponderant United States was determined to prevent it from legitimately exercising international influence commensurate with its growing capabilities to shape a new post–Cold War order in the region.

With the transformation of the old international system and emerging concerns about the nature of the new one, Sino-American cooperation increasingly gave way to Sino-American conflict at the end of the twentieth century. Although the mix of cooperation and conflict in bilateral relations clearly shifted toward the latter, U.S.-China relations were not yet driving a new Cold War. Still, it seemed increasingly likely that the real question was not whether sharp rivalry could be avoided, but rather whether it could be managed so that the United States and China could avoid becoming implacable adversaries. The answer to that question remains elusive and will ultimately depend on the choices that leaders in Washington and Beijing make. In subsequent chapters, I mainly examine China's choices—its emerging strategy for coping with the security challenges it perceives. But because Beijing views the role that a preponderant United States plays to be the single greatest international constraint it faces in pursuing its interests, before closely analyzing China's choices, I offer a few brief observations about the American side of the relationship. By the end of the 1990s, the United States loomed ever larger in China's calculations not only because of the unmatched capabilities the world's sole remaining superpower deployed, but also because of the extent to which Washington's strategic-military attention had begun to shift away from Europe and toward Asia.

U.S. Grand Strategy Reconsidered

As George W. Bush had promised during the 2000 presidential election campaign, upon assuming office his administration initiated a sweeping strategic review.[9] The new vision it suggested, and the reallocation of resources it im-

[9] For the thinking of national security experts close to the Bush campaign, see Condoleezza Rice, "Campaign 2000—Promoting the National Interest"; and Eliot A. Cohen, "Defending America in the Twenty-First Century." The three key documents that would emerge during the first two years of the Bush administration were the "Quadrennial Defense Review Report"; "The National Security Strategy of the United States of America"; and "The Nuclear Posture Review." The last of these remains classified, but for a description of its contents, see Bradley Graham and Walter

plied, aimed to deal with the alleged obsolescence of a military posture whose basic contours had been shaped by forty years of Cold War struggle. Although the review was not narrowly focused on China, one of its major themes—the call for a shift in America's global priorities—had a direct bearing on the United States' China policy. The September 11 terrorist strikes against the United States altered the focus of the review to new missions and priorities, but they also reinforced the determination to transform the American military in ways that the Pentagon under Defense Secretary Donald Rumsfeld had already anticipated.

After the decline and collapse of the Soviet empire, the American military had initially continued to focus on European contingencies that imagined a revived Russian threat. By the mid-1990s, however, it became clear that for the foreseeable future Russia would have difficulty simply retaining its credentials as a great power, and in any case it would remain at a substantial military and geopolitical disadvantage relative to a robust, indeed expanding, NATO. Although U.S. military planners soon came to accept the implausibility of a revived superpower threat originating in Moscow, during the 1990s changes in the American force posture (mainly reductions in aggregate spending and deployments) were remarkably modest. The experience of the Persian Gulf War of 1990–91 did result in a shift in contingency planning, with the emphasis placed on the need to prepare to respond nearly simultaneously to "two major regional conflicts." But although planning incorporated new weapons systems and underscored the novel logistical challenges of far-flung operations, it essentially mandated a modified Cold War–style military for the United States.[10]

By the late 1990s, however, critics (especially those who advocated embracing the "revolution in military affairs") viewed this posture and the regional contingencies to which it was geared as dated in two respects. First, as the conventional capabilities of the prospective adversaries that motivated the strategy atrophied, the likelihood of the scenarios it envisioned (major ground wars in the Persian Gulf and on the Korean peninsula) diminished. The more likely military challenge for the United States would be attempts by Iraq or North Korea to threaten the use of weapons of mass destruction. As a result, the United States would need to shift from preparing to deploy heavy ar-

---

Pincus, "Nuclear Targeting Draft Shifts Focus From Russia; More Emphasis Given to China, N. Korea, Mideast"; Michael R. Gordon, "U.S. Nuclear Plan Sees New Weapons and New Targets."

[10] See William W. Kaufmann and John D. Steinbruner, *Decisions for Defense: Prospects for a New Order;* William W. Kaufmann, *Assessing the Base Force: How Much Is Too Much?*

mored combat divisions to exploiting advanced weapons technology (missile defenses, smart bombs, superior intelligence and logistics) to cope with the risks such states might pose if already potent deterrent threats of punishment failed to dissuade them. Second, there was a sense that early post–Cold War strategic planning had paid insufficient attention to the growing strategic significance of Asia in general and China in particular.[11]

In this context, the Bush administration commenced a strategic review in 2001 coordinated by Defense Secretary Donald Rumsfeld (and reportedly inspired by the intellect of Andrew Marshall). To the extent the review identified China as the most plausible great power concern for U.S. planners and potentially the most dangerous adversary that should guide thinking about the military, economic, and political means that best ensure U.S. interests in the world's most dynamic region, it had all the markings of an American grand strategy for the twenty-first century. When the 9/11 strikes occurred, however, long-range planning to deal with prospective threats took a backseat to the immediate need to deal with existing dangers. Did the shift to an emphasis on the war against terrorism and denying potential state sponsors of terrorism weapons of mass destruction also signal an end to the reorientation of American strategy that was paying greater attention to East Asia?

American planners certainly face a daunting challenge from nonstate terrorist groups and some of their potential state sponsors, both because these enemies may be hard to find (in the case of terrorists) and because they may operate according to a calculus that is not much affected by traditional worldly considerations of blood and treasure (this applies both to terrorists and allegedly to the leaders of "rogue" states).[12] But however nettlesome these strategic problems may be, the threat that such adversaries pose to the United States is hardly comparable in scale or scope to the threat a great power adversary could pose. In contrast with the security concerns motivating current U.S. military actions in the global war on terrorism, the stakes in the mid-twentieth-century struggle against the Axis powers (which motivated an anti-fascist united front strategy) and the Cold War struggle with the Soviet Union (which motivated a strategy of containment), for example, were clearly much higher, more wide-ranging, and, especially in the latter case, perhaps existen-

---

[11] Although critics questioned the Clinton administration's China policy, it had not ignored Asia's importance. On the contrary, after an early post–Cold War interlude of uncertainty, it clearly articulated the U.S. determination to remain fully involved in Asian security affairs. See the East Asian Security Reports the U.S. Department of Defense issued in 1995 and 1998 (*The United States Security Strategy for the East Asia-Pacific Region*).

[12] See "The National Security Strategy of the United States of America."

tial.[13] It would be unusual, then, if an American grand strategy for the twenty-first century did not at least consider the possibility of such great power threats emerging, threats that could overshadow the currently pressing concern about terrorist networks and middle-power rogue states. Not surprisingly, therefore, even as the Bush administration's quadrennial defense review and its resulting national security strategy appropriately increased the attention paid to immediate dangers, it also carried through with the anticipated focus on the strategic implications of a rising China.[14] How does the new strategy envision dealing with what it sees as the most plausible potential great power challenge to international American interests?

The United States has ostensibly adopted a hybrid strategy combining elements from the alternatives of "containment" and "engagement" that had dominated the debate about China policy in the 1990s.[15] Current policy hedges against substantial uncertainty about China's future capabilities and intentions (the concern of those who had advocated straightforward containment) while seeking to avoid an unfortunate self-fulfilling prophecy of mutual hostility (the fear of those who had argued for engagement). Insofar as it prepares for the possibility that China might pose a threat (mainly military) to the interests of the United States and its allies in Asia against which Washington must hold the line, the present approach taps the logic of containment. Insofar as it endorses a proactive policy (mainly economic) designed to nurture elements within China who would define their nation's interests in ways that are largely compatible with the interests of the United States and its allies, the present approach taps the logic of engagement.[16]

Does this hybrid policy toward China, one that some have labeled "congagement," serve U.S. strategic interests in the early twenty-first century? By definition, strategy is always about interdependent choice. The wisdom of a grand strategy drafted in Washington cannot be assessed without some insight

[13] Although the history of international relations suggests that the actual mortality rate for states in the modern world has been remarkably low, the fear that another state might be able to determine their political fortunes has led most states to act as if their survival were at stake.

[14] See "Quadrennial Defense Review Report"; see also "The National Security Strategy of the United States of America"; Gordon, "U.S. Nuclear Plan Sees New Weapons and New Targets." On the remaining, if muted, focus on China as a potential threat in the Quadrennial Defense Review, and its implications for U.S. policy in the longer term, see Wu Xinbo, "The Promise and Limitations of a Sino-U.S. Partnership."

[15] See David Shambaugh, "Containment or Engagement of China: Calculating Beijing's Responses"; Gerald Segal, "East Asia and the 'Constrainment' of China."

[16] See Zalmay M. Khalilzad et al., *The United States and a Rising China: Strategic and Military Implications*, pp. 72–75.

into the approach being embraced in Beijing. Put differently, to grasp the implications of Washington's strategy, it is essential to anticipate Beijing's response. Is congagement more likely than containment or engagement to discourage a Chinese challenge and encourage Chinese cooperation? The answer, of course, cannot be known in advance. But while scholars may be willing to wait, leaders will have to act and, therefore, seek answers that will help them craft prudent policy. As they do so, familiarity with China's perceptions of its own interests and anticipation of its most likely reactions to U.S. policy are crucial.

To this end, the remainder of this book explores the broad contours of China's grand strategy at the start of the twenty-first century. It examines how the regime in Beijing is pursuing what it sees as China's interests in light of the country's growing capabilities and the constraints of the international context within which they must operate. It argues that after an unsettled period of several years, during which China was dealing with the new challenges that accompanied the end of the Cold War, by 1996 a rough consensus on a basic foreign policy line began to emerge among China's top leaders, a consensus that constitutes a de facto grand strategy guiding the country's international behavior. The grand strategy aims to engineer China's rise to great power status within the constraints of a unipolar international system that the United States dominates. It is designed to sustain the conditions necessary for continuing China's program of economic and military modernization as well as to minimize the risk that others, most importantly the peerless United States, will view the ongoing increase in China's capabilities as an unacceptably dangerous threat that must be parried or perhaps even forestalled. China's grand strategy, in short, aims to increase the country's international clout without triggering a counterbalancing reaction.

The basic approach to implementing this grand strategy that the leaders in Beijing settled on during the late 1990s is detailed in subsequent chapters. At its core are two components. One is diplomacy that focuses on establishing various types of partnerships with other major powers. This effort aims to create linkages that make China an indispensable, or at least very attractive, actor on whose interests the system's key actors are reluctant to trample. The other component is an activist international agenda designed to establish China's reputation as a responsible member of the international community and mute widespread concerns about how Beijing is likely to employ its growing capabilities, thus reducing the incentives for others to unite in opposition to China.[17]

Why have China's leaders settled on this approach to guide their foreign

[17] For a brief discussion of many of these changes, see M. Taylor Fravel and Evan S. Medeiros, "China's New Diplomacy."

policy? If this vision in fact reflects a choice, what are some of the alternative grand strategies from which their choice may be distinguished? How has this strategic vision been manifest in Beijing's foreign policy? Has it been yielding the results China's leaders anticipated? Are they likely to adhere to this approach in the coming years? What are the implications of China's grand strategy for international security in the early twenty-first century? These are some of the questions to which subsequent chapters respond.

Chapter 2 provides an overview of the historical background and international context that help clarify the path China followed in embracing the grand strategy its leaders had settled upon by the late 1990s. It looks at change and continuity in the security challenges Beijing faced after the Cold War, defining the major problems and the choices available as China's leaders sought to cope with them. Chapter 3 assesses China's growing capabilities in the mid-1990s and the potentially dangerous reaction they provoked, a reaction that prompted Beijing to recalibrate its post–Cold War foreign policy. On the one hand, China's greater economic and military resources were helpful for ensuring the country's international interests. On the other hand, the perception of a rising China was aggravating the problems Beijing faced as others responded to what they viewed as the potential threat a stronger China might pose. Chapter 4 examines the logic driving these concerns about China's growing power and the worry that its continued rise might increase the likelihood of international conflict. Chapter 5 looks more closely at the proximate causes of China's response to the concerns its growing power was generating, especially Beijing's reaction to what looked like a chronically troubled, post–Cold War security environment in which the power of a preponderant United States would sharply limit China's foreign policy choices. Chapter 6 describes the two main features of the de facto grand strategy on which China's leaders settled by the second half of the 1990s, focusing on the steps they took to dampen perceptions of a "China threat" and to ensure a more favorable environment for the country's rise to true great power status. Chapter 7 provides a detailed account of one of the two central features of the new approach, China's major power diplomacy designed to establish partnerships with the countries that Beijing anticipates will define the international landscape in the coming decades. Chapter 8 assesses the durability of China's present grand strategy, and chapter 9 considers its consequences for international security and Sino-American relations in the early twenty-first century.

2

China's Changing Strategic Landscape

Much of the debate about the rise of China since the early 1990s has addressed two questions: How fast are China's economic and military capabilities increasing? And how should the world, especially the United States, respond to this emerging great power?[1] These are important questions, and I will return to them in subsequent chapters. But the ongoing debate about them has diverted attention from an equally important question: What is China's grand strategy? For reasons set forth in the introduction, assessing the significance of China's growing capability, whatever its trajectory, and the advisability of alternative ways of responding to it requires a grasp of the way leaders in Beijing seek to realize their nation's interests given the constraints imposed by their own resources and the international context within which they must operate.

Absent some informed judgment about China's purposes, countries that see their interests strategically interdependent with China's are left to focus on capabilities and to argue that prudence requires hedging against the most troubling possibilities, since intentions reflected in policy can change more quickly than capabilities. Such worst-case analysis might be sensible for intellectual exercises that are designed to consider the range of scenarios against which real trends can be compared. But it makes little sense for policy makers to privilege the worst-case scenario without supporting evidence, not only because resources to prepare for potential problems are limited, but especially because the likelihood of such worst-case scenarios will depend in part upon choices China makes in response to policies that others adopt. The emerging dynamic, especially for the Sino-American relationship that has largely molded China's post–Cold War grand strategy, reflects the logic of what international relations scholars refer to as "the security dilemma."

[1] See Michael E. Brown et al., eds., *The Rise of China.*

The International Context for Choice:
China and the Security Dilemma

The security dilemma describes the difficult choice that states face because they find themselves in the inherently uncertain and potentially dangerous condition of anarchy, a defining feature of the international system's structure. In contrast to domestic political systems, in which more or less effective central governments wield power and authority, in international politics there is no government standing above states that can reliably enforce agreements or resolve disputes. Each state, therefore, has incentives to hedge its bets against the need to take care of itself and deal with unpredictable adversaries and an unknowable future. The steps that states take to act on these concerns may worry other states, which see such actions as a reason they, too, should hedge their bets. The resulting dilemma each state faces is the following: should it attempt to ensure its security by arming itself if doing so might provoke a response from others that could wind up increasing the threat it originally faced? Or should it eschew actions that others might deem provocative, even if such restraint entails tolerating a degree of vulnerability that a military buildup might reduce, especially when the state cannot be sure whether restraint will be reciprocated?[2]

Although the condition of anarchy that produces the security dilemma confronts all states, the intensity of the security dilemma varies depending on the nature of military technology, strategic beliefs, and perceptions about the belligerence of the potential adversary.[3] At one extreme—when it is difficult to distinguish offensive from defensive weaponry, when military advantages are expected to accrue to the side that gets in the first blow, and when the other party is viewed as hostile—the security dilemma can drive intense, competitive peacetime military buildups. The U.S.-Soviet arms race during the Cold War in part reflected these circumstances.[4] Such intense security di-

---

[2] In addition to building arms, states may choose to hedge against potential threats by collaborating with others. This gives rise to the similar but distinct "alliance security dilemma" (the decision to form or refrain from forming alliances), which has its own vexing dynamics that are set forth by Glenn Snyder, "The Security Dilemma in Alliance Politics."

[3] See Robert Jervis, "Cooperation under the Security Dilemma"; Thomas J. Christensen and Jack Snyder, "Chain Gangs and Passed Bucks: Predicting Alliance Patterns in Multipolarity." With the exceptions noted below, security dilemmas are most vexing when it is difficult to distinguish status quo states from aggressors by observing the types of weapons they deploy and the military doctrines they embrace.

[4] Beliefs—even if they may not have been sensible, or even relevant to what either side would have chosen to do if war seemed imminent—drove behavior. Although

lemmas may even create conditions conducive to the outbreak of war, as occurred with the pressures for competitive mobilization that immediately preceded World War I. At the other extreme, however, the security dilemma plays little role in shaping relations between states despite the condition of anarchy and regardless of prevailing military technology or strategic beliefs. In two circumstances the attributes of states overwhelm these other factors and render the uncertainty about the meaning of military deployments that usually feeds the security dilemma largely irrelevant.[5] In one, states have high confidence that each state sees the use of force as almost unthinkable for resolving disputes that may arise. This conviction, conducive to "best-case planning," has been reflected in relations between the United States and Britain since the mid-twentieth century. A second and exactly opposite possibility, however, is that the uncertainty feeding the security dilemma loses its importance because states see military force as almost the only way to resolve their disputes. This conviction, conducive to "worst-case planning," may well have been reflected in relations between the United States and Saddam Hussein's Iraq in the years leading up to the war of 2003.

The U.S.-China relationship falls in a middle range where the vexing logic of the security dilemma is highly relevant, though not necessarily intense. Both countries consider the use of force possible but not inevitable. Both recognize that they have common and conflicting interests (they are neither unshakable friends nor implacable foes). And strategic uncertainties prevail about the advantages of offense versus defense (continuing innovations in weapons technology raise doubts about the effectiveness of offensive, defensive, and deterrent options). In such cases military deployments and diplomacy do not provide conclusive proof of hostile or benign intentions. Each side sees hedging one's bets as at least prudent, and the unavoidable uncertainty they face provides incentives to closely monitor and sometimes respond to the preparations the other is making. Although the Sino-American security dilemma cannot be eliminated because its fundamental cause is the condition of anarchy in which these two potentially rival states find themselves, its intensity

---

some analysts emphasized the robustness of a stable deterrent balance, a view often reflected in declaratory nuclear doctrine, operational planning emphasized the importance of militarily effective first use that provided plenty of incentives for each side to continue building up its capabilities. See Bruce G. Blair, *The Logic of Accidental Nuclear War.*

[5] See Thomas J. Christensen, "The Contemporary Security Dilemma: Deterring a Taiwan Conflict," pp. 8–11. On the link between middling levels of trust and the uncertainty about preferences that feeds the security dilemma, see Andrew Kydd, "Trust Building, Trust Breaking: The Dilemma of NATO Enlargement."

may be mitigated by more clearly grasping the strategic purposes that guide China's policies. To be sure, improved understanding will not create harmony where there are, or may one day be, genuine differences of interest. But given the interdependent nature of Sino-American relations, it can at least help reduce the danger of acting on imagined rather than real conflicts of interest and unnecessarily aggravating a security dilemma these countries cannot escape.

Grand Strategy

However helpful it might be to grasp the strategic vision guiding China's foreign policy, is it feasible? My account of China's emerging grand strategy in the post–Cold War era does not refer to a formal and detailed plan contained in a "smoking gun" document issued by the Chinese Communist Party's Central Committee. Instead it identifies a rough consensus on China's basic foreign policy that became entrenched among party leaders during 1996 and has since provided a guide for the country's international behavior. Although some elements of this approach appeared during the early 1980s, its content ultimately reflected new challenges that China faced following the end of the Cold War. This foreign policy consensus, I suggest, constitutes a grand strategy for China in the sense the term is often employed by international relations scholars: the distinctive combination of military, political, and economic means by which a state seeks to ensure its national interests.[6] But is grand strategy, then, simply a convenient shorthand for referring to the collection of foreign policies a state adopts? What, if anything, makes grand strategy distinctive?

Although much has been written about grand strategy, little has dealt with it as a general concept or theorized about its meaning and significance. The literature discussing grand strategy instead is comprised mainly of historical analysis examining the grand strategies that states have adopted in the past, or policy analysis examining the merits of alternative grand strategies that today's states might consider. Typically, authors stipulate a definition of grand strategy (sometimes briefly identifying its advantages and occasionally acknowledging

---

[6] See Paul Kennedy, "Grand Strategy in War and Peace: Toward a Broader Definition"; Barry Posen, *The Sources of Military Doctrine: France, Britain, and Germany Between the World Wars*, p. 13. Some states may define their interests as little more than ensuring their territorial and political integrity; others may have interests that are more expansive. See Edward N. Luttwak, *Strategy: The Logic of War and Peace*, p. 182. Few states are as ambitious as history's aspiring hegemons (Napoleon's France, Hitler's Germany, Hirohito's Japan), but leading states have usually sought to shape, and not just survive in, their international environment, typically in ways that will further enhance their wealth, power, and status.

its limitations) and then use it to frame the case they are studying.[7] A partial exception to this pattern can be found in Iain Johnston's work on China's strategic culture and grand strategy. In addition to his historical analysis of China, Johnston provides a theoretically informed, critical evaluation of existing typologies of grand strategy and, based on the shortcomings that he identifies, offers an alternative way to categorize them. He does not, however, offer a full-blown theory of grand strategy itself.[8] Why not? Given his bold theorizing about the effects of strategic culture and his careful parsing of the logical problems with much of the existing literature about grand strategy, the omission may seem surprising. Yet this apparent gap is arguably not a failing of Johnston or others writing about this subject. Grand strategy may simply not be the sort of phenomenon that calls for a distinct theoretical literature; it may best be understood as one of many topics illuminated by theories about strategy in general.

Strategic theory explains how actors employ available means to achieve their goals in a setting of interdependent choice. What makes any study of strategy distinctive is the assumption that actors do not just devise plans to realize objectives, but do so in a context where they must anticipate the likely response of others whose reactions could thwart or facilitate their efforts.[9] Theories about military strategy, for example, identify the logic behind the ways states pursue their goals by planning to use the forces they command (the land, sea, or air forces they may harness to defensive, offensive, or deterrent strategies) in a context where it is understood that others may well offer opposition. Adapted for differences in the means employed and the problems confronted, theories about economic strategy or diplomatic strategy similarly address questions about means, ends, and interdependent choice.

[7] Examples include Edward N. Luttwak, *The Grand Strategy of the Roman Empire: From the First Century A.D. to the Third*; Edward N. Luttwak, *The Grand Strategy of the Soviet Union*; Alastair Iain Johnston, *Cultural Realism: Strategic Culture and Grand Strategy in Chinese History*; Thomas J. Christensen, *Useful Adversaries: Grand Strategy, Domestic Mobilization, and Sino-American Conflict, 1947–1958*; Richard Rosecrance and Arthur A. Stein, eds., *The Domestic Bases of Grand Strategy*; Barry R. Posen and Andrew L. Ross, "Competing Visions for U.S. Grand Strategy"; Robert J. Art, "Geopolitics Updated: The Strategy of Selective Engagement"; Robert J. Art, *A Grand Strategy for America*; Walter Russell Mead, *Power, Terror, Peace, and War: America's Grand Strategy in a World at Risk*.

[8] Johnston, *Cultural Realism*; see esp. pp. 109–17.

[9] Strategic theory has clear links with contemporary research in game theory. See John C. Harsanyi, "Game Theory and the Analysis of International Conflict"; Thomas C. Schelling, *The Strategy of Conflict*. See also Luttwak's emphasis on the paradoxical logic of strategy that follows from interdependent choice (Luttwak, *Strategy*).

In this view, what distinguishes *grand* strategy as a concept is not its nature, but rather its scope. It is labeled "grand" because it refers to the guiding logic or overarching vision about how a country's leaders combine a broad range of capabilities linked with military, economic, and diplomatic strategies to pursue international goals.[10] Grand strategy in this sense refers to the way a state may coordinate its policies in various domains to reduce the likelihood that they will work at cross-purposes.[11] Grand strategy, then, is *not* simply a label for a comprehensive description of a state's various foreign policies. Rather, it refers to the central logic that informs and links those policies, the regime's vision about how it can most sensibly serve the nation's interests (goals) in light of the country's capabilities (means) and the international constraints it faces (the context of interdependent choice).[12]

Given the daunting intellectual challenge of reconciling means and ends while also anticipating the reactions of others, one might expect that "grand strategy" must refer to a fairly elaborate, carefully crafted government plan. In some cases, it is true, one can identify more or less clear statements that set forth the key elements of a country's grand strategy. The U.S. government, for example, drafted an initial formalization of its Cold War grand strategy of containment in the document NSC-68.[13] Often, however, a state's grand strategy is not expressed in such an explicit fashion. Sometimes it is only possible to identify a state's grand strategy as it becomes clear over time that foreign policy choices are reflecting a relatively consistent vision that provides a rough guide leaders use to assess the appropriateness of particular military,

[10] See André Beaufre, *An Introduction to Strategy*, pp. 19–31; Mead, *Power, Terror, Peace, and War*, p. 13.

[11] Coordination may succeed or fail. Posen identifies the dangers of what he labels "disintegrated" grand strategy. See *Sources of Military Doctrine*, pp. 24–25, 52. See also Luttwak, *Strategy*, p. 181; Rosecrance and Stein, *The Domestic Bases of Grand Strategy*, p. 4.

[12] Steve Walt has suggested that a state's grand strategy ultimately reflects a regime's theory (explicit or implicit) about the nature of international politics. See Stephen M. Walt, *The Origins of Alliances*, p. 2. See also Art, *A Grand Strategy for America*, pp. 1–2. For views that emphasize the internal as well as external goals that affect regime choices, see Rosecrance and Stein, *The Domestic Bases of Grand Strategy*, pp. 20–21 and passim.

[13] The basic logic of containment was originally articulated by Sovietologist George Kennan during and immediately after World War II. Despite the consensus among Americans on the need to make containing the threat Moscow posed to U.S. interests a top priority, sharply divergent views about how best to practice containment were evident from the very start. For the classic account of these variations in U.S. containment policies, see John Lewis Gaddis, *Strategies of Containment: A Critical Appraisal of Postwar American National Security Policy*.

economic, or diplomatic initiatives.[14] Indeed, this is the case with China's current grand strategy, whose logic became apparent after the mid-1990s. It emerged from a process of change in Beijing's approach to foreign affairs that actually began in the early 1980s but was completed only after China's leaders figured out how their approach would need to be modified to cope with the dramatic changes that followed the collapse of the Cold War international order. Subsequent chapters discuss the logic that defines this largely implicit grand strategy and describe its contents. First, however, I briefly recount the more explicit strategy China embraced during the preceding decades. This historical background provides a useful point of contrast that highlights the distinctiveness of the grand strategy that guides China's foreign policy today.

Historical Background for Choice: From Mao to Now

The strategic logic driving China's foreign policy during most of the Cold War era had its roots in the 1930s, when Mao Zedong championed an approach that helped the revolutionary movement of the Chinese Communist Party (CCP) achieve victory.[15] Mao's vision was, in essence, a variation on the familiar realpolitik theme described in the international relations literature about the balance of power. The blueprint called for the CCP to give top priority to coping with the most serious threat that the party faced at any given time (the "principal contradiction" in the Maoist argot), and to be willing to set aside ideological differences with potential supporters in order to form the broadest possible coalition of allies wiling to cooperate in parrying this main threat. If the nature of the principal adversary changed, so should the cast of allies with whom the CCP formed a coalition. Thus, between 1935 and 1945 Mao called for a broad coalition of Chinese patriots, with little regard to class background or party affiliation, to fight the Japanese occupation. The result was a massive expansion of the CCP's base of support that enabled it to mount impressive, though not decisive, operations against the Japanese occupying China.[16] After Japan's defeat in World War II, short-lived attempts at

[14] See Mead, *Power, Terror, Peace, and War*, p. 19.

[15] On Mao's strengthening leadership of the CCP's revolutionary strategy after 1927, see Benjamin I. Schwartz, *Chinese Communism and the Rise of Mao*; Chalmers A. Johnson, *Peasant Nationalism and Communist Power: The Emergence of Revolutionary China, 1937–1945*; Lucien Bianco, *Origins of the Chinese Revolution, 1915–1949*.

[16] On the dramatic surge in support for the CCP after it embraced Mao's strategy of building a nationalist united front to resist Japan, see Johnson, *Peasant Nationalism and Communist Power*. Although the Chinese fighters inflicted pain and suffering on occupying forces, Japan only surrendered and withdrew from China after the United States had defeated it in August 1945.

creating a coalition government for China failed and Civil War erupted. In this context, Mao argued that the principal threat not just to the CCP but also to the nation was a domestic enemy, the Kuomintang (KMT) regime of Chiang Kai-shek. Its incompetence and corruption were allegedly jeopardizing realization of the popular nationalist goal of building a more prosperous and powerful China, a goal that Sun Yat-sen had set forth early in the twentieth century. Mao again called for a broad (though this time somewhat less inclusive) united front of all Chinese who agreed that the KMT regime had forfeited its right to lead the country and had to be replaced.[17] The Communist Party's success in isolating Chiang and his most conservative supporters within Chinese society, together with increasingly effective military operations, enabled the communists to achieve a surprisingly rapid military victory by late 1949.

After Mao's CCP gained control of China, the strategy that emphasized forming coalitions against a principal adversary that had proven its worth in the struggle for power was retained as a guide for determining the new regime's grand strategy. Between 1949 and 1976, the approach informed Mao's analysis of international threats to China and led him to identify a changing cast of main enemies that resulted in three different applications of this grand strategy.[18] In the 1950s, China perceived a mortal danger posed by a hostile and powerful U.S.-led capitalist camp and therefore allied with the Soviet-led socialist bloc. In the mid-1960s, China perceived a growing threat of exploitation by the colluding American and Soviet superpowers and briefly attempted to forge a coalition of the "revolutionary forces of the third world." And after 1969, when China saw the rising power of a more hostile Soviet Union as the new main threat to its interests, it aligned with the United States and all others willing to resist the "socialist-imperialist hegemon." This Maoist approach emphasizing the importance of flexibly rallying broad support against a principal enemy prevailed not only for the four decades Mao dominated CCP politics, but also in the years immediately following his death in September 1976. Because Mao's successors saw their Soviet neighbor as still powerful and potentially dangerous, they carried forward the late Chairman's strategy of building a united front against Moscow, even as they began to criticize and abandon most of his other policies.

[17] In addition to Johnson, *Peasant Nationalism and Communist Power*, see Suzanne Pepper, *Civil War in China: The Political Struggle, 1945–1949*.

[18] For an analytical survey of China's foreign policy from the founding in 1949 to the early post–Cold War period, see Thomas W. Robinson, "Chinese Foreign Policy from the 1940s to the 1990s."

Predictably, however, when the post-Mao leaders concluded that the So-viet threat was diminishing during the 1980s, they reconsidered China's strat-egy and decided to loosen its alignment with a less essential American partner. But before the implications of a declining threat from Moscow had been fully digested, the Soviet Union itself collapsed. As the post–Cold War era dawned, the relevance of the counterhegemonic, realpolitik, strategic principles Mao had put in place was no longer obvious for two reasons. One reason was that China was increasingly secure. It did not face the sort of direct and immediate great power military challenge it had confronted during the Cold War. Grave insecurity had previously required Beijing to subordinate other interests to the overriding need for a counterbalance to dire threats. Simply put, absent a clearly dangerous "principal adversary" and a serious risk of war, the argu-ment for forging a united front had lost its urgency. A second reason for the demise of Maoist grand strategy was the end of bipolarity and the advent of a unipolar world. Beijing began to worry about the ways the United States, as the world's sole surviving superpower, might challenge China's vital interests. But in a unipolar world there were no peer competitors of the United States to whom China could turn as allies. Consequently, while Beijing's concerns about coping with unfettered American power grew, forging a counterhe-gemonic united front no longer seemed a viable option.

Change and Choice: Deng and After

Beijing's initial response to the different strategic challenges the end of the Cold War posed, like the response of many to the novelty and uncertainty it presented, was ad hoc. Only as the nature of the post–Cold War international system and China's interests in it became clearer during the 1990s did Bei-jing's foreign policy begin to gain a measure of coherence. By the second half of the decade, the broad contours of China's current grand strategy could be discerned. The approach that emerged at that time, however, was not as ex-plicit as the sequence of counterhegemonic foreign policy lines evident during the Maoist era. In part, this is because the old incentive for a very explicit strategy had been lost—the sort of clear and present existential dangers China faced during the bipolar Cold War era that had made it simpler to identify friends and enemies. Yet, in part, reduced clarity about policy also reflected the reduced stature of the top leaders in Beijing (compared with Mao Zedong and his immediate successor as paramount leader, Deng Xiaoping). To be sure, Mao and especially Deng did not simply issue edicts; even they had to ensure a modicum of support for their preferred policies, at least among key elements of the central elite.[19] After Deng's health began to fail in the early 1990s, however, policy making increasingly was characterized by careful compromise and consensus building.[20] This is a process that works against the clear articulation of a sharply defined personal vision. Nevertheless, while the vision may be less explicit or less forcefully articulated, China's foreign policies since the mid-1990s have been marked by a consistency that reflects the logic of a de facto grand strategy, one that is acceptable to a broad cross-section of the elite.[21] What is this approach and how is it expected to enable China to realize its national purposes?

As ever, China's current grand strategy first attends to potential threats to vital interests (territorial and political integrity). But these, too, have changed since the end of the Cold War. Indeed, by the early 1980s the likelihood of superpower military operations against the PRC had already begun to diminish, especially because China's nuclear capability finally began to provide Beijing with a crude but sufficiently frightening deterrent.[22] After the Cold War, China no longer faced blunt military challenges, but instead threats to its interests that were more subtle or indirect (concerns about the corrosive political effects of economic and cultural exchanges with the West; the risk of elite division or popular instability that could follow Taiwan's defiance of Beijing's claim that it is part of China's sovereign territory) and involved peripheral rather than core territorial interests (concerns about lingering disputes with China's maritime neighbors in the East and South China Seas). The old approach of building a coalition against a clearly defined, most dangerous military adversary seemed to offer few answers for dealing with these new sorts of problems.

Moreover, Beijing needed a strategy that not only served the "negative purpose" of protecting core national interests against external threats, but also

[19] See Carol Lee Hamrin, "Elite Politics and the Development of China's Foreign Relations," pp. 82–83. On the varying extent to which Mao was constrained by his colleagues and the challenges of maintaining order in China, see Avery Goldstein, *From Bandwagon to Balance-of-Power Politics: Structural Constraints and Politics in China, 1949–1978*.

[20] See Cheng Li, *China's Leaders: The New Generation*; Joseph Fewsmith, *Elite Politics in Contemporary China*; Joseph Fewsmith, *China since Tiananmen: The Politics of Transition*.

[21] Michael Swaine and Ashley Tellis, taking a longer historical view, similarly argue that they can discern various Chinese grand strategies even though one does not find them "explicitly presented in any comprehensive manner by its rulers." See Swaine and Tellis, *Interpreting China's Grand Strategy: Past, Present, and Future*, pp. 8, 81.

[22] See Avery Goldstein, *Deterrence and Security in the 21st Century: China, Britain, France and the Enduring Legacy of the Nuclear Revolution*.

served an increasingly salient "positive purpose"—to engineer the country's rise to the status of a true great power that can shape, rather than simply respond to, the international system in which it operates. China's pursuit of this goal would be part of and contribute to a long-term global trend transforming the currently unipolar system in which the United States is the sole superpower into a multipolar system in which China would be one of several great powers.[23] Beijing expected this change to finally loosen the tight international constraints a relatively weak China had faced under Cold War bipolarity and still faces today under unipolarity. In addition, under multipolarity, crosscutting interests were expected to condition more varied patterns of alignment, reducing the risk that others might one day forge a united coalition aimed at China.[24] Although Beijing did not see such a strategic alignment as an imminent danger in the early 1990s, as noted below, it had begun to worry that the United States might be preserving and redefining its Cold War vintage security pacts with China's Asian neighbors as a trellis on which an encircling coalition could be built in the future.

China's post–Cold War foreign policy line, then, has been designed in part to usher in what Beijing expects will be a more favorable multipolar international order, rather than merely waiting and hoping for it to form "naturally."[25] But because the international distribution of power put the United States at such a dramatic advantage, after briefly entertaining the unrealistic hope of a quick shift to multipolarity, China's leaders reluctantly resigned themselves to a very long period of transition. By the mid-1990s they were concluding that the process would take at least several decades. In addition, it had become clear that the challenges they faced while fostering a transition away from unipolarity would be especially tough—not only because China would have to sustain its recently impressive record of economic growth for several more decades if it were going to emerge as one of the great powers in a future multipolar world order, but also because by the mid-1990s China's increasing, yet still quite limited, capabilities had *already* begun to elicit worried reactions from the United States and Asian neighbors. Beijing, therefore, sought to ensure that in

[23] See Zhu Tingchang, "Xin Shiji Zhongguo Anquan Zhanlüe Gouxiang" [China's security concept for the new century], p. 12.

[24] China's view echoes the arguments of those international relations theorists who argued that multipolarity diffuses hostility and reduces the dangers of war. See Karl W. Deutsch and J. David Singer, "Multipolar Power Systems and International Stability." For the view that bipolar systems are likely to be more peaceful, see Kenneth N. Waltz. "International Structure, National Force, and the Balance of World Power."

[25] Ye Zicheng, "Zhongguo Shixing Daguo Waijiao Zhanlüe Shizai Bixing" [The imperative for China to implement a great power diplomatic strategy], pp. 6–9.

the decades before the dawn of multipolarity, their quest to become a great power did not provoke a preventive reaction from either the United States or its Asian friends and allies who might share American concerns about the prospect of China's rise. The challenge for Deng Xiaoping's successors was, in short, to devise policies that would facilitate a continuing increase in the country's power relative to others while minimizing the likelihood that this trend would stimulate potential adversaries to offset China's efforts.[26]

To meet this challenge, China's leaders embraced a grand strategy that attempts to reconcile their long-term goals and short-term limitations. Some of the key elements of the strategy had actually been articulated during the early 1980s.[27] Even before the Cold War had decisively ended, tensions with the Soviet Union ebbed, and Deng Xiaoping envisioned China embracing an increasingly independent foreign policy. China would take advantage of a less threatening international environment in which he expected bipolarity and the risk of superpower war to give way to multipolarity and the opportunity to focus on economic development.[28] Anticipating a reduced need to deal with immediate military challenges, Deng foresaw a shift to a focus on the tasks of modernization that would provide the essential foundation for realizing the century-old nationalist goal of making China a rich, powerful, and respected member of the community of modern states. But it was only in the mid-1990s that Beijing would fully embrace the strategic logic of Deng's admonition for a policy emphasizing independence, peace, and development. Importantly, it did so under circumstances significantly different than those

[26] Swaine and Tellis aptly refer to China's current approach as "the calculative strategy," emphasizing this very tough challenge China faces in trying to become a peer competitor of the currently dominant United States. See *Interpreting China's Grand Strategy*, p. xi. For theoretical discussion of the alternative possibilities for adjusting relations between a dominant and rising power, see Robert Powell, *In the Shadow of Power: States and Strategies in International Politics*.

[27] See Ye, "Zhongguo Shixing Daguo Waijiao Zhanlüe Shizai Bixing"; also Deng Xiaoping, "We Must Safeguard World Peace and Ensure Domestic Development, May 29, 1984."

[28] Michael Pillsbury, focusing most importantly on the arguments of "Deng Xiaoping's national security adviser," Huan Xiang, details China's early expectation about a transition to multipolarity that emerged in the mid-1980s (Pillsbury, *China Debates the Future Security Environment*, pp. xxiv, 3, 9–10, 55). At that time, the transition was expected to proceed in two stages, with "the big triangle" of the United States, the Soviet Union, and China to be followed by the addition of Western Europe and Japan. Thus, bipolarity would give way to tripolarity, and then pentapolarity (ibid., p. 11). Even so, Deng remained cautious about forsaking China's strategic ties to the United States in the 1980s while the future of Soviet policy remained unclear.

Deng had originally anticipated.[29] Three differences stood out. First, the risk of world war remained low, but the risk of China's involvement in limited military conflicts triggered by sovereignty disputes along its periphery had grown. Second, the Chinese Communist Party retained its firm grip on power, but the domestic political challenge of 1989 and the serial collapse and partial disintegration of one-party communist states elsewhere between 1989 and 1991 had elevated the salience of "unity and stability" at home as an important security consideration for policy makers in Beijing. Third, the bipolarity of the Cold War had indeed faded, but it had given way to an unexpected, and most likely prolonged, era of American unipolarity rather than a smooth transition to multipolarity.

Under these more trying circumstances, China's foreign policy-makers by the mid-1990s faced a new triple challenge: 1) to reduce the growing risk that neighbors would act on their budding fears about the PRC's increasing power and more assertive behavior in East Asia; 2) to ensure continued growth of the civilian economy, on which domestic political stability increasingly depended; and 3) to cope with the potential dangers Beijing saw in surprisingly robust American primacy—reflected both in the stunning demonstrations of U.S. military superiority in the Persian Gulf and the Balkans as well as the remarkable performance of the U.S. economy during the first decade of the post–Cold War era. After several years during which China's foreign policy had failed to deal adequately with the seriousness of these challenges, in 1996 Beijing began to adjust its approach.[30] The result of these adjustments was an emerging logic guiding China's choices that I identify as its current grand strategy. The strength of the broad commitment to this foreign policy vision became increasingly evident as it survived the test of debates about its suitability after 1996. Events such as the U.S. bombing of the Chinese embassy in Belgrade in 1999, the EP-3 spy plane collision in 2001, and recurrent tensions in the Taiwan Strait provided more than one opportunity for advocates of an alternative to China's current grand strategy to make their case. On each occasion, as detailed in chapters 7 and 8, they failed to do so and Beijing's leaders chose to stay their newly established course.

[29] Ye, "Zhongguo Shixing Daguo Waijiao Zhanlüe Shizai Bixing," pp. 5–6. See also Ye Zicheng, "Carrying Forward, Developing and Pondering Deng Xiaoping's Foreign Policy Thinking in the New Situation."

[30] See Yan Xuetong, "Dui Zhongguo Anquan Huanjing De Fenxi Yu Sikao" [Analysis of and reflections on China's security environment], p. 6.

Continuity and Choice

Although China's current grand strategy reflects recent changes in the country's capabilities as well as the changed post–Cold War setting in which it is now constrained to operate, it also bears the imprint of three important continuities.

First, while the international system's polarity has changed, its ordering principle has not. China must pursue its interests and cope with American primacy within what remains an anarchic international system. Under anarchy, states face substantial uncertainty about the future and cannot depend on essentially unenforceable international agreements, and thus have strong incentives to hedge their bets. One consequence of anarchy is the security dilemma described above. Another is the premium placed on self-help. China, like all countries, may try to cultivate commitments from other states or international organizations to provide assistance if its interests are threatened, or try to head off threats through deals with potential adversaries. But because there is no central international authority to enforce agreements, depending on others to fulfill their terms is risky. This consideration does not lead states to pursue a costly policy of total self-reliance, but it does encourage states to weigh and manage the risks of too heavily relying on, or too fully trusting in, others. In the new century, as during the Cold War, China's grand strategy is unavoidably conditioned by such concerns and the incentives for self-help that anarchy generates.

Second, while advancements in military technology yield ever more sophisticated hardware and software, the changes usually captured by the phrase "revolution in military affairs" (RMA) have not yet reversed the strategic verdict of the nuclear revolution that occurred in the mid-twentieth century.[31] Although the search for effective defenses against nuclear weapons continues, there is little prospect that defensive systems capable of fully neutralizing the arsenals within reach of major powers will be deployed in the foreseeable future. To undo the revolutionary strategic effects of nuclear weapons, leaders having such a defensive system would need to be completely confident that its operation, perhaps in conjunction with massive preemptive strikes, would eliminate even the slimmest possibility of nuclear retaliation. Short of this point, they continue to face the terrifying chance that a nearly disarmed victim of a massive first strike might yet succeed in launching a small and ragged

---

[31] See Robert Jervis, *The Meaning of the Nuclear Revolution: Statecraft and the Prospect of Armageddon*; Michael Mandelbaum, *The Nuclear Revolution: International Politics before and after Hiroshima*; Goldstein, *Deterrence and Security in the 21st Century*.

but (if it manages to evade or otherwise foil the prepared defenses of the at-
tacker) potentially catastrophic retaliatory blow. This nagging uncertainty
about the residual vulnerability of even the most heavily defended, technologically sophisticated, and powerful state is the bedrock of the nuclear revolution. Among nuclear states, the risk of swift and devastating punishment endures. This risk tightly constrains the use of force by such states when it means
courting great power war.

Of course, the nuclear revolution did not render conventional military capabilities irrelevant or make war itself obsolete. Nuclear powers have continued to plan for both major and minor contingencies, military crises have
erupted, and force has been used in support of national policy. But since the
mid-twentieth century, when the interests of rival great powers have been in
play, the shadow of escalation that could entail the catastrophic use of nuclear
weapons has dramatically altered the significance of conventional capabilities.
Nuclear-armed states can ensure their vital interests as long as they deploy
conventional capabilities that make it unlikely an adversary could threaten
them with a fait accompli and avoid facing the risk of escalation. The revolution in military affairs has, however, begun to alter the challenges states face in
deploying the conventional capabilities needed to complement the nuclear
trump card. Stronger powers like the United States have to worry about
weaker states exploiting new vulnerabilities that heavy reliance on sophisticated technologies create. Less powerful states like China have to worry about
their ability to muster the quantity and quality of resources necessary to deploy conventional forces that are not woefully obsolete and vulnerable to swift
destruction by states better able to fully exploit the RMA. As long as such
states possess a nuclear retaliatory capability, they need not have the forces to
prevail in a conventional conflict, but they do need forces sufficient to test the
resolve of adversaries they cannot defeat, forces that require such adversaries to
face the risk of unacceptable escalation. Much of the selective modernization
of China's military undertaken after the end of the Cold War, and described
in chapter 3, aimed to provide Beijing with exactly this sort of capability for
use in possible confrontations with its most plausible great power adversary,
the United States. The legacy of the nuclear revolution, then, continues to
shape the military environment in which Beijing formulates its grand strategy.
It establishes the quantity and quality of conventional as well as nuclear forces
required to ensure China's vital interests. It also modifies the consequences of
unipolarity insofar as escalation risks temper the strategic importance of the
substantial American military advantage when it confronts even a weaker nuclear power like China.

A third continuity that conditions China's strategic choice is geopolitical.

Despite playing a new role on a changed world stage, China finds itself performing in the same old theater. Because China is moving up but cannot move out, geography and history combine to pose daunting problems for the country's foreign policy makers. Although China faces no immediate great power threat along its borders (indeed, its periphery is arguably less directly threatened by great powers than at any time since the early nineteenth century), there are no guarantees that this favorable circumstance will continue indefinitely. China is surrounded by great, or potentially great, powers (as well as a number of minor powers) with whom it has a checkered history. None may be enemies today, but prudence requires a strategy for coping with the problems that a deterioration in relations with any of them might pose for Beijing tomorrow. Moreover, China's border regions (especially Tibet, Xinjiang, and Inner Mongolia) are populated by national minorities whose questionable loyalty to Beijing ensures concerns that neighboring countries could exploit ethnic unrest if relations with China deteriorate.[32] And though not tied to important ethnic cleavages, the political dispute with Taiwan and the possibility that it could result in a military clash involving the United States establish this front as another serious—arguably the most serious—potential security challenge on the country's periphery. Finally, a newer concern reflecting China's unchanged geographic circumstances was added in the post–Cold War era and became more prominent with the unfolding American war on terrorism in the early twenty-first century, that is, the uncertain implications of an expanded U.S. military role in Central Asia just beyond China's western borders (either an ongoing physical presence or access to facilities in states allied with Washington).

Choosing a Course: China's Grand Strategy Emerges

In this context of both change and continuity, what grand strategy made sense for China as a rising but not yet fully risen great power interested in elevating its international influence under circumstances where it faced an array of potential adversaries, most of whom had close ties to the world's only superpower and many of whom were nervous about China's intentions? By the late 1990s, the leaders in Beijing settled on an approach characterized by two broad components. The first, great power diplomacy focused on establishing various types of partnerships, is designed to make China an indispensable, or at least very attractive, actor on whose interests the system's major powers are

---

[32] As discussed in chapter 6, after 1996 a key Chinese aim within the Shanghai Five (later the Shanghai Cooperation Organization) has been to ensure that the states of Central Asia will not lend their support to separatist elements in China.

reluctant to trample. The other component of China's strategy embraces an activist agenda designed to establish Beijing's reputation as a responsible international actor, reducing the anxiety about China's rise that CCP leaders recognized might prompt others to oppose it, individually or jointly. China's strategy may hopefully look forward to what Beijing expects will eventually become a multipolar system in which crosscutting interests will make it more difficult to rally a coalition based on a single concern. But it also realistically remains sensitive to the stark constraints China now faces, especially the current limits on China's capabilities and the resulting need for it to cope with challenges to its interests that American preponderance can present in the near term. In subsequent chapters I examine the advent of the strategy and detail its contents. In the remainder of this chapter, I distinguish China's present approach from four broad alternative grand strategies—hegemony, balancing, bandwagoning, and isolation.[33] All these strategic options have shortcomings that suggest why Beijing did not choose them at the end of the twentieth century.

Hegemony

Under a hegemonic strategy China would strive to maximize its power relative to all rivals by diverting as much national wealth as possible from civilian economic needs to military modernization, and by attempting to exploit its power advantages wherever possible. A rising power embracing such a strategy seeks to equal and eventually surpass its more powerful rivals. Germany under Hitler and arguably the Soviet Union, especially under Stalin after World War II, offer examples of the single-minded pursuit of greater power built on military armaments that one expects to see from an ambitious challenger that adopts this sort of strategy. They also provide examples of the typical problems an aspiring hegemon can encounter. Because the grasp for domination reveals worrisome intentions and raises questions about how the future hegemon would employ its power advantage if it were realized, other states have clear incentives to respond with their own efforts to forestall its hegemony. Their self-interest in avoiding the dangers of vulnerability and possible victimization encourages others to counter the aspiring hegemon— separately through competitive armament or jointly by forming an opposing

[33] For Chinese assessments of the grand strategies some of the leading states in international political history adopted, see Guo Shuyong, "21 Shiji Qianye Zhongguo Waijiao Dazhanlüe Chuyi" [A modest proposal for China's diplomatic grand strategy on the eve of the twenty-first century], p. 92. Such seemingly arcane discussions in China's journals typically are intended as object lessons for present day policy makers.

coalition.[34] Although Hitler's rivals may have been slow to respond, in the end his drive for supremacy (like Napoleon's a century earlier) triggered a reaction that not only frustrated his ambitions but also resulted in his country's crushing defeat.

The Soviet Union during the Cold War offers a different, and somewhat less clear-cut, example of the problems that may result from a rising power adopting a hegemonic strategy. Yet it is one that Chinese analysts have taken to heart. The lesson to draw from the Soviet example is less obvious because the strength of Soviet ambition was not as consistently clear as Hitler's (or Napoleon's) and because the practical, as opposed to rhetorical, significance of promoting a communist world order dimmed over time as hegemony became an ever more unrealistic goal. Nevertheless, the Soviet Union's emphasis after World War II on building a military machine that would give it increasing clout relative to its neighbors and ultimately relative to its superpower rival, the United States, did lead Moscow to adhere to a distorted development program expected to serve its hegemonic grand strategy. The Soviet approach and the national priorities it created, however, ultimately proved counterproductive, though not exactly in the same way as had Germany's. Moscow's apparent post–World War II ambitions induced others to respond by increasing their armaments and to cooperate against the potential Soviet threat. And because a strategy that emphasized increasing military capabilities led the Soviet leaders to shortchange the domestic economic and political foundations of national strength, their determined pursuit of power mortgaged the regime's future by weakening its domestic base of support. By the time a leadership dedicated to dramatically altering the country's grand strategy and adjusting its domestic priorities in a decisive way had come to power, it was too late. The defeat of the Soviet Union, unlike that of other aspiring hegemons, was largely self-inflicted. As will be noted below, however, the peacefulness of its demise did not negate the impact on Beijing of the lesson it contained about the risks of embracing a hegemonic grand strategy. China's contemporary leaders have been especially sensitive to the Soviet example as a cautionary tale, not only about the shortcomings of the Stalinist economic model, but also about the potentially catastrophic political consequences of attempting to maximize international military clout at the expense of domestic development.

[34] The determination with which such states go about amassing power encourages others to worry about the threat they might pose. Thus, the reaction they call forth is consistent with the expectations of both Waltz's balance-of-power theory as well as Walt's balance-of-threat theory. See Kenneth N. Waltz, *Theory of International Politics*; Walt, *The Origins of Alliances*.

Balancing

Under a balancing strategy China would strive to offset the potentially threat-ening dominance of powerful rivals through a determined but more modest effort at military modernization and forming alliances with states sharing its security concerns. A rising power embracing such a grand strategy is moti-vated primarily by a concern with enhancing its own security rather than achieving dominance over others. Worried about exposure to powerful and potentially hostile rivals, a state that adopts a balancing strategy attempts to augment its own ability to counter foreseeable threats and cultivates coopera-tive arrangements with others who have parallel security concerns. These ef-forts, what international relations scholars usually label internal and external balancing, have been manifest throughout history in competitive arms build-ups and alliance formation. Soviet grand strategy under Stalin prior to the Cold War reflected this sort of approach. The Soviet investment in a budding military-industrial complex, entering the Molotov-Ribbentrop Pact, the nonaggression treaty with Japan, and later realigning to side with the Allies against Nazi Germany all reflected the imperatives of balancing that an inse-cure, besieged state confronts. China's alliance with the Soviet Union in 1950 and its request for Moscow's assistance in modernizing its military, Beijing's determination to develop its own independent nuclear deterrent, and eventu-ally China's decision to realign and cooperate with the United States in op-posing the Soviet Union, as noted above, reflected the requirements of the balancing strategy that China embraced during most of the Cold War.

A state that adopts a grand strategy emphasizing balancing may not en-counter the problems aspiring hegemons have faced, but this approach, too, has its costs. First, although the burden may be lighter than that required to amass the capabilities needed to dominate others, investing in the military forces needed to ensure one's security against powerful external threats does have opportunity costs. Put otherwise, the choice of guns over butter may not be as skewed for a balancer as for an aspiring hegemon, but the balancer will still need to divert national wealth from other useful domestic purposes as it seeks to augment its ability to deal with potentially serious external threats. This burden will be more or less imposing depending on the particular cir-cumstances a state faces. A state that seeks only to ensure that others will leave it alone may sometimes be able to opt for relatively inexpensive military forces that dissuade potential adversaries by making a successful challenge seem ex-traordinarily difficult or too costly. But a state (like China) that believes its geopolitical circumstances, the nature of military technology, or significant international interests make it necessary to have an elaborate and expensive capability to parry powerful rivals is likely to find it must shoulder a heavier burden to balance potential threats. In short, while a balancing grand strategy is unlikely to carry the economic price tag of a hegemonic grand strategy, it is not necessarily cheap or easy to implement.

Moreover, balancing typically means incurring noneconomic costs. If in addition to augmenting its own ability to counter potential threats a balancer also attempts to pool resources and cooperate with others sharing its threat perceptions, it may find that it has to tailor its policies to ensure solidarity with its partners.[35] Sometimes this political price is steep and produces tensions in or even a rupture of the alliance, a problem with which leaders in Beijing are intimately familiar. Early in the Cold War, when China faced grave threats from the United States, the CCP apparently believed it had little choice but to accept the deference its Soviet partner expected as leader of an alliance that was deemed essential for their country's security. But Beijing's (and especially Mao's) unhappiness with Moscow's leadership grew during the 1950s, and the perception that distasteful deference was not worth the security dividend the Soviets were prepared to provide contributed to tensions that destroyed the alliance. By the end of the decade Beijing decided instead to accept the risks it would face in relying on its own wherewithal to develop and deploy forces to balance against the United States, especially as that threat and China's vulnerability to it appeared somewhat less pressing by the end of the 1950s. A decade later, however, China again faced a serious military threat, this time from the Soviet Union. Because Beijing was still not confident of its ability to counter a strongly motivated superpower enemy, it initiated a process that resulted in strategic entente with the United States. For most of the rest of the Cold War, Beijing's balancing grand strategy required it to accept cooperation with an ideologically distasteful partner, and one that refused to abandon its ties to the CCP's political rivals on Taiwan. As long as China believed the dangerous Soviet threat dictated a grand strategy of counterhegemonic balancing, however, it had little choice but to subordinate its political preferences to military necessity. With the end of the Cold War, this constraint eased.

There were strands of China's initial post–Cold War foreign policy, noted in chapter 5, that suggested it might continue to rely on a grand strategy of balancing revised to cope with the new challenges it saw in a world dominated by a potentially hostile American superpower. By the mid-1990s, however, the leaders in Beijing recognized that such an approach was not feasible. Because of the difficulties China faced in significantly increasing its own capabilities (inter-

---

[35] See Hans Morgenthau, *Politics among Nations*, pp. 181–88; Waltz, *Theory of International Politics*, pp. 166–70.

nal balancing), the absence of powerful allies interested in hedging against an American threat (external balancing), and the need to develop a grand strategy that promised more than a simple ability to fend off threats to survival, Beijing instead adopted the approach described in subsequent chapters expecting that it would better serve China's interests as a rising power in a unipolar world.

Bandwagoning

Under a bandwagoning strategy China would not seek to increase its own military capabilities or to collaborate with others to score gains relative to potential rivals as in the first two strategies. Instead, it would choose to accommodate the preferences of the system's most powerful state, hoping to realize the absolute gains of increased international economic exchange and to enjoy the security benefits the hegemon would provide as a collective good. A state embracing such a grand strategy may do so because it finds the alternatives implausible or believes that its security and prosperity are best served by currying favor with a more powerful state it would be foolish to provoke and that is not seen as posing a serious threat to vital national interests. Such a strategy should not, however, be confused with mere subordination to the will of a hegemonic power, in which case weaker states may profess loyalty to the strong because they recognize they have little choice but to comply with its wishes or be forced to acquiesce. A bandwagoning strategy is designed to advance a state's interests, not simply avoid unacceptable punishment, to score gains and not merely avoid losses.[36] Such bandwagoning may, for example, be reflected in the post–Cold War foreign policies of many American allies in Europe and Asia. Once the necessity of balancing against a Soviet superpower evaporated in 1991, the United States was no longer a counter to a clear security threat but instead the anchor of a militarily peaceful and economically open international order from which others could benefit.[37]

Allowing a powerful state like the United States to shoulder many international risks and burdens has its obvious advantages, and it would seem to make

[36] On the importance of distinguishing bandwagoning from subordination, see Goldstein, *From Bandwagon to Balance-of-Power Politics*; Randall L. Schweller, "Bandwagoning for Profit: Bringing the Revisionist State Back In."

[37] Japan and Germany during the Cold War may also provide imperfect examples of this approach. The examples are imperfect in at least two senses. First, their close relations with the United States were nurtured also by a desire to balance against the perceived threat from the Soviet bloc. Second, their foreign policies were tightly constrained by the consequences of devastating defeat in World War II that limited the possibility of considering the full range of strategic options open to "normal" states, even if they had wanted to.

bandwagoning an attractive alternative compared with the hegemonic or balancing grand strategies. The obvious drawback, however, is the vulnerability that states embracing the strategy accept. If they have miscalculated the benign intentions and generosity of the more powerful state with whom they cast their lot, or if its sincerely benign intentions change as interests evolve over time, states once pleased with the benefits all enjoy under the established order may instead begin to worry about the distribution of those benefits and how uneven gains may enable the strong to threaten the weak. If there are ways in which material advantages can be translated into military or economic power that jeopardizes a state's security or requires it to compromise on core political preferences, as realist international relations scholars have argued, leaders will be increasingly concerned about relative rather than absolute gains.[38]

For China, the prospect of adopting a grand strategy of bandwagoning with the United States in the post–Cold War era was not very attractive. Beijing wanted to reduce rather than accept its relative weakness, worried about the liberal political agenda a powerful United States might impose on China, and rejected American hegemony as a legitimate ordering principle for international relations. Yet in some respects the strategy a rising China adopted after the mid-1990s reflected an interest in enjoying the benefits the United States provides as leader of the unipolar world. A key feature of China's foreign policy, as emphasized in the following chapters, has been to ensure that the country is able to reap the benefits of the U.S.-fashioned international economic order because it is essential to the success of China's economic reforms and growth. In the security realm, as well, even though China worries about the potentially hostile purposes of American military power and alliances in the western Pacific, especially now that the rationale of the Soviet threat has evaporated, it also recognizes that it derives benefits from the pacifying influence of the American presence, especially given China's concerns about the possibility of conflict on the Korean peninsula and the prospect of Japan adopting a more independent, less predictable security policy. Thus, while China did not embrace a grand strategy of bandwagoning with the world's superpower, the logic behind bandwagoning did partly inform the policies Beijing ultimately embraced.

[38] In the 1980s and 1990s, international relations scholars disagreed about whether anarchy necessarily constrains states to focus on maximizing relative rather than absolute gains they may obtain from international cooperation. For a sample of the wide-ranging debate, see Robert M. Axelrod, *The Evolution of Cooperation*; David A. Baldwin, ed., *Neorealism and Neoliberalism: The Contemporary Debate*; Robert Powell, "Guns, Butter, and Anarchy"; and, Powell, *In the Shadow of Power*.

Isolationism

Under an isolationist strategy China would invest in military capabilities only insofar as they were essential to the minimal goal of ensuring the inviolability of the country's territorial and political integrity while also seeking to maximize economic independence through autarky. Although modern technology has eroded the viability of isolationism that depends on geographic separation and hard-to-surmount physical obstacles (e.g., mountains and oceans), it has also provided nuclear weapons that enable states to embrace a new form of isolationism if they so choose. In some respects it may be an attractive choice. A state embracing an isolationist grand strategy can avoid costs the other three alternatives entail. In the modern world, a state embracing this strategy need only invest in a minimal nuclear deterrent and then combine its effectiveness for dissuading serious threats to vital interests with a modest investment in daunting conventional defenses along the country's periphery. As long as it possesses delivery systems that can inflict the retaliatory blow essential for effective deterrence, the state does not have to make a heavy investment in typically expensive power projection assets (troops, weapons, and logistical capabilities for long-range air, land, and sea-based operations) that are essential under a hegemonic strategy and often important under a balancing strategy. Beyond this economic advantage, an isolationist grand strategy may enable the state to avoid the political costs of compromising its policy preferences in order to maintain solidarity with allies as may be necessary if one opts for balancing, or to please a dominant state that supplies benefits to its supporters as may be necessary if one opts for bandwagoning.

Yet an isolationist grand strategy has its own, if different, costs. While enabling the state to avoid heavy military burdens and many international obligations or entanglements, it also limits the state's ability to influence events beyond its borders. An isolationist grand strategy, then, is not suitable for a state that has significant interests abroad, that would prefer to enhance its security by shaping international events in ways that preclude the emergence of new dangers, or that aspires to wield the type of international influence historically identified with great powers.[39] In addition, although an isolationist grand strategy may reduce military burdens and political costs, it is also likely to limit the opportunity for a country to reap the benefits available through active participation in international affairs. Extensive engagement with the intellectual and especially the economic life of an increasingly interdependent world is a valu-

---

[39] American isolationism, for example, may explain the lag between growing U.S. capabilities in the late nineteenth century and its arrival as a true great power.

able complement to internal strengths, even for major powers with large domestic markets. Opting out entails opportunity costs likely to stunt development. Depending on changing military technology, lagging development may eventually undermine a country's competitiveness in ways that jeopardize its security against external threats. And, if isolationism retards economic growth, it can also create domestic political risks for a regime whose legitimacy depends heavily on satisfying the people's demand for an ever-rising standard of living, as it does in China.

In light of these costs, perhaps it should not be surprising that few states have embraced a truly isolationist grand strategy, or, if they have, they have not stuck with it for very long.[40] China, however, did at least briefly flirt with such an approach. From the Great Leap Forward in the late 1950s through the early years of the Cultural Revolution in the mid-1960s, Mao willingly scuttled the tattered Sino-Soviet alliance; strongly backed the rapid development of a Chinese nuclear deterrent; proudly proclaimed the relevance of his self-reliant People's War strategy, warning potential adversaries of the punishment that a huge (if obsolete) mobilized military and militia would inflict on any invader; and touted the virtues and viability of extreme economic self-sufficiency when combined with dispersal of the country's infrastructure to minimize its vulnerability to external pressure or attack.[41] This stubbornly independent vision for China's security policy was effectively abandoned after 1969, however, when even Mao recognized its inadequacy for responding to an increasingly dire Soviet threat, a threat that provided stark incentives for China to return to the strategy of using one superpower to balance the other.

[40] Conventional wisdom often portrayed the geopolitically distinctive United States as the classic isolationist state for much of its history before the mid-twentieth century. Walter McDougal has explained why this caricature was not a very accurate portrayal of the American experience. See Walter A. McDougall, *Promised Land, Crusader State: The American Encounter with the World since 1776.* Just after the Cold War, Eric Nordlinger recommended a modified isolationist strategy for the United States. In his view, military isolationism could be combined with the use of what Joseph Nye refers to as "soft power" to promote American economic and political interests abroad. This approach, however, reintroduces the constraints of international life since it would be necessary to negotiate the terms of economic (and other nonmilitary) relations with others. In any case, a key to Nordlinger's proposal is the physical separation of the U.S. homeland from its potential military adversaries. As noted above, China does not enjoy the same geopolitical advantage. See Eric A. Nordlinger, *Isolationism Reconfigured: American Foreign Policy for a New Century.*

[41] See Harvey W. Nelsen, *Power and Insecurity: Beijing, Moscow, and Washington, 1949–1988,* pp. 89–90; Barry Naughton, "The Third Front: Defence Industrialization in the Chinese Interior."

But unlike the security crisis of 1969 that discredited the policy of extreme military self-reliance, Mao's emphasis on economic autarky, though stunting China's growth, did not produce a domestic crisis severe enough to prompt him to abandon this strand of his isolationist strategy. Only after Mao's death did China's leaders finally address the problems of economic stagnation that isolationism exacerbated and initiate the "opening to the outside" that catalyzed a remarkably successful modernization program. For Mao's successors, the legacy of China's experiment with an isolationist grand strategy, then, was not only the lesson they learned about the security risks it entails for a state that is weaker than its most potent rivals but eschews strategic partners. It was also the lesson they learned about the especially severe economic costs of autarky for a developing country that deprives itself of the benefits of exchange with others.

China's Transitional Strategy

The approach to which China has committed itself since the mid-1990s differs from each of the four broad alternatives just described. China's current grand strategy differs not only in substance (described below), but also insofar as it is a strategy that necessarily has an "expiration date." Its logic addresses the circumstances of what is expected to be a period of transformation lasting from the end of the bipolar Cold War era to the end of the unipolar post–Cold War era the United States dominates. As such, the approach could be labeled a "strategy of transition." The strategy is tailored to fit the requirements of an emerging China, to chart a course for its rise during the era of unipolarity; it is not designed to guide China once it has risen and circumstances are fundamentally different. This temporal limitation is also reflected in one of the labels for the approach that some Chinese began to invoke in November 2003—the "strategy of peaceful rise."[42] China's national capabilities and the international constraints it now faces put a premium on sustaining a peaceful environment

[42] In chapter 7 I return to the Chinese debate about "peaceful rise," a label first introduced by Zheng Bijian at the 2003 Boao Forum. The label fell victim to domestic criticism in spring 2004 when some apparently believed that its prominence might send the wrong signals by 1) alarming those who worried about the consequences of China's rise, and 2) unwisely limiting China's options for ensuring its interests, especially in the Taiwan Strait, where threats of force could not be eschewed. See Evan S. Medeiros, "China Debates Its 'Peaceful Rise Strategy'"; Zheng Bijian, "New Path for China's Peaceful Rise and the Future of Asia"; Wen Jiabao, "Turning Your Eyes to China"; Ruan Zongze, "Through Diplomatic Efforts, China Is Now Putting up a Platform for Its Own Peaceful Rise"; "Peaceful Rise: Strategic Choice for China"; Wang Yiwei, "The Dimensions of China's Peaceful Rise."

necessary for the growth that will enable it to rise to the position of a true great power. What course China will follow if the strategy succeeds is unclear.

It is true that leaders and analysts in the PRC frequently insist that their country's international behavior will not change even when it becomes stronger and unipolarity ends. They may ultimately be proven correct. The future, however, will depend on the policies China and others choose to embrace once its current strategy has run its course, the transition is complete, and China has risen to the ranks of the great powers.[43] At that time, different leaders in Beijing will make choices that reflect their country's new capabilities and transformed international constraints that cannot be confidently foreseen. Might China then become a peer competitor actively and self-reliantly balancing the system's other great powers? Might it become a great power seeking allies because its own clout continues to lag significantly behind others'? Or might it become a dominant power seeking to refashion the international order to its liking?[44] From the perspective of China's leaders whose thinking is informed by the current transitional strategy, such speculation is premature at best and unwisely provocative at worst. Instead, they focus on the problem of coping with immediate and foreseeable challenges to their country's security in ways that also serve their general interest in expanding China's international role, even as the precise nature of that role in the more distant future is not yet clearly defined.

Beijing's present strategy is distinguished not only by its focus on managing China's rise during the era of American unipolarity. It is also distinguished by a pragmatic recognition of the advantages and disadvantages I have linked with the four broad alternative grand strategies introduced above. China's current foreign policy line entails efforts to develop national capabilities and cultivate international partners, but it also aims to avoid the provocative consequences of the more straightforward hegemonic and balancing strategies. And while the current foreign policy line entails international economic and diplomatic engagement designed to maximize the benefits of interdependence, it also tries to steer a middle course between the risks of vulnerability associated

[43] I return to this point in the concluding chapter. Claims of benign intent are often discounted, not only because others know that an aggressive rising power has incentives to misrepresent its intentions, but also because (as the literature about the security dilemma emphasizes) intentions may change when new circumstances arise. See Dale C. Copeland, *The Origins of Major War*, pp. 22–23, 37, 245.

[44] Chinese analysts disagree in their forecasts. Some see China emerging as simply a stronger regional power, others as a regional power with global influence, and still others as a true global power. Author's interviews, Beijing, June–July 1998, March–April 2000, October 2000.

with bandwagoning and the opportunity costs associated with isolationism.

The following chapters detail the choices China made in the mid-1990s and afterward. Before I proceed, however, a final comment about my characterization of China's policies as reflecting a "grand strategy" is in order. Some might argue that the term overstates the coherence of Beijing's approach to international affairs. To be sure, in China as elsewhere, the numerous individuals and organizations responsible for formulating and implementing policy over the range of issues that arise ensures something well short of full coherence. Moreover, as noted above, it is also true that the power of the paramount leader in Beijing today is less than it was under Mao or Deng; in foreign as well as in domestic policy debates among the central elite, divergent opinions play a greater role. Nevertheless, the Chinese communist regime's Leninist structure endures and, especially on major foreign policy matters, enables the party center to provide the broad direction within which actors must operate. And while there are differences about the wisdom of particular policy choices, on the most important issues a consensus on the basic foreign policy line has formed—one that seeks to maintain the conditions conducive to China's continued growth and to reduce the likelihood others will unite to oppose China.[45]

This consensus in Beijing on a broad approach for dealing with the world, China's transitional grand strategy designed to sustain a peaceful environment for the country's rise to great power status, reflects not just China's capabilities and the constraints of a unipolar international system but also the hard lessons of experience learned during the Cold War and especially its immediate aftermath. What were these lessons?

Leaving the Cold War Behind: False Start

As indicated above, during the Cold War China had pursued its foreign policy interests within the tight constraints and resulting clear incentives bipolarity provided. Given the country's meager national wealth and the scope of the threat each of the superpowers posed, Beijing's foreign policy for most of the four decades after 1949 was driven, in conformity with the principles of realpolitik, by a survivalist logic that frequently trumped other regime prefer-

---

[45] See Paul Heer, "A House United." In short, as there were disagreements in the United States during the Cold War about the best way to practice containment, there are disagreements between hard- and soft-liners, but these typically reflect disagreements about details rather than fundamental strategy. On the U.S. case, see Gaddis, *Strategies of Containment.* On the issue of coherence in grand strategy, see Posen, *The Sources of Military Doctrine.*

ences. The imperatives of international structure derived not merely from the relatively clear implications of bipolarity, but also the tightness of its constraints for a state so closely involved in the system's superpower-dominated competitive politics.[46] Any Chinese government with the limited capabilities Beijing commanded would have faced strong incentives to embrace a similar strategy—relying on one superpower to counter the threat the other represented (a consequence of bipolarity), even as it sought to improve the prospects for self-reliance because of worries about the wisdom of depending on foreigners (a consequence of anarchy).[47]

During the early 1980s, however, the need to cultivate a close Sino-American strategic alignment that had driven China's foreign policy since 1969 diminished as a consequence of three developments.[48] First, China began to perceive an easing of the Soviet threat.[49] Second, after years of denouncing détente as a delusion and encouraging the West to arm itself against the dangerous Soviet hegemon, Beijing saw its wishes more than fulfilled in the mas-

---

[46] China's borders served as the venue for the superpowers' three biggest foreign military operations of the Cold War era (Korea, Vietnam, and Afghanistan), as well as the site for several escalation-threatening crises between Beijing and the system's duopolists (the Taiwan Strait during the 1950s, the Sino-Soviet border in 1969, and Indochina in 1979). China's Cold War strategy suggested that the country represented the unusual case in which structural constraints are so tight that personality and national attributes need only play a distant secondary role in analyzing its foreign policy. For a debate about the usefulness and limitations of structural-realist explanations of foreign policy, see Colin Elman, "Horses for Courses: Why Not Neorealist Theories of Foreign Policy?"; Kenneth N. Waltz, "International Politics Is Not Foreign Policy"; Colin Elman, "Cause, Effect and Consistency: A Response to Kenneth N. Waltz." See also Avery Goldstein, "Structural Realism and China's Foreign Policy: Much (but Never All) of the Story."

[47] See Avery Goldstein, "Discounting the Free Ride: Alliances and Security in the Postwar World."

[48] For a survey of China's varying willingness to set aside differences in its negotiations with the United States see Robert S. Ross, *Negotiating Cooperation: The United States and China, 1969–1989*.

[49] As indigenous resistance efforts in Afghanistan and Cambodia garnered international support and effectively hamstrung Moscow's and Hanoi's efforts to consolidate their military occupations, Beijing's sense of alarm about events on its periphery ebbed. Ahead of their Western counterparts, some Chinese analysts even began to argue that the Soviets had, to use Paul Kennedy's term, entered the phase of imperial overstretch, suggesting that the shortcomings of the Soviet economy were finally limiting Moscow's ability to meet the ever-escalating demands (quantitative and qualitative) of military competition in the bipolar world. See Paul Kennedy, *The Rise and Fall of the Great Powers*; Wenqing Xie, "U.S.-Soviet Military Contention in the Asia-Pacific Region"; Jia Bei, "Gorbachev's Policy toward the Asian Pacific Region."

sive military buildup undertaken by President Reagan's United States and, to a lesser extent, other leading NATO countries and Japan. Third, Beijing's nuclear arsenal was beginning to include a small number of longer-range weapons that posed a serious risk of devastating retaliatory punishment against the Soviet Union's European heartland in the event a clash with China ever escalated uncontrollably. Thus, by the 1980s, the "existential deterrence" benefits of China's nuclear arsenal finally reinforced the "existential alliance" benefits of the Sino-American relationship that China had enjoyed since the Nixon opening of 1972.[50]

Consequently, Deng's anti-Soviet balancing grand strategy after 1980 differed from Mao's in that it was less tightly constrained by the need to cultivate a de facto alliance with the United States.[51] It also differed from Mao's insofar as the political, economic, and military content of the strategy began to change along with the domestic reforms Deng and his colleagues initiated in 1979. Politically, with the end of class-struggle rhetoric, China no longer relied on the Marxist categories of "revisionism" versus "revolution" to explain threatening Soviet behavior. Economically, with the abandonment of the Maoist development model, China sought to combine domestic institutional changes (*dui nei gao huo*) with an opening to the outside world (*dui wai kai fang*) to stimulate rapid economic growth that might eventually provide a foundation for national strength. Such growth would in turn reduce the need to depend on powerful patrons when facing future international threats. Militarily, with the demythologization of Mao, the People's Liberation Army was able to reduce, if not eliminate, the longstanding emphasis on adhering to the techniques that had proven helpful in the 1930s and 1940s (the doctrine of People's War), and to begin the arduous process of creating a professional army with the personnel and equipment suited to the modern battlefield that could complement China's small nuclear deterrent.[52]

---

[50]"Existential deterrence," or the idea that a state's possession of just a few nuclear weapons that *might* survive attack and inflict horrifying retaliatory damage should induce extreme caution and that the balance of capabilities is largely irrelevant, was popularized by McGeorge Bundy. The term "existential alliance" is used here to indicate that despite the absence of a formal security treaty, Sino-American rapprochement after 1972 created the possibility of military coordination that Soviet military planners could not safely ignore. See Goldstein, *Deterrence and Security in the 21ˢᵗ Century*.

[51] Compared with some of his colleagues, however, Deng remained wary about too quickly improving relations with the Soviets because of the great importance he attached to the economic as well as strategic benefits of good ties with the West. See Lu Ning. *The Dynamics of Foreign-Policy Decisionmaking in China*, pp. 95, 97, 151, 152.

[52] On the policies and priorities during the early stages of China's post-Mao reforms, see Harry Harding, *China's Second Revolution: Reform after Mao*. On the initial

During the 1980s, then, China's grand strategy was characterized by continuity in its fundamental purpose (hedging against potentially dangerous Soviet power), but its content was changing. Beijing viewed the advanced West, especially the United States, less as a military partner essential to China's short-term interest in coping with a pressing security threat and more as an economic partner essential to China's long-term interest in modernization. And although China still worried about a Soviet challenge, it also pursued improved relations with its northern neighbor.[53] When Moscow's "new thinking" under Mikhail Gorbachev's leadership more clearly heralded an inward turn by the country whose expansionist tendencies China had feared, a flurry of diplomacy quickly moved Sino-Soviet relations from the phase of reduced tension and dialogue initiated in the early 1980s to an era of full normalization capped by Gorbachev's state visit to Beijing in May 1989.

Nearing the end of the Cold War, China's international situation could hardly have seemed brighter.[54] Neither superpower posed a serious threat to China's security, and both seemed willing to nurture good relations with an economically awakening China. "Peace and development," as Deng Xiaoping argued, indeed seemed to be "the trend of the times." But the apparent dawn of a golden age for Chinese foreign policy in the "new world order" was not to be. Political and economic countercurrents were at work both within China and abroad that soon required Beijing to scramble for a strategy that was more than "status quo plus."

China's spectacular economic performance during the early 1980s had actually begun to take a turn for the worse after 1986. Heightened job insecurity and raging inflation together with political dissatisfaction among China's intellectuals and broad-based frustration with official corruption created a volatile mix that set the stage for nationwide demonstrations in the spring of 1989.[55] This unanticipated challenge to the CCP's monopoly on political

---

wave of post-Mao military modernization, see Paul H. B. Godwin, *The Chinese Defense Establishment: Continuity and Change in the 1980s*; Ellis Joffe, *The Chinese Army after Mao*; Charles D. Lovejoy and Bruce W. Watson, eds., *China's Military Reforms*; Larry M. Wortzell, ed., *China's Military Modernization*.

[53] On some of these changes, see Liu Di, "Deng Xiaoping's Thinking on Diplomatic Work—Interview with Liang Shoude, Dean for College of International Relations for Beijing University." See also Liu Huaqiu, "Strive for a Peaceful International Environment."

[54] Sun Jianshe, "Shiji Zhijiao Dui Woguo Anquan Huanjing De Sikao" [Reflections on our country's security environment at the turn of the century], p. 20.

[55] A set of three fortuitous circumstances "opened a window" for the airing of these grievances. First, the death of Hu Yaobang in April made it unseemly to prevent students from taking to the streets to engage in public mourning activities; once there,

power emerged just as China's leaders were attempting to consolidate what seemed to be their newly favorable position in a less threatening world. President George Bush had visited Beijing two months before the demonstrations began, suggesting a continuation of the friendly Sino-American ties that had taken root since President Nixon's visit in 1972. And Soviet general secretary Gorbachev arrived in early May for a visit that China's leaders had planned as a foreign policy triumph marking the end of the Cold War in Asia. But when continuing demonstrations in central Beijing precluded the scheduled public ceremonies and overshadowed the Sino-Soviet meetings, Gorbachev's visit instead became a diplomatic embarrassment for Deng and the CCP.[56] The regime's brutal crackdown on the demonstrators that followed in June instantly transformed Western perceptions of the PRC (whose political warts had been glossed over while it had been a valued strategic partner against the Soviets). These events also awakened new strategic concerns among China's leaders.[57]

Beijing's security environment no longer seemed so benign.[58] To be sure, neither the United States nor the Soviet Union posed an immediate *military* threat (as had been the case during most of the Cold War). Yet both posed a challenge to China's national security. The United States threatened China not only because it spearheaded the initial post-Tiananmen effort to isolate Beijing and impose sanctions, but also because its subsequent effort to resume constructive engagement carried the risk (for Americans, the promise) of what Beijing referred to as "peaceful evolution"—a process of fundamental political change that the CCP believed would lead to domestic unrest, if not regime collapse.[59]

---

they combined expressions of grief with support for the more ambitious political reform agenda with which Hu had been identified and which had cost him his job as general secretary of the CCP in January 1987. Second, the officially sanctioned presence of the international press corps who were invited to cover and help publicize the Sino-Soviet summit in May provided the demonstrators with both a platform and a belief that security forces would act with atypical restraint in front of the cameras. Third, the seventieth anniversary of nationalist, proreform demonstrations that gave China's May Fourth movement its name might have been seen as offering patriotic political cover for demands that Beijing focus on the challenges of political modernization.

[56] Even as they debated how to respond to the massively popular demonstrations, China's leaders fretted over the possibility that this was the beginning of "blowback" from reforms in the Soviet bloc that followed those the PRC had initiated a decade earlier but, in terms of politics, were more ambitious. Author's interviews, Beijing, June–July 1998.

[57] See Yan, "Dui Zhongguo Anquan Huanjing De Fenxi Yu Sikao," p. 8.

[58] On the deteriorating security environment during the 1990s, see Sun, "Shiji Zhijiao dui Woguo Anquan Huanjing de Sikao," p. 20.

[59] One leading analyst labeled the peaceful evolution approach "the theory of

The Soviet Union, its successor states, and its erstwhile satellites threatened China by example. Just as China's economic reformers had been inspired by newly industrialized countries in East Asia a decade earlier, China's political reformers might be inspired by newly democratized countries in the former Soviet bloc, especially during the first flush of optimism about their prospects that followed the serial collapse of communist regimes in the early 1990s.[60]

As if the "democratic threat" from abroad were not enough, at the same time Beijing soon found that it also faced a frustrating renewed challenge on a matter it had long defined as an absolutely vital national interest—sovereignty over Taiwan. After decades of harsh rhetoric about "liberating Taiwan," beginning in 1979 the CCP had floated a series of proposals for peaceful unification that emphasized patience on timing and tolerance of differences (ultimately offering to allow Taiwan to maintain its own political, economic, and military institutions if it would only acknowledge Beijing's claim to sovereignty).[61] During the early post-Mao era, Beijing might have had high hopes for this more generous approach since it was directed at Taiwan's authoritarian ruling party (the KMT), whose leaders, however ideologically hostile to communism they might have been, were at least committed to the idea that

---

China's collapse." See Liu, "Strive for a Peaceful International Environment." Michael Pillsbury notes that in 1991–92 China saw the U.S. policy of "containment and 'peaceful evolution'" as a main cause of the Soviet collapse. Only after 1992 did the Chinese begin to emphasize the Soviets' own mistakes, especially "stagnation and isolation . . . along with [their] highly centralized planning and an excessive military budget" (*China Debates the Future Security Environment*, p. 188; see also pp. 185–87. On the importance of concerns about domestic order as a key consideration shaping China's grand strategic choices, see Swaine and Tellis, *Interpreting China's Grand Strategy*, pp. 9–20, chapter 2.

[60] On some of the CCP's concerns, see John W. Garver, "The Chinese Communist Party and the Collapse of Soviet Communism."

[61] Deng Xiaoping described some of these conditions: "Different systems may be practiced, but it must be the People's Republic of China alone that represents China internationally. . . . After reunification with the motherland, the Taiwan special administrative region will assume a unique character and may practice a social system different from that of the mainland. It will enjoy independent judicial power, and there will be no need to go to Beijing for final adjudication. What is more, it may maintain its own army, provided it does not threaten the mainland. The mainland will not station anyone in Taiwan. Neither troops nor administrative personnel will go there. The party, governmental and military systems of Taiwan will be administered by the Taiwan authorities themselves." See Deng Xiaoping, "An Idea for the Peaceful Reunification of the Chinese Mainland and Taiwan, June 26, 1983." For a survey and analysis of China's Taiwan policy in the post-Mao era, see Michael D. Swaine, "Chinese Decision-Making Regarding Taiwan, 1979–2000." On the initial post-Mao moderation, see ibid., pp. 311–13.

Taiwan was part of China. As Taiwan began to democratize in the late 1980s, this commitment was in jeopardy. Younger KMT politicians with roots on the island rather than the mainland and newly active opposition politicians, especially in Taiwan's Democratic Progressive Party (DPP), envisioned a continuation of de facto independence and, increasingly, moves toward de jure independence. If the passage of time meant greater democratization on Taiwan, and increased democratization meant an end to Taipei's traditional commitment to unification, a policy of patience and tolerance would no longer be so appealing in Beijing. Moreover, the end of the Cold War had not ended the relevance of liberal-democratic ideology as a driving force in U.S. foreign policy, but instead actually elevated its importance. Consequently, the likelihood of American support for democratic Taiwan against communist China (especially in the wake of the brutal 1989 crackdown that vividly illustrated the authoritarian credentials of the government in Beijing) had increased to levels unmatched since Nixon's historic visit in 1972.[62]

Thus, in the early 1990s, China's Cold War grand strategy was dead, but a new direction was not yet clear. Until 1992, Beijing focused mainly on addressing the immediate internal political and economic problems that had emerged at the end of the 1980s. Foreign policy was limited essentially to small steps to undo the setbacks in economic and diplomatic relations that followed the international outrage about Tiananmen Square.[63] After 1992, apparently satisfied that it had weathered the political storm of communist collapses and had righted its economic ship, the regime began to evince greater self-confidence at home and abroad.[64]

With a decisive push provided by Deng Xiaoping and sustained by his designated successor Jiang Zemin, aggressive economic reforms reignited rapid growth catalyzed by large-scale foreign trade and investment. The economic attractiveness of China, whose communist regime was no longer

[62] Several of my interlocutors stressed the importance of the contrasting images of "democratizing Taiwan" and "Tiananmen China" that prevailed in the United States after 1989, arguing that these made Americans more receptive to Taipei's initiatives to elevate its independent international profile.

[63] China's cooperation, or at least acquiescence, at the United Nations during the Persian Gulf crisis of 1990–91 was a noteworthy part of Beijing's effort to rebuild Sino-American relations. Deng Xiaoping called for China to maintain a low profile during this troubled time. See "Beijing Urged to Keep Regional Power Focus."

[64] In retrospect, Liu Huaqiu, director of the Foreign Affairs Office under the State Council, asserted that China had "withstood the impact from the drastic changes in Eastern Europe and the disintegration of the Soviet Union [and] smashed Western sanctions" ("Strive for a Peaceful International Environment"; author's interviews, Beijing, June–July 1998).

deemed to be on the verge of collapse, led others to seize the opportunity China's new openness provided.[65] The resulting boom had international political spillover effects. Beijing refocused on peace and development as the central themes of its international diplomacy, reaffirming the emphasis that Deng had introduced during the last decade of the Cold War. China also renewed its efforts to improve relations with neighboring states, engaging in constructive dialogue about border disputes, normalizing state-to-state relations, and working to manage "problems left over from history." Booming foreign trade even had a beneficial political impact on the delicate matter of relations with Taiwan. In 1993, China and Taiwan opened unofficial talks and began to establish a framework for expanding economic, social, and academic exchanges. And in 1994, with memories of the CCP's brutal 1989 crackdown fading, U.S. president Bill Clinton, despite his earlier campaign trail rhetoric that warned about "coddling Chinese dictators," shifted to an emphasis on engagement with an economically rebounding China and called for an end to the annual effort to link most-favored-nation trade status with Beijing's domestic political practices and foreign policy.[66] China's international prospects were clearly brightening.

Yet even as a domestically more secure Beijing reemerged from the shadow of Tiananmen and became more internationally active, China faced a world that was more suspicious and less forgiving than it had been in the 1980s. Consequently, China's international position quickly deteriorated again during 1995–96 when others began to respond to what they viewed as an increasingly powerful PRC's assertive behavior in the South China Sea (where it used military force to buttress its claim to disputed territory) and the Taiwan Strait (where it undertook military exercises and missile tests to highlight the risks for Taipei if it abandoned the goal of reunification). By March 1996, Beijing confronted an international environment potentially more dangerous than at any time since the late 1970s. Its actions were antagonizing the states that comprised the Association of Southeast Asian Nations (ASEAN), crystallizing the view of an important segment of the U.S. foreign policy elite that China represented an emerging challenge to American interests in Asia, and even arousing Japan's fears about the PRC's future role in the region.[67]

[65] See Suisheng Zhao, "Deng Xiaoping's Southern Tour: Elite Politics in Post-Tiananmen China"; Nicholas R. Lardy, *China in the World Economy.*

[66] "Text of President Clinton's Address About China."

[67] See Aaron Friedberg, "Ripe for Rivalry: Prospects for Peace in a Multipolar Asia"; Denny Roy, "Hegemon on the Horizon? China's Threat to East Asian Security"; Michael G. Gallagher, "China's Illusory Threat to the South China Sea." On the greater challenges facing China and the contrast with those of the late Cold War years,

Although a modernizing China was impressively increasing its capabilities during the 1990s, greater capabilities did not seem to be enhancing the country's security because others were reacting with alarm to what China believed were simply efforts to ensure its own interests. Beijing was, in short, caught in the familiar dynamic of the security dilemma.[68] Initially, China's leaders focused less on their own role in provoking a nervous reaction and more on what they saw as others' unwarranted fears.[69] As explained in chapter 5, however, they soon grasped the need to devise an approach that more effectively addressed the concerns an emerging China was generating. The result was the consensus that formed during 1996 and has since provided the core logic for a grand strategy designed to facilitate China's peaceful rise. Before describing that consensus and the contents of the grand strategy that rests upon it, I look more closely at the nature of China's increasing capabilities and its foreign policy during the early post–Cold War era that clarified the problems with which its leaders would have to cope.

---

see Ye, "Zhongguo Shixing Daguo Waijiao Zhanlüe Shizai Bixing," p. 5; Allen S. Whiting, "ASEAN Eyes China: The Security Dimension"; author's interviews, Beijing, June–July 1998.

[68] One Japan Defense Agency analyst, for example, explained the nervous reaction to a rising China by pointing not just to "China's assertion of territorial rights without the approval of concerned nations, rapid economic growth, justification of the use of military capabilities, modernization of weapons, and lack of transparency in military spending, but [also to] China's erstwhile about-face in diplomatic stances. . . . When one deals with any country that is prone to about-faces, one cannot avoid a sense of insecurity" (Nobuyuki Ito, "Reading the World: The Strategic Environment in the 21st Century").

[69] Such a lack of empathy is certainly not unique to Chinese leaders (see Robert Jervis, "Hypotheses on Misperception"). The sharp limits on domestic debate about the PRC's foreign policy combined with an ideological insistence that socialist states are pacific and capitalist states cause wars, however, may exacerbate the problem. See Pillsbury, *China Debates the Future Security Environment*, pp. xxxi–xxxii.

3

Growing Capabilities, Growing Problems

Within just a few years after the collapse of the Soviet Union, it became nearly conventional wisdom that China was an emerging great power and that its arrival would pose some of the most difficult questions for international security in the post–Cold War era. In short order, most analysts thinking about the dynamics of the international system in the twenty-first century were asserting that it was essential to consider the rise of China and its implications.[1] Yet the foundation for this expectation was not entirely clear. In what sense was China's power increasing? To what extent did the new claims of a rapidly rising China reflect reality as opposed to perceptions? This chapter examines the fit between objective indicators and judgments about China's power that quickly took root during the first half of the 1990s.[2] These assess-

[1] The new wave of scholarly interest in East Asian security and China emerged in about 1993. One of the more influential publications heralding the shift in attention was Aaron Friedberg, "Ripe for Rivalry: Prospects for Peace in a Multipolar Asia." Just two years earlier, Asia and China received relatively short shrift in one of the first serious comprehensive overviews of the post–Cold War global landscape. See Robert J. Art, "A Defensible Defense: America's Grand Strategy after the Cold War." By 1996, the spirit of the emerging "China-mania" was reflected in popular media as well as academic circles. See Ian Buruma, Seth Faison, and Fareed Zakaria, "The 21st Century Starts Here: China Booms. The World Holds Its Breath"; Michael E. Brown, Sean M. Lynn-Jones, and Steven E. Miller, eds., *East Asian Security*.

[2] My focus is on conditions that triggered the adoption of China's current grand strategy during the mid-1990s, not on the entire process of military modernization that predates this period, as noted below, and continued afterward. For a recent comprehensive assessment of China's military modernization since the end of the Cold War that includes coverage of forces, doctrine, and spending, see David Shambaugh, *Modernizing China's Military: Progress, Problems, and Prospects*.

ments set the stage for a reconsideration of China's international role that in turn helped shape the grand strategy Beijing would embrace.

Perhaps the early post–Cold War focus on China's growing international role should not have been altogether surprising, inasmuch as it is a country that had long possessed three of the attributes considered among the traditional prerequisites for membership in the great power club: it had vast territory, rich resources, and a large population. And, during the second half of the twentieth century, other key requirements for international influence had been successively met. The victory of the Chinese Communist Party that ended China's Civil War in 1949 resolved a century-long pattern of internal political disunity that had facilitated a series of foreign encroachments on the country's sovereignty. During the four decades of the Cold War, the new regime's leaders gradually enhanced their international prestige and eventually overcame attempts at diplomatic isolation to assume their role as the sole legitimate representatives of the Chinese state in key international bodies, most notably the United Nations Security Council. In addition, during the Cold War China invested heavily in the rapid development of the modern era's military badges of great power status—nuclear warheads and the ballistic missiles to deliver them.

Nevertheless, until the last decade of the Cold War China remained only a "candidate" great power because it had failed in its efforts to promote domestic development that could serve as the basis for comprehensive economic and military strength at world-class levels. Instead, in the bipolar world dominated by the United States and the Soviet Union, China remained a developing country, though one that had a vast army supplied with obsolete conventional and crude nuclear weaponry. These limitations kept it in the group of second-ranking powers, and among them perhaps the least capable.[3] But in the decade after 1979, while the Soviet Union was retrenching internationally and then imploding, new leaders in Beijing instituted a series of sweeping reforms that resulted in high-speed growth—both quantitative expansion and qualitative improvements.[4] Although the results realized by the end of the Cold War were modest, China appeared to be poised for an economic takeoff. This prospect led many to begin extrapolating in ways that pointed to a seemingly inescapable conclusion: China was finally adding the last pieces to its great

[3] See Avery Goldstein, "Robust and Affordable Security: Some Lessons from the Second-Ranking Powers During the Cold War," pp. 478–79, 519; Avery Goldstein, *Deterrence and Security in the 21st Century.*

[4] For overviews of the initial wave of China's reforms, see Harry Harding, *China's Second Revolution*; Kenneth Lieberthal, *Governing China.*

power puzzle. Beijing would soon have the wealth and expertise to be a leading player in international economic affairs, assets that might also provide the foundation for a first-class military capability.[5] Many who had comfortably spoken about a Chinese great power some time in the future began to take seriously the implications of China sooner, rather than later, having the ability to more assertively pursue its own interests. Often, those thinking about this prospect believed it spelled trouble for international security, at least in East Asia and perhaps beyond.[6]

This changing view of China's prospects became the root of concern about a possible "China threat" that complicated Beijing's foreign policy during the 1990s. China's political leaders and its foreign policy analysts challenged the basis for such worries. Their objections centered on disagreements about the pace and the extent to which China's capabilities were increasing and included denials that China would use its capabilities, however impressive they might seem, to threaten others. Setting aside the question of intentions, to what extent was the belief in increasing Chinese power that took hold in the mid-1990s warranted?

Interpreting China's Power

Although it might seem that an assessment of China's power should have been a straightforward exercise, important differences in the way its capabilities were portrayed confused the issue. Some who began to point to a rising China in the mid-1990s discussed its power in absolute terms. Such descriptions provided a current snapshot of the quantity or quality of Chinese economic and military capabilities. In part because of the country's huge population, observers could point to big numbers that seemed to speak for themselves, drawing attention to impressive levels of consumption, large government budgets, and a vast array of military personnel.[7] But for analysts whose

---

[5] For a forecast anticipating this outcome as the Cold War was about to end, see Paul Kennedy, *The Rise and Fall of the Great Powers,* pp. 447–58.

[6] On the increased importance of China for U.S. foreign policy, see U.S. secretary of state Warren Christopher's May 1996 speech, "'American Interests and the U.S.-China Relationship': Address by Warren Christopher." See also Friedberg, "Ripe for Rivalry"; Denny Roy, "Hegemon on the Horizon"; Michael G. Gallagher, "China's Illusory Threat to the South China Sea"; Richard K. Betts, "Wealth, Power, and Instability: East Asia and the United States after the Cold War"; Richard Bernstein and Ross H. Munro, *The Coming Conflict with China*; and Andrew J. Nathan and Robert S. Ross, *The Great Wall and the Empty Fortress: China's Search for Security.*

[7] Because of China's huge population, of course, per capita figures are less impressive than national totals. Which data are most useful depends on the purposes of one's

interest in China was piqued by the international implications of its rise, the measurement of absolute capabilities was less important than assessments of relative capabilities.

Broadly speaking, there are two ways to distinguish work that discusses power in relative, as opposed to absolute, terms.[8] One is whether the analysis is national or international in scope. A national assessment is one that draws comparisons between a state's present and past capabilities, the sort of developmental story often told in the literature that details the history of a particular country. An international assessment is one that draws comparisons between one state's capabilities and others'. A second broad distinction can be drawn within the realm of such international assessments. They may entail either synchronic comparison of current capabilities relative to other states (depicting an existing balance of power, for example), or diachronic comparison that traces changes in such relations over time (depicting the rise and fall of great powers).

With a few important exceptions, analysts who began to focus on China's ascent during the 1990s chronicled growing power either by describing the

---

analysis. A ruthless political leadership may be able to extract funding for massive military investment from a large economy even while per capita income remains low, as happened in the Soviet Union. Whether such efforts are sustainable over the long term is a separate question and has been raised in debates about the reasons for the Soviet collapse in 1991.

[8] Two additional caveats are worth noting. First, "power" is a highly contested term, and the debate about its meaning cannot possibly be resolved in this space. For a brief introduction to the debate and references to some of the key positions, see William C. Wohlforth, *The Elusive Balance*, esp. pp. 3–10. Second, and perhaps ironically, in this case it is easier to deal with the theoretical-interpretive issues than the empirical ones. Since 1979 Western scholars have been better able to interview relevant policy makers, academics, and military personnel to gather the increasing volume of publications in China, as well as to obtain many imperfectly controlled "internal-circulation-only" (*neibu*) materials often discovered on the shelves of China's bookstores. But the CCP still remains relatively cool to the notion of transparency in the military-security realm. On the strategic rationale for China resisting transparency, see Goldstein, "Robust and Affordable Security," pp. 485–91, 500–503; Alastair Iain Johnston, "China's New 'Old Thinking': The Concept of Limited Deterrence," p. 31 n. 92. China's Defense White Paper in 1995 was an unrevealing disappointment. Subsequent white papers have been only slightly more forthcoming. See "White Paper—China: Arms Control and Disarmament"; Banning N. Garrett and Bonnie S. Glaser, "Chinese Perspectives on Nuclear Arms Control"; Christopher Bluth, "Beijing's Attitude to Arms Control"; Barbara Opall, "Skeptics Doubt Value of PLA White Paper." English translations of all of these white papers are available at http://english.peopledaily.com.cn/whitepaper/home.html.

country's absolute capabilities (implicitly suggesting their impressiveness) or by identifying significant changes relative to China's own past. Such accounts offered measures of what William Wohlforth has termed "estimated power," looking at indicators that many believe are the building blocks of international influence.[9] The most important sets of indicators in the Chinese case were economic statistics, military spending, and modernization of the PLA's forces.

Economic Indicators

By the mid-1990s, economic statistics that described the size or growth rate of China's aggregate and per capita gross domestic product (GDP) as well as the expanding volume and changing composition of China's international trade provided a startling picture of transformation. During the 1980s China's GDP had doubled in size, and in less than a decade it was doubling again.[10] Although per capita income remained low, some began to assert that this statistic understated the fundamental improvements in the standard of living of most of China's citizens, changes better captured by changing patterns of consumer behavior.[11] At the same time, China's trade volume had ballooned from $38.2 billion to more than $250 billion,[12] and the composition of imports and exports had shifted as China went from being an exporter of raw materials and importer of foodstuffs to being an exporter of labor-intensive consumer goods and an importer of industrial products.[13] Moreover, a string of trade surpluses was yielding a stunning increase in the country's foreign exchange reserves.[14] Simply put, by the mid-1990s China's profile had been transformed; no

[9] William C. Wohlforth, "The Perception of Power: Russia in the Pre–1914 Balance."

[10] See Lieberthal, *Governing China*, p. 126; also "Statistical Communiqué of the State Statistical Bureau of the People's Republic of China," released annually each March and available in *Beijing Review*.

[11] See Li Dong and Alec M. Gallup, "In Search of the Chinese Consumer," p. 19; "Diversifying Consumer Purchases in China." Even so, a substantial fraction of the Chinese population remained mired in poverty. See Patrick E. Tyler, "In China's Outlands, Poorest Grow Poorer."

[12] See Nicholas R. Lardy, *China in the World Economy*, p. 2; "China Confident in Fulfilling Foreign Trade Target for This Year."

[13] Lardy, *China in the World Economy*, pp. 29–33.

[14] From roughly $15 billion at the end of the 1980s, China's foreign exchange reserves reached $84.3 billion by August 1996, ranking China fifth in the world. Its reserves topped $100 billion by November 1996 and were headed for $150 billion by mid-1997. Nicholas R. Lardy, "The Future of China: China's Growing Economic Role in Asia," p. 7; "China's Forex Reserves Not Too High—Official"; "China Growth Seen at 9.8 Pct, Reserves at $140 Bln."

longer a reluctant and minor participant in the international economy, it was emerging as an eager and major actor following a development strategy that other East Asian countries relying on export-led growth had pioneered.

Military Spending

The focus on China's emerging military capabilities initially lagged behind the interest in its improving economic performance. In part this reflected the fact that the 1980s had been a decade in which People's Liberation Army's (PLA) budgets were kept relatively low while Beijing accorded highest priority to domestic economic growth in an effort to lift the standard of living of the Chinese people from the meager levels achieved under Maoist socialism. To be sure, those specializing in the study of China's military had been tracking basic changes in force structure and doctrine that the regime initiated beginning in the early 1980s.[15] But it was only during the early 1990s that a broader community began to pay much attention to evidence suggesting quantitative increases and qualitative improvements in China's military capabilities. One of the triggers for the upsurge in interest was the beginning of a succession of large peacetime increases in military spending. Some of the increase could be explained, as Beijing claimed, by the need to offset the effects of inflation and to compensate for a decade of relative budgetary neglect. Most analysts, however, concluded that the magnitude of the official increase, especially when combined with the many hidden sources of PLA revenue that comprise its funding base, demonstrated Beijing's determination during the 1990s to significantly upgrade China's armed forces.[16]

Estimates of the size and interpretation of the meaning of increases in the

[15] See Paul H. B. Godwin, *The Chinese Defense Establishment*; Harlan Jencks, "People's War under Modern Conditions: Wishful Thinking, National Suicide, or Effective Deterrent?"; Paul H. B. Godwin. "The Chinese Defense Establishment in Transition: The Passing of a Revolutionary Army?"; Ellis Joffe, *The Chinese Army after Mao*; Larry M. Wortzell, *China's Military Modernization*.

[16] On the reduced PLA budgets of the 1980s, see Paul H. B. Godwin, "Force Projection and China's National Military Strategy," p. 77. Figures on China's military spending ranged from the low official report of about $8 billion to foreign estimates well in excess of $50 billion. For a discussion of the technical and practical complexities of calculating China's defense spending that produced such conflicting results, see "China's Military Expenditure." See also David Shambaugh, "Growing Strong: China's Challenge to Asian Security," p. 54; Shaoguang Wang, "Estimating China's Defence Expenditure: Some Evidence from Chinese Sources"; and the estimates published in the U.S. Arms Control and Disarmament Agency's *World Military Expenditures and Arms Transfers* and the Stockholm International Peace Research Institute's *Yearbook*.

military budget in the early 1990s remained uncertain. But for at least four reasons, the belief that China was rapidly increasing its military capabilities was unduly alarmist. First, despite the assumption that international arms sales contributed a hidden increment to the official budget, the annual cash value of China's arms exports in the first half of the 1990s actually "dropped significantly from levels posted in the late 1980s" (as much as $3.1 billion) to a level of roughly $1.2 billion annually.[17] Second, those positing the highest totals for PLA budgets (in excess of $50 billion) assumed that the Chinese military's commercial enterprises contributed some $5 to $20 billion. In fact, these operations added between $1.2 and $1.8 billion annually.[18] Third, although this thriving military-business complex was providing hidden revenues, it was also exacting hidden costs, spreading corruption within the military, diverting the PLA's attention from its principal responsibility to ready itself for possible armed conflict, and redirecting the focus of China's defense industry away from strategically important military, to economically profitable civilian, production.[19] These problems would, in fact, lead China's political leaders in 1998 to order the PLA to rapidly shed its commercial ventures. And fourth, whatever the precise level of China's military spending during the 1990s may have been, much of the inflation-adjusted annual increases of 4 percent went to ever more costly operations and maintenance, not new weapons procurement.[20] To be sure, some of this increase represented an investment that would produce a more effective fighting force, but some was also absorbed by the need to deal with the growing problem of poor living standards for mili-

[17] Bates Gill, "The Impact of Economic Reform Upon Chinese Defense Production," pp. 153–54; John Frankenstein, and Bates Gill, "Current and Future Challenges Facing Chinese Defence Industries," p. 427.

[18] The officially announced figure understated the total at less than $1 billion. See Tai Ming Cheung, "China's Entrepreneurial Army: The Structure, Activities and Economic Returns of the Military Business Complex," pp. 184–87. For the higher estimates, see Solomon M. Karmel, "The Chinese Military's Hunt for Profits," p. 106; Bernstein and Munro, *The Coming Conflict with China*, p. 72.

[19] See Cheung, "China's Entrepreneurial Army"; Arthur S. Ding, "China's Defence Finance: Content, Process and Administration"; Gill, "The Impact of Economic Reform," pp. 150–52. On the difficulties posed by China's Soviet legacy of a well-insulated military-industrial complex, see Eric Arnett, "Military Technology: The Case of China."

[20] Michael D. Swaine, "Don't Demonize China; Rhetoric About Its Military Might Doesn't Reflect Reality." See also Frankenstein and Gill, "Current and Future Challenges," pp. 411, 420–21. A strong case could be made for estimates of total military spending during the mid-1990s in the $30 billion range. See "China's Military Expenditure," pp. 270–75.

tary personnel and to compensate for the increased cost of purchasing goods at higher market prices as China continued to move further away from the fixed and artificially low prices that had prevailed in its Soviet-style command economy.

Force Modernization

Improvements in the PLA's deployed capabilities by the mid-1990s seemed to point in the same direction as increases in the military budget and provided additional evidence that contributed to the impression that China was a rapidly rising power whose implications for international affairs needed to be more seriously addressed. Moreover, deployed forces arguably provide a more direct, if still imperfect, index of actual national power than economic statistics and budgetary trends that may only suggest the potential for, or interest in, augmenting military strength.

China's program of force modernization that attracted widespread attention in the 1990s was guided by a shift in doctrine that actually began in the early 1980s. At that time, Beijing began to heavily discount the likelihood of major, potentially nuclear, war with the hostile Soviet superpower. A new view, formally articulated by the Central Military Commission in 1985, stressed instead the need to prepare to fight limited, local wars, for which neither the People's War doctrine of protracted national resistance nor China's small nuclear arsenal would be very useful.[21] The PLA began to revamp itself in line with this change in strategic outlook during the late 1980s, but the most dramatic tangible changes emerged only in the next decade. The breathtaking American demonstration of advanced military technology in the 1991 Gulf War and the intensification of disputes about the status of Taiwan and territories in the South China Sea—areas effectively beyond the PLA's largely continental range of operation—provided China's leaders with stronger incentives to accelerate a modernization program that increasingly emphasized the importance of "limited war under high-technology conditions."[22]

The continuing strength of China's growing economy and the availability of advanced armaments from an economically strapped Russian military in-

[21] For an overview of these doctrinal shifts, see Nan Li, "The PLA's Evolving Warfighting Doctrine, Strategy and Tactics, 1985–1995: A Chinese Perspective"; Paul H. B. Godwin, "From Continent to Periphery: PLA Doctrine, Strategy and Capabilities Towards 2000."

[22] Li, "The PLA's Evolving Warfighting Doctrine," p. 448; Godwin, "From Continent to Periphery," pp. 472–73.

dustry provided a golden opportunity to act on these incentives.[23] What were the results? During the early 1990s, "pockets of excellence" began to emerge within the ground, air, and naval forces of the PLA. These pockets were reflected most clearly in the development of elite units, so-called "fist" or rapid-response forces, that were better supplied and designed to take the lead in using more advanced equipment to master the techniques of combined arms and joint service operations. By the mid-1990s analysts estimated that between 15 and 25 percent of the PLA (i.e., several hundred thousand troops) was comprised of such elite forces designed for airborne and marine assault as well as ground attack missions.[24] Even so, there were questions about just how much of an immediate improvement this ostensibly dramatic reorganization represented. Widely publicized exercises displaying new weapons and techniques (such as the simultaneous deployment of forces from multiple services) did not definitively demonstrate that the new units had the training, the doctrinal understanding, and the command-and-control capabilities that would be essential for genuinely effective combined arms operations. Enduring shortcomings in the PLA's ability to coordinate tactical air power with quickly evolving ground or sea operations added to doubts about the likely effectiveness of China's newly created elite units.[25]

By the mid-1990s, however, China's military modernization was not only leading to increased spending and selective reorganization, but was also providing the PLA with new equipment. In this effort, too, the immediate goal was to create pockets of excellence; comprehensive force modernization remained a distant goal to be achieved perhaps in the middle of the twenty-first century.[26] The most noteworthy aspect of the procurement effort in the early 1990s was the selective purchase of foreign equipment for the PLA Air Force (PLAAF) and Navy (PLAN) in order to quickly compensate for the most serious shortcomings in China's capabilities and, if possible, to catalyze the production of better indigenously produced equipment.[27] What were the key im-

[23] See Godwin, "Force Projection," pp. 79–81.

[24] Chong-pin Lin, "The Power Projection Capabilities of the People's Liberation Army," pp. 110–11; Godwin, "From Continent to Periphery," pp. 469–70, 482.

[25] See Dennis J. Blasko, Philip T. Klapakis, and John F. Corbett Jr., "Training Tomorrow's PLA: A Mixed Bag of Tricks," pp. 488, 517; also Dennis J. Blasko. "Better Late Than Never: Non-Equipment Aspects of PLA Ground Force Modernization," esp. 130–35; Shambaugh, "Growing Strong," p. 53; Godwin, "Force Projection," pp. 83–86.

[26] Godwin, "From Continent to Periphery," p. 484.

[27] New equipment for the ground forces was apparently assigned a lower priority than that for air, naval, and ballistic missile forces. See Blasko, "Better Late Than Never," p. 126.

provements in the PLA's equipment, and to what extent were these significantly increasing China's military power?

Air forces. With an eye to improving both the combat effectiveness and range of forces that would play a key role in any effort by China to project power across the Taiwan Strait or in the South China Sea (two of the most plausible contingencies for PLA action), in the 1990s the PLAAF began to overhaul a fleet dominated by thousands of obsolete first- and second-generation fighter aircraft based on 1950s Soviet designs (the MiG-19-based J-6 and MiG-21-based J-7).[28] The longstanding weaknesses of China's aircraft industry limited Beijing's ability to rely on indigenous production of modern fighters and bombers, and even to upgrade existing platforms without foreign assistance. Plans in the 1980s to upgrade China's J-8 with modern avionics from abroad were dealt a serious blow by the U.S. sanctions imposed following the Tiananmen Square crackdown in June 1989. Shortly afterward, however, the collapse of the Soviet Union and the diplomatic fence mending with Russia gave China the opportunity to obtain advanced aircraft from a major new supplier. Beijing purchased twenty-four Su-27 fighters (designated J-11 in China) in 1991 and another twenty-two in 1995, and by 1996 Moscow had agreed to a proposal for coproduction.[29] At the same time, China continued working toward deployment of an indigenously produced J-10 aircraft whose design benefited from cooperation with Israel Aircraft Industries and its work on the canceled Lavi project.[30]

---

[28] In September 1996 Taiwan's deputy chief of the General Staff estimated that only about one-quarter of China's air force was operational (Barbara Opall, "China Boosts Air Combat Capabilities"). There were also reports that China had ceased operating its nuclear strategic bombers (Barbara Starr, "China Could 'Overwhelm' Regional Missile Shield"). Production of the most obsolete aircraft was sharply reduced during the 1980s (Frankenstein and Gill, "Current and Future Challenges," pp. 412–13). Other upgraded Chinese aircraft—the J-7MG, J-8II, and the FC-1 (being co-developed with Pakistan)—were continuing production mainly for the export market (Richard D. Fisher, "The Accelerating Modernization of China's Military").

[29] In addition to providing the PLAAF with its first truly modern (fourth-generation) fighter aircraft, Russia also began supplying China with a package of advanced capabilities including Sorbtsiya ECM jamming pods and AA-10 Alamo and AA-11 Archer infrared-guided air-to-air missiles with helmet-mounted sighting. See "Arms Exports to China Assessed, Moscow"; Fisher, "Accelerating Modernization"; Richard D. Fisher, "China's Purchase of Russian Fighters: A Challenge to the U.S." The upgraded version of the Su-27 could be fitted with the even more advanced Russian AA-12 air-to-air missile (Robert Karniol, "China Is Poised to Buy Third Batch of Su–27s").

[30] Godwin, "From Continent to Periphery," p. 480; Fisher, "Accelerating Moderni-

Compared with the fighters available to the PLAAF just a decade earlier, these new additions promised a dramatic upgrade in capabilities and led some to expect that China would field a contingent of several hundred more modern aircraft perhaps as early as the first decade of the twenty-first century. But given China's poor track record in air force modernization, a legacy that partly explained the turn to foreign suppliers despite Beijing's traditional preference for self-reliance, it was likely that actual deployment would proceed more slowly, as turned out to be the case.[31] Shortcomings in China's aerospace industry limited its ability to maintain the advanced equipment it was importing and coproducing.[32] And because maintenance was an issue, training was often constrained by an interest in minimizing wear and tear on equipment. Such problems limited the PLAAF's ability to translate new equipment purchases and production into *operational* pockets of excellence, especially since the latter depended on having highly trained personnel integrate better equipment with revised doctrine for its use.

Similar challenges faced the PLAAF in the 1990s when it sought in-flight refueling systems and AWACS (airborne warning and control systems) that would be essential for China to project increased power any significant distance beyond its coastline and sustain air operations across the relevant theaters in East Asia. Again, the PLAAF looked abroad to fill gaps, turning not only to Russia but also to Israel, Iran, and Pakistan.[33] And again, foreign pur-

---

zation," esp. n. 60; Chong-pin Lin, "The Military Balance in the Taiwan Straits," pp. 587–88. The U.S. Office of Naval Intelligence argued that this multirole fighter "may be more maneuverable than the U.S. F/A-18 E/F" but with "less sophisticated radar and countermeasures" ("China Develops Stealthy Multi-Role Fighter"). See also "Air Forces of the World—China" and "Catching Up." For an assessment of the J-10 program available from the Federation of American Scientists' Military Analysis Network, see http://www.fas.org/man/dod–101/sys/ac/row/j–10.htm.

[31] Andy Chuter, "China's Fighter Skips Generation."

[32] The enduring shortcomings of China's military industry are in part a legacy of the Maoist-era practice of "copy production" and "reverse engineering" (Gill, "The Impact of Economic Reform," pp. 147–49; see also Frankenstein and Gill, "Current and Future Challenges," pp. 414–15; Lin, "Power Projection Capabilities," p. 107). On challenges facing China's indigenous combat aircraft industry, including quality control, limited funding, and competition from Russian imports, see Gill, "The Impact of Economic Reform," pp. 152–53. Such problems also raised doubts about China's ability to bring to fruition the XXJ advanced stealth multirole fighter program projected for sometime in the second decade of the twenty-first century (Joseph C. Anselmo, "China's Military Seeks Great Leap Forward").

[33] See Lin, "The Military Balance in the Taiwan Straits," p. 587; Lin, "Power Projection Capabilities," p. 104; David Shambaugh, "China's Military in Transition: Politics, Professionalism, Procurement and Power Projection," p. 293; Opall, "China

chases were not easily leveraged into substantially improved capabilities. Limits on China's ability to maintain and repair new equipment constrained the training of personnel and the frequency of exercises essential for mastering the delicate techniques of in-flight refueling using new tankers and modified aircraft.[34] A different challenge hampered the deployment of AWACS, which should have been more straightforward since Beijing sought only to marry the Russian Il-76 (with which its air force already had experience) to Israel's sophisticated Phalcon radar. But this promising plan was blocked by U.S. diplomatic pressure that ultimately convinced Tel Aviv to abrogate its part of the deal. Although China moved ahead, it had to settle for a fully Russian system rather than the superior hybrid it had hoped to deploy.[35]

Naval forces. China's navy, too, initiated a process of determined, if selective, modernization focused on deploying vessels with greater range, greater survivability, and more lethal weapons systems than the largely obsolete, vulnerable, coastal defense force China possessed at the end of the Cold War.[36] Shortcomings in China's shipbuilding industry, as in its aircraft industry, led Beijing's naval modernization effort to depend heavily on importing foreign equipment and technology even as it attempted to combine this with or adapt it to indigenous production.

Key improvements in PLAN equipment were emerging by the mid-1990s. Older classes of Chinese destroyers and frigates were being upgraded and new ones were being introduced that incorporated significant elements of more advanced Western propulsion and weapons technologies.[37] China's navy also

---

Boosts Air Combat Capabilities." China is reported to have modified up to five of its H-6 bombers to refuel J-8II Finback fighters; U.S. intelligence reportedly estimated that China might convert up to twenty H-6 bombers into air-to-air refueling aircraft. The Su-27s purchased in the 1990s were not modified for air-to-air refueling, but this capability could be acquired later. See Fisher, "China's Purchase of Russian Fighters: A Challenge to the U.S."

[34] See Shambaugh, "China's Military in Transition," p. 295; Godwin, "From Continent to Periphery," pp. 478–80; Godwin, "Force Projection," p. 86.

[35]"Russia and Israel to Supply Airborne Radar to China." Between one and four such AWACS systems, at $250 billion apiece, were to be assembled for China by Elta, an Israel Aircraft Industry subsidiary ("AWACS for China"); Amotz Asa-El and Robert Daniel, "Bulls in a China Shop."

[36] The goal is to transform the PLA Navy, in successive steps, from a navy that operates within close range of the mainland to a genuine blue-water navy that can project power at great distances on the high seas. On China's naval plans, see John Downing, "China's Evolving Maritime Strategy, Part I," pp. 129–33; John Downing, "China's Evolving Maritime Strategy, Part II," pp. 186–91; "Plans for the Predictable Future."

[37] Upgrades for two of China's seventeen aging Luda-class destroyers and its

began to improve its ability to sustain forces at sea by deploying additional, more sophisticated oilers and stores ships (especially the Dayun class for vertical replenishment), as well as its ability to transport troops and undertake amphibious landings with the addition of the Qiongsha attack transport and a small number of newer LSTs (the Yukan and Yuting class).[38] The most dramatic aspect of the mid-1990s effort to modernize the surface fleet, however, was the December 1996 announcement that China would purchase from Russia two Sovremenny-class guided missile destroyers, larger, less vulnerable, and much more lethal ships than any in the PLAN's inventory.[39] Equipped with upgradeable missile packages, the Sovremenny destroyers would at a minimum raise the risks for American aircraft carrier battle groups if they intervened in the Taiwan Strait, a key planning assumption for China after the minicrisis of 1995–96, as indicated below. Complementing this improvement in the surface fleet, China also began to replace its obsolete and noisy Romeo-class conventional and unreliable Han-class nuclear attack submarines. Beijing initiated production of the quieter Song-class vessel, continued development of a replacement for the troubled Han SSNs, and purchased four Russian-built Kilo-class conventional submarines whose advanced versions were superior to anything China was likely to produce itself.[40]

As a result of these wide-ranging efforts, during the mid-1990s China's navy was beginning to deploy an array of modern forces necessary if it was to

---

twenty-nine Jianghu-class frigates included "C901 SSM launchers, improved missile and gun fire control electronics suites, a towed variable-depth sonar system and improved torpedo capabilities . . . [and] facilities for . . . Z-9a helicopters" (Godwin, "From Continent to Periphery," pp. 474–75). See also Frankenstein and Gill, "Current and Future Challenges," pp. 416–17. The new ships included two Luhu-class destroyers and five Jiangwei-class frigates incorporating U.S.-built General Electric turbine engines, French Crotale surface-to-air missile systems, C801 ship-to-ship missiles based on the French Exocet, and improved antisubmarine capabilities based on Italian torpedo launchers and torpedoes along with French Dauphin 2–based Z9A helicopters (Godwin, "From Continent to Periphery," pp. 474–75).

[38] Godwin, "From Continent to Periphery," pp. 475–76

[39] Carrying "a balanced suite of weapons: 8 SS-N-22 ['Sunburn'] anti-ship missiles, 44 surface-to-air missiles, and one anti-submarine warfare helicopter, plus advanced radar, sonar and systems to defend against incoming missiles and torpedoes," the Sovremenny-class destroyers pose a threat to aircraft carriers and other surface ships, even those armed with advanced Aegis systems (Fisher, "Accelerating Modernization"; "Russian-Chinese Military-Technical Cooperation Background"; Anselmo, "China's Military Seeks Great Leap Forward").

[40] Two of the Kilos were the advanced "project 636" version rated by the U.S. Office of Naval intelligence as comparably quiet to the Los Angeles–class SSN. Godwin, "From Continent to Periphery," pp. 476–78.

undertake operations in regional conflicts at greater distances from the main-land. But again, issues of training and maintenance set limits on the pace at which this potential could be realized. Moreover, even within these antici-pated naval "pockets of excellence" glaring shortcomings remained that would continue to limit effectiveness. In particular, most of the surface fleet was still fitted with inadequate air and missile defense systems.[41] The resulting vulnerability not only clouded the PLAN's prospects for projecting power, but also helped explain the repeated delay, if not cancellation, of China's de-cision about whether to purchase or construct an aircraft carrier. The enor-mous investment (procurement, maintenance costs, and personnel training) required to deploy an aircraft carrier battle group that must include surface and submarine forces for the carrier's protection made it an unattractive proposition unless its chances for survival were good. As long as it seemed plausible that China could instead rely on the PLAAF to combine longer-range aircraft, in-flight refueling, and AWACS-assisted command and control to extend the range of military operations in the nearby regions most impor-tant for the foreseeable future, a massive diversion of resources to deploy vul-nerable carriers was unlikely.[42]

Missile forces. In addition to the modernization of China's air and naval forces during the 1990s, China's continued investment in its missile program was seen as further evidence of its rising power.[43] Analysts reported that China, with an eye to improving survivability, expanding target coverage, and foiling anticipated missile defenses, was pushing ahead with development of a second generation of long-range nuclear-armed ICBMs (DF-31, DF-41) and an SLBM (JL-2).[44] But even if these programs proved more quickly successful

---

[41] See Godwin, "Force Projection," pp. 87–88.

[42] See Godwin, "From Continent to Periphery," p. 480; "Force Projection," pp. 96–97.

[43] Beijing had long assigned high priority to investment in ballistic missiles. See John W. Lewis and Xue Litai, *China Builds the Bomb*; John Wilson Lewis and Hua Di, "China's Ballistic Missile Programs: Technologies, Strategies, Goals"; John W. Lewis and Xue Litai, *China's Strategic Seapower*; Goldstein, *Deterrence and Security in the 21st Century*.

[44] See Alastair I. Johnston, "Prospects for Chinese Nuclear Force Modernization: Limited Deterrence Versus Multilateral Arms Control," esp. 562–63; also Johnston, "China's New 'Old Thinking'"; James A. Lamson and Wyn Q. Bowen, "'One Ar-row, Three Stars': China's MIRV Programme, Part I"; James A. Lamson and Wyn Q. Bowen, "'One Arrow, Three Stars': China's MIRV Programme, Part II"; Godwin, "From Continent to Periphery," pp. 482–84; Wyn Q. Bowen and Stanley Shephard, "Living under the Red Missile Threat."

than their forerunners, this investment in missile modernization was not going to yield an operational capability until at least well into the first decade of the twenty-first century. In the intervening years China's long-range nuclear arsenal would be limited to a small number (perhaps twenty) of first-generation, liquid-fueled ICBMs (the DF-5) initially deployed in the last decade of the Cold War.

The key area of growth in China's missile capabilities that attracted the most interest during the 1990s was instead the deployment of medium- and short-range mobile, conventional (or dual-capable) ballistic missiles (DF-11, DF-15, and DF-21). Beijing increased the numbers of missiles available for regional contingencies while working hard to improve their accuracy by incorporating data from global-positioning satellite systems and providing warheads with terminal guidance packages.[45] China also invested more heavily in defensive missile technologies useful not only as antiaircraft systems, but also as an incipient antimissile capability against regional threats (despite Beijing's vociferous opposition to such systems for the United States and its allies in Asia).[46]

In sum, by the mid-1990s increased spending and accelerating force modernization were beginning to transform China's military profile. The changes being wrought to the obsolete Maoist PLA that the reformers had inherited were impressive. Yet the practical significance of observed changes could easily be exaggerated if the problems of translating forces into effective fighting capacity were overlooked. More importantly, such purely national assessments that compared China's present with its past did not in itself answer questions about the implications of this change for international security. After all, concerns about China's rise in the 1990s were rooted in beliefs about the consequences of China's growing capabilities relative to others. How did China's military forces stack up against those of potential adversaries? By this measure, the PLA's strength was also increasing, but it was limited to an extent by ongoing improvement in the forces other regional actors deployed.

[45] China also began to pursue advanced guidance and ramjet technologies from Russia and Israel in order to develop long-range supersonic cruise missiles. See Bowen and Shephard, "Living under the Red Missile Threat"; Fisher, "Accelerating Modernization."

[46] China purchased one hundred Russian SA-10 surface-to-air missiles and reportedly sought to combine this technology with that derived from a Patriot missile purchased from Israel to synthesize an improved HQ-9 SAM system. In addition, China began to beef up its air defenses around Beijing and at the Wuhu and Suixi air bases for the PLAAF's Su-27s by deploying Russian built S-300 systems (Fisher, "Accelerating Modernization"; Opall, "China Boosts Air Combat Capabilities").

China's Benchmarks

Unlike during the Cold War, the most important contingencies for the use of China's military in the 1990s no longer entailed ground engagements on the Asian mainland.[47] Instead, the active disputes and most plausible contingencies for crises or direct confrontations for China in the post–Cold War era lay across the ocean (in decreasing order of importance) with the rival regime on Taiwan, with Southeast Asian states making territorial claims in the South China Sea, and with Japan over the Diaoyu (Senkaku) Islands. In these areas of concern, China's growing military power needed to be measured against four prospective adversaries—Taiwan, the ASEAN states with competing claims in the South China Sea, Japan, and (because of its power projection capabilities and stated interests in the region) the United States. China's modernization by the mid-1990s was lifting the PLA from what had been a position of near impotence against all but the smallest of these potential regional adversaries, but still left it short of achieving dramatic military advantages and even well short of meaningful parity in most respects.

China's improved air and naval capabilities were beginning to give it an edge over any individual ASEAN state it might face in the South China Sea. But although ASEAN states could not hope to match the quantity of forces China could deploy, many had more experience with their modern air and naval equipment and almost all had been augmenting their capabilities in response to China's programs. While the ASEAN states usually looked first to the United States as the preferred source for prized modern fighters (especially the F-16 and F-18), they also turned to France and, like China, they tapped the Russian market.[48] Because these countries were better prepared than

[47] This was a welcome development for Beijing since ground-force modernization was proceeding at a very modest pace. See Blasko, "Better Late than Never," p. 141. This assertion sets aside the possible use of the PLA as a last-ditch internal security prop for the communist regime. In the 1990s, China's People's Armed Police (PAP) were simultaneously being revamped to be better able to play this role in any future domestic crisis. On the roles of the PLA and PAP, see Tai Ming-Cheung, "The People's Armed Police: First Line of Defence."

[48] See Gallagher, "China's Illusory Threat to the South China Sea"; Godwin, "Force Projection," pp. 78, 90–91; Godwin, "From Continent to Periphery," p. 485; Michael Klare, "East Asia's Militaries Muscle Up: East Asia's New-Found Riches Are Purchasing the Latest High-Tech Weapons." See also "Philippines Studying Russian Offer of Mig–29s"; "Russia Offers Its Jetfighters to Indonesia." By the mid-1990s, ASEAN air forces included the following modern combat aircraft: Malaysia had eight F/A-18C/Ds and eighteen MiG-29s, Thailand thirty-six F-16As, Singapore seventeen F-16As, Indonesia eleven F-16As; Vietnam three Su–27s, and three more on order.

China to integrate modern (third-generation) fighter jets into their militaries, their upgrades reflected a sensible choice to exploit a comparative advantage in quality to compensate for what they expected would be an inevitable disadvantage in quantity relative to their huge northern neighbor. More important, if China were to confront not isolated ASEAN adversaries but a coalition of at least several of these small neighbors made nervous by a more assertive regional heavyweight, Beijing would have little prospect of achieving the decisive air superiority essential for it to project naval power in the region. And, as in most of the other plausible contingencies discussed here, without a high probability of swift success it was unlikely that the PLA would be eager to put at risk its best new equipment that constituted the few gems in its pockets of excellence.[49] Given China's growing edge in sheer numbers (when one includes the larger inventory of less-modern equipment), during the 1990s it might have been moving closer to an ability to prevail through a war of attrition. But for the foreseeable future, this outcome would ultimately rest not so much on any significant shift in the military balance of power relative to its adversaries in Southeast Asia as on China's determination, a determination shaped by both the terrific military and diplomatic price Beijing would have to pay even if it achieved victory.[50]

Against Taiwan the effects of Beijing's military buildup during the first half of the 1990s were offset by Taipei's efforts geared specifically (and more ex-

[49] See Gill, "The Impact of Economic Reform," pp. 160–61. Depending on the scenario, China could, of course, find itself facing a coalition that included not just ASEAN members but also forces from Australia, New Zealand, and Britain who conduct exercises with Singapore and Malaysia under the Five-Power Defense Arrangement (Godwin, "Force Projection," p. 91). Intervention by extraregional powers, especially the United States and Japan, would erase any Chinese force advantage in the South China Sea. See Lin, "Power Projection Capabilities," pp. 113–14.

[50] Some military analysts are fond of the axiom "quantity has a quality all its own." While a massive quantitative advantage can offset qualitative shortcomings, two interconnected considerations must be kept in mind. First, the technologically inferior side must be willing to suffer greater rates of attrition. Second, the required quantitative offset and rates of attrition that must be accepted can be dauntingly steep if the adversary has significantly more sophisticated equipment. In the modern era, the latter consideration is far from trivial because weapons technology and sophisticated command and control can result in exchange ratios that are remarkably lopsided. The record of the Israeli Air Force from the 1960s through the 1980s in its clashes with technologically outclassed Arab adversaries, and the U.S. experience fighting a huge but technologically inferior Iraqi military in 1991 when the Americans took advantage of superior intelligence, more precise targeting, and greater weapons range to ensure a decisive victory both suggest the substantial challenges of converting "quantity" into "quality" in today's world.

plicitly than for the ASEAN countries) toward dealing with the challenge China's PLA might pose. As China was selectively modernizing its air, naval, and ballistic missile forces in ways that made long-range operations in and across the Taiwan Strait technically more feasible, Taiwan was substantially upgrading its own military capabilities. While the PLAAF prepared to deploy Russian Su-27s, Taiwan prepared to deploy a fleet of modern fighters comprised of 150 American F-16s, 60 French Mirage 2000s, and 130 of its domestically produced Indigenous Defense Fighters, all supported by E2C Hawkeye AWACS. While the PLAN was deploying more sophisticated destroyers, frigates, and submarines, Taiwan was upgrading its surface fleet by adding at least twenty modern American, French, and indigenously produced frigates and improving its ship- and land-based antisubmarine warfare capabilities.[51] And while China's Second Artillery was deploying more numerous and sophisticated missiles that placed the entire theater within range, Taiwan was deploying ever more sophisticated, if imperfect, ballistic missile defenses.[52]

The point is not that Taiwan could be confident it would always be able to defeat easily an increasingly modern PLA's assault. Rather, the point is that Taiwan's military modernization in the 1990s ensured that for the foreseeable future it would remain very costly for the PLA to prevail, even if others, most importantly the United States, chose to remain aloof, something about which China could not be certain. Indeed, as noted below, during the 1990s American intervention became a central planning assumption in China's thinking about the possibility of conflict in the Taiwan Strait. Nevertheless, leaders in Taipei understandably worried that Beijing's determination to ensure Taiwan's reunification with the mainland, certainly stronger than its determination to have its way in possible clashes with its Southeast Asian neighbors, might lead it to opt for military action despite the risks it would entail. Even so, during the 1990s China's growing military capabilities were not resulting in an increase in strength relative to Taiwan that would make such a blunt

[51] See Godwin, "From Continent to Periphery," p. 485, Godwin, "Force Projection," pp. 92–94; Lin, "The Military Balance in the Taiwan Straits," pp. 580–83; John W. Garver, "The PLA as an Interest Group in Chinese Foreign Policy," pp. 260–61. Taiwan purchased the Mirage 2000-5 and a version of the F-16A/B, called the F-16 MLU (mid-life upgrade), reportedly "nearly as good" as the F-16 D/C. See "Taiwan to Take Delivery of Five More U.S. F-16s."

[52] They included U.S. Patriot systems upgraded after the Gulf War and the indigenously developed and improved Tiangong SAM systems. See Bowen and Shepherd, "Living under the Red Missile Threat"; Lin, The Military Balance in the Taiwan Straits," p. 579.

and direct use of force much more attractive than it had been in the recent past.

Because increases in the PLA's power were not decisively tipping the cross-strait balance of power, the most plausible approaches for Beijing to deal with Taiwan remained diplomatic and economic pressure. And if those proved inadequate the most likely military approach remained the *indirect* use of force, as was evident in China's actions during the minicrisis of 1995–96.[53] To deter Taiwan from challenging the status quo and moving toward independence, or to compel Taiwan to accept changes in the status quo that presaged eventual reunification, Beijing could threaten military actions that might not ensure victory but would gravely harm what Taiwan values (especially disrupting its trade-dependent economy). This was, however, a possibility that predated the growth in China's capabilities resulting from the initial post–Cold War modernization drive. Because China already possessed the ability to inflict grave punishment, the effectiveness of Beijing's indirect use of force against Taiwan continued to rest more on the balance of resolve than on the balance of power. The PLA's modernization effort was not producing a military advantage for China that opened fundamentally new possibilities. It was instead producing a modest increase in the means available for carrying out Beijing's existing options that emphasized coercion based on the threat to harm an adversary it still could not defeat.[54]

China's other two potential adversaries that provided a benchmark for measuring the significance of the PLA's improving military capabilities after the end of the Cold War were Japan and the United States. By the mid-1990s it had became increasingly plausible that either or both might confront China if Beijing's actions were judged a threat to their vital interests in the region. Japan's concerns centered not only on the territorial dispute over the Diaoyu

[53] Even after nearly another decade of PLA modernization, China still faced daunting challenges in threatening or using military force against Taiwan. See Shambaugh, *Modernizing China's Military,* pp. 307–27. See also Lin, "The Military Balance in the Taiwan Straits," pp. 591–95; Lin, "Power Projection Capabilities," pp. 111–13.

[54] For analyses that explore the new challenges that such improving capabilities present, see Thomas J. Christensen, "Posing Problems without Catching Up: China's Rise and Challenges for U.S. Security Policy"; Robert S. Ross, "Navigating the Taiwan Strait: Deterrence, Escalation Dominance, and U.S.-China Relations." For discussion of China's improving submarine capabilities and their relevance to crises in the Taiwan Strait, see Michael A. Glosny, "Strangulation from the Sea? A PRC Submarine Blockade of Taiwan"; Lyle Goldstein and William Murray, "Undersea Dragons: China's Maturing Submarine Force."

(Senkaku) Islands, but also on the potential threat to shipping lanes in East and Southeast Asia (including the Malacca and Taiwan Strait), and more generally the consequences of possible Chinese regional hegemony. Other than the Diaoyu Islands dispute, U.S. interests were similar and could be broadly defined as the preservation of regional stability, ensuring freedom of the seas, and preventing the use of force to alter the status quo. With Japan or the United States providing the benchmark for assessing the PLA, the balance of capabilities in the 1990s was starkly simple, clear, and basically unchanged. Compared with the air and naval forces of either Japan or the United States, the PLA was still and, at least well into the first decade of the twenty-first century, would remain outclassed, even if China's determined effort at military modernization proceeded smoothly. Despite an economic slowdown, Japan was continuing its own program of selective military modernization that most notably included adding about 130 F-2 (formerly FSX) fighters to an air force that already possessed 180 F-15Cs.[55] The capabilities at the disposal of the United States for force projection in East Asia were not limited to, but only most clearly reflected in, the awesome assets of the U.S. Navy's Pacific Fleet dedicated to the region.[56]

Nevertheless, as indicated with respect to the situation in the Taiwan Strait, China's significant military disadvantage relative to even these most potent prospective adversaries was not the only relevant strategic consideration. While military modernization during the 1990s was not increasing the PLA's power to the point it could expect to prevail against better-equipped Japanese and American forces, it was increasing China's ability to punish adversaries it could not defeat. Improvement in the forces China deployed, or would soon deploy, was already making it more dangerous for either state to confront Beijing in regional disputes. Adding well-armed Su-27s, Sovremenny destroyers, and Kilo-class submarines would not turn the waters of East Asia into a Chinese lake, but it would mean that not only Japan but even the United States could no longer expect to dominate China easily (i.e., at minimal cost) in limited conventional military engagements. Combined with its improving ballistic missile capabilities, China's ability to preclude swift, decisive, and

[55] See Chen Lineng, "The Japanese Self Defense Forces Are Marching toward the 21st Century"; Swaine, "Don't Demonize China"; "SDF to Deploy F-2 Fighter Jets by 2000"; Hidemichi Katsumata, "Dream of Domestic Jet Fighter Realized."

[56] The assets of the U.S. Navy's Seventh Fleet were especially impressive. See the weekly update of this Pacific Fleet's web pages, http://www.cpf.navy.mil/. For a review that questioned the durability of the military advantage the United States enjoyed in the 1990s, see Fisher, "China's Purchase of Russian Fighters: A Challenge to the U.S."

painless outside intervention and to require its most potent adversary to run both the risk of suffering significant casualties in conventional warfare and the small but terrifying risk of nuclear escalation was increasing Beijing's leverage in confrontations over interests it deemed vital.

During the 1990s, then, China's capabilities were increasing and its military was improving, both compared with its own recent past and relative to others. Yet its modest increase in power hardly seemed to justify the alarmed reaction it elicited, and it was this reaction that would shape China's emerging grand strategy. Instead, the surge in interest in and concern about China's allegedly rapid rise by the middle of the decade seems to have been driven more by changes in what William Wohlforth labels "perceived" power than by real, but less dramatic, changes in "estimated" power.[57]

Perceived Power

Wohlforth's work explains that perceptions of power are not entirely detached from reality, but are shaped by factors that go beyond a straightforward assessment of available evidence. What, then, accounted for the perception that set in during the mid-1990s that China had begun a swift rise to great power status? Four influences fostered this view: historical context, the low level from which the latest era of growth started, the systems in which military modernization was concentrated, and two adventitious events that catalyzed a change in perceptions.

First, history had established the expectation that China was a country in some sense deserving a place in the ranks of the great powers. Part of this expectation was rooted in China's role as regional hegemon during much of its imperial past. Part, however, was rooted in the more recent anointing of China as at least a candidate great power by others during the mid-twentieth century. During World War II, mainly at the behest of a sympathetic Roosevelt administration in the United States, the Republic of China (ROC) was initially included as one of the Big Four allies participating in summits planning military strategy to defeat the Axis. The divergence between this lofty formal status and the reality of China's limited capabilities (along with the reluctance of Chiang Kai-shek's government to put China's forces in harm's way) soon became clear, especially to Britain's prime minister, Winston Churchill. By the last phases of the war, China's role as a great power ally had lost most of its practical significance.[58] Yet after the war the fiction that the

[57] See Wohlforth, "The Perception of Power: Russia in the Pre-1914 Balance."

[58] Churchill was shocked at the Americans' inflated perception of China. See Herbert Feis, *The China Tangle*, p. 11. Allied policy eventually adjusted to the reality of the

ROC government in exile was a great power endured in the symbolic form of its seat allegedly representing China on the UN Security Council through 1971, again a status based on U.S. support rather than tangible capabilities. And when the People's Republic of China replaced the ROC as the internationally recognized representative of China at the UN in 1971, the switch occurred because the United States no longer insisted on blocking the move. The change in American policy was part of the Nixon administration's effort to anoint Beijing once again a great power because it was expected to serve U.S. strategic interests. Bolstering China's international status, the country's deficient economy and obsolete military equipment notwithstanding, would provide the United States with additional leverage over its Soviet rival.[59]

As a consequence of history, then, "great power China" had become what cognitive theorists refer to as an "unfilled concept," and one with deep roots; analysts were primed to accept evidence that the promise was at last being realized.[60] In such circumstances, there may be an inclination to exaggerate the significance of limited data. The tendency to see China fulfilling preconceived expectations may have been reflected not just in the way that other nations quickly credited it with military achievement yet to be fully realized, but also in the rush to accept limited evidence that China was emerging as a global economic power. A readiness to embrace this conclusion may have been further fed by the emergence in the 1970s of the "Asian tigers" (South Korea, Taiwan, Hong Kong, and Singapore), rapidly industrializing countries following patterns of export-led growth. Once observers concluded that reform-minded leaders in Beijing had transformed the country's economic foundations in the 1990s, it became plausible and then fashionable to see the evidence of high-speed growth in GDP and booming exports as confirmation that China would be the next East Asian country to fill the role of an Asian tiger.[61]

---

limited military clout of Chiang Kai-shek's China. China was simply to be discouraged from seeking a separate peace with Japan in order to ensure that large numbers of Japanese troops would remain tied down in operations on the Chinese mainland.

[59] See Kenneth N. Waltz, *Theory of International Politics*, p. 130. Ironically, perhaps, China's role in the event of a war with the Soviets would almost certainly have been to tie down the enemy's forces on a second front, the same role it played in World War II.

[60] On unfilled concepts, see Robert Jervis, "Hypotheses on Misperception." The opening subheading ("This Time It Is Real") of Nicholas Kristof's article "The Rise of China" also reflects this longstanding expectation.

[61] See Jim Rohwer, "Rapid Growth Could Make China World's Largest Economy by 2012."

A second influence on perceptions was the low level from which China's economic and military growth began.[62] China's economic expansion in the 1980s and 1990s was unquestionably impressive and had resulted in genuine improvements in the people's standard of living as well as the country's aggregate wealth. But the perception of breathtaking change was enhanced partly because the opening of the country in 1979 had enabled observers to pierce the veil of Maoist propaganda that had been in place since 1949 and to grasp just how impoverished China had remained during the first thirty years of communist rule. As reformers more successfully tapped what many believed were China's inherent economic strengths, it was easy to conclude that this was the beginning of an era during which the country's potential would be realized, rather than a brief surge resulting from extraordinary policies and efforts that could not be sustained. The perception of China's economic future was not, then, that it would be characterized by a significant downward correction or a leveling off, but rather that rapid growth would continue as China quickly rose through the ranks of the world's leading economies. The belief in the robustness of China's growth trajectory was reinforced when it became clear that the CCP had succeeded in riding out the storm of international outrage that followed its bloody suppression of domestic protests in 1989 and then survived the collapse of communism throughout the former Soviet empire. Defying a brief flurry of pessimistic predictions about its prospects for sticking to the reform agenda, in relatively short order Beijing resumed and then in 1992 even accelerated the shift to a market-based economy, posting the high growth rates and expanding trade volumes that drew widespread attention by the mid-1990s.[63]

Unlike ignorance about China's true economic conditions during the Maoist era, the backward state of China's armed forces was well known even before Deng Xiaoping's reforms opened the country. Most observers had long recognized that the PLA lacked most of the accouterments of a great military power. Most also recognized that rectifying its broad and deep deficiencies was going to require much more than marginal increases in investment and deployment. Yet, in a sense, the dismal state of the PLA in the late 1970s merely provided a background that more starkly highlighted the significance of each initiative in the new wave of military modernization described above. In addition, the projection that China's growing economic strength would

[62] On the importance of baselines, see Wohlforth, "The Perception of Power," p. 374.

[63] On the decisive political impetus for accelerating reforms that Deng Xiaoping provided in spring 1992, see Suisheng Zhao, "Deng Xiaoping's Southern Tour."

provide the wealth and technology to sustain the sort of military modernization drive necessary for the PLA to become a world-class power lent greater
significance to the observation that China was engaged in a concerted
buildup. Together with confidence in the robustness of its economic expansion, the relatively modest fraction of national wealth China was devoting to
the PLA (even when the highest estimates for budgets were used) fed the expectation that China would be able to sustain its military modernization at a
pace that would narrow the gap between China and the world's leading powers.[64] In this respect, China looked different than the defunct Soviet Union,
whose regime had tapped a huge proportion of its relatively stagnant economy
in a desperate, and ultimately self-defeating, attempt to stay in the game of superpower military competition. Moreover, the perceived significance of China's military growth was further enhanced because it was becoming most pro-
nounced in the early 1990s, a time when most other major powers were implementing post–Cold War reductions in military spending.

A third factor affecting perceptions of a rising China was the extent to
which military modernization focused on improving capabilities that would
be most useful as Beijing sought to play a more active international role.[65] The
drive to increase the number and variety of ballistic missiles, field improved
strategic nuclear warheads, and fashion a usable power projection capability
by reorganizing and reequipping air and naval forces all contributed to the
impression that China might not be content with forces designed only to discourage others from challenging the country's territorial integrity. Instead,
although realization of its goals might be years away, Beijing's investment in
forces of greater range and lethality suggested to some an interest in the sorts
of capabilities that would better enable it to play the role of a great power
whose military could support a more activist posture and influence events well
beyond its borders.

Finally, two unpredictable events in the 1990s had a catalytic effect, accelerating the change in perceptions about China's present and likely future international role. First, in 1993 the International Monetary Fund (IMF) decided to modify its method of calculating the national wealth of the world's
countries. Instead of relying only on currency exchange rates to estimate
GDP, the IMF began to formulate estimates based on purchasing power parity

[64] As noted above, such expectations assumed what, in the Chinese case, is prob-
lematic—that increasing national wealth can easily be translated into military power.
For doubts about the ease of tapping this potential, see Gill, "The Impact of Economic
Reform"; Arnett, "Military Technology: The Case of China."

[65] For similar influences on perceptions of Russia's power prior to World War I, see
Wohlforth, "The Perception of Power," p. 374.

(PPP).[66] Normally, the esoterica of economic methodology and the decisions of international organizations would draw little public attention. In this case, however, the recalculation resulted in a flurry of major media reports that China's GDP was actually four times larger than previously thought. The announcement ostensibly portrayed a breathtaking change in the world economic order as it was, and would be. China immediately advanced from having the tenth largest GDP in the world to third, narrowly behind Japan, and on a course to surpass the United States relatively early in the twenty-first century.[67] Nothing had actually changed overnight, of course. Indeed, the higher figures associated with the purchasing power parity method had been put forward in less visible publications prior to the IMF announcement.[68] And for the small community of China experts and businesspeople familiar with the situation on the ground, the reports merely corrected what had long been understood to be the old statistics' gross understatement of the economic vitality of those parts of China that had benefited from the reforms.[69] But for others, these reports were a wake-up call that helped crystallize the view of China as East Asia's newest economic dynamo.

The second catalyst that accelerated a changing view of China was the re-intensification of the dispute over Taiwan in 1995–96. Fearful of permitting Taiwan's leadership to pursue a more independent international role, Beijing responded to what it saw as dangerous U.S. complicity in this effort by abandoning the fruitful diplomacy that had characterized cross-strait relations during the early 1990s. Following a U.S. decision to reverse policy and issue a

[66] Any method of cross-national comparison introduces distortions. Rather than converting China's GDP as reported in yuan into U.S. dollars, the PPP method attempts to compensate for the incomparability of price structures across economies by estimating the costs of sample baskets of goods and services in each country. Ideally, these provide the basis for figuring out what constitutes parity in the purchasing power of different currencies. For a helpful discussion with illustrations, see Werner Antweiler, "Purchasing Power Parity."

[67] Steven Greenhouse, "New Tally of World's Economies Catapults China into Third Place"; "Revised Weights for the World Economic Outlook; Annex IV."

[68] See "U.S. Report Projects China's Economic Rise in 2010."

[69] See Rohwer, "Rapid Growth Could Make China World's Largest Economy by 2012"; William H. Overholt, *The Rise of China*. For competing estimates of Chinese GDP and an attempt to evaluate their merits, see Lardy, *China in the World Economy*, pp. 14–18. Although most analysts prefer the PPP calculations to those based on exchange rates, the partial nature of price reform and the persistence of a black market in China introduce distortions in prices that weaken confidence in the figures upon which PPP calculations must rely. I thank Mark Groombridge for explaining this complication to me.

visa to Taiwan's president, whose May 1995 trip to Cornell University then became part of his effort to elevate the island's international stature, China decided to signal relevant audiences in both Washington and Taipei that it would not tolerate a drift toward, let alone an outright declaration of, independence. Between the summer of 1995 and the spring of 1996, Beijing deployed ground, air, and naval forces to the Taiwan theater and staged military exercises that included the repeated launching of missiles disrupting the sea lanes around the trade-dependent island. While events unfolded, Chinese military officers also reminded a prominent American visitor that the situation was no longer the same as that which prevailed in the 1950s when confrontations over Taiwan pitted a vulnerable China against a distant and invulnerable United States that could comfortably rattle its nuclear saber. Because China had finally deployed long-range missiles tipped with nuclear warheads, if the United States became directly involved in any cross-strait confrontation in the 1990s, the United States, and not just China, would have to worry about the risks of nuclear escalation that could touch the homeland.[70]

Beijing's vigorous response to what it saw as dangerous developments in the Taiwan Strait crystallized the perception that China was a country increasingly inclined to use whatever capabilities it had to serve its international interests.[71] Less alarmist defense analysts noted, as emphasized above, that Beijing lacked a military capability to do more than inflict punitive damage on Taiwan and frighten its trading partners. Yet China's actions aroused concerns about the implications of the PLA's modernization program, especially its power projection component, concerns aroused with less fanfare by Beijing's earlier efforts to pursue its claims to disputed territory in the South China Sea.[72] Prior

---

[70] Initial reports apparently exaggerated the prominence and explicitness of China's reference to its nuclear deterrent in the meeting with Chas. Freeman. See Patrick E. Tyler, "As China Threatens Taiwan, It Makes Sure U.S. Listens"; Patrick E. Tyler, "Beijing Steps up Military Pressure on Taiwan Leader"; Jim Wolf, "China Aides Gave U.S. Nuclear Warning, Official Says." Chas. Freeman clarifies the exchange in Chas. Freeman, "China's Changing Nuclear Posture."

[71] See House National Security Committee, *Testimony of Floyd D. Spence: National Security, Security Challenges, China*; also David Morgan, "Gingrich Calls for U.S. Defense against Nuclear Attack."

[72] See Jeffrey Parker, "China Taiwan Drills 'Proof' of PLA Modernization." For China's claims about the success of its missile tests, see "China Claims Readiness for 'Future War.'" The military maneuvers in the Taiwan Strait and China's final series of nuclear weapons tests in 1996 also provoked alarm in Japan (including explicit comments added to its Defense White Paper). See Nicholas D. Kristof, "Tension with Japan Rises Alongside China's Star"; Gerald Segal, "The Taiwanese Crisis: What Next?" pp. 269–70; Brian Williams, "Japan Sees China as Growing Military Challenge."

to the mid-1990s, analysts specializing in Asian affairs may have pondered the possibility that China would replace the former Soviet Union as the main great power challenger to the status quo in Asia and become the principal focus for many countries' military contingency planning. It was the Taiwan Strait confrontation of 1995–96, however, that grabbed the attention and shifted the perceptions of a much broader cross-section of foreign policy analysts, most importantly in the United States.[73] Events in the Taiwan Strait were significant not because they had demonstrated China's newfound power (if anything, they again revealed the PLA's shortcomings),[74] but because they catalyzed the perception that China's first steps in modernizing its military should be interpreted as foreshadowing a trajectory of growth whose consequences had not been fully appreciated.

China's Self-perception

The preceding discussion addressed some of the reasons for a change in the way the outside world began viewing China. Was China's view of its own position also changing? Absent access to declassified internal Communist Party documents or greater access to top decision makers than is currently available, analysis of Chinese views must be inferred from circumstantial evidence or interpretation of policies and statements that may, or may not, reflect actual beliefs.[75] With such limitations in mind, I offer the following brief sketch, because such views are relevant to the interaction between China and the outside world that conditioned its emerging grand strategy in the mid-1990s. Beijing's reaction to the changing perceptions of other states would in part depend upon whether it believed such perceptions were reasonable or instead were disingenuous distortions of reality that reflected malign intentions.

The reforms Deng Xiaoping initiated after 1978 resulted in economic expansion and growing foreign trade and investment that in turn altered Beijing's view of its international position. At the beginning of the "opening to

[73] At about this time the public debate developed its focus on a choice between "containment" and "engagement." See "Containing China"; Shambaugh, "Containment or Engagement of China"; Segal, "East Asia and the 'Constrainment' of China."

[74] See Patrick E. Tyler, "Shadow over Asia: A Special Report; China's Military Stumbles Even as Its Power Grows."

[75] As indicated above, access to documentary sources has improved, though problems of selectivity in a filtering process controlled by the CCP authorities remain. The written record is augmented by greater possibilities for interviews by the few scholars who have cultivated the proper contacts. Still, the difficulties caused by Chinese officials' biased self-reflection and the remaining limits on the scope of interviewing exacerbate problems scholars confront even in more open polities.

the outside" in the early 1980s, China mainly played the role of economic suitor, simply attempting to entice foreign investors with preferential tax arrangements, a large supply of relatively inexpensive, submissive labor, and the ever-present lure of a potentially huge domestic market's demand for consumer goods. By the mid-1990s, however, Beijing was moving beyond viewing itself in this role of suitor. Having established its economic credentials, a more confident China began to act as a major player, one that had the strength to more assertively negotiate the terms on which it would participate in the international economy. Beijing's hard bargaining to gain admission to the World Trade Organization (WTO) as a charter member without relinquishing its demand that it be granted some of the concessions to which developing countries were entitled reflected its attempt to become more of a force in the councils of international economic power while retaining the advantages China enjoyed during the early stages of its economic takeoff.[76]

The CCP also seemed to be more confidently playing what it saw as its stronger hand of economic cards as a diplomatic tool. In the past, China had been the state threatened with economic sanctions as punishment for various policy infractions, most notably the recurrent U.S. warnings that most-favored-nation trading status would be revoked if China's domestic and international behavior did not meet certain standards. By the mid-1990s, Beijing was not only continuing to stand fast against such economic pressure; despite its prior claims that political disagreements should not complicate mutually beneficial economic exchange, Beijing was also beginning to use its own economic leverage to signal unhappiness with U.S. objections to China's human rights policy, its export of arms and dual-use technologies, and more important, to demonstrate anger at the Clinton administration's policy in the Taiwan Strait.[77]

[76] On China's negotiating posture with respect to joining the WTO, a stance that prevented it from accession as a founding member in January 1995 (and ultimately delayed its entry until 1999), see "Beijing Has Fulfilled GATT Terms"; Guy De Jonquieres, "China Pressed over WTO Entry—EU and U.S. Say Beijing Must Accept World Trade Body's Rules"; Geoffrey Crothall, "Beijing Threatens GATT Talks Boycott If 'Final Offer' Rejected"; "China and WTO." See also Nicholas R. Lardy, *Integrating China into the Global Economy*. And despite suggestions that China should be invited to join the G7 (now G8) after the revision of IMF calculations in 1993, Beijing did not push to join the G7, probably to avoid discrediting its claim to being a developing country entitled to preferential trading arrangements within the WTO. "China Bucks G–7 Membership, Wants WTO."

[77] For Chinese premier Li Peng's suggestion that U.S. business leaders should use their influence to move U.S. government policy toward China in a more positive di-

Though the extent to which economic development was changing China's self-perception is unclear, Beijing's behavior during the mid-1990s (including also its growing activism at the annual meetings of the APEC forum) suggested that it saw itself in a transition from object to subject in the international economy.

China's view of its international role had also begun to change in the military realm. During the Cold War, China had essentially been a survivalist state husbanding its limited capabilities and adjusting to the givens of its precarious position in a dangerous environment. By the 1990s, China had become a thriving state basically secure against foreign threats, one seeking to increase its ability to shape, and not just cope with, a fluid if still potentially dangerous environment. This major change constituted a shift from the role China had been constrained to play in the bipolar Cold War world to the one it hoped to craft for itself in a post–Cold War world it expected would eventually move beyond American-led unipolarity.

From 1950 through the late 1980s, China's foreign policy had reflected the clear understanding among leaders in Beijing, rhetorical flourishes notwithstanding, that their country was militarily outclassed by the superpowers that dominated the international system. Under these circumstances, the regime's goal was to ensure its survival through self-reliant military preparation combined with grudging dependence on the support of one superpower against the danger posed by the other. Over more than three decades, a series of serious American and then Soviet threats were parried, after which the worrisome activism of each alleged "hegemon" in East Asia declined.[78]

The waning Cold War and then the collapse of the Soviet Union led to a shift in China's military-strategic goals at the same time the country's economic takeoff was beginning. For China to reclaim its rightful role among the world's great powers, it would need a military that could more self-reliantly advance the country's international interests. But Beijing understood that the military modernization described above was only the beginning of a long and difficult process. China faced a daunting challenge if its modernization efforts were to succeed in closing the gap with the world's more powerful states, especially the preponderant United States. While China's leaders were undoubtedly proud of the strides they were making in military modernization by

---

rection, see "PRC: Li Peng Meets Boeing's Board Members." See also Rajiv Chandra, "China: European, U.S. Aircraft Producers Compete for Boom Market."

[78] For a discussion that emphasizes China's pursuit of more than its narrow military security objectives in managing its relations with the United States during the last decades of the Cold War, see Robert S. Ross, *Negotiating Cooperation.*

the mid-1990s, they saw their achievements as modest improvements from a rather low baseline. Consequently, Beijing viewed the concerns about China's rising power that others had begun to express as patently absurd exaggerations; these unfounded claims were allegedly part of an attempt to justify efforts to "keep China down." Indeed, as noted in chapter 5, the contrast between external perceptions of a sharp rise in China's capabilities and Beijing's own understanding of its limited achievements fueled the CCP's initially angry reaction to the new "China threat theory" that began circulating among Western analysts by the mid-1990s.

Fit between Estimated Power, Perceptions, and Reality

Estimated power and perceived power—that is, data usually thought to reflect the influence a state can bring to bear internationally and the beliefs of policy makers about such influence—are unlikely to coincide. The degree of disparity varies for some of the reasons discussed above, but in addition is also likely to vary with the occurrence of events that provide for the hard test of actual competition in the international arena. Crises, militarized conflicts, and wars provide the best, if still imperfect, guide to real power relations; the absence of such direct tests provides the greatest opportunity for uncertain or faulty estimates as well as distorted perceptions.[79] Power tests enabling China and others to assess the country's clout and its determination to act on its foreign policy preferences were relatively frequent during the first three decades of the PRC's existence. The Korean War in 1950, crises in the Taiwan Strait in 1954–55 and 1958, war with India in 1962, border clashes with the Soviets in 1969, and the brief invasion of Vietnam in 1979 helped clarify China's actual capabilities relative to its adversaries at different points in time. After 1979, however, seventeen years passed before there was anything that might qualify as a clarifying event seriously testing China's ability to wield military power. Moreover, 1979 also marked the beginning of the reform program that set the stage for claims about China's growing power. Thus, while all could agree that the reforms were enabling China to modernize its military, in the 1990s

[79] Wohlforth, "The Perception of Power," pp. 377–78. Such tests remain imperfect since international outcomes reflect not just capabilities, but also the relative resolve of the adversaries and the extent to which the issue in dispute is one for which military and economic power are decisive. On the limited usefulness of military force to solve political problems of governance, as demonstrated by the U.S. experience in Vietnam, see Waltz, *Theory of International Politics*, pp. 188–91. For discussion of the reasons why relative power may not reliably predict outcomes in war, see Andrew Mack, "Why Big Nations Lose Small Wars: The Politics of Asymmetric Conflict"; Ivan Arreguin-Toft, "How the Weak Win Wars: A Theory of Asymmetric Conflict."

analysts could debate but not resolve the key question, "Was China becoming stronger compared to others and, if so, how much stronger?"[80]

The Taiwan Strait military exercises in 1995–96 provided some, though not much, information about China's rise. First, they signaled that Beijing was prepared, as it had repeatedly stated, to use force if necessary to ensure that the island's political reunification with the mainland remained on the agenda. Second, they demonstrated that the PLA had the ability to rely on missiles to coerce Taiwan, either through disrupting its economic lifeline of trade or through engaging in a campaign of strategic bombardment of the island designed for punitive purposes. Such a capability could serve to frighten the Taiwanese in order to dissuade them from moving toward independence or, if dissuasion failed, could serve as the means to compel Taiwan to reverse steps that Beijing found intolerable. Third, the military exercises revealed the enduring limits on the PLA's ability actually to project power, even in China's own backyard. China's continuing lack of air superiority over the Taiwan Strait precluded the amphibious assault that an offensive would require, whether or not the United States chose to assist the island in its defense.[81] And fourth, the Clinton administration's decision to maneuver two aircraft carriers to the vicinity of Taiwan in March 1996, together with repeated warnings about the gravity with which Washington viewed the situation, sent a clear signal to Beijing: Despite elements of ambiguity in U.S. policy toward Taiwan since diplomatic relations were severed in 1979, an assault against the island would almost certainly result in some sort of American military response; the PLA would, therefore, encounter U.S. forces against which it still could not match up.[82] If the events of 1995–96 clarified power relations, then they

[80] This situation parallels that Wohlforth observed with regard to Russia just prior to World War I. See Wohlforth, "The Perception of Power," pp. 377–78. A similar uncertainty may have characterized France's position just prior to the 1870 war with Prussia. I thank Tom Christensen for pointing this out.

[81] For a May 1996 U.S. Office of Naval Intelligence assessment, see Jim Wolf, "U.S. Navy Says China Rehearsed Taiwan Invasion"; also Peer Slevin, "China Could Not Easily Overwhelm Taiwan, Analysts Agree."

[82] Ambiguity dates to the 1972 Shanghai Communiqué, which provided a framework for Sino-American relations in the years following President Nixon's visit. See Alan D. Romberg, *Rein in at the Brink of the Precipice.* Continuing ambiguity may have led China to underestimate the likelihood of a forceful U.S. reaction in 1995–96. See "Perry Criticized on Taiwan." After the March 1996 exercises, the United States more clearly signaled it would respond to Beijing's future use of force against Taiwan. See Paul Basken, "Clinton: U.S. Wants 'Peaceful' One-China." See also Robert S. Ross, "The 1995–96 Taiwan Strait Confrontation: Coercion, Credibility, and the Use of Force."

did so by underscoring the fact that the fruits of China's military modernization drive were not yet significantly altering Beijing's ability to assert its interests beyond China's continental borders.

*   *   *

Few doubted that China's capabilities had been increasing in the decades
after Mao's death in 1976. It remained more difficult, however, to accurately
assess the magnitude and significance of China's growing economic and military power, especially absent clear tests of strength against its prospective rivals
in Asia. China's leaders were proud of the achievements of their modernization program and happy to be seen as a country "on the rise." But they were
shocked when observers began to view their country as anything other than
relatively poor and still developing, and they were angered when others labeled a rising China a potential military threat. I have suggested that contemporary estimates and perceptions in the mid-1990s on balance exaggerated the
speed and extent of China's growing capabilities. Nevertheless, even if more
accurate assessments might have moderated the concerns some began to express about China, it was the trend itself rather than its debatable pace that
they saw as worrisome. Why did the prospect of China's ascent, however
rapid, ring alarm bells? Although policy makers and other attentive observers
rarely invoked academic arguments, the sorts of concerns about China's rise
that circulated beginning in the mid-1990s often reflected reasoning prominently featured in leading theories of international relations. For the most part
these theories suggested reasons to expect that as China's power grew, potentially dangerous international conflicts involving China would become more
likely. Chapter 4 briefly examines these arguments and their implications for
the way the world was responding to China's growing capabilities, a response
that in turn encouraged leaders in Beijing to develop the policies that comprised the grand strategy on which they settled during the second half of the
1990s.

4

China's Growing Power: Why the Worry?

In this chapter, I set aside doubts about the validity of claims that China's rise to great power status would be relatively swift and instead consider some of the reasons why those who took this trend for granted by the mid-1990s believed it would pose a danger for international peace and security. Concerns about the implications of China's ascent often rested on arguments whose logic, at least implicitly, reflected strands of international relations theory about the causes of military conflict. Indeed, most such theories offer grounds for pessimism about the likely consequences of China's growing power. I will also, however, discuss two theories that suggest why inevitable disputes need not result in military conflict; one of these theories offers persuasive reasons why the worst-case scenario of major power war should, in any event, remain implausible.

Power Perspectives

Hegemons and Challengers

International relations theories that explicitly focus on the dynamics of changing power relations support some of the most troubling predictions. Two such theories—Robert Gilpin's power preponderance theory and A. F. K. Organski and Jacek Kugler's power-transition theory—focus on the consequences of a shift in power between a dominant state and a rising challenger.[1]

Power preponderance. Gilpin depicts international relations as a political system in which governance functions are performed by a leading state that draws

---

[1] Robert Gilpin, *War and Change in World Politics*; A. F. K. Organski and Jacek Kugler, *The War Ledger*.

on its wealth, power, and status to set the rules of the game.[2] Over time, how-ever, economic and technological diffusion proceeds during eras of peace and other states are empowered. As the burdens of international governance drain and distract the reigning hegemon, challengers eventually emerge who seek to rewrite the rules of governance to their advantage. With its relative power ebbing, the erstwhile hegemon may become desperate enough to resort to force to forestall the increasingly urgent demands of a rising challenger. Or the challenger, as its power grows, may be tempted to press its case with threats to use force. It is "the rise and fall of the great powers" (as Paul Kennedy put it in his account of international political history) that creates the circumstances under which major wars, what Gilpin labels "hegemonic wars," break out.[3]

This power preponderance theory logically encourages pessimism about the implications of a rising China. It leads to the expectation that international trade, investment, and technology transfer will result in a steady diffusion of American economic power, benefiting the rapidly developing states of the world, including China. As the United States scurries to put out the many brushfires that threaten its far-flung global interests (the classic problem of over-extension), it will be unable to devote sufficient resources to maintaining or re-storing its former advantage over emerging competitors like China. While the once-clear American advantage erodes, the United States will find it increas-ingly difficult to preserve the order in Asia that it created during its era of pre-ponderance. The expectation is an increase in the likelihood of the use of force—either by a Chinese challenger able to field a stronger military in support of its demands for greater influence over international arrangements in Asia, or by a besieged American hegemon desperate to head off further decline.

Power transition. A related but distinct argument of this sort focused on the ominous consequences of an emerging great power is the "power-transition theory" set forth by Organski and Kugler. They envision the international system as a hierarchy of contending states in which the distribution of benefits reflects the interests of the system's dominant actor (the hegemon). When a strong contender believes it has the power to recast the international hierar-chy, it is likely to be the aggressor in a major war "to redraft the rules by which relations among nations work" and gain "the greater benefits and privileges" that accompany dominance.[4] Although similar to power prepon-

---

[2] Gilpin, *War and Change in World Politics.* For a more detailed historical discussion that mirrors the logic Gilpin depicts, see Paul Kennedy, *The Rise and Fall of the Great Powers.*

[3] Kennedy, *The Rise and Fall of the Great Powers.*

[4] Organski and Kugler, *The War Ledger,* pp. 19–20, 23. Gilpin, by contrast, does not indicate whether the rising or the falling power will be the "aggressor."

derance theory insofar as it emphasizes the importance of shifts in the capabilities of a dominant state and a rising challenger, Organski and Kugler's power-transition theory focuses a bit more closely on what it views as the dangerous phenomenon of "crossover"—the point at which a challenger is about to overtake the established leading state. When the power gap narrows, the dominant state becomes increasingly desperate to forestall, and the challenger becomes increasingly determined to realize, the transition to a new international order whose contours are defined by the system's leading state. The stakes of this change are clearly quite high. Each state, therefore, is strongly motivated to consider all available means, including war, to affect the outcome of a possible transition.

Though suggesting why a rising China may ultimately present grave dangers for international peace when its capabilities make it a peer competitor of the United States, the power-transition theory is less clear about the dangers posed while the challenger is still struggling to catch up. This is important since China's military capabilities in the 1990s were still at least several decades away from being in the same league as those of the United States. One might conclude, then, that the sort of logic described by power-transition theory was not feeding the concerns about a still-weak China that emerged shortly after the end of the Cold War. But pessimism about the consequences of China's rise did in a sense reflect this theory's logic, even though a challenge in the near term seemed unlikely. Because a dominant state may worry about the mere prospect of being overtaken in the future and believe that it is wise to move early to preclude a transition while the task is more manageable (embracing the logic of preventive action), the theory at least suggests the possibility of serious conflict well before any predicted crossover. Indeed, among the historical occurrences illustrating the dangers that power-transition theory sets forth, Germany's decisions on the eve of World War I may have reflected precisely this sort of projection about future dangers that an allegedly rising Russia could pose rather than fear of an imminent power transition.[5]

---

[5] See William C. Wohlforth, "The Perception of Power." Dale Copeland argues that power shifts matter and explain the outbreak of war between major powers, but not in the way that Organski and Kugler or Gilpin suggest. In Copeland's "dynamic differentials theory," war results from a dominant power's fear of decline rather than a rising power's impatience. Rising powers, Copeland asserts, would always be better off waiting until they are stronger before risking war; dominant powers have incentives to launch preventive wars before they have lost their advantage (Dale C. Copeland, *The Origins of Major War*). Yet, if it is clear that the dominant state has incentives to act preventively at some point, there should be circumstances under which the rising state will believe it is better to attack rather than wait and respond after it has been struck.

What expectations about the consequences of China's growing economic and military strength follow from these theories that focus on the challenge a rising power may pose to a reigning hegemon? The expectation is that an ever more capable Beijing would demand a larger role in the management of international affairs hitherto dominated by the world's leading power, the United States. To the extent the United States resists, either because it is unaccustomed to accommodating others' international interests in governing the system or because it is fearful that others' gains come at the United States' expense, the stage is set for intense and potentially dangerous struggle.[6]

Were such problems evident in the 1990s? Even though hard facts suggested that China was at best in the early stages of a long process that might make it a peer competitor of the United States, by the mid-1990s worrisome signs that Sino-American relations would reflect the logic highlighted in these theories emphasizing the importance of shifting power were already emerging. Predictions, noted in chapter 3, that China's growth would give it the world's largest GDP (aggregate, not per capita) sometime in the first few decades of the twenty-first century rather quickly triggered anxiety among some about a potentially dangerous challenge to American economic leadership in Asia.[7] Recurring trade deficits with China of the sort that had previously led to fears about Japan's economic gains at the United States' expense also generated concern in Washington about unfair economic competition as the Chinese economy boomed in the mid-1990s. And although one might expect that the huge gap between Chinese and American military capabilities (especially in terms of technological sophistication) would have precluded comparable anxiety in this area, similar concerns were manifest in the arguments of those who

---

This choice depends on many considerations—such as the countries' relative strength and their levels of resolve—that are more readily captured in the bargaining model of shifting power offered by Robert Powell. See *In the Shadow of Power,* chapter 4.

[6] There is also the potential for racial or cultural differences to exacerbate great power rivalry if Beijing believes the United States and perhaps its Western allies are determined to deny China its rightful role because they cannot tolerate an Asian power rising above second-class status. In the post–Cold War era, sensitivity to the potential significance of cultural, if not simply racial, tensions in international relations was reawakened by Samuel Huntington's work, which received substantial attention in China. See Samuel P. Huntington, "The Clash of Civilizations?"; Samuel P. Huntington, *The Clash of Civilizations and the Remaking of World Order.*

[7] Steven Greenhouse, "New Tally of World's Economies Catapults China Into Third Place"; "Revised Weights for the World Economic Outlook; Annex IV"; Jim Rohwer, "Rapid Growth Could Make China World's Largest Economy by 2012"; William H. Overholt, *The Rise of China;* Nicholas R. Lardy, *China in the World Economy,* pp. 14–18.

warned of a looming "China threat."[8] Occasionally alarmist reports about the purchases of advanced Russian air and naval equipment as well as suspicion that Chinese espionage might contribute to an erosion of the American advantage in nuclear and missile technology stoked fears about a narrowing of the power advantage a preponderant United States enjoyed over China at the end of the twentieth century.[9] But perhaps most telling, remarkably early in the post–Cold War era China had begun to supplant the defunct Soviet Union in thinking about potential great power threats to U.S. interests. Beijing's military modernization and regional assertiveness in the South China Sea and especially the Taiwan Strait resulted in scenarios for conflict with China, a country that had been a virtual American ally during the last two decades of the Cold War, quickly becoming important contingencies for assessing the adequacy of U.S. conventional and nuclear forces.[10]

Meanwhile Beijing's actions in some respects also conformed with the expectations these theories generate about a "challenger" dissatisfied with the dominance of a "hegemon." China vociferously criticized U.S. human rights policy as an effort to impose American values on the rest of the world, and criticized U.S. international economic policy, especially with respect to the terms under which China could accede to the WTO, as an attempt to preserve American dominance.[11] And, as noted in chapter 3, in the military realm China's modernization program by the mid-1990s was focused on acquiring a capability to advance its interests in the Taiwan Strait, which China believed American preponderance put at risk.

[8] See especially Richard Bernstein and Ross H. Munro, *The Coming Conflict with China.*

[9] The espionage concerns eventually led to a U.S. congressional investigation, and by the late 1990s the U.S. Congress had mandated annual reports to assess the potential dangers a rising China might pose for American interests. For the Cox Committee report on Chinese espionage, see "Select Committee on U.S. National Security and Military/Commercial Concerns with the People's Republic of China." But see also the devastating criticisms of the report in Alastair Iain Johnston, W. K. H. Panofsky, Marco DiCapua, and Lewis R. Franklin, *The Cox Committee Report: An Assessment Center for International Security and Cooperation*; Walter Pincus, "Hill Report on Chinese Spying Faulted, Five Experts Cite Errors, 'Unwarranted' Conclusions by Cox Panel." For annual updates of two of the most important efforts to report on the implications of China's changing economic and military capabilities, see *Annual Report on the Military Power of the People's Republic of China; The National Security Implications of the Economic Relationship between the United States and China; Report to Congress of the U.S.-China Economic and Security Review Commission.*

[10] See William W. Kaufmann, *Assessing the Base Force*; Michael O'Hanlon, *Defense Planning for the Late 1990s.*

[11] See "China Slams U.S. Demands for WTO Entry."

Balance of Power

Like those experts who saw trouble emerging from the conflicting interests of a hegemon and challenger, those whose interpretations of international politics were informed, implicitly or explicitly, by balance-of-power theory also saw reason to worry about the potentially disruptive effects of a rising China. The logic of balancing suggests not only that Beijing would worry about U.S. power, globally as well as in Asia, and seek to offset the threat it might pose to Chinese interests, but also that China's increasing capabilities would trigger a reaction among its neighbors concerned about the ways in which Beijing might use its growing clout.[12] As Stephen Walt has emphasized, great power in and of itself may not always be deemed a threat requiring a response, but geography as well as the region's experience with China's dominance prior to the arrival of Western imperialism in the nineteenth century suggested reasons to expect that it would be hard for Beijing to allay regional fears about how it might wield its growing capabilities.[13] Lesser regional actors would most likely believe they needed to hedge their bets by arming themselves or courting partners whose assistance would be essential if it ever became necessary to actively counter a stronger China.[14] By the mid-1990s, there were already at

[12] Three of the seminal works in contemporary theorizing about balancing behavior are Kenneth N. Waltz, *Man, the State, and War: A Theoretical Analysis*; Kenneth N. Waltz, *Theory of International Politics*; and Stephen M. Walt, *The Origins of Alliances*. Although the logic of balancing is clear, the connections between the theories and their application are complicated and sometimes inconsistent. Discussion of these theoretical problems falls outside the scope of this book, but two points should be noted. First, some states may engage in what amounts to anticipatory balancing against projected power (regional actors seeing a need to prepare to cope with a stronger China); others may balance against current power (China's interest in countering a dominant United States). Second, the reaction to current and projected power is also shaped by national interests, not just power. Explaining the foreign policy choices of particular states requires the consideration of many national attributes (including perceptions of intent, shared history, and ideology) that are omitted from Waltz's balance-of-power theory about broad patterns of behavior in the system, but included in Walt's balance-of-threat application to the choices individual states make.

[13] For a different interpretation of regional actors' understanding of their experience with Imperial China, see David C. Kang, "Getting Asia Wrong: The Need for New Analytical Frameworks."

[14] The response to China's international renaissance has been mixed, since balancing only makes sense if states can muster sufficient resources, individually or collectively. Absent great power allies, self-interested East Asian states may conclude they have no alternative to accommodating Chinese interests. See Avery Goldstein, "Balance-of-Power Politics: Consequences for Asian Security Order."

least rumblings of the sort that such balance-of-power reasoning would predict, including reactive arms buildups in the region, noted in chapter 3, and regional actors seeking allies to compensate for their limited national strength (most notably, tentative consultations among the ASEAN states as well as Japan's and Australia's reinvigorated security agreements with their American partner discussed in chapter 5).[15]

While balance-of-power theory does not argue that the interactive process it depicts inevitably results in war, it does view the use of force as one of the options available to states should they conclude that diplomacy backed by military power is ineffective. The logic of balancing provides reason to worry that the perception of China as a rapidly rising power could lead to military conflict in one of two ways. Prospective adversaries might see a sustained effort at countering Beijing's growing power as intolerably burdensome and resort to the use of force to end the competition. Or, China itself might conclude that relying on its military clout is the most feasible way to offset the dangers posed to its international interests (whether modest or ambitious) by the power others possess. Balance-of-power theory only suggests the resort to force is possible, not inevitable. What, then, might determine its likelihood? Some have argued that one of the decisive factors determining whether balancing will be peacefully conducted or result in war is the number of great powers in the international system, distinguishing between bipolar and multipolar eras.[16] What does such reasoning suggest about the prospects for balancing to remain peaceful as China's power grows?

[15] See President Clinton's speech to the Japanese Diet in "Clinton: Japan, U.S. Must Continue to Be Partners"; also "United States to Retain Strong Presence in Pacific: Christopher." See also Desmond Ball, "Arms and Affluence: Military Acquisitions in the Asia-Pacific Region"; "SE Asians Arming up to Protect Their Resources"; David Shambaugh, "Growing Strong," p. 44; "Singapore's Lee Warns of Growing Power of China"; and "Asian Reaction Swift to China's Maritime Expansion." Japan has the capability to take the lead in efforts to hedge against the need to counter growing Chinese strength, but the domestic and regional legacy of Japan's behavior during the Second World War makes this unlikely. See Charles Lane, "TRB from Washington: Re-Orient," p. 6.

[16] Which sort of system is more likely to be peaceful, however, remains an unsettled issue among international relations scholars despite a long-running debate during the Cold War. For three articles that helped trigger the polarity debate, see Karl W. Deutsch and J. David Singer, "Multipolar Power Systems and International Stability"; Richard N. Rosecrance, "Bipolarity, Multipolarity, and the Future"; and Kenneth N. Waltz, "International Structure, National Force, and the Balance of World Power." See also Thomas J. Christensen and Jack Snyder, "Chain Gangs and Passed Bucks"; Barry R. Posen, *The Sources of Military Doctrine*; John J. Mearsheimer, "Back to the Future: Instability in Europe after the Cold War"; Steven Van Evera, "Primed for

Polarity. During the early 1990s many, including the Chinese, believed that the post–Cold War world would relatively quickly move beyond a brief era of American unipolarity and that a new multipolar world would emerge.[17] Yet the details of the expected transition remained unclear, especially within the East Asian region where China's interests were greatest and its growing influence would first be felt. It was at least plausible that bipolarity might return, if only temporarily, anchored this time by the United States and China, with an internally weakened, Eurocentric Russia and a militarily self-limited Japan playing marginal roles. If so, China's rise could pose the dangers identified as the risks associated with balancing under bipolarity—especially hostile overreaction to a single adversary on which each duopolist focuses its attention. In this respect, it was troubling that early in the post–Cold War era, even before a rising China could be considered a peer competitor of the United States in a new bipolar setting, both Beijing and Washington were already closely focusing on one another and viewing one another's actions as potentially threatening. Each was already worrying about shifts in the balance of military power and mutual perceptions of resolve. Early indications, then, suggested a bipolar East Asia would be primed for recurrent Sino-American conflict reminiscent of the dangerous Soviet-American rivalry during the Cold War.

But most analysts initially expected that the unipolar post–Cold War order would soon give way to multipolarity rather than restored bipolarity. Would balancing be less dangerous if a rising China emerged not as the sole great power rival of the United States, but instead as one of several key actors in a multipolar East Asia (including not just the United States, but also a less restrained Japan, a resurgent Russia, and perhaps even a widely engaged and more powerful India)? Balance-of-power theorists were not optimistic. As Aaron Friedberg noted, key political influences that reduced the dangers of multipolarity in Europe after the Cold War (consensus on the lessons from the past fighting of wars, long experience at international diplomacy, the homogeneity of domestic political orders) were absent in East Asia.[18] Moreover, military-strategic considerations that allegedly can contribute to the peacefulness of balancing under multipolarity might also be absent. It is not clear, for example, that a need for allies would exert much of an inhibiting effect on China since many scenarios under which it was thought to be a potentially disruptive in-

---

Peace: Europe after the Cold War"; Thomas J. Christensen, "Perceptions and Alliances in Europe, 1865–1940."

[17] For an early post–Cold War Western assessment of China's prospects that took multipolarity for granted, see William T. Tow. "China and the International Strategic System."

[18] Aaron Friedberg, "Ripe for Rivalry," pp. 9–10, 27–28.

fluence in the region, such as the South China Sea territorial disputes, were not likely to require Beijing to plan on joint action.[19] Balance-of-power theorists have also noted the special temptation of military adventurism that multipolarity can encourage when a state believes others will "pass the buck" rather than accept a share of the burden and take the risks to balance against its assertive actions. According to such thinking, in a multipolar setting China could be tempted to use force to advance its interests, despite the risks of conflict, if it thought that prospective rivals would fail to balance in a timely fashion. Throughout history, such gambles on a lack of opposition have sometimes turned out to be based upon disastrously incorrect predictions and have contributed to the outbreak of catastrophic wars. Yet their recurrence provides another reason for those whose thinking is informed by balancing logic to worry about the consequences of China's rise under multipolarity.

In short, balancing looked potentially dangerous whether the world in which China would emerge as a great power turned out to be bipolar or multipolar. But what were the likely implications of China's rise if the post–Cold War international system instead remained unipolar, with the United States as the sole superpower for decades rather than years? Scholarly debates about the links between polarity and peacefulness have ignored what many have presumed to be the implausible condition of unipolarity. Yet an enduring unipolar order was exactly what was coming more clearly into focus by the middle of the 1990s. The extreme power disparities that prevailed under unipolarity seemed to preclude traditional attempts at balancing by other states, including China. Indeed, Beijing soon recognized that it had neither the option of flexibly allying with others (an option that would have been available under multipolarity), nor the option of self-reliance (an option that would be available if China were to become a peer competitor of the United States under bipolarity). Consequently, as noted in the next chapter, Beijing rather quickly backed away from any serious attempt to balance U.S. power in ways that might have provoked conflict. Instead, China's leaders embraced a more subtle grand strategy designed to advance their country's interests while also coping with the potential dangers they faced during a protracted period of American preponderance.

Security dilemma. Theorizing about the security dilemma, closely related to balance-of-power theory, suggests additional reasons why some expected China's growing power to increase the risk of international conflict. As noted in chapter 2, in an anarchic system where it is impossible to establish binding

---

[19] See Van Evera's "drunk tank" analogy to explain the beneficial restraining influence of allies in a multipolar world ("Primed for Peace," p. 39).

commitments, the difficulty of interpreting others' capabilities and intentions means that each state's effort to enhance its own security poses a potential threat to which others are likely to respond.[20] In the 1990s, China's policies and the reaction to them did suggest an intensifying security dilemma. Beijing's investment in power-projection capabilities, reassertions of sovereignty over waters and territory from the Diaoyu (Senkaku) Islands to Taiwan to the Spratlys, and the limited military actions China had undertaken contributed to growing consternation in Tokyo, Taipei, the capitals of the ASEAN countries, and most openly in Washington, D.C. While the buildup of the PLA's air and naval forces might simply have reflected Beijing's belief that it needed to be able to mount a forward defense in the event conflict were forced upon a reluctant China, these capabilities could also be used to undertake offensive military operations. It is precisely such uncertainty about intentions and how they might change over time that drives the security dilemma.

As the literature about the security dilemma would predict, the PRC's Asian neighbors and the United States responded to what they saw as a potentially dangerous China by hedging against the possible challenges an even more powerful China could pose to their interests in the future.[21] Beijing, in turn, saw the fears others cited as at best groundless and at worst disguising their true motivation—to keep China down.[22] Beijing instead noted its own relative weakness, not its emerging strength, and explained its policy statements and military deployments as no more than what was necessary to defend the nation's vital interests. China's leaders argued that the exaggeration of the PLA's capabilities and the questioning of their motives were really a smokescreen—a pretext to justify revived Japanese militarism and a U.S.-sponsored strategy of containment aimed at China, operationalized through military assistance to regional actors and the cultivation of anti-China alli-

---

[20] See John H. Herz, "Idealist Internationalism and the Security Dilemma"; Waltz, *Theory of International Politics*, pp. 186–87; Glenn Snyder, "The Security Dilemma in Alliance Politics." As also noted in chapter 1, the literature does suggest variations in strategic beliefs and military technology that may dampen this dynamic. See Robert Jervis, "Cooperation Under the Security Dilemma"; Christensen and Snyder, "Chain Gangs and Passed Bucks."

[21] See "Vietnam, China in Dispute over Offshore Drilling"; "U.S. Forces Welcome in South China Sea"; Nicholas D. Kristof, "Tension with Japan Rises alongside China's Star." On Japan's 1996 Defense White Paper's inclusion of a call to keep a cautious eye on China's buildup and activism, see Brian Williams, "Japan Sees China as Growing Military Challenge."

[22] See, for examples, "China Defense Minister Says Threat Theory Absurd"; Shambaugh, "Growing Strong," p. 43; Benjamin Kang Lim, "Beijing Slams West for Playing up China Threat."

ances.[23] In short, by the mid-1990s the situation in East Asia was one in which malign mutual perceptions seemed to be feeding worst-case (or at least "bad-case") planning that could trigger dangerous spirals of conflict. The intensifying security dilemma was concisely summarized by one of the leading experts on China's military modernization, David Shambaugh: "From China's perspective, its build-up [was] a legitimate effort to acquire armed forces commensurate with its rising status as a global economic power and protect its perceived national interests. But from the perspective of many of China's neighbors an alarming trend [had] begun."[24]

Nowhere were the troubling consequences of balancing fueled by the security dilemma becoming more apparent than in the tension across the Taiwan Strait.[25] By the mid-1990s, both China and Taiwan (with its informal ties to the United States) were again worried that their political dispute might result in the use of force, though this outcome was not seen as inevitable. Both China and Taiwan remained uncertain about the intentions of the other; the forces deployed in and near the prospective theater of conflict were not unambiguously identifiable as offensive, defensive, or deterrent weapons but could be used for any of these missions; analysts disagreed about whether attackers or defenders would have the military advantage; and, perhaps distinctive to this case, the parties even disagreed about what constituted a threat to the status quo that might justify military preparations. Under these ambiguous circumstances, each side's improving capabilities (including deployment of new weapons, redeployment of existing forces, and military exercises) could be viewed as increasing the potential threat and provided incentives for the other to respond. Restraint looked too risky because each worried that restraint might not be reciprocated, but instead exploited by the other to gain a strategic advantage. Thus, unsure about one another's current and future intentions, each side prudently made the effort necessary to counter the im-

---

[23] For criticism of U.S. motives, see Jane Macartney, "China Army Wants Nuclear Arms Destruction, Test End"; "China Says Future U.S. Ties Hinge on Taiwan." U.S. policy statements were not entirely clear. See "Testimony before the House International Relations Committee Subcommittee on Asia and the Pacific, by Admiral Richard C. Macke, U.S. Navy Commander in Chief, United States Pacific Command"; also "China Building up for Spratlys—U.S. Official"; "American Interests and the U.S.-China Relationship." On China's suspicion of Japan's motives, see Thomas J. Christensen, "Chinese Realpolitik"; "China's Jiang Zemin Warns against Japan Militarism"; Holly Porteous, "China's View of Strategic Weapons."

[24] Shambaugh, "Growing Strong," p. 44.

[25] See Thomas J. Christensen, "The Contemporary Security Dilemma: Deterring a Taiwan Conflict." See also Thomas J. Christensen, "Posing Problems without Catching Up."

proving military capabilities of its potential adversary. As a result, the sort of vexing cycle described by the security dilemma prevailed in the Taiwan Strait.

Although China claimed that new military deployments were meant to discourage provocative attempts by the leaders on Taiwan who might otherwise lurch toward independence, triggering a war, Taiwan (and its American supporters) saw China's capabilities not as a hedge against Taipei's adventurism, but rather as a sign of the mainland's preparation for offensive action to force the Taiwanese to accept integration on Beijing's unacceptable terms. When Taiwan responded by deploying new forces of its own as well as weaponry purchased from the United States and sought reassurance that the United States would offer additional support in the event of a military challenge from the mainland, China saw these efforts as proof that Taiwan's leaders were determined never to reunite with the mainland. The United States, indirectly caught in the dilemma, tried to strike a delicate balance between the need to hedge against the threat that China's capabilities could pose to Taiwan and the need to avoid unintentionally encouraging Taiwan to believe the United States would back provocative moves toward independence.[26] Yet Washington's approval of military transfers to and support for Taiwan, even though they were strictly limited to enhancing the island's defensive capabilities, alarmed leaders in Beijing who saw it as increasing the challenge they faced and requiring a response. Leaders in Taipei then interpreted Beijing's reaction as further evidence of the growing threat from China. When Beijing demanded that Washington halt its arms sales to Taiwan to end the cycle and facilitate a peaceful resolution of the dispute, Washington called on Beijing to first renounce the use of force against Taiwan. Because China feared its generosity would not be reciprocated, however, it rejected the American suggestion, predictably stoking suspicion and causing consternation in Taipei and Washington. In short, the intense rivalry that reemerged in the Taiwan Strait in the 1990s seemed to be a classic example of the security dilemma, illustrating why some worried that the growth of Chinese power and reactions to it would result in dangerous balancing behavior and increase the chances of military conflict.

[26] For the United States this is the challenge of practicing "dual deterrence." See Andrew J. Nathan, "What's Wrong with American Taiwan Policy"; Brett V. Benson and Emerson M. S. Niou, "Comprehending Strategic Ambiguity: US Policy toward Taiwan Security."

Regime Perspectives

Some observers and policy makers believed that the principal reason to worry about the potentially disruptive effect of China's rise was not its impact on the distribution of power among states, or even the uncertainties associated with life in an anarchic international system, but rather the nature of the political regime ruling China. Two strands of international relations theory provided an intellectual foundation for the claim that China's domestic politics might make it an especially troublesome emerging great power.

Democratic Peace Theory

The first such argument pointed to the likelihood that China's growing power would be internationally disruptive because it is not a liberal democracy. After the Cold War, the logic of this position no longer rested on the belief that all communist states were driven to spread their way of life. Instead, in the new vision China's communist credentials were important mainly because they indicated that it remained a brutal dictatorship all too willing to resort to force rather than reason to settle disagreements at home and abroad. Among academics, the arguments supporting this view have been referred to loosely as "democratic peace theory."[27] It suggests that the distinctive domestic institutions and political values of liberal democracies ensure peace among them, though not between such states and nondemocracies.

Because leaders of liberal democracies face domestic institutional restraints and are committed to the norm of resolving political disputes through discussion and compromise rather than violence, they share the expectation that the use of military force is neither necessary nor desirable in their bilateral relations. Leaders of liberal democracies view the policies of their counterparts in other liberal democracies as legitimately representing the will of their people and thus worthy of respect. They also are likely to have confidence in the reliability of international agreements negotiated with such leaders, despite the absence of a supranational enforcer in the anarchic international system, because commitments among democracies are made not just by individuals but by individuals accountable to effective institutions. By contrast, democracies willingly use force against nondemocracies that fall outside the liberal "zone of

[27] The locus classicus of the contemporary democratic peace argument is Michael W. Doyle, "Kant, Liberal Legacies, and Foreign Affairs." For work that began to raise questions about the logic and evidence supporting the assertion of a democratic peace, see Christopher Layne, "Kant or Cant: The Myth of the Democratic Peace"; Henry S. Farber and Joanne Gowa, "Polities and Peace"; Edward D. Mansfield and Jack Snyder, "Democratization and the Danger of War."

peace." Leaders of democracies do not presume that the leaders of dictator-
ships represent the views of their people, and they worry about the reliability
of agreements negotiated with rulers not bound by the institutions of representative government. Against authoritarian states, democracies may have to
use force in self-defense, or they may choose to use force to expand the zone
of peace by defeating and then converting authoritarian enemies.

What are the implications of this reasoning for the consequences of China's
rise that many saw in the offing by the mid-1990s? If an authoritarian China
were to become a great power, it would not only be outside the zone of
peace, but it would also have the wherewithal to be a belligerent in a great
power war. Against a Chinese regime that rejected liberal democratic values
and in which the foreign policy decision-making process on crucial security
matters was not much constrained by representative institutions but rather
monopolized by, at most, a handful of leaders only loosely accountable to a
slightly larger elite, this perspective suggested that democratic great powers
would feel justified in embracing confrontational policies.[28] And because
China's small, authoritarian ruling group believed that the West was engaged
in a campaign designed to subvert communist rule without a fight ("peaceful
evolution"), hostility and intransigence would be reciprocated.[29] In short, the
perception in the mid-1990s that China was growing powerful but was not
democratic contributed to the nervousness about the implications of its rise.

Democratic Transition Theory

The "democratic transition theory" offered by Edward Mansfield and Jack
Snyder suggests a different argument about the international dangers an
emerging great power's domestic political order might pose. It explains why
some states in the midst of a shift from authoritarianism to democracy are
likely to adopt disruptive foreign policies.[30] Mansfield and Snyder argue that
competitors for leadership in such regimes may endorse highly belligerent

[28]On lower priority matters the foreign policy process is less centralized and more
bureaucratized. See Michael D. Swaine, "The PLA in China's National Security Policy: Leaderships, Structures, Processes"; David Shambaugh, "Containment or Engagement," pp. 196–201; A. Doak Barnett, *The Making of Foreign Policy in China:
Structure and Process.*

[29] See Shambaugh, "Growing Strong," p. 50; David Shambaugh, "The United
States and China: A New Cold War?" p. 244.

[30] Mansfield and Snyder, "Democratization and the Danger of War." They subsequently refined the argument by stipulating the institutional conditions under which
the belligerence they explain is most likely to arise. See Edward D. Mansfield, and Jack
Snyder, "Democratic Transitions, Institutional Strength, and War."

policies because this stance enables them to garner popular support by tapping nationalist sentiments or to garner elite support by placating the institutional remnants of authoritarian rule, especially the military.

But why would such ideas be relevant to the concerns about a rising China that surfaced in the 1990s? China, after all, was clearly still an authoritarian regime. Nevertheless, while Beijing's sweeping efforts to reform its centrally planned economy after 1979 grabbed most of the attention, China's leaders were also undertaking a less heralded, admittedly halting, and intentionally modest program of political relaxation. And with it, the potential for the sorts of problems Mansfield and Snyder identified grew.[31] Importantly, in the 1990s observers noted a deep-seated nationalism taking root among a more attentive, aware, and outspoken Chinese public.[32] Its manifestations included not just pride in China's recent economic progress, but also popular resentment at past and present mistreatment by foreigners, feelings nurtured by the CCP's standard account of the country's century of humiliation that began with the British victory in the Opium War and lasted through the brutal Japanese invasion and occupation of World War II. This strident strand of nationalism provides the country's leaders with a collection of hot button issues that democratic transition theory suggests might have disturbing consequences for China's international behavior.

One concern is the possibility that China's communist leaders may be

[31] The revised version of their theory actually raises greater concern about the Chinese case, since they now acknowledge that the existence of strong political institutions during the period of transition can offset the dangerous effects they emphasize. One of the distinctive features of contemporary China is the remarkably underdeveloped state of political institutionalization, even as dictatorial controls are relaxed. This condition is not coincidental and seems unlikely to change. Ever since the reform era began in 1979, the CCP has insisted on adhering to "four cardinal principles" or "four upholds" that cannot be challenged. The regime has repeatedly invoked two of these principles, "upholding the dictatorship of the proletariat" and "upholding the leading role of the Communist Party," to prevent competing sources of institutional power, such as courts, a free press, and rival parties, from taking root.

[32] See Joseph Fewsmith and Stanley Rosen, "The Domestic Context of Chinese Foreign Policy: Does 'Public Opinion' Matter?"; Gerald Segal, "China Takes on Pacific Asia"; Allen S. Whiting, "Chinese Nationalism and Foreign Policy after Deng"; Michel Oksenberg, "China's Confident Nationalism"; Jonathan Unger, ed., *Chinese Nationalism*; Fei-ling Wang, "Ignorance, Arrogance, and Radical Nationalism: A Review of China Can Say No"; Hongshan Li, "China Talks Back: Anti-Americanism or Nationalism? A Review of Recent 'Anti-American' Books in China." Most such assessments have relied on anecdotal evidence. Survey research suggests a wider variety of nationalist views in China. See Alastair Iain Johnston, "The Correlates of Nationalism in Beijing Public Opinion."

tempted to adopt a more belligerent foreign policy to rally nationalist support behind their tottering regime whose legitimacy has grown otherwise tenuous (having lost its former ideological appeal and still lacking a well-institutional-ized basis for its exercise of authority). Another concern, more directly linked to Mansfield and Snyder's theory, is that belligerence might result from the pressures of competition within the CCP as elite contenders seek to outshine or discredit their rivals by tapping volatile nationalist sentiments.[33] Under such circumstances, there would be reason to worry that China's leaders, having roused public opinion, would find it more difficult to compromise in conflicts with other states if their domestically motivated foreign policy initiatives re-sulted in disputes touching on sensitive nationalist legacies. Two obvious can-didates for trouble of this sort are the Taiwan problem, in which Chinese leaders could cast the United States (perhaps assisted by the island's former colonial ruler, Japan) as the foreign stumbling block to a peaceful resolution, and the Diaoyu (Senkaku) Islands dispute with Japan, in which Beijing could portray Tokyo's intransigence as reflecting a broader refusal to acknowledge its affronts to the Chinese nation between 1895 and 1945.

To be sure, in the 1990s China's authoritarian rulers did not yet face either the sort of intense internal elite competition or the degree of accountability to a mass electorate that Mansfield and Snyder emphasize. But the more collec-tive form of leadership already evident as the old revolutionary strongmen passed on, the diminished effectiveness of political controls over the Chinese people gaining greater access to information as a result of the post-Mao eco-nomic and social reforms, and the insecurity of communist rulers who could no longer rely on Marxism to justify their grip on power had already begun to increase the importance of attending to nationalist popular opinion.[34] Mansfield and Snyder's work alerts one to the possible dangers this can pres-ent.

Finally, the continuing role of the military in China's politics added yet another concern that figures prominently in the democratic transition theory. Despite signs early in the reform era that a professionalizing PLA would re-move itself from participation in politics, the chronic weakness of China's ci-vilian institutions kept the military in the position of, at a minimum, political kingmaker.[35] Even as the regime shifted away from what had been decades of

[33] Shambaugh, "The United States and China," p. 247.

[34] Expressions of nationalist outrage and anticipation of such outrage may have con-strained the regime's reaction to events as varied as the 1993 decision against awarding China the 2000 Olympics, the U.S. bombing of China's embassy in Belgrade in 1999, and the April 2001 EP-3 spy plane incident.

[35] The PLA played a decisive political role at least twice in the PRC's history, re-

nearly one-man rule, those who hoped to rise to the top still needed to earn the support of the PLA. In the 1990s, that support sometimes required a commitment not just to large defense budgets, but also to permitting the military to plan for contingencies that would demonstrate its credentials as an international fighting force rather than as tool of domestic dictatorship ("the Taiwan Strait, not Tiananmen Square"). This need for civilian elites to curry favor with the military is yet another way in which conditions in a rising China seemed to resonate with Mansfield and Snyder's concerns about the potential belligerence of regimes moving away from strict authoritarian rule.[36]

Institutional Perspective

Other analysts worried that a more powerful China might increase the risks of conflict because Beijing would be at best weakly constrained by international institutions. Institutionalist approaches to explaining international political outcomes assert that formal and informal organizational practices mitigate the effects of anarchy, dampen conflict, and enhance the prospects for cooperation.[37] Unfortunately, the conditions that contributed to the pacifying effects of institutionalization in post-World War II Europe seemed absent in early post–Cold War Asia. Organized attempts at international cooperation on economic and security affairs in Asia had a comparatively short history in comparison to Europe: conflicting rather than common interests were salient,

---

storing a modicum of order when the Cultural Revolution descended into chaos and suppressing the challenge posed by massive prodemocracy demonstrations in spring 1989.

[36] On the changing role of the PLA and the relevance of this political consideration for the Taiwan Strait military exercises of 1995 and 1996, see Shambaugh, "Containment or Engagement," pp. 190–91; also David Shambaugh, "China's Commander-in-Chief: Jiang Zemin and the PLA." On the web of military–political elite ties, see Ellis Joffe, "Party-Army Relations in China: Retrospect and Prospect"; Swaine, "The PLA in China's National Security Policy"; Richard Baum, "China after Deng: Ten Scenarios in Search of Reality." Notably, in 2002–3, as party and state leadership passed from the "third" to the "fourth" generation, the transition in civilian control of the military was delayed, with the semiretired Jiang Zemin retaining his role as chairman of the Central Military Commission until September 2004, even after stepping down as chairman of the Party and president of the PRC.

[37] See, for example, Stephen D. Krasner, ed., *International Regimes*; John Gerard Ruggie, "Multilateralism: The Anatomy of an Institution," p. 7. For a flavor of the intense debate with realists about the importance of international institutions, see John J. Mearsheimer, "The False Promise of International Institutions" and the exchange of views it provoked in *International Security* 20, no. 1 (1995).

cultures were diverse, and an overarching transnational identity and sense of community that might undergird institution building were lacking.[38]

Perhaps most troubling, in the early 1990s China's clear preference for bilateral rather than multilateral approaches to resolving its international conflicts seemingly diminished the prospects for developing more effective regional institutions. As noted in chapter 6, Beijing was sometimes willing to participate in international regimes and multilateral efforts at problem solving, but not when it worried that China's vital interests, especially historically sensitive issues of territorial sovereignty, might be at stake.[39] Most notably, in forcefully pressing its claims to the Spratly Islands during the early 1990s, China had generally undermined the region's most significant effort at building international institutions to dampen security conflicts, the ASEAN Regional Forum (ARF).[40] In response, states concerned about China's maritime aspirations initially resorted to more traditional realpolitik methods for coping with their insecurity.[41] The ongoing efforts of regional and extraregional states to nurture the ARF continued, but its weak institutional arrangements did not seem to promise much of a constraint on the international behavior of an increasingly powerful China.[42] Pessimism prevailed about the prospects for Beijing's meaningful participation in East Asian international institutions and about their effectiveness for managing the numerous interstate disputes involving China. Though such pessimism about the future of multilateralism in Asia would in retrospect seem misplaced, in the mid-1990s it was yet another reason for trepidation about the increasing military power Beijing was expected to soon have at its disposal.

In light of the multiple lines of reasoning that suggested why China's rise could pose problems for international security, it is hardly surprising that the

[38] See Friedberg, "Ripe for Rivalry," pp. 22–23, 24; Ruggie, "Multilateralism: The Anatomy of an Institution," p. 4. See also Charles A. Kupchan and Clifford A. Kupchan, "Concerts, Collective Security, and the Future of Europe," pp. 124–25.

[39] See Alastair Iain Johnston, "Prospects for Chinese Nuclear Force Modernization," pp. 575–76. On possible differences within China's leadership about the acceptability of multilateralism, see Shambaugh, "China's Commander-in-Chief," pp. 234–35; David Shambaugh, "China's Military in Transition," p. 273.

[40] See Michael Leifer, *The ASEAN Regional Forum*, pp. 37, 43–44; Mark J. Valencia, *China and the South China Sea Disputes*. On other confidence- and security-building measures at the time, see Ball, "Arms and Affluence."

[41] On Indonesia's bilateral security treaty with Australia, see Leifer, *The ASEAN Regional Forum*, pp. 50–52. On the Philippine's efforts to rejuvenate its military alliance with the United States after clashing with China over Mischief Reef in 1995 and Scarborough Shoal in 1997, see "Philippines to Seek Revision of Defense Pact with U.S."

[42] Leifer, *The ASEAN Regional Forum*, pp. 53–60.

perception of its growing capabilities elicited widespread concern in the last decade of the twentieth century. Yet pessimism was not universal. Some believed such concerns were overdrawn. Two strands of international relations theorizing provided an intellectual foundation for a more sanguine outlook.

Interdependence Perspective

Literature emphasizing the importance of increasing economic interdependence offered one line of reasoning justifying optimism about the likely impact of China's growing capabilities. This literature highlights the incentives for states to contain their international disputes when the costs of conflict are great (because one would alienate valued economic partners) and the benefits from the use of force are small (because the foundations of modern economic and military power depend less on assets that can be captured, such as manual labor and natural resources, and more on enterprising personnel, knowledge, and technological innovation).[43] Such considerations would arguably be important for China, since its rise was mainly based on rapid economic development fueled to a significant degree by dramatically increased levels of international trade and investment. Sharp reductions in international economic activity would seriously damage China's ability to sustain the high rates of growth that would be necessary, if not sufficient, for it to emerge as a great power.

From this perspective, China's leaders would be wary of alienating their most valued economic partners, the Americans, Japanese, and Europeans, a nearly certain result if Beijing decided to resolve international disputes or pursue its interests by using its increased military power. As long as China's leaders were concerned about preserving the conditions essential for promoting their country's welfare under circumstances where international trade and investment remained crucial, they would be reluctant to resort to the use of force. In this view, the arms of an interdependent state like China might not

[43] Robert O. Keohane and Joseph S. Nye, *Power and Interdependence*; John E. Mueller, *Retreat from Doomsday: The Obsolescence of Major War*; Steven Van Evera, "Why Europe Matters, Why the Third World Doesn't: American Grand Strategy after the Cold War"; Stephen G. Brooks, "The Globalization of Production and the Changing Benefits of Conquest." For criticism of this line of reasoning, see Kenneth N. Waltz, "The Myth of National Interdependence"; Robert J. Art, "To What Ends Military Power?"; Peter Liberman, "The Spoils of Conquest"; Norrin M. Ripsman and Jean-Marc F. Blanchard, "Commercial Liberalism under Fire: Evidence from 1914 and 1936." For China, the interest in not disrupting vital economic patterns of trade and investment would have to be weighed against the temptation to seize valuable natural resources, especially oil, in disputed maritime territories.

be tightly chained by economic concerns, but they are likely to be loosely bound in ways that reduce the prospects for military conflict and increase the incentives to sustain international cooperation. As suggested in the following chapters, Beijing's grand strategy did in fact reflect the salience of these economic considerations by the late 1990s.

Nuclear Peace Perspective

What might be termed "nuclear peace theory" provided perhaps the strongest reason to expect that any dangers associated with China's growing capabilities would be limited. This theory asserts that the advent of nuclear weapons, especially thermonuclear weapons that can be loaded atop ballistic missiles, revolutionized international politics by fundamentally transforming the costs of conflict among the great powers. Because none can confidently eliminate the risk of unacceptable retaliation by its adversary, nuclear powers dare not engage one another in military battles of the sort that have a real potential to escalate to unrestrained warfare. Among the great powers, even where capabilities are severely imbalanced, the nuclear revolution allegedly results in easily established relationships of mutual deterrence. These not only provide a robust buffer against general war, but they also tightly constrain crisis behavior and the fighting of limited wars.[44] Crises and limited wars between nuclear states with survivable retaliatory forces may yet occur, but their outcomes will no longer be determined mainly by traditional estimates of the balance of military power. Instead, in the nuclear age, such encounters become a competition in risk taking whose outcome is likely to be determined by the balance of political interests that underpins each actor's resolve.[45]

Nuclear peace theory, then, suggests that the alarmist implications for international security of China's rise to power were being overstated, mainly because analysts failed to explain why the familiar nuclear constraints would not apply for a Chinese decision maker and his counterpart in a rival great power.[46]

---

[44] See Bernard Brodie, *War and Politics*, esp. chapter 9; Kenneth N. Waltz, "Nuclear Myths and Political Realities"; Robert Jervis, *The Illogic of American Nuclear Strategy*; Jervis, *The Meaning of the Nuclear Revolution*; Goldstein, *Deterrence and Security in the 21st Century*. Not all analysts share this nuclear optimism. For debate about the logical and empirical validity of nuclear deterrence theory, see the special issue of *World Politics*, vol. 41, no. 2 (January 1989).

[45] See Richard K. Betts, *Nuclear Blackmail and Nuclear Balance*.

[46] Nuclear peace theorists would dismiss the recent Chinese interest in a nuclear war–fighting capability as another example of the futile attempt to "conventionalize" strategy that has often emerged among those who must plan for the use of the state's armed forces. See Alastair Iain Johnston, "China's New 'Old Thinking.'" Nuclear

According to this line of reasoning, any uncertainties about relative capabilities that might develop as China's strength grew would be overshadowed by certainty about the unacceptable damage even a small nuclear exchange could cause. This stark strategic reality would sharply limit the consequences of conflicts that might arise for the reasons more pessimistic perspectives suggested—anxiety and ambition linked to shifting power, fear about the type of regime wielding greater capabilities, and concern about the weakness or reliability of international institutions. In this view, China's military pressure on Taiwan or adventurism in the South China Sea and elsewhere in East Asia, whatever their causes, would be feasible only as long as the risk of an escalating conflict with a nuclear-armed rival was virtually zero. If such risk-laden military engagement became a serious possibility, leaders in Beijing and any nuclear adversary would feel the same pressure to find a negotiated solution that leaders in Washington and Moscow had felt during their various Cold War crises. In short, China might rise, but the strategic consequences of the nuclear revolution that have sustained a long era of peace among the great powers would endure.

*   *   *

By the mid-1990s, assessments of China's growing strength and forecasts about its implications for peace and security were raising troubling questions. While others pondered the meaning of China's rise, however, leaders in Beijing were increasingly worried about their ability to cope with the intensifying challenges they believed they faced. From their perspective, potential adversaries already seemed to be responding nervously to the anticipation that a relatively weak China would soon become strong and begin wielding the clout of a true great power. The following chapter, therefore, examines Beijing's understanding of its interests under the difficult conditions it saw emerging and how this perception shaped the grand strategy it embraced.

---

peace theorists see such conventionalization as at best irrelevant and at worst recklessly wasteful, but they do not see it as strategically destabilizing because the dominant deterrent logic prevails when leaders are forced to make war/peace decisions. For pessimistic views of the effects of nuclear weapons in East Asia, especially under conditions of multipolarity, see Friedberg, "Ripe for Rivalry"; Christensen and Snyder, "Chain Gangs and Passed Bucks"; Christensen, "Perceptions and Alliances in Europe, 1865–1940."

5

Stimuli for a New Strategy

The potential threat from the United States topped the list of Beijing's security concerns in the mid-1990s. Following a very brief transition period after the end of the Cold War during which China's analysts speculated about the possibility of a sharply reduced American role in East Asia, Beijing's fears about the United States grew rapidly.[1] The basic worry was that unmatched U.S. capabilities were being harnessed to a global strategy of engagement and enlargement that established an ambitiously expansive definition of American national security interests likely to challenge China. Beijing saw an unchecked United States, following the demise of its Soviet rival, that was quick to undertake repeated military interventions around the globe, quick to engage in "frequent crude interferences in the internal affairs of other countries," and eager to update and upgrade its network of Cold War alliances as a vehicle for ensuring America's continued international dominance.[2] As the decade progressed, China's concerns deepened and came more clearly into focus.

Chinese analysts worried about U.S. success in strengthening its bilateral military relations with Japan, South Korea, the Philippines, Australia, and Thailand (what one termed a "five-finger strategy" in the Asia Pacific to consolidate U.S. interests). Such fears were reinforced by joint military exercises that continued in Northeast Asia despite the end of the Cold War, by Washington's closer military cooperation in Southeast Asia with the Philippines, Malaysia, Thailand, and Singapore (including exercises that focused on the South China Sea), and by newly emerging American defense ties in Cen-

---

[1] See Lu Youzhi, "Chongxin Shenshi Zhongguo De Anquan Huanjing" [A fresh examination of China's security environment], pp. 58–59; Fang Hua, "Yatai Anquan Jiagou De Xianzhuang, Qushi Ji Zhongguo De Zuoyong" [The current Asia-Pacific security framework: trends and China's role], p. 12.

[2] Fu Liqun, "Several Basic Ideas in U.S. Strategic Thinking."

tral Asia.[3] Chinese analysts cast these activities in geopolitical terms and characterized them as an American effort to build a firewall around China that might also enhance Washington's ability to pressure Beijing. This line of reasoning would soon tap into ideas set forth by former U.S. national security adviser Zbigniew Brzezinski, and portray NATO expansion and a revised U.S.-Japan security relationship as complementary components of an American shift to an offensive, militarily activist alliance posture designed to control the Eurasian heartland and prevent the emergence of any peer competitors who might challenge American power.[4] In the Chinese telling, the crux of the East Asian facet of this post–Cold War U.S. strategy entailed exploiting the notion of a "China threat" to "sow divisions [among the region's states and] . . . to prevent China from becoming developed and powerful."[5] Of the various events in the 1990s that fed these fears, the most worrisome was the nearly simultaneous strengthening of two U.S.-led Pacific alliances, with Australia and Japan, that Beijing believed were developing an anti-China focus.[6]

U.S.-Australia Alliance

The July 1996 declaration "Relations of Strategic Partners of the 21st Century between Australia and the United States" clearly troubled the Chinese. Australia's "security outlook" was said to embrace a belief "that potential security risks existed in its area . . . , that countries in that area were building up their militaries," and that instability in "the Korean Peninsula . . . the Taiwan Strait . . . and the Nansha [Spratly] Islands" required the "forward deployment of the U.S. military in Australia . . . to effectively handle future regional and global challenges." Beijing interpreted this declaration as reflecting barely concealed concerns about a rising China. Defense Secretary William Perry's assertion that Australia, along with Japan, was one of two U.S. "anchors in the Asia-Pacific Region" (what one Chinese analyst termed the "claws of the crab") simply reinforced Beijing's view that the United States was cultivating

---

[3] See Fang, "Yatai Anquan Jiagou De Xianzhuang," p. 12.

[4] See Chu Shulong and Wang Zaibang, "Guanyu Guoji Xingshi He Wo Duiwai Zhanlüe Ruogan Zhongda Wenti De Sikao" [Reflections on some important questions about the international situation and our external strategy], p. 20. For the arguments drawing on Zbigniew Brzezinski's book, *The Grand Chessboard: American Primacy and Its Geostrategic Imperatives*, see Lu, "Chongxin Shenshi Zhongguo De Anquan Huanjing," pp. 58–59.

[5] Fu, "Several Basic Ideas in U.S. Strategic Thinking." See also Zhang Dezhen, "Qianghua Junshi Tongmeng Buhe Shidai Chaoliu" [Strengthening alliances is not in keeping with the times], p. 6.

[6] Lu "Chongxin Shenshi Zhongguo De Anquan Huanjing," pp. 58–59.

a "triangular security framework in the Asia Pacific region" as part of an incipient anti-China containment policy, Australia's protestations to the contrary notwithstanding.[7]

Beijing also viewed plans for joint U.S.-Australian military exercises, intelligence and logistical cooperation, and permission for the United States "to
build a ground relay station in Australia" as laying a key part of the foundation
for the advanced warning system the Americans required if they were to deploy ballistic missile defenses.[8] This connection to missile defense linked
China's objections about the evolving U.S.-Australia relationship to a larger
regional concern. Missile defense plans rankled Beijing because they raised the
prospect of a whole new range of U.S. military deployments in Asia that
could vitiate one of the PRC's few areas of regional military strength. The
possibility of employing even crude ballistic missiles to punish prospective adversaries against whom the PLA could not match up in other respects provided China with leverage it did not want to lose.

In the short term, a new generation of U.S. defenses might frustrate Beijing's ability to rely on the threat of ballistic missile strikes to discourage others
from taking steps that jeopardized China's interests, especially its interest in
preventing Taiwan's permanent political separation. In the longer term, missile defenses could become a crucial component of the U.S. effort to establish
a ring of encirclement around China. Even if fully effective missile defense
might be years away, in the interim Beijing was concerned that the joint efforts to prepare for eventual deployment would not only strengthen military

---

[7] See Li Xuejiang, "The 'Two Anchors' of the United States." By April 1997 Japan
and Australia were in fact engaged in a dialogue to expand their bilateral defense ties,
and to cooperate in facilitating a U.S. military presence in the region. "Australia, Japan:
Hashimoto, Howard Discuss Security Issues, Environment." Australia's foreign minister, Alexander Downer, recognizing the sensitivity that Beijing had demonstrated in
1996–97, quickly discounted the prospect of any agreement that would alarm China
when the Bush administration in July 2001 floated the idea of an Asian security alliance
that would bring together the United States, Australia, Japan, and South Korea. See
"Australia Denies Proposed Asian Security Alliance with U.S. Aimed at China."

[8] Zhu Feng, "TMD Yu Dangqian Zhongmei Guanxi" [TMD and current Sino-
American relations], p. 10. See also Tang Guanghui, "Behind the Warming of Austra-
lian-U.S. Relations," pp. 19–21; "Australia: PRC Criticism over Security Pact with
U.S. Noted"; Zhang, "Qianghua Junshi Tongmeng Buhe Shidai Chaoliu." In addition, New Zealand doubled the power of its Waihopai spy station to facilitate intelligence-gathering efforts with the United States, Australia, and Britain, allegedly to
maintain the ability to monitor China that was forfeited when Hong Kong reverted to
PRC rule. See "New Zealand: Spying Capacity Upgrade in New Zealand Linked to
China."

integration between Washington and its Asian allies but also increase their dependence on the United States.[9] Moreover, if theater missile defenses were a precursor to national missile defenses that would protect the U.S. homeland against retaliation, the era of American hegemony would likely be extended. National missile defenses would make it difficult for states to count on clever asymmetric nuclear strategies as a cost-effective way to offset American military superiority. Rising powers, including China, might find that they instead had to invest in the full range of advanced conventional capabilities that the wealthy United States could already deploy. From the perspective of the first post–Cold War decade, such competition with the industrial and technological might of the United States was not an inviting prospect. Missile defense, in short, would both complicate China's ability to manage its regional security problems and also raise higher still the barriers China faced if it hoped to enter the great power club.

U.S.-Japan Alliance

Largely because of the missile defense issue, Beijing was nervous about the evolving U.S.-Australia alliance. But it found the prospect of a simultaneously changing U.S.-Japan alliance much more alarming. Historically rooted Chinese skepticism about Japan's commitment to a peaceful foreign policy colored Beijing's interpretation of the revised guidelines for U.S.-Japan military cooperation in the post–Cold War era being hammered out in 1996 and 1997.[10] The comments of Li Jijun, lieutenant general and deputy commandant of the Academy of Military Sciences, typified a concern about Japan's intentions that was frequently articulated in the mid-1990s: "A half century has passed, and facts show that Japan's strategic culture has really made no appreciable progress." Li contrasted Japan's refusal to fully confront its militarist past with "the kind of self-introspection" the Germans had undertaken and that had "promoted European reconciliation."[11] Others offered more alarmist

[9] See Thomas J. Christensen, "Theater Missile Defense and Taiwan's Security"; Chen Ying, "Zhanqu Daodan Fangyu Xitong Yu Dongya Anquan Xingshi" [Theater missile defense and East Asia's security situation], pp. 28–30.

[10] Bilateral consultations followed Japan's post–Cold War review of its self-defense forces, intensified with the statement issued upon President Clinton's visit to Tokyo in April 1996, and culminated in the new security guidelines issued in September 1997. See "Japan-U.S. Joint Declaration on Security—Alliance for the 21st Century"; "The Guidelines for Japan-U.S. Defense Cooperation."

[11] Li Jijun. "On Strategic Culture," pp. 8–15. Another commentary similarly argued, "After World War Two, and unlike Germany, Japan has only grudgingly and under pressure acknowledged its history of aggression. It has never made any serious

views, arguing that "[in] recent years, the 'pacifist' trend in Japan that has dominated for a long time in the post-war period has weakened, with an obvious rightist political trend developing through such things as the glorification of aggressive wars, requesting revision of the peace constitution, and advocating the 'right to collective defense' in joint operations with the United States."[12]

This view of Japan fed Chinese skepticism about the explanation that Washington and Tokyo offered for plans to revise their guidelines for defense cooperation as a hedge against unspecified threats to stability in the region. The allies claimed that this was merely an updating of longstanding bilateral security ties made necessary by the end of the Cold War and, especially after the 1994 Korean nuclear crisis, by concerns about coordinating any response to renewed conflict on the peninsula. The revisions, they explained, were most important to preclude the possibility of an American backlash against a lack of Japanese burden sharing if the United States undertook military operations in Korea. But Chinese analysts routinely dismissed as unbelievable the idea that such politically sensitive changes in a major alliance were designed to deal with a minor power like North Korea. Instead, Beijing saw the revised security guidelines as an ominous portent of collaborative efforts to limit the PRC's international influence.[13]

China, in fact, asserted that the heart of the planned revision was the section of the agreement that called for Japan to assume greater responsibilities in the event a crisis emerged "in areas surrounding Japan that will have an important influence on Japan's peace and security."[14] Although the limited support activities to which Tokyo committed itself and the absence of collective self-defense language suggested this represented only a marginal adjustment, and despite the fact that the most likely contingency for Japanese-

---

attempt to realistically examine its role and its actions" (Da Jun, "True Threat Comes from Those Trumpeting 'China Threat.'")

[12] Ma Junwei, "Political Trends in Japan Following the General Election," pp. 11, 14–16. See also Xia Liping, "Some Views on Multilateral Security Cooperation in Northeast Asia," pp. 12–15.

[13] Author's interviews, Beijing, June–July 1998. Similar Chinese skepticism greeted subsequent U.S. claims that the purpose of missile defenses was to deal with an incipient North Korean ballistic missile threat. Japan's embrace of American arguments about a "China threat" was also alleged to be behind Tokyo's reactivation of the Diaoyu Island dispute in 1996, which was interpreted as part of Japan's participation in an incipient U.S. strategy of containment aimed at China. See He Chong, "The International Plot Behind the Diaoyu Islands Dispute Provoked by Japan."

[14] See the final text in "The Guidelines for Japan-U.S. Defense Cooperation."

American cooperation was a conflict in Korea, China strongly objected on three grounds.

First, although small, the change was allegedly more evidence of a disturbing trend in Japan's military policy. Over half a century, Japan had progressed "from having no army to having a modernized 'self-defense force' and from only protecting Japan's own territory to the possibility of entering 'Japan's peripheral regions' [*Riben zhoubian diqu*]." China insisted that, at best, the change represented a deviation from Japan's proclaimed postwar path of peace and development; at worst, it was an attempt to provide legal cover for Japan's constitutional proscriptions on international military activity (the Chinese referred to it as "edgeballing," invoking a ping-pong metaphor whose closest English equivalent is "salami tactics"). Second, because the concept "areas surrounding Japan" was vague, and because it was not "not geographic but situational," at any time the periphery could be arbitrarily expanded; Beijing, of course, worried that it might be expanded to include the area around Taiwan. And third, the pretext for this change (that in Japan's peripheral regions after the Cold War there are still unstable and untrustworthy factors) revealed that the real motive was a concern about China.[15] In short, the basic Chinese view was that the revision reflected the "China threat theory" circulating in both the United States and Japan, a theory that fulfilled the allies' need for a new common enemy to replace the defunct Soviet threat, and that the revision was intended to cover the most likely contingency for a U.S. military confrontation with China—conflict in the Taiwan Strait.[16]

---

[15] Zhang Guocheng, "Ling Ren Guanzhu de Xin Dongxiang—Rimei Xiugai Fangwei Hezuo Fangzhen Chuxi" [A new trend catching people's attention—The emerging Japan-U.S. Revised Guidelines for Defense Cooperation]; Zhang Guocheng, "Hewei 'Zhoubian You Shi'?—Xie Zai Xin 'Rimei Fangwei Hezuo Fangzhen' Qiaoding zhi Shi" [What's the meaning of "situations arising on the periphery"?—Written in the new "Japan-U.S. Joint Defense Guidelines"]. Indeed, the language of the 1996 U.S.-Japan Declaration's assessment of regional security made this interpretation plausible: "instability and uncertainty persist in the region. Tensions continue on the Korean Peninsula. There are still heavy concentrations of military force, including nuclear arsenals. Unresolved territorial disputes, potential regional conflicts, and the proliferation of weapons of mass destruction and their means of delivery all constitute sources of instability." See "Japan-U.S. Joint Declaration on Security." This language was a bit stronger than concerns about political uncertainties and instability contained in *The United States Security Strategy for the East Asia-Pacific Region* (1995). The stronger language was incorporated in the 1998 version of the report, *The United States Security Strategy for the East Asia-Pacific Region*, p. 62.

[16] See Ni Feng, "Meiri Tongmeng Yu Diqu Anquan" [The U.S.-Japan alliance and regional security], pp. 69, 72.

Beijing was determined to minimize the anti-China potential of the evolving U.S.-Japan alliance. Its immediate goal was to convince Japan to exclude Taiwan and its surrounding waters from the peripheral regions for joint action that the new guidelines would cover. Motivated by the Sino-American military tensions that had developed during the 1995–96 Taiwan Strait crisis, Beijing repeatedly sought clarification on this point. Tokyo's standard reply remained simple, if unsatisfying to Beijing: The U.S.-Japan security treaty is a bilateral matter neither targeting any third country nor aimed at interfering in others' internal politics; Japan's stance on Taiwan has already been clearly stated in a Sino-Japanese joint declaration; and Tokyo has no plan to change its policy of maintaining only informal relations with Taiwan.

However diplomatically proper, this position fell short of what China wanted to hear. The absence of formal links to Taipei did not rule out the possibility that Japan could, under the terms of the revised U.S.-Japan security guidelines, support American military operations in the area around Taiwan if a crisis developed. Indeed, leading Japanese politicians instead pointedly refrained from providing China the explicit assurances it sought.[17] Perhaps most telling, when the *Yomiuri Shimbun* reported that the peripheral region to be covered under the revised guidelines "would be 'the Far East and its vicinity,' including the Taiwan Strait and the Spratly Islands, the Government immediately denied that it would decide in advance which areas should be covered by the guidelines. Instead, said Kanezo Muranoka, the Government's chief Cabinet Secretary, a decision will be deferred until an emergency arises."[18] China's defense minister, Chi Haotian, would later sum up Beijing's official reaction to Tokyo's unchanging position during his February 1998 trip to Japan: "the important reason for China's concern about the questions of Japanese-American security cooperation involves the Taiwan problem. If the Japanese side could further clarify its attitude about Taiwan and the Japanese-U.S. Security Treaty, it would help eliminate our misgivings about Japanese-American security cooperation."[19]

---

[17] Some explicitly linked Japan's concerns about Taiwan to concerns about China's growing military strength, a view sure to raise Beijing's ire. See comments by Koichi Kato, secretary general of Japan's Liberal Democratic Party (Gerald Curtis, "Japan: Kato on Domestic, International Politics," pp. 28–43.).

[18] Sheryl WuDunn, "Japanese Move to Broaden Military Links to the U.S.," p. A6.

[19] "Chi Haotian Yu Riben Fangweiting Zhangguan Huitan, Huijian Riben Zimindang Ganshizhang He Zhengtiaohuizhang" [Chi Haotian holds consultations with the director of Japan's Defense Agency, meets with Japan's LDP secretary general and the head of the LDP Policy Research Council]. Press reports in late summer 1998 indicated that Jiang Zemin postponed his state visit to Japan not because of the massive floods in China, but because Japan's leaders were rejecting a summit communiqué that

Yet, even more forthcoming statements from Tokyo would not likely have eliminated China's lingering fear that Japan might decide to support the United States if it militarily intervened during a new confrontation in the Taiwan Strait. Invoking the right words, however much Beijing might have welcomed the gesture, would not have dispelled a strong Chinese belief that Japan's own interests would ultimately encourage it to cooperate with U.S. action there. The interests Chinese analysts cite include the following: 1) Leaders in Tokyo see China as an obstacle that might prevent Japan from one day resuming a great power role. They therefore generally support American policies that help block China's rise, including efforts to block national unification; 2) Leaders in Tokyo view the Taiwan Strait as a crucial transit route for Middle East energy resources on which Japan depends; 3) Significant members of Japan's political elite have longstanding social ties to Taiwan and even personal ties to its leaders, some established during Tokyo's half century of colonial rule over the island that ended in 1945; 4) Because of geographic proximity, Japan would worry that a crisis in the Taiwan Strait could spill over into conflict over the Diaoyu (Senkaku) islands claimed by both Japan and China; and 5) Resurgent right-wing forces in Japan see Taiwan as an issue they can exploit to advance their political agenda.[20]

In sum, then, Beijing interpreted the reorientation of Cold War–vintage U.S. alliances with both Australia and Japan as part of a generally dangerous reaction to unfounded concerns about the putative threat a more powerful China might pose, although the specific concerns differed in each case. During the early 1990s, China also faced new worries about the strategic posture of some its Southeast Asian neighbors. As the PRC had begun to clarify its sovereignty claims to disputed territory in the South China Sea, the ASEAN states had grown more nervous about Beijing's future plans in the area and appeared to be hedging their bets in ways that China found unsettling.

---

would include the sort of firm pledges (the "three noes") about Taiwan's status that President Clinton had issued during his 1998 trip to the PRC. See "Chinese President Jiang's Visit to Japan May Be Delayed to Next Year"; also "Japan Rejects Any Chinese Pressure over Taiwan." Many interlocutors expressed very strong skepticism about Japan's intentions regarding China's claim over Taiwan. As one explicitly expressed the view implicit in what others said, "Japan's leaders are not less meddlesome on the Taiwan matter, but only much more 'cunning' than the U.S." (author's interview, Beijing, July 1998).

[20] See Wang Yiwei, "Dui Tai Junshi Douzheng Dui Shijie Zhanlüe Geju De Yingxiang Chutan" [A preliminary exploration of the effects on the international strategic situation of military action against Taiwan], p. 28; Liu Changmin, "Shixi Dangjin Riben Zhengzhi De Youqinghua" [A tentative analysis of the right-wing drift in contemporary Japanese politics], p. 24.

Southeast Asia

In 1992 China had declared its "Law on the Territorial Sea and the Contiguous Zone" that asserted an expansive and unequivocal claim that the "PRC's territorial land includes the mainland and its offshore islands, Taiwan and the various affiliated islands including Diaoyu Island, Penghu Islands, Dongsha Islands, Xisha Islands, Nansha (Spratly) Islands and other islands that belong to the People's Republic of China."[21] Worries about China's claims to the disputed territories and the perception that China was willing to use military force in support of them quickly fostered anxiety among ASEAN states as well as the United States. Despite Beijing's occasionally reassuring rhetoric indicating that it would be prepared to discuss ways to build economic cooperation in the South China Sea, its stance on sovereignty was defiantly uncompromising. Especially disconcerting was Beijing's fortification of Mischief Reef in 1995 soon after it had ostensibly agreed to avoid military solutions to outstanding disputes in the region.[22] Together with the broader perception that began to take root in the mid-1990s that China's economic and military capabilities were rapidly increasing, China's actions in support of these territorial claims raised red flags in the region about a challenge to the status quo.

Acting on their tacit concern about China, several Southeast Asian states increased their bilateral security cooperation with the United States (which included organizing joint military exercises), Indonesia and Australia inked a new security agreement, and Washington clarified its long-standing concern about freedom of navigation through potential maritime choke points—freedom that some of China's assertions about territorial waters in the area seemed to call into question.[23] From Beijing's perspective, then, diplomatic

[21] See "Law on the Territorial Sea and the Contiguous Zone of the People's Republic of China." ASEAN states issued their own Declaration on the South China Sea in July 1992, calling for the peaceful resolution of outstanding territorial disputes and urging all "all parties concerned to exercise restraint with the view to creating a positive climate for the eventual resolution of all disputes" ("ASEAN Declaration on the South China Sea Manila, Philippines").

[22] See Allen S. Whiting, "ASEAN Eyes China: The Security Dimension"; Masashi Nishihara, "Aiming at New Order for Regional Security—Current State of ARF"; Michael Leifer, *The ASEAN Regional Forum*, pp. 37, 43–44; and Mark J. Valencia, *China and the South China Sea Disputes.*

[23] See Lu Jianren, "Yatai Daguo Zai Dongnan Yazhou Diqu De Liyi" [Asia-Pacific great powers' interests in Southeast Asia], pp. 41, 45; Fang, "Yatai Anquan Jiagou De Xianzhuang," p. 12. The U.S. government emphasized that "maintaining freedom of navigation in the area was a fundamental interest of the US," and its State Department spokesman warned, "The US would . . . view with serious concern any maritime

trends in Southeast Asia, as elsewhere in the Western Pacific, were beginning to serve the American five-finger strategy to contain China. Regional deals were being cut that would help maintain the United States as the dominant power in Southeast Asia by ensuring its command of the region's seas for commercial and military ships, while limiting China's ability to operate air and naval forces in the theater, not to mention keeping China from gaining a territorial foothold by establishing control over the scattered Spratly Islands.[24]

As a result of these developments, by mid-decade China faced an array of increasingly suspicious states in an arc stretching from Northeast to Southeast Asia, a change that seemed to pose the real risk of a steadily deteriorating international environment. What could Beijing do about this disturbing trend whose continuation might have resulted in China confronting an encircling coalition incorporating virtually all of the major and minor powers in the region as well as the heavily involved and internationally dominant United States? In chapter 2, I suggested broad alternative grand strategies for a rising power that contrast with the approach China ultimately adopted in 1996. Below, I look at the somewhat more specific choices open to China in the mid-1990s and indicate why they were not embraced.

Responding to the Danger: China's Strategic Alternatives in the Mid-1990s

Assertive Self-reliance

One option Beijing might have pursued was a more determined effort to augment the PLA's capabilities while hoping that this would not be offset by any countermeasures China's rivals could undertake. Essentially, this approach would have represented a bet against the logic of the security dilemma, or at least a gamble on the inefficiency of others' attempts to counterbalance a Chinese buildup via arming or allying. At first glance such an approach might seem to have been more plausible than ever because of China's improving

---

claim, or restriction on maritime activity, in the South China Sea that was not consistent with international law" (Felix Soh, "US Warns against Restrictions in South China Sea, Block Press Tour to Spratlys"). On a visit to the Philippines in August 1995, U.S. secretary of state Warren Christopher in discussing the disputes in the South China Sea stated, "Maintaining freedom of navigation is a fundamental interest of the United States" (Greg Torode, "Philippines Offered US Jets; Manila Warns over Continued Chinese Construction Work on Mischief Reef"). See also Michael Richardson, "China's Push for Sea Control Angers ASEAN."

[24] Lu, "Yatai Daguo Zai Dongnan Yazhou Diqu De Liyi," pp. 41, 45; See also Fang, "Yatai Anquan Jiagou De Xianzhuang," p. 12.

economic situation in the 1990s. Beijing's military modernization was, after all, making impressive progress, even if (as chapter 3 suggests) its pace and extent were exaggerated in many foreign analysts' great leaps of faith about the operational significance of equipment purchases and doctrinal revision. Yet China could not quickly transform the PLA into a first-class great power fighting force able to take on all comers. China's economy was incapable of providing the quantity and, more importantly, the quality of resources necessary for a serious effort at militarily outpacing its chief competitors, especially the United States and its allies, whose actions already suggested a clear determination to respond in kind. China's analysts pragmatically understood that "objective conditions" did not yet afford their country the option of great ambition and required instead a focus on the protracted struggle of comprehensive modernization that would eventually make it possible to play a bigger international role. For the foreseeable future, then, China would need a grand strategy that offered some other way to face up to three stark realities: an international order dominated by the United States, China's substantial economic interdependence with that international order, and nervous neighbors inclined to look to the United States as a hedge against the possible risks that might arise for them if China aspired to become the dominant power in East Asia.[25]

Resource constraints aside, more assertive self-reliance was unattractive because China's leaders were wary of repeating what they understood to be the Soviet Union's fatal mistakes, only one of which was excessive military spending that distorted its economy with disastrous domestic political consequences. Beijing could be confident that its reforms placing top priority on developing the civilian economy were enabling the PRC to avoid the "Soviet disease" at home, but by the mid-1990s its foreign policy seemed to be increasing the risk that China could suffer the "Soviet disease" abroad.[26] By this

[25] See Guo Shuyong, "21 Shiji Qianye Zhongguo Waijiao Dazhanlüe Chuyi" [A modest proposal for China's diplomatic grand strategy on the eve of the twenty-first century], pp. 92–93, 95; see also Yan Xuetong, "Dui Zhongguo Anquan Huanjing De Fenxi Yu Sikao" [Analysis of and reflections on China's security environment], p. 10; Michael D. Swaine and Ashley J. Tellis, *Interpreting China's Grand Strategy: Past, Present, and Future*, pp. 121–29, chapter 4.

[26] Author's interviews, Beijing, June–July 1998. See also the analysis of the Chinese debate about lessons learned from the Soviet collapse in Michael Pillsbury, *China Debates the Future Security Environment*, pp. 185–89. On the centrality of modernization in China's foreign policy calculus because it is the key to increasing the country's "comprehensive national power" that determines a country's international standing, see Zalmay M. Khalilzad et al., *The United States and a Rising China: Strategic and Military Implications*, pp. xi, xiii–xiv, 3–5. On lessons learned by China from the link between

I mean a condition in which a lesser great power's assertive international behavior, political character, and geographic location lead a broad coalition of
states to oppose it because, contrary to balance-of-power logic, they view it as
a more dangerous threat than the world's most powerful state. As the 1990s
unfolded and some worried about what they saw as the PRC's ambitious program of military modernization, assertive regional behavior, and anachronistic
domestic political system, China faced a real risk that it could find itself, like
the Cold War Soviet Union, surrounded by fearful states prompted to align
with, rather than balance against, the dominant and active United States.[27] Indeed, China's policy shifts described below were specifically designed to discourage others from embracing such a new strategy of containment against
China justified by the perception that it was potentially more threatening
than, even if not yet as capable as, the United States.

Fortress China

A more affordable and technically plausible second option was for China to
adopt a strategy of well-armed isolation. Such an approach would simply seek
to ensure that the homeland remained free from foreign occupation forces and
was safe from seriously damaging military strikes. The PRC's modest but improving nuclear arsenal already fulfilled the basic requirements of such a strategy by dissuading others from jeopardizing China's vital interests because it
would necessarily entail running the risk of escalation to a horrifying missile
exchange. Though he did not endorse the strategy, Yan Xuetong, who
emerged as one of China's most prominent security analysts during the 1990s,

---

Moscow's effort to challenge the United States and the subsequent Soviet collapse, see
Guo, "21 Shiji Qianye Zhongguo Waijiao Dazhanlüe Chuyi," p. 93. On the need for
China to prevent a situation in which the United States could reprise the containment
policies it used to deal with the Soviet Union, see Chu and Wang, "Guanyu Guoji
Xingshi He Wo Duiwai Zhanlüe Ruogan Zhongda Wenti De Sikao," p. 21. Jiang
Zemin reportedly resisted calls for massive increases in military spending, in part on the
grounds that "the arms race during the cold war was an important reason for the col-
lapse of the Soviet Union" ("Chuanwen Jiang Zemin Zhishi Gaibian Zhonggong De
Guofang Zhengce" [Jiang Zemin said to indicate a change in CCP national defense
policy]).
    [27] Steve Walt has described how such perceptions of the Soviet threat, rather than
American capabilities, induced patterns of alignment that defied the logic of balance-
of-power theory (Stephen M. Walt, "Alliance Formation and the Balance of World
Power" and *The Origins of Alliances*). Swaine and Tellis note that China's military
spending "has increased at a pace that is intended neither to undermine the attainment
of essential civilian development priorities nor to unduly alarm both the peripheral
states and the major powers" (*Interpreting China's Grand Strategy*, p. 129).

acknowledged its blunt effectiveness for ensuring the homeland's political and territorial integrity:

> As long as new military technology does not neutralize this risk [of nuclear escalation], in particular as long as ballistic missile defense technology is unable effectively to protect against large-scale nuclear strikes, the possibility of any local regional wars escalating to world war is very small. For the same reason, the danger of a military crisis in the Taiwan Strait causing our county to suffer a large scale invasion by a foreign military power is also small.[28]

Nevertheless, armed isolation was not an entirely satisfactory strategy for China at the end of the twentieth century, mainly because the regime had goals that went beyond mere survival. The regime's vision of a future in which China would be one of several great powers in a multipolar world, its determination to elevate the country's often affronted international status, and its expanding international interests linked with the foreign trade and investment essential to maintain the growth rates on which domestic political stability depended all diminished the attractiveness of what would have amounted to a "fortress China" approach.[29] Moreover, however well suited such a strategy might have been for preserving the status quo (as Yan's comment above suggests), it would not have provided much hope for breaking the stalemate over Taiwan, a central goal for Beijing. On the contrary, the tense if peaceful mutual deterrent posture it emphasizes would most likely encourage a further strengthening of U.S. military ties to the island regime. During the 1990s, Beijing already saw American concern about Taiwan's security, especially in Congress, bolstering such ties and facilitating an "independence trend" that seemed likely to make peaceful reunification ever more difficult.[30]

Public Relations

A third option for stemming the disquieting international trend China's leaders faced in the mid-1990s was for Beijing to attempt to discredit what it claimed was the trend's root cause—the exaggerated fears others harbored about a China that in reality was still weak and whose intentions, in any case, were benign. Government spokesmen did in fact attempt to do precisely this, frequently denouncing the "China threat theory" as absurd and explaining

[28] See Yan, "Dui Zhongguo Anquan Huanjing De Fenxi Yu Sikao," p. 8.

[29] Author's interviews, Beijing, June–July 1998. See also Daniel Kwan, "Beijing Urged to Keep Regional Power Focus," p. 10; Ye Zicheng, "Carrying Forward, Developing and Pondering Deng Xiaoping's Foreign Policy Thinking in the New Situation."

[30] Yan, "Dui Zhongguo Anquan Huanjing De Fenxi Yu Sikao," pp. 7–8.

that the purpose of the PRC's measured military modernization was purely defensive.[31] Beijing typically stressed three main points in support of its public critique of the "China threat theory": 1) shortcomings in the country's economic conditions would continue to require it to place top priority on domestic development rather than excessive military spending;[32] 2) China's own bitter experience with imperialism ensured that it would never seek hegemony over others;[33] and 3) the incipient steps that others seemed to be taking in response to a nonexistent threat from China could create a tragic self-fulfilling prophecy.[34] Beijing's best efforts to discredit the "China threat theory," however, failed to reassure regional and global actors. "Cheap talk" about ultimately opaque and changeable intentions predictably mattered less than the uncertainties about the future that perceptions of China's growing capabilities and occasionally assertive behavior (in the Taiwan Strait and South China Sea) were creating.

[31] Huai Chengbo, "Behind the Fear of a 'China Threat,'" p. 10; Su Huimin, "View of a 'China Threat' Groundless," pp. 10–11; "'China Threat' Fallacy Refuted (Western Allegations)," p. 6; Yang Ge, "China's Rise: Threat or Not? (International Community's Fears of Chinese Supremacy)," pp. 23–25; Chi Haotian, "Zou Fuhe Woguo Guoqing Bing Fanying Shidai Tezheng De Guofang Xiandaihua Jianshe Daolu" [Follow the path of modernizing national defense suited to our national conditions and the characteristics of our times], p. 10; Ren Xin, "'China Threat': Theory Untenable," pp. 10–11. For a particularly virulent attack on the "China threat theory" as a latter-day version of the "yellow peril theory," as actually a "'threat to China' theory," and as a "trick to intimidate and hold China back," see Li, "On Strategic Culture." See also Pillsbury, *China Debates the Future Security Environment*, p. xxx.

[32] See "Tulao De Wudao" [Futile misdirection]; "Jieshou Meiguo Youxian Xinwen Dianshiwang Jizhe Caifang, Jiang Zemin Changtan Zhongmei Guanxi Ji Taiwan Deng Wenti" [Giving an interview to an American CNN reporter, Jiang Zemin speaks freely about Sino-American relations, Taiwan, and other questions]; Liu Huaqiu, "Strive for a Peaceful International Environment"; "Jundui Yao Shiying Gaige He Fazhan De Xin Xingshi, Gengjia Zijue Fucong Fuwu Dang He Guojia Da Ju" [The army must adapt to the new situation of reform and development, be even more aware of complying with and serving the Party's and country's overall situation].

[33] See "Jiu Zhongmei Guanxi, Taiwan Wenti, Zhongguo Renda Zhidu Deng Wenti: Qiao Shi Jieshou Meiguo Jizhe Caifang" [Qiao Shi takes questions from American reporters on Sino-American relations, the Taiwan problem, the National People's Congress system, etc.]; "Chi Haotian Zai Riben Fabiao Yanjiang, Zhuozhong Chanshu Zhongguo Guofang Zhengce" [Chi Haotian's lecture in Japan setting forth China's national defense policy].

[34] See Wang Jisi, "Shiji Zhi Jiao De Zhongmei Guanxi" [Sino-American relations at the turn of the century].

Alliance

A fourth option for the PRC was to seek an ally (or allies) to counter the forces that seemed poised to array themselves against China. But the lack of credible partners sharing China's concerns limited the feasibility of this approach. It is true that one significant bright spot for China's diplomacy, especially early in the 1990s, was its warming relationship with the new Russia. After the United States imposed military sanctions following the 1989 crackdown in Tiananmen Square, Russia emerged as the key vendor of modern military hardware that the PRC could not produce for itself. But, as noted in chapter 3, the purchase of Russian weaponry could not provide a decisive counter to the more advanced, and with American backing potentially larger, military forces of China's most plausible rivals in the mid-1990s in theaters ranging from the Spratlys to Taiwan to the Diaoyus. Nor would alliance with an enfeebled, struggling Russia advance one of China's key international goals—deepening integration with the global economy to ensure that foreign trade and investment continued to play its role in the country's rapid development. On the contrary, the opportunity costs of cultivating a real anti-American alliance were too high. A turn toward hostile alliance systems would jeopardize the benefits of participation in the relatively open post–Cold War international economic system essential to China's (and Russia's) continued modernization.[35] Shared resentment of U.S. international dominance (in Russia about having to accept NATO's plans for eastward expansion, in China about the strengthened U.S. alliances in Asia and American leadership of the West's demands that China meet standards set by the developed industrial states on matters from human rights to market access) did produce Sino-Russian joint statements condemning Washington's policies. Yet, however heartfelt, "antihegemony" rhetoric was no more helpful for actually dealing with the difficult challenges China faced in the 1990s than similar Maoist rhetoric had been in the 1960s when Beijing briefly flirted with the notion that solidarity with the third world might serve as an effective counterweight to the superpowers. Nor could a militarily and economically stumbling Russia provide the sort of tangible security benefits that China's ties to the United States had offered in the last two decades of the Cold War. In short, a Sino-Russian alliance was not a viable option.

The unattractiveness or impracticality of the aforementioned alternatives for dealing with China's precarious situation in the mid-1990s led to a con-

---

[35] Author's interviews, Beijing, June–July 1998. See also Ye Zicheng, "Carrying Forward, Developing and Pondering Deng Xiaoping's Foreign Policy Thinking in the New Situation."

sensus among the elite in Beijing supporting the policies that, taken together, I label its new grand strategy. These policies were designed to head off the danger that China would find itself confronting an encircling coalition incorporating virtually all of the major and minor powers in the region as well as the heavily involved United States. They reflected the leaders' pragmatic acceptance of their county's limited capabilities and limited diplomatic options for responding to the potentially dangerous, if perplexing, anxiety about China's growing power that had taken root so quickly in the 1990s.[36] Whereas Beijing's initial reaction to China threat arguments had been righteous indignation, it began to mellow into a realistic recognition that, however misplaced, such worries reflected the nervousness that normally accompanies the emergence of a new great power. Analysts also recognized that these concerns were developing in a post–Cold War setting that was less forgiving for China. Without the unifying common threat (the Soviet Union) that had previously encouraged many neighboring states to set aside their political and ideological disagreements with Beijing, it was not surprising that long muted differences were resurfacing.[37]

*   *   *

The next chapter describes how Beijing dealt with the distinctive challenges a rising China faced in the era of American unipolarity. It summarizes the purpose, logic, and content of the approach that became entrenched as the core of a grand strategy designed to maintain the peaceful environment crucial for China's rise during the transition to a multipolar world it expected to emerge sometime in the mid-twenty-first century.

[36] Swaine and Tellis note that the tough challenge facing China in attempting to lift itself into the same league as the world's sole remaining superpower leads it to embrace a "weak-strong" security approach, the hybrid, cautious grand strategy they label "the calculative strategy" (*Interpreting China's Grand Strategy*, chapter 4). See also Guo, "21 Shiji Qianye Zhongguo Waijiao Dazhanlüe Chuyi," pp. 92–93.

[37] Author's interviews, Beijing, June–July 1998. For a frank recognition of the concerns that China's growing power triggered among neighboring countries, especially in Southeast Asia, see Guo, "21 Shiji Qianye Zhongguo Waijiao Dazhanlüe Chuyi," p. 94. China's shifting tone may also have reflected the growing professionalism of China's policy analysts. By the 1990s many had either been trained in the West or benefited from exchanges with their Western counterparts. Some aspired to a style of analysis that was both less ideological and less Sinocentric than the work they had been able to produce in the politically restrictive Maoist era or its immediate aftermath.

6

China Adjusts

Neither growing capabilities nor the modest benefits of closer ties to a troubled Russia during the first half of the 1990s seemed likely to ensure Beijing's ability to advance China's national interests in a context where others were becoming nervous about its rise. To address the shortcomings of its foreign policy, from mid-1996 China's leaders responded by shifting their emphasis to two broad efforts. First, they emphasized actions, and not just words, to reassure China's neighbors and to enhance the PRC's reputation as a more responsible and cooperative player. The principal manifestations of this new emphasis were Beijing's more active embrace of multilateralism—including its effort to foster a peaceful resolution of the nuclear crisis on the Korean peninsula and its effort to facilitate cooperation with Southeast Asia—and its widely touted self-restraint during the wave of currency devaluations that accompanied the Asian financial crisis. Second, the leaders in Beijing began a concerted effort to improve bilateral relations with the world's leading states in order to reduce the likelihood that they would unite to prevent China's slow but steady rise to the ranks of the great powers. By cultivating various types of partnerships, Beijing sought to increase the perceived benefits that other great powers would gain by working with China and to underscore the opportunity costs of working against it.[1]

The following section discusses each of these major elements of China's grand strategy. It should first be reiterated, however, that although this strategy gained coherence in 1996, it did not represent a sharp break with the past.

[1] Taylor Fravel and Evan Medeiros also discuss such changes in "China's New Diplomacy." China's careful cultivation of partnerships after the mid-1990s focused on the major powers, in contrast with an earlier, less formal focus on partnerships with third world countries that Harry Harding noted. See Harry Harding, "China's Cooperative Behaviour," pp. 392–97.

As indicated in chapter 2, some of the themes of China's transitional strategy to ensure a peaceful environment for its rise to great power status can be traced to the 1980s. In the waning years of the Cold War, Deng Xiaoping had anticipated that Beijing would be able to adopt a more independent foreign policy that took advantage of a changing international environment in which bipolarity and the risk of superpower war would give way to multipolarity and an opportunity for peaceful economic development.[2] In other respects, too, China's current grand strategy builds on foreign policy initiatives evident in the early post–Cold War period, including China's attempt to resolve disputes with bordering states and promote good relations with neighbors, its determination to repair relations with the West and Japan after sanctions were imposed following the crackdown on protestors in 1989, its decision to eschew traditional security alliances, and its interest in playing a constructive role in international organizations.[3] Thus, the strategy that emerged in 1996 was not so much a bold new departure for China as a refinement reflecting a clearer consensus among the leaders in Beijing that they needed to more effectively adjust their foreign policy to the circumstances China faced in the post–Cold War era. What distinguished China's grand strategy after 1996 was its greater coherence, the increased level of international activism, and the stepped-up effort to mollify the concerns and suspicions about China's intentions that others had begun to develop.

Reassurance

Multilateralism

In the early post–Cold War period China engaged in multilateral diplomacy, but mainly in order to symbolize the PRC's status as an actor that must be included when deliberating matters of regional or global importance. Its partici-

---

[2] See Deng Xiaoping, "We Must Safeguard World Peace and Ensure Domestic Development"; Ye Zicheng, "Zhongguo Shixing Daguo Waijiao Zhanlüe Shizai Bixing" [The imperative for China to implement a great power diplomatic strategy], pp. 5–10; Michael Pillsbury, *China Debates the Future Security Environment*, pp. xxiv, 3, 9–10, 11

[3] On the early 1990s, see Zhu Qizhen, "China's Foreign Policy: Independent Policy of Peace"; Qian Qichen, "Adhering to Independent Foreign Policy"; Qian Qichen, "An Independent Foreign Policy of Peace: Excerpts from Chinese Foreign Minister Qian Qichen's March 12, 1992 Speech"; Xing Hua, "China's Successful Diplomacy"; Liu Huaqiu, "China's Diplomatic Achievements in 1992"; Chen Qimao, "New Approaches in China's Foreign Policy: The Post–Cold War Era"; Bonnie S. Glaser, "China's Security Perceptions: Interests and Ambitions"; Wei Zhengyan, "China's Diplomacy in 1993."

pation seemed reluctant and to reflect a belief that these forums, especially in the Asia-Pacific, were subject to manipulation by the United States and Japan, which might encourage others to gang up against China.[4] For solving issues touching on its vital interests, China clearly preferred bilateral diplomacy. Multilateralism would not only vitiate the power advantage China otherwise enjoyed over many of the region's countries, but it also meant more complicated negotiations. By 1996, however, experience suggested that Beijing's original calculation of the costs of multilateralism and benefits of bilateralism was mistaken. Even in its dealings with relatively small powers in the South China Sea disputes, bilateralism was not providing Beijing with the leverage it hoped for. When disputes intensified (e.g., over China's fortification of Mischief Reef), regional adversaries whose unity China did not want to face within multilateral settings united anyway.[5]

In the mid-1990s, China began to evince a new appreciation of the benefits of multilateralism.[6] Beijing apparently concluded that if it helped ease its neighbors concerns, accepting the constraints that come with working in multilateral settings was preferable to the risk of isolation and encirclement its more aloof stance and assertive behavior had been creating.[7] Beijing expected that its shift to a receptive posture on multilateralism would help foster a reputation for responsible international behavior, offering a more effective counter to troubling "China threat" perceptions than its dismissive, and apparently unconvincing, rhetoric.

At every opportunity China began to point proudly to its participation in multilateral regional efforts. In April 1996 cooperation among China, Russia, Kazakhstan, Kyrgyzstan, and Tajikistan resulted in "the first multilateral treaty . . . to build confidence in the Asia-Pacific region"; Beijing cited it as a

[4] See "Analyst Interviewed on APEC's Prospects"; Han Hua, "Zhang Yishan [Chinese Foreign Ministry Official] on China's Multilateral Diplomacy," p. A2.

[5] See Noel M. Morada and Christopher Collier, "The Philippines: State Versus Society?"

[6] Many of my interlocutors emphasized this shift. At the fifteenth CCP Congress in September 1997, General Secretary Jiang's report put a new emphasis on multilateral diplomacy. See Liu Di, "Deng Xiaoping's Thinking on Diplomatic Work and China's Diplomatic Policy"; also Fang Hua, "Yatai Anquan Jiagou De Xianzhuang, Qushi Ji Zhongguo De Zuoyong" [The current Asia-Pacific security framework: Trends and China's role], p. 15; Wu Xinbo, "The Promise and Limitations of a Sino-U.S. Partnership."

[7] See Masashi Nishihara, "Aiming at New Order for Regional Security—Current State of ARF," pp. 35–40; also Alastair Iain Johnston and Paul Evans, "China's Engagement with Multilateral Security Institutions," pp. 258–61; "ARF Support Group Meeting Ends in Beijing."

"powerful rebuttal of the 'China threat theory,'" and evidence that "instead of being a 'threat,' China actually plays a constructive role in preserving peace and stability in its peripheral areas."[8] As this group reconvened to solve regional problems, it acquired an identity as the "Shanghai Five" (because of the site of their original meeting), met on a regular basis, and widened its agenda. By June 2001, it would return to the city of its founding, add a sixth member, Uzbekistan, and formally institutionalize its existence as the Shanghai Cooperation Organization (SCO). With China exercising strong and active leadership, then, this group became a major multilateral forum for the exchange of views on regional security concerns whose prominence has consistently expanded since 1996.[9]

Though less fully developed than its SCO diplomacy, Beijing's other significant forays into multilateralism after 1996 also reflected its concerted effort to allay fears about the international role a rising China would play in the future. Among the more prominent manifestations of the warmer embrace of multilateralism were Beijing's decisions that signaled stronger support for the various components of the international nuclear nonproliferation regime. In August 1996, Beijing announced its intention to sign the Comprehensive Test Ban Treaty, despite the fact that this step would make it more difficult for China to modernize its fledgling nuclear arsenal. In 1998, it joined most of the international community in condemning India and Pakistan for their nuclear weapons tests that challenged the regime's nonproliferation norm. And at the end of the decade, Beijing began to play a more active role in facilitating tension reduction on the Korean peninsula, reflecting China's new role in encouraging multilateral efforts to address the proliferation dangers that North Korea's nuclear program posed. China strengthened its support for the 1994 Agreed Framework addressing concerns about North Korea's nuclear ambitions, decided to participate in four-party talks about the peninsula's future, and then intensified its efforts to convince the North Koreans to accept an American offer of multilateral talks to dampen the crisis provoked by Pyongy-

---

[8] See Xia Liping, "Some Views on Multilateral Security Cooperation in Northeast Asia"; "Five-Nation Agreement Provides Model in Peaceful Conflict Resolution," p. 4; Willy Wo-Lap Lam, "Singing a Different Tune to the US."

[9] Especially in the post–9/11 context, the group has turned its attention to the challenge of combating terrorism. At their summit in May 2003, the SCO heads of state issued the Moscow Declaration, in which they announced that they had "decided to set up two permanent institutions—the SCO Secretariat in Beijing and the Anti-Terrorist Regional Center in Bishkek" (Zhang Shuo, "The Shanghai Cooperation Organization Holds Its Third Summit, Issues 'Moscow Declaration'"). See also "Anti-Terrorist Exercises of SCO to Be Held in Kazakhstan, China."

ang's apparent nuclear recidivism in2002–2003.[10] China's role in multilateral efforts to cope with the North Korean proliferation problem marked a significant change for Beijing. Not only had others previously suspected China of directly or indirectly assisting North Korea's covert nuclear weapons programs (in part because of its alleged links to the Pakistani program with which China had a well-established connection), but, perhaps more importantly, the longstanding assumption had been that the role Beijing was most likely to play was as the sole ally of the unpredictable and apparently dangerous regime in Pyongyang. Although the accuracy of these prevailing perceptions was questionable, beginning in the mid-1990s China more actively began to adjust its policies in ways that would result in it being seen as a responsible participant in international efforts to discover a solution that preserved both peace on the Korean peninsula and the norm against nuclear nonproliferation.[11]

Yet another prominent manifestation of Beijing's new embrace of multilateralism that it expected would help dampen fears of an emerging China threat was its increased flexibility on settling differences with the ASEAN states.[12] This became clearest when China indicated a greater willingness in the late

[10] See Tao Wenzhao, "China's Position Towards the Korean Peninsula"; Ding Shichuan and Li Qiang, "Chaoxian Bandao Heping Jizhi Ji Qi Qianjing" [A peace mechanism for the Korean peninsula and its prospects], pp. 42–44; Zhang Guocheng, "Quadripartite Talks Enter Substantive Stage," p. 6; "PRC Outlines 5 Principles to Reduce Tension in Koreas." On China's initial reservations about the four-party talks, see "PRC Spokesman: Beijing Hopes for Negotiations on Korea"; Kay Moeller, "China and Korea: The Godfather Part Three," p. 38.

[11] China's normalization of diplomatic relations with South Korea in 1992 had initiated a booming economic and eventually a warming political relationship with Seoul while at the same time contributing to a steady souring of its relationship with a chagrined Pyongyang. See Qi Deliang and Tang Shuifu, "Li, Yi Yong-Tok Discuss Economic Ties." In the early 1990s, China's foreign policy toward the peninsula was already tailored to meet China's national interests (a peaceful environment conducive to economic development in which neighboring states do not become pawns of any foreign power hostile to the PRC) rather than to meet the obligations of the 1961 treaty with Pyongyang signed when ideology underpinned a relationship of fraternal communist parties who were allegedly as close as "lips and teeth." See Mao Xuncheng, "Chaoxian Bandao Jushi De Fanfu Ji Qi Yuanyin" [The causes of the recurrent situation on the Korean peninsula), pp. 100–102; Tao, "China's Position Towards the Korean Peninsula"; Weixing Hu, "Beijing's Defense Strategy and the Korean Peninsula"; Banning Garrett and Bonnie S. Glaser, "Looking across the Yalu: Chinese Assessments of North Korea."

[12] See "Roundup: China Becoming Active Force in Multilateral Cooperation"; "ARF Support Group Meeting Ends in Beijing"; Fang, "Yatai Anquan Jiagou De Xianzhuang," p. 15; "Text of Chinese Foreign Minister's Speech to ASEAN."

1990s to accommodate ASEAN's expressed preference to devise multilateral "rules of the road" minimizing the potential for unintended conflict in the South China Sea while sovereignty disputes remained unresolved, and also to create a nuclear weapons–free zone in Southeast Asia. On both issues Beijing began gradually to shift away from its position emphasizing problems with the ASEAN proposals that might pose a threat to China's national interests. The evolution of Beijing's stance that unfolded after the mid-1990s and China's more constructive participation in multilateral discussions began to yield tangible results in the opening years of the twenty-first century. In August 2002, Foreign Minister Tang Jiaxuan announced that the PRC was ready to become the first nuclear weapon state to sign the protocol to the Treaty on the Southeast Asia Nuclear-Weapon-Free Zone, a position Premier Zhu Rongji reaffirmed in November 2002.[13] And after a number of false starts, at the sixth China-ASEAN Summit in November 2002, China and its Southeast Asian neighbors finally agreed to the Declaration on the Conduct of Parties in the South China Sea, which indicated that "pending the peaceful settlement of disputes, the parties concerned vowed to intensify efforts to seek ways, in the spirit of cooperation and understanding, to build trust and confidence between and among them" and "stressed the determination to seek a peaceful settlement of the disputes over the South China Sea through friendly coordination and negotiation."[14] In each of these cases, China not only embraced multilateralism over bilateralism, but also emphasized enhancing cooperation to realize joint benefits over the competitive pursuit of relative advantage. In-

[13] "Tang Jiaxuan Attends and Speaks at China-ASEAN Foreign Ministerial Dialog Meeting." See also Mi Ligong and Lei Bosong, "Premier Zhu Rongji Attends Sixth China-ASEAN Summit"; Fang, "Yatai Anquan Jiagou De Xianzhuang," p. 15. China had initially signaled its willingness to sign the protocol to the Bangkok Treaty in July 1999 after it became convinced that ASEAN would amend the protocol to deal with concerns about the geographical scope of the treaty, including disputed continental shelves and exclusive economic zones in the South China Sea. See Lee Kim Chew, "China Agrees to an ASEAN N-Arms Ban"; Xie Meihua, "PRC Ambassador for Disarmament Speaks at UN Session"; "Tang Jiaxuan Supports Nuclear-Free Southeast Asia"; "Southeast Asia Nuclear-Weapon-Free Zone Treaty (Treaty of Bangkok)"; "China-ASEAN Foreign Ministers' Informal Meeting Held in Qingdao."

[14] See *Declaration on the Conduct of Parties in the South China Sea, Phnom Penh*; "China, ASEAN Sign Declaration on Code of Conduct in South China Sea"; "Roundup: China Becoming Active Force in Multilateral Cooperation." On the preceding efforts to draw up acceptable "Norms for Behaviour in the South China Sea Region," see the comments by China's foreign minister, Tang Jiaxuan, at the July 2000 ARF meetings ("Text of Chinese Foreign Minister's Speech to ASEAN"); also "ASEAN, China Hope to Sign South China Sea Code of Conduct This Year"; "China Pushes Peace but Ignores Spratlys Code."

deed, on the code of conduct and the nuclear weapons–free zone, China basically agreed to accept the preferred positions of its smaller neighbors. Beijing's
growing interest in regional multilateralism culminated with a flurry of
agreements in 2002–2004 that included an ambitious plan for establishing a
China-ASEAN Free Trade Area by 2010 and China's accession to the Treaty
of Amity and Cooperation in Southeast Asia (the first non-ASEAN state to
take this step).[15]

Active multilateralism was expected to foster the general perception of a
more responsible China and undercut the force of China threat arguments. But
multilateralism also serves specific strategic interests for Beijing. The Shanghai
Cooperation Organization improves China's access to Central Asian energy
supplies and promises to help Beijing cope with its growing concern about the
risks of foreign support for Islamic separatism in the country's western prov-
inces. Beijing's efforts to bolster the nonproliferation regime are expected to
slow any increase in the number of potential nuclear adversaries as well as to
limit the size and technological sophistication of the existing arsenals against
which the adequacy China's modest deterrent had to be measured. Support for
tension reduction and nuclear abstinence on the Korean peninsula serves Beijing's multiple and potentially conflicting interests in saving face with its historical allies in North Korea, ensuring the health of its close economic ties with
South Korea, dampening pressures for the United States and its allies to deploy
ballistic missile defenses, and reducing the chance that a unified Korea in the
future would become a hostile neighbor backed by the United States or Japan.[16]
Agreeing to set aside sovereignty claims in the South China Sea while working
on practical measures to manage differences with ASEAN countries at the ARF
and its associated venues facilitates China's access to the resources and sea lanes
in the region at a time when Beijing lacks the power-projection capability to

---

[15] See *Framework Agreement on Comprehensive Economic Co-operation between the Asso-
ciation of South East Asian Nations and the People's Republic of China; Protocol to Amend the
Framework Agreement on Comprehensive Economic Co-operation between the Association of
South East Asian Nations and the People's Republic of China; Instrument of Accession to the
Treaty of Amity and Cooperation in Southeast Asia; Agreement on Trade in Goods of the
Framework Agreement on Comprehensive Economic Co-operation between the Association of
Southeast Asian Nations and the People's Republic of China; Agreement on Dispute Settlement
Mechanism of the Framework Agreement on Comprehensive Economic Co-Operation Between
the Association of Southeast Asian Nations and the People's Republic of China; Plan of Action
to Implement the Joint Declaration on ASEAN-China Strategic Partnership for Peace and Prosperity.* On the warm reception for visiting Chinese leaders within Southeast Asia in
2003, see Philip P. Pan, "China's Improving Image Challenges U.S. in Asia."

[16] See Avery Goldstein, "Across the Yalu: China's Interests and the Korean Peninsula in a Changing World."

decisively support its claims. Perhaps equally important, its embrace of ASEAN multilateral initiatives is expected to help counter the adverse reaction to China's growing capabilities and alleged assertiveness that had been evident by the mid-1990s (especially the reaction to the fortification of Mischief Reef), thereby permitting Beijing to focus on more pressing concerns such as resolving the Taiwan issue and preventing the American effort to strengthen bilateral military ties in the Asia-Pacific from becoming a full-blown strategy of containment aimed at China.[17] And finally, though perhaps least obvious, an expanding role in regional multilateralism provided Beijing with forums within which it expected to find support for its "hard" view of sovereignty that emphasizes the absolute right of each state to decide how best to manage its own internal affairs. Multilateralism, then, seemed to offer a possible way for China to strengthen its hand against the strong Western criticism of its record on political, religious, and human rights issues that had developed after the 1989 crackdown, pressure that Beijing labeled foreign meddling and that the CCP deemed a threat to domestic political stability.[18]

[17] On China's recognition of potential interaction between the South China Sea and Taiwan disputes, see Wang Jianwei, "China's Policy Towards Territorial Disputes in the South China Sea." Nevertheless, ASEAN reaction to the outbreak of hostilities in the Taiwan Strait is unpredictable and its member countries could well break ranks on the issue, with some supporting China's claim to Taiwan based on the principle of recognized sovereignty, while others seize the opportunity to assert their claims to territory in the South China Sea. See Wang Yiwei, "Dui Tai Junshi Douzheng Dui Shijie Zhanlüe Geju De Yingxiang Chutan" [A preliminary exploration of the effects on the international strategic situation of military action against Taiwan], p. 28. On China's continued concern about ASEAN perceptions of China as a potential threat, see Defense Minister Chi Haotian's comments in "China Aims to Change Perception as 'Potential Aggressor,' Says Malaysia."

[18] See "Quanmian Kaichuang Jiushi Niandai Waijiao Xin Jumian-Dang De Shisida Yilai Woguo Waijiao Gongzuo Shuping" [Comprehensively initiating the new situation in 1990s diplomacy—A review of our country's diplomatic work since the Fourteenth Party Congress]; "China Will Never Seek Hegemony, Said Chinese Premier." China's hard-sovereignty stance was reflected not only in its desire to uphold the "noninterference" principle in disputes about human rights, but also in its stance toward arms control. In this sphere, China positions itself as the champion of the developing states' preference that agreements remain sensitive to their sovereignty concerns about matters such as intrusive verification (that could expose weaknesses), rather than privilege principles, such as maximum transparency acceptable to advanced states (willing to reveal their strengths). See "Wo Caijun Dashi Zai Lianda Yiwei Qiangdiao, Ying Fangzhi Ba Caijun Mubiao Yinxiang Fazhanzhong Guojia" [Our disarmament ambassador at the General Assembly's first session emphasizes, [we] should guard against making the developing countries the target of disarmament]; "Wo Daibiao Tan Junshi Touming Wenti, Chanshu Kongzhi Xiao Wuqi Wenti Lichang" [Our repre-

Beijing's growing multilateral activity after the mid-1990s, then, represented a symbolic change in style but also served substantive purposes. It reflected neither a conversion to supranational values nor a new set of inviolable
diplomatic principles; rather, it was understood to be a useful component of
China's grand strategy that would advance national interests. Indeed, Beijing
still viewed military power as the primary guarantee of "comprehensive security" and its embrace of multilateral diplomacy was, therefore, partial and
conditional.[19] China not only flatly rejected suggestions that disputes about
matters it regards as unquestionably internal (specifically Taiwan) be open to
multilateral discussion, but also continued to resist suggestions that other less
sensitive sovereignty disputes be settled, rather than simply set aside, in such
forums. Even as China moved to accommodate ASEAN preferences, for example, on the eve of the July 2000 ARF session a Chinese official indicated
that "China expected its Southeast Asian neighbors to abide by previous ARF
understandings to keep its South China Sea territorial dispute with many
ASEAN states off the multilateral agenda. . . . We've made it clear that this is
an issue to be tackled bilaterally."[20] China apparently remained worried that
ASEAN states might still attempt to rely on multilateralism and perhaps the
inclusion of outside powers such as the United States to improve their lever-

---

sentative discusses the question of military transparency, sets forth our stance on controlling small arms]; "Wo Dashi Zai Lianheguo Caijun Weiyuanhui Zhichu, Jianli
Wuhequ Youli Heping" [Our ambassador at the UN Conference on Disarmament
points out, establishing nuclear-free zones is good for peace].

[19] In discussions about the nonmilitary (e.g., economic, environmental) components
of "comprehensive security," or what are elsewhere referred to as "nontraditional" security concerns, analysts acknowledge that such matters are increasingly important but
also assert that military security remains "the effective means for ensuring comprehensive security" or a prerequisite for dealing with these nontraditional concerns. See
Zhou Guiyin, "Xin Shiji De Guoji Anquan Yu Anquan Zhanlüe" [International security and security strategy in the new century], p. 69; Yan Xuetong, "Dui Zhongguo
Anquan Huanjing De Fenxi Yu Sikao" [Analysis of and reflections on China's security
environment], p. 9; "China Pushes Peace but Ignores Spratlys Code." China's clearly
instrumental view of multilateralism distinguishes it from more expansive definitions of
multilateralism like that articulated by John Ruggie. See Ruggie, "Multilateralism:
The Anatomy of an Institution." In this respect, China's stance toward supranational
organizations and values is little different than that exhibited by most other states.

[20] See "China to Take Missile Shield Opposition to ASEAN." At the level of "track
two" discussions, Beijing's view of multilateralism was more relaxed, even permitting
some unofficial exploration of the Taiwan dispute. The practical significance of such
unofficial activities is questionable, however. Its chief virtue, according to some of my
interlocutors, is that Beijing is under no obligation to accept the advice or results that
emerge. Author's interviews, Beijing, June–July 1998.

age when facing China in negotiations about disputed territory.[21] In the late 1990s, China also worried that some ASEAN states might be reconsidering their commitment to the principle of noninterference in the internal affairs of sovereign states as a way to curry favor with the economically booming United States, which was promoting a "new interventionism" enunciated while it undertook military operations to support human rights in Serbia's Kosovo province.[22] These concerns did not fundamentally alter China's strengthened commitment to multilateralism. They did, however, serve as a reminder that even as Beijing more warmly embraces the post–Cold War multilateralism that ASEAN had helped foster, its pragmatic focus on the presumed benefits and the feared potential costs are never far below the surface.[23]

In sum, multilateralism, once seen as a potential vehicle for outside pressure on China, after the mid-1990s was to be harnessed to serve China's grand strategy. It became one of the tools for Beijing to counter the more hostile and suspicious views of China that had been shaping the region's strategic environment. Through its participation, China would seek to prevent multilateral institutions from simply reinforcing U.S. capabilities and alliances in the Asia-Pacific, and instead seize the opportunities they offered to counter the risks it saw in American primacy and, over time, to help hasten the end of the unipolar era.[24] To this end, China began to argue that the flowering of multilateral diplomacy reduced the need for others to deploy more advanced weapons systems in the region (especially ballistic missile defenses) and to depend on military alliances (especially those with the United States).[25] Although Bei-

[21] See Zhou, "Xin Shiji De Guoji Anquan Yu Anquan Zhanlüe," p. 70.

[22] See Fang, "Yatai Anquan Jiagou De Xianzhuang," pp. 13, 14.

[23] On the instrumental value of participation (China gains access and say-so) as well as the image value (avoiding opprobrium but also creating opportunities for "back patting"), see Johnston and Evans, "China's Engagement with Multilateral Security Institutions."

[24] Yan, "Dui Zhongguo Anquan Huanjing De Fenxi Yu Sikao," p. 10; Fang, "Yatai Anquan Jiagou De Xianzhuang," pp. 11, 14; Chu Shulong, "Lengzhanhou Zhongguo Anquan Zhanlüe Sixiang De Fazhan" [The development of China's thinking about security strategy after the Cold War], pp. 11–13; Sa Benwang, "Woguo Anquan De Bianhua Ji Xin De Pubian Anquanguan De Zhuyao Tezheng" [The change in our country's security and the main features of the new concept of universal security], p. 51; Xiao Feng, "Dui Guoji Xingshizhong Jige Redian Wenti De Kanfa" [Perspective on several hot issues in the international situation], p. 3; Wang, "Dui Tai Junshi Douzheng Dui Shijie Zhanlüe Geju De Yingxiang Chutan," p. 28.

[25] Xia, "Some Views on Multilateral Security Cooperation in Northeast Asia"; see also Johnston and Evans, "China's Engagement with Multilateral Security Institu-

jing recognized that the regional security architecture based on bilateral ties with the United States would remain in the "dominant position" in the short run, it asserted that multilateral cooperation based on a "new security concept" should be given greater play in the long run. Consonant with "the five principles of peaceful coexistence" first articulated at the Bandung Conference of the 1950s, this new security concept emphasizing dialogue and cooperation would be the basis for an alternative to the American-led order.[26]

Currency responsibility

A second element in China's attempt to transform the reputation it was acquiring by 1995–96 as a potentially disruptive and dangerous rising power was its response to the Asian financial crisis that deepened and threatened to spread around the globe in late 1997. As its neighbors' currencies fell in value, Beijing decided not to devalue the yuan (or *renminbi*) and, more importantly, to clearly announce that this decision was a costly step China took to help stabilize a precarious international situation. Although some foreign economists noted that there were also very sound self-interested economic reasons for the decision (the net economic effect for China if it devalued the yuan might have been negative),[27] Beijing's repeated assurances that it was not going to devalue its currency to maintain the competitiveness of Chinese exports paid significant international political dividends. These dividends grew as observers intermittently predicted that China would soon change its policy, especially because declining exports were hurting national growth in a period when the

---

tions." Some in China's foreign policy elite also assert that multilateralism is an integral part of the diplomatic portfolio any country must possess if it is to be considered a true great power in the modern era. See Thomas J. Christensen, "Parsimony Is No Simple Matter: International Relations Theory, Area Studies, and the Rise of China," pp. 35–36.

[26] However "new," this regional vision would also strictly uphold one "old" principle of international relations well established since the seventeenth century, the traditional "hard" or "absolute" view of state sovereignty that Beijing held dear. See Fang, "Yatai Anquan Jiagou De Xianzhuang," pp. 11–15; also Sa, "Woguo Anquan De Bianhua Ji Xin De Pubian Anquanguan De Zhuyao Tezheng," p. 51. See also "Former Vice-Premier Calls for New Dimensions to Five Principles of Peaceful Coexistence"; "China Will Never Seek Hegemony, Said Chinese Premier." Yan Xuetong argues that regional security cooperation can enhance China's security by diluting American leverage (Yan, "Dui Zhongguo Anquan Huanjing De Fenxi Yu Sikao," p. 10).

[27] See especially Thomas G. Moore and Dixia Yang, "Empowered and Restrained: Chinese Foreign Policy in the Age of Economic Interdependence," pp. 215–22. On China's ability to substitute other measures for devaluation, see Nicholas Lardy's comments in Gerrit Gong et al., "China into the Abyss?"

regime was undertaking a painful new round of domestic economic reforms. The more observers speculated, the greater the payoff for Beijing's reputation each time it reiterated its pledge even as China's economy slowed during 1998.

Justifiably or not, others began to cite Beijing's actions as evidence of a responsible internationalism that seemed to contrast with the narrowly self-interested approaches of its neighbors. In early 1998, British prime minister Tony Blair "joined [French president] Chirac in lavish praise of China's responsible behavior during the Asian financial crisis and described Beijing as a pillar of stability and responsible behavior. . . . Chirac declared that by choosing not to devalue the yuan, Beijing had shown 'an extremely responsible and co-operative attitude.' "[28] China's leaders clearly recognized the usefulness of this reaction to its currency policy. Their thinking was forthrightly summarized by the editors of the pro-Beijing Hong Kong newspaper, *Ta Kung Pao*: "Recently China would rather suffer losses by itself by persistently guarding against devaluation of *renminbi*. By demonstrating to all people in the world its image of being a large country that assumes responsibility and honors its word, China is extensively praised by the international community."[29] Indeed, on his visit to Beijing in October 1998, European Commission president Jacques Santer reacted to assurances from China's central bank governor that the PRC would hold the line on the yuan in 1999 "as part of [its] 'responsible attitude' to the Asian financial crisis," by echoing the comments from Blair and Chirac and lauded China as "the pillar for the region's economic and financial stability."[30]

Even if the crisis had eventually compelled China to decide that currency devaluation was an unavoidable economic necessity, the longer Beijing could delay such a decision, the more likely it would have been able to portray the step as a result of others' (in particular, Tokyo's) protracted failure to shoulder their share of the burden for fostering a regional recovery while China had done more than its part. In the event, because Beijing believed that the political benefit was worth the economic cost (real or perceived) of refraining from devaluation, it stuck with its currency pledge through 1999. By then, signs of a regional recovery had begun to appear. But even after the period passed during which others might have criticized Chinese devaluation as a "beggar

[28] "Blair Looks to Profit in Beijing."

[29] "China's International Status Is in the Ascendance"; see also Peng Shujie and Liu Yunfei, "News Analysis: Partnership Promotes China's All-around Diplomacy."

[30] See "Yuan Must Remain Stable, Says China's Central Bank Governor"; "EU Chief Congratulates China as Pillar of Asian Economy"; "China's New Premier Takes Centre Stage but Avoids Limelight."

thy neighbor" policy, Beijing remained quite leery of damaging its carefully cultivated reputation for responsible behavior, as was reflected in the heavily qualified and quickly disavowed trial balloons about possible devaluation of the yuan floated in May and June 2000.[31]

In sum, beginning with the Asian financial crisis, Beijing's grand strategic concerns, rather than a purely economic calculus, were shaping its currency decisions. Moreover, to the extent others were convinced that China had been making sacrifices during the financial crisis, the policy not only boosted the country's reputation, but by demonstrating the sort of responsible posture leaders exhibit, it also helped build the case that a booming China should soon play a more prominent role in an increasingly integrated global economy.[32]

Great Power Diplomacy: Partnerships and Linkage

Policies to reassure others and transform China's international reputation were important features of Beijing's new approach, but its principal strategic focus was great power diplomacy. The change on this front that emerged in 1996 was China's broadened effort to cultivate "partnerships." Of these, the most im-

[31] See "China Could Float the Yuan This Year: Prominent Economist"; Sara French, "U.S. Rates and Yuan to Weigh on Growth," p. 3; Christine Chan, "Time Not Ripe for Yuan Float," p. 6; Hiang Whai Quak, "Flexible Yuan Won't Hurt Hk£ Money Chief," pp. 1, 2. By 2003, China was under pressure to go further and revalue its currency. Predictably, China's premier, Wen Jiabao, first reminded everyone about China's record from the late 1990s: "'The Chinese government has always held a serious and responsible attitude towards the [currency] issue,' said Wen. He said that during the Asian financial crisis in 1997, China did not devalue the RMB and maintained its exchange rate, while many countries around China devalued their currencies. China's efforts had contributed to the stability of the economy and financial well being of the region and the world, he said" ("Stable RMB Exchange Rate Benefits World Economy: Premier Wen"). As China began to respond to demands for revaluation, it again carefully managed the debate to ensure that it could protect not only its economic interests but also its political reputation. The most plausible outcome would be a cautious repegging (perhaps against a basket of currencies) that Beijing would explain as a potentially painful and risky step that it was taking as a responsible member of the international economic community. China's continuing emphasis on its role as a responsible actor is reiterated in "China Denies Selling of USD Assets." Not all foreign economic analysts agreed that the Chinese currency should be revalued. See Stephen Roach, "The Hypocrisy of Bashing China," p. 17.

[32] Ye, "Zhongguo Shixing Daguo Waijiao Zhanlüe Shizai Bixing," p. 10. By 2004, China's growing role was prompting calls for it to be added to the G-8 meeting of leading world economies. See Thomas L Friedman, "Maids vs. Occupiers," p. 29; David R. Francis, "How to Make the G-8 'Club' a Little Less Cozy," p. 17; "Commentary: China for the G-8."

portant were at first labeled "strategic partnerships," a term reserved for bilateral ties with those countries China saw as most likely to define the multipolar international system it insisted would eventually supplant the unipolar world of American primacy that prevailed at the start of the twenty-first century.[33] China's purpose in forging partnerships was to enhance its attractiveness to the other great powers without the sacrifice of flexibility that might have been necessary if it sought to build traditional alliances. Such partnerships were in fact explicitly crafted to be bilateral relations that fall in a middle ground between those that identify others as allies and those that identify others as adversaries: "In these partnerships we won't find a clearly us-against-them characteristic. . . . These new strategic partnerships often have a two-fold nature. More often than not, the two sides are both partners and competitors."[34]

In cultivating these bilateral ties, China's leaders expected that they would

[33] See Peng and Liu, "News Analysis: Partnership Promotes China's All-around Diplomacy"; "China: Qian Qichen on 'Constructive' Strategic Partnerships"; Lu Jin and Liu Yunfei, "New Analysis: From Beijing to Washington and from Moscow to Beijing—A Revelation of New-Type Relations between Major Powers"; Zhang Yifan, "From 'Playing Card' to Establishing Strategic Partnership: Special Interview with Yang Chengxu, Director of the China Institute of International Studies," p. 5. On relations with smaller states, see "Quanmian Kaichuang Jiushi Niandai Waijiao Xin Jumian-Dang De Shisida Yilai Woguo Waijiao Gongzuo Shuping"; Han Hua, "Jiang Zemin to Go to Kuala Lumpur in Mid-December to Attend East Asia–ASEAN Summit, China to Establish Partnership with ASEAN," p. A1; "Chinese President Tells ASEAN Summit of Hopes for "Good-Neighbourly Partnership"; "Text of Chinese Foreign Minister's Speech to ASEAN."

[34] "Interview with Song Baotian, Deputy Director of the China Institute for International Relations." On the alleged obsolescence of alliances in the post–Cold War world, see "Gouzhu Xin Shiji De Xinxing Guoji Guanxi" [Building a new type of international relations for the new century], p. 6. On China's refusal to pursue its interests by traditional means, see Liu, "Deng Xiaoping's Thinking on Diplomatic Work," p. A6. See also Michael D. Swaine and Ashley J. Tellis, *Interpreting China's Grand Strategy: Past, Present, and Future*, pp. 114–21. One analyst argued that partnerships fit in with China's broader new approach defined by one basic principle (independent and peaceful diplomacy rather than unconditional cooperation), two basic links (developing Sino-American relations and entering international institutions), and three strategic fulcrums (strategic partnerships with other great powers, good neighborly partnerships with bordering countries, and basic partnerships with developing countries). Unlike less contingent alternative postures that China might have chosen (leader, outsider/bystander, challenger), the partnership approach also enables China to enjoy the advantages of free-riding on the security and global economic stability the U.S. hegemon supplies (Guo Shuyong, "21 Shiji Qianye Zhongguo Waijiao Dazhanlüe Chuyi" [A modest proposal for China's diplomatic grand strategy on the eve of the twenty-first century], pp. 91, 92, 95, 96).

establish a simple linkage: if partners, especially great power partners, opted to press Beijing on matters important enough to sour relations, they would jeopardize significant benefits such as opportunities for trade and investment, as well as complicate cooperation on managing urgent security problems such as weapons proliferation and international terrorism. By highlighting the advantages of mutually beneficial relations and clarifying the costs of acting contrary to China's interests, Beijing sought to maximize its leverage over those who could be the weightiest members of any hostile coalition.[35] It even envisioned the possibility that states would compete to cultivate their ever more valuable partnerships with the PRC. When the European Union approved a new China policy "establishing a comprehensive partnership with China" in June 1998, Beijing's media outlets in Hong Kong claimed this was evidence that the United States and the EU were "vying with each other to develop their relations with China thanks to the ever-increasing enhancement of China's national strength" and argued that the EU's action demonstrated China's indispensability—"Because China is the largest country in the world in terms of population, many difficult global questions cannot be settled without its participation. Thus, China's words and actions can hold the balance."[36]

China's leaders also anticipated that cultivating partnerships would help them cope with the immediate constraints of American power while hastening the advent of a multipolar world in which the United States would no longer be so dominant. Chinese observers regularly emphasized that its partnerships were both a sign of emerging multipolarity and a force accelerating this transformation of the international system's structure.[37] As described in the next chapter, Beijing hoped that partnership with the EU would augment the

[35] See Shi Nangen, "1997: A Fruitful Year in China's Multi-Dimensional Diplomacy," p. 7; "Prospects of China's Diplomatic Activities in 1998"; Guo, "21 Shiji Qianye Zhongguo Waijiao Dazhanlüe Chuyi," pp. 92–94. Several of my interlocutors in Beijing frankly asserted that implicit threats to transfer of arms or dual-use technology to states like Iran was one of the few cards in China's hand when dealing with the world's other great powers to discourage them from ignoring China's interests.

[36] "China's International Status Is in the Ascendance." Such arguments resonate with the analysis by Zbigniew Brzezinski, former U.S. national security adviser, whose views receive much attention in China. Brzezinski asserted that the PRC ultimately hoped to create a situation in which others, especially the United States, would see China as a needed and natural partner (*The Grand Chessboard*, pp. 170, 173).

[37] In his review of China's debate about international security in the post–Cold War era, Michael Pillsbury noted the Chinese assertion that it would be possible, for example, to "assist the trend toward multipolarity and increase its pace," in part by helping to elevate the EU's role on the international stage. Pillsbury, *China Debates the Future Security Environment*, p. 54.

influence of a power center that might one day rival the United States. Meanwhile, Beijing hoped that forging closer ties with the biggest European states would provide China with partners better positioned to persuade Washington it should gracefully accept the inevitable and embrace the potential virtues of emerging multipolarity.[38]

Creating a multipolar world was something China's leaders saw as highly desirable, but that was not the main immediate strategic purpose for which the partnerships were being forged. In the wake of repeated displays of striking U.S. military superiority during the early post–Cold War era and given a resurgent American economy, by the second half of the 1990s the leaders in Beijing had already concluded that multipolarity was a distant goal.[39] Their top priority, therefore, was to ensure China's interests while coping with the stark constraints of a unipolar world in which a potentially hostile United States would long remain the dominant power. This was the overriding consideration that led Beijing to conclude that the cultivation of great power partnerships, especially one with the United States, should be a central feature of a prudent strategy for China. Partnerships would enable China to address its concerns about U.S. preponderance without resorting to the more directly confrontational and (given the array of international interests and capabilities described in chapter 5) seemingly futile alternative of a straightforward attempt

[38] See Ye, "Zhongguo Shixing Daguo Waijiao Zhanlüe Shizai Bixing," pp. 7–8.

[39] Public rhetoric and scholarly debate sometimes sought to finesse the point. One approach, for example, was to suggest that the world was at least *becoming* multipolar, though for a time there would still be only one superpower. Another approach was to suggest that "unipolarity" obscured the fact that the world would soon be best described as having one superpower and several great powers (*yichao, duoda*). Such debates, however, revolved around semantic ruses to soften the reality of an international system that remained unipolar—a world with only one true great power and a handful of lesser regional powers. Yet Chinese analysts hopefully looked for signs of change, sometimes reprising arguments about American decline that had been popular in the West during the late 1980s (author's interviews). See also Fu Fuyuan, "Zhiyi Shidai De Qiwen" [Questioning *Time's* weird story]; "Iraq Crisis Revealed Collapse of US Global Authority: Chinese Analysts"; "Yici Yiyi Zhongda Yingxiang Shenyuan De Fangwen-Zhuhe Jiang Zhuxi Fang E Yuanman Chenggong" [A trip of great significance and far-reaching influence—Congratulations on President Jiang's completely successful Russian visit]; Liu Huaqiu, "Strive for a Peaceful International Environment"; Tang Tianri, "Relations between Major Powers Are Being Readjusted"; "Jiu Zhong'e Liangguo Zui Gaoji Huiwu, Shuangbian Guanxi Deng Wenti, Jiang Zhuxi Jieshou Eluosi Jizhe Caifang" [President Jiang's interview with Moscow reporters, about the Sino-Russian Summit Meeting, bilateral relations, etc.]; "Li Peng Zai Mosike Jishou Jizhe Fangwen" [Li Peng's interview with reporters in Moscow]; Peng and Liu, "News Analysis: Partnership Promotes China's All-around Diplomacy."

to counterbalance American power. Beijing saw its subtler approach as a way to instead avoid irrevocably alienating those a traditional alliance strategy would have targeted (the economically attractive United States and its prosperous allies) while also easing the concerns of others who, even if they were not designated as adversaries, would have been wary of joining any direct challenge to America's international leadership that allowed them to benefit from the collective goods of peace and prosperity.[40] Finally, and of lesser importance, by cultivating partnerships rather than alliances, Beijing anticipated a propaganda advantage. It could label a central theme of U.S. foreign policy—the effort to reinvigorate, expand, and redirect its military alliances in Asia and Europe—as reflecting a stubbornly anachronistic Cold War mentality that China, embracing partnerships (and multilateralism), had discarded. Defense Minister Chi Haotian emphasized the point for U.S. defense secretary William Cohen during his January 1998 visit to Beijing, claiming, "at present, relations between major powers are undergoing a strategic readjustment. In the new situation, neither expanding military alliances [i.e., NATO] nor strengthening military alliances [i.e., U.S. alliances with Japan and Australia] is conducive to maintenance of peace and security."[41] Old-fashioned alliances, in Beijing's vision, were to be supplanted by international partnerships.

What, then, defined these partnerships? Beijing did not provide a formal and explicit explanation.[42] In practice, however, China's partnerships were defined by a commitment to: 1) building stable bilateral relations without targeting any third party; 2) promoting extensive economic intercourse; 3) muting disagreements about domestic politics in the interest of working together on matters of shared concern in international diplomacy; and 4) routinizing official visits, especially military-to-military exchanges and regular summit meetings between top government leaders.[43] Beijing, it must also be emphasized again, did not ex-

[40] Ye, "Zhongguo Shixing Daguo Waijiao Zhanlüe Shizai Bixing," p. 8. This view of the benefits supplied by a leading state is emphasized by international relations scholars advancing "hegemonic stability theory." See Charles P. Kindleberger, *The World in Depression, 1929–1939*; Robert O. Keohane, *After Hegemony: Cooperation and Discord in the World Political Economy*; Robert Gilpin, *War and Change in World Politics*.

[41] "China: Expanding Military Contacts Part of Diplomatic Strategy"; also Zhao Gangzhen, "Daguo Guanxi, 'Huoban Re'" [Big power relations: 'Partnership fever'"].

[42] Each of my interlocutors provided a fairly detailed description of what they *thought* the term meant, but most also professed substantial confusion, indicating that the party center preferred to keep the definition malleable.

[43] Peng and Liu "News Analysis: Partnership Promotes China's All-around Diplomacy"; see also Sun Baoshan, "Shilun Lengzhanhou Guoji Guanxizhong De Huoban Guanxi" [Preliminary discussion of partnerships in post–Cold War international relations], pp. 84–90; "Editorial: Great Success in China's Big-Nation Diplomacy."

pect such partnerships to yield purely cooperative relations. On the contrary, it anticipated that differing national interests, culture, and political ideology would generate conflicts between partners. What Beijing expected instead was that partners would be committed to managing unavoidable conflicts so that they could continue to work together on vital areas of common interest. Since 1996 China has sought to establish some sort of partnership with each of the world's major powers. Especially important were those with Russia and the United States, initially designated "strategic partnerships" because they were expected to have the greatest significance for the evolution of regional and international security affairs. The following chapter explores the distinctive bilateral relationships that China fostered with these two states as well as other major powers in the years after 1996.

7

China and the Major Powers

China and Russia

The strategic partnership China formed with Russia set the pattern for Beijing's preferred approach to bilateral relations with the major powers. Boris Yeltsin's initial state visit to China in December 1992 had laid the groundwork for improving Sino-Russian ties in the post-Soviet era and resulted in the September 1994 joint announcement during Jiang Zemin's return visit that China and Russia were establishing a "constructive partnership." At a third summit meeting in Beijing in April 1996, the relationship was redefined and labeled a "strategic cooperative partnership." The Chinese then began to tout this partnership as a "new type of state-to-state relations—non-alliance, non-confrontation, and not directed against any third country," hailing it as "the first of its kinds [sic] in the history of bilateral relations between counties in the world, particularly between large countries."[1]

The actual significance of the term used was not immediately obvious, and some wondered whether the arrangement was in fact simply a first step toward an old-fashioned alliance, especially because 1) it emerged amidst shared and deepening concerns about U.S. international dominance in Europe and Asia; 2) Moscow had already become a prized vendor of military hardware that Beijing could not produce for itself; and 3) China's military purchases were a rare bright spot for the troubled Russian economy. Despite these mutual interests in fostering close ties, however, for reasons outlined in chapter 5, an alliance targeting the United States was not particularly attractive to China or Russia.[2] Beijing understood that the weapons Russia was willing to sell, while

[1] Fang Yinwan and Yang Guojun, "Beneficial Enlightenment for Large Countries to Build a New Type of Relationship"; "Zhong'e Zui Gaoji Huiwu" [Sino-Russian summit meeting]; Wu Songzhi and Yi Shuguang, "Gongzhu Mulin Youhao Hezuo Guanxi" [Building together cooperative good neighborly relations].

[2] When the constructive strategic partnership was announced, the foreign ministers

valuable, would not provide it with a decisive counter to U.S. military power. Some in Moscow, meanwhile, were already growing nervous about the risks of helping to create an increasingly powerful China on their country's doorstep. But, most importantly, an anti-American alliance would entail steep opportunity costs for both Russia and China as it would jeopardize their vital interest in continued modernization that required integration with an international economic system in which the United States and its allies remained the key players. As one Chinese assessment frankly put it, "Especially in the area of economic trade and technology, Sino-American relations, Sino-Japanese relations, Russian-American relations, and Russian-German relations are even more important than Chinese-Russian relations."[3]

Shared anxiety about an unchecked American superpower, therefore, resulted not in an old-fashioned alliance, but instead in the first and most stable of Beijing's new great power partnerships.[4] In this close partnership, as in a

---

for Russia and China explicitly stated, "the furthering of a Sino-Russian partnership is of strategic significance, but the seeking of comprehensive common interests and closer co-operation does not mean that the two countries will form an alliance" ("PRC: Qian Qichen, Primakov Hold Breakfast Meeting"). This stance has endured. China quickly shot down Russian premier Primakov's trial balloon (subsequently disavowed by President Yeltsin) suggesting a Russia-India-China defense alliance. See "China Cautious on Primakov Plan." And, as will be noted below, in 1999, when some Chinese security experts argued that the U.S. bombing of the Chinese embassy in Belgrade indicated an American threat so dire that Beijing should lose no time allying with Moscow, their views were rejected as inconsistent with China's basic national interest in unallied diplomacy (*bu jiemeng de waijiao zhengce*) (Zhou Guiyin, "Xin Shiji De Guoji Anquan Yu Anquan Zhanlüe" [International security and security strategy in the new century], p. 1). China's leaders have adhered to the view that a Sino-Russian combination would be too weak to do much to check an overwhelmingly dominant United States. See Ye Zicheng, "Zhongguo Shixing Daguo Waijiao Zhanlüe Shizai Bixing" [The imperative for China to implement a great power diplomatic strategy], p. 7. For the view that the Sino-Russian cooperative strategic partnership is a "quasi-alliance" that could be transformed into a formal alliance if Sino-American relations irreversibly deteriorate, see ibid., pp. 9–10.

[3] Huang Zongliang, "Miandui Beiyue Xin Zhanlüe Chonggu Zhong'e Guanxi" [Reassessing Sino-Russian relations in the face of NATO's new strategy], pp. 25–28. See also Ye Zicheng, "Carrying Forward, Developing and Pondering Deng Xiaoping's Foreign Policy Thinking in the New Situation."

[4] See Francesco Sisci, "Neighbours Push for Better Ties with Russia—China: Military Transfers Get Boost after Talks"; also Ye, "Zhongguo Shixing Daguo Waijiao Zhanlüe Shizai Bixing," p. 7. Nevertheless, some of my Chinese interlocutors expressed doubts about the practical significance and durability of the Sino-Russian partnership. They argued it was dependent on the warm personal ties between top Russian and Chinese leaders after the end of the Cold War and had rather shallow roots in their

traditional alliance, the importance of parallel strategic interests provided strong incentives for Moscow and Beijing to mute areas of disagreement. Both were uneasy about U.S. capabilities and intentions. While Russia worried about the geopolitical implications of NATO's eastward expansion, Chinese analysts saw NATO's emerging post–Cold War strategy as part of a larger American design to ensure its global hegemony. Beijing thought it discerned the possibility that the United States could simultaneously threaten China from the west (as it began to expand its military ties with Central Asia) and from the east (as it strengthened its existing military ties to Japan). Russia and China were reacting not only to these changes in U.S. security relations on their periphery and unmatched U.S. capabilities, but also to what they viewed as America's growing appetite for foreign military intervention and its ever-clearer determination to deploy ballistic missile defenses.[5]

Operations in the Persian Gulf and especially the Balkans during the 1990s that proved to be relatively pain-free for the United States suggested that neither prospective adversaries nor international organizations would any longer pose much of a constraint on American decisions about where and when to act abroad. Because Moscow and Beijing each have territories over which they seek to secure sovereign control (for Russia, Chechnya; for China, Taiwan), both were increasingly wary of the role that a more fearless United States might decide to play. Therefore, when China's official news agency described the most important features of the strategic partnership with Russia it not only emphasized "close and regular contact between the two state leaders, and departments of foreign affairs, national defenses, law enforcement, economics, science, and technology," and the general need to resist "hegemonism and power politics." It also specifically highlighted the partners' joint opposition to "attempts to amend the basic principles of international law, to threaten others by force or to interfere in other countries' internal affairs" and their pledge to "respect each other's independence, sovereignty and territorial integrity and firmly oppose any attempts to split the country from within or outside the country" based on their "understand[ing] and support" for "each other's efforts to safeguard national unification, sovereignty and territorial integrity." More to the point, Moscow reciprocated Beijing's support for its stance against foreign meddling on Chechnya by explicitly reaffirming

---

countries' national interests (noting in particular that Sino-Russian trade fell well short of targets Beijing and Moscow set during the 1990s). See also Zhao Longgeng, "Zhong'e Zhanlüe Xiezuo Huoban Guanxi Maixiang Jianshi Zhi Lu" [Strides towards strengthening the Sino-Russian strategic cooperative partnership], pp. 32–33.

[5] See Huang, "Miandui Beiyue Xin Zhanlüe Chonggu Zhong'e Guanxi."

its support for Beijing's unwavering "one China principle" with respect to Taiwan.[6]

U.S. missile defense plans that gained new momentum in the late 1990s further reinforced Sino-Russian concerns about continued "hegemony" that American interventionist behavior helped nurture. As it became clear Washington was unlikely to allow existing treaty obligations (the 1972 ABM Treaty) or technological difficulties (a series of disappointing tests) to stand in the way of the U.S. missile defense program, Moscow and Beijing stepped up the frequency and vehemence of their objections. Their shared position eventually culminated in an explicit Sino-Russian joint statement issued during Russian president Putin's July 2000 visit to Beijing. The document not only criticized U.S. efforts to move forward with hitherto prohibited national missile defenses and its related attempts to revise the ABM Treaty to remove legal constraints it posed. It also explicitly raised objections to U.S. plans to deploy already permissible theater missile defenses (TMD) in Asia that might neutralize the strategic leverage China's ballistic missiles provided and that promised to result in increased military integration between the United States and its Pacific allies or, even more worrisome from Beijing's perspective, Taiwan.[7]

[6] In the immediate wake of the 1996 confrontation in the Taiwan Strait, the Sino-Russian partnership's joint stance against foreign interference in others' internal affairs clearly reflected Beijing's concerns about the potentially interventionist role the United States might play in the future. See "PRC: More on Sino-Russian Strategic Partnership." See also "China, Russia Issue Beijing Declaration." Nevertheless, the Chinese do not confidently count on more than rhetorical support from their Russian strategic partner in the event of trouble in the Taiwan Strait. Their experience during the 1950s clarified for both parties that Taiwan is a vital interest for China but not Russia. This history leads to the expectation that Russia would probably hesitate if supporting its China partner in a renewed Taiwan crisis meant running a significant risk of confrontation with the United States. Historically rooted suspicion even led one Chinese analyst to suggest that Moscow might actually prefer that the Taiwan situation not be resolved too quickly. Tension there, after all, diverts substantial U.S. military attention from European to Asian contingencies. See Wang Yiwei, "Dui Tai Junshi Douzheng Dui Shijie Zhanlüe Geju De Yingxiang Chutan," pp. 28–29.

[7] "Nonstrategic missile defense that is not prohibited by the 'ABM Treaty' . . . should not harm the security interests of other countries, should not lead to the establishment or strengthening of close-type military or political blocs. . . . China and Russia are seriously worried about, and firmly oppose, a certain country's plan to deploy in the Asia-Pacific region a nonstrategic missile defense system that might have the aforesaid negative impacts. Incorporating Taiwan into a foreign country's missile defense system in whatever form is unacceptable and will seriously undermine regional stability" ("Joint Statement by the PRC President and the Russian Federation President on the Antimissile Issue").

Missile defenses posed a serious challenge for Russia and China because they raised the specter of an altered military environment that would be distinctly disadvantageous for both. In the existing strategic setting, Russian and Chinese missile forces offered an affordable asymmetrical offset to the many quantitative and qualitative advantages the U.S. military enjoyed on the modern battlefield. Ballistic missiles were useful not mainly as a means to turn the tide of fighting in a given theater, but rather because they introduced the risk of unacceptable, potentially nuclear, escalation Moscow and Beijing could exploit to induce even the most powerful adversary to behave more cautiously than would otherwise be the case. In a world with effective missile defenses, however, Russia and China would have to worry about the possibility that great power strategic competition would be decided absent the fear of escalation and be confined to the arena of advanced conventional armaments where U.S. economic and technological strengths promised to give it a huge and, for the foreseeable future, enduring advantage.[8]

The actual prospect for such a dramatic change in the strategic environment might well be remote since there are so many relatively simple methods to foil missile defenses and because their performance must approach perfection to be meaningful if the adversary's missiles might carry nuclear warheads. But while academic strategic analysts can coolly recommend relying on simple and cheap countermeasures against imaginable defenses, civilian and military officials tend to plan conservatively and to worry about underestimating the adversary's prowess. The consequences if the United States successfully deployed highly effective missile defenses would be sufficiently dramatic that prudent military planners and responsive political leaders in Moscow and Beijing worried that they might feel constrained to hedge against this possibility by increasing their investment in expensive advanced conventional armaments as well as counters to anticipated missile defenses.

Despite their shared concern about missile defenses, these strategic partners pursued different approaches to coping with the prospect of American deployment. The greater size, sophistication, and diversity of Russia's nuclear arsenal enabled Moscow to entertain the notion of a deal with the United States that would set limits on deployed defensive systems (a tack abandoned when President Bush in 2002 simply invoked the clause permitting the United States to withdraw from the ABM Treaty). In contrast, China's very small and slow-to-modernize ICBM force made it more difficult for Beijing to accept even very limited U.S. national missile defenses. Moreover, theater missile

---

[8] See Zhu Feng, "TMD Yu Dangqian Zhongmei Guanxi" [TMD and current Sino-American relations], p. 12.

defenses complicated the Sino-American agenda in ways that were not relevant to Russia's thinking. Deployed TMD would cast doubt on the usefulness of China's shorter-range missiles that Beijing saw as necessary to discourage Taiwan from adopting separatist policies, to encourage it to negotiate the terms for reunification, and to dissuade the United States from intervening. China also worried that Japan's announced intention to cooperate with the United States in developing and deploying TMD would enable Tokyo to acquire advanced missile technologies, further enhancing its potential, if it ever decided to shift course, to quickly become a major nuclear power (because it already has a wide range of advanced military technologies and possesses a large quantity of fissile material).

Thus, while Russia and China were both anticipating that American missile defenses might require them to shoulder a much heavier military burden simply to maintain their current levels of security in an extended era of American unipolarity, China's concerns ran deeper.[9] China's analysts argued that missile defenses were in fact another element in the broader U.S. response to China's rise. One interpretation suggested that a key reason the United States was so eager to deploy missile defenses was because they would weaken China's limited strategic deterrent, hedge against China's growing military power, and thereby forestall the shift from unipolarity to multipolarity.[10] Another interpretation suggested that American missile defenses were actually a trap designed to draw China into an arms race that would play to the U.S. economic and technological advantages and weaken China by leading it to repeat the Soviet mistake of unsustainable military competition derailing or distorting domestic economic development.[11]

[9] Lu Youzhi, "Chongxin Shenshi Zhongguo De Anquan Huanjing" [A fresh examination of China's security environment], p. 59; See also "Political Scientist Criticizes Planned Reform of Russian Missile Forces"; Fred Weir, "Putin Tries Big Shift in Military Strategy," p. 1; "Chuanwen Jiang Zemin Zhishi Gaibian Zhonggong De Guofang Zhengce" [Jiang Zemin said to indicate a change in CCP national defense policy].

[10] See Lu, "Chongxin Shenshi Zhongguo De Anquan Huanjing," p. 59; Chen Ying, "Zhanqu Daodan Fangyu Xitong" [Theater missile defense and East Asia's security situation], p. 28. Zhu, "TMD Yu Dangqian Zhongmei Guanxi," p. 12. For American assertions that the most important purpose for U.S. missile defenses is indeed to cope with a more powerful China, see Gay Alcorn, "China 'Real Reason' for Missile Shield"; Peter Brookes, "The Case for Missile Defense." On China's need to invest in efficient countermeasures, see "Chuanwen Jiang Zemin Zhishi Gaibian Zhonggong De Guofang Zhengce."

[11] Chen, "Zhanqu Daodan Fangyu Xitong Yu Dongya Anquan Xingshi," p. 28. During the summer of 2000 President Jiang Zemin's worry that looming U.S. missile

Shared, if far from identical, international security concerns in the 1990s provided the foundation for a robust Sino-Russian strategic partnership. The strength of these concerns overshadowed other frustrations in the relationship. The high profile of Chinese nationals in Russia's far eastern regions intermittently resulted in tensions for which no easy remedies could be found. More troubling, despite the partners' professed intention to boost trade and investment, Sino-Russian economic relations remained profoundly disappointing.[12] In the mid-1990s, with the partnership blooming, Russia and China had set the target for two-way trade volume at $20 billion by the turn of the century. As the new millennium dawned, trade volumes remained in the $5–6 billion range, with Russian sales of raw materials and modern weapons the only real bright spots. When President Putin visited Beijing in July 2000, he and Jiang Zemin found themselves reprising the basic pattern Yeltsin and Jiang had established in the mid-1990s. Once more they emphasized a common interest in opposing and hastening the end of American-led unipolarity, warning against outside intervention in others' internal affairs and against deploying allegedly destabilizing missile defenses. But there was little the leaders could do to produce a substantial deepening of a bilateral economic relationship until Russia managed to overcome the domestic reasons for its enduring weakness.[13]

Because ties to Russia provided China with important benefits— eliminating the old threat from the north and permitting the PLA to turn its attention to security concerns in the east and south; complicating U.S. attempts to isolate China on matters such as missile defense and Taiwan; and making weaponry available that Beijing could neither produce itself nor purchase elsewhere—the Sino-Russian strategic partnership remained vital to China. The relationship, however, did not provide the economic benefits

---

defenses might result in a sharp deterioration of China's strategic environment led him to call for a bold review of the country's policies on modern weapons development (including countermeasures) and arms control. See Cary Huang, "Jiang Zemin Reportedly Urges Development of Strategic Weapons"; "Chuanwen Jiang Zemin Zhishi Gaibian Zhonggong De Guofang Zhengce."

[12] See Chen Xiaoqin, "Buru 21 Shiji De Zhong'e Guanxi" [Sino-Russian relations entering the 21st century], pp. 31–35; Zhao, "Zhong'e Zhanlüe Xiezuo Huoban Guanxi Maixiang Jianshi Zhi Lu," pp. 32–33; Gilbert Rozman, "Sino-Russian Relations in the 1990s: A Balance Sheet," pp. 93–113.

[13] See "News Agency Interviews Russian President on Visit to China"; "China, Russia Issue Beijing Declaration"; "Joint Statement by the PRC President and the Russian Federation President on the Antimissile Issue." See also Rozman, "Sino-Russian Relations in the 1990s"; "PRC Academics Interviewed on Putin's Visit to China," p. A15; Michael Pillsbury, *China Debates the Future Security Environment*, pp. 155, 169.

Beijing knew were necessary for China to sustain its great power aspirations. Moreover, mutual suspicions rooted in recent history, as well as the belief that rivalry between big neighbors is natural and will be hard to avoid once Russia recovers from its economic downturn, were never very far beneath the surface. China, therefore, carefully limited its partnership with Russia by drawing the line short of alliance and also by working to build partnerships with other great powers that could better serve Beijing's grand-strategic interest in modernization.[14] In this latter effort, China's relations with the United States were the top priority.

China and the United States

The importance of ties to the United States reflected three considerations. First, stable bilateral relations were crucial for Beijing to maintain confidence that the international environment would be peaceful enough to safely focus on the domestic economic development essential to China's rise. Second, as the Chinese economy boomed in the mid-1990s the United States had become an essential market for goods and a source of capital, technology, and managerial expertise that China lacked. And third, U.S. policy toward China and Taiwan would clearly have a direct bearing on the prospects for realizing the goal of national reunification.[15] Thus, an acceptable grand strategy had to provide China with a satisfactory approach to managing relations with the world's sole superpower, relations that had been recurrently troubled since the late 1980s. Beijing's effort to work with Washington in establishing China's second strategic partnership was expected to serve this purpose.

Laying a Foundation

In July 1996, almost immediately following the Sino-American confrontation over Taiwan, Beijing and Washington began talks aimed at arranging summit meetings to repair strained relations.[16] By July 1997, China's foreign minister, Qian Qichen, and the U.S. Secretary of State, Madeleine Albright were holding their fourth meeting of the year on the sides of a session at the

[14] Huang, "Miandui Beiyue Xin Zhanlüe Chonggu Zhong'e Guanxi."

[15] Ye, "Zhongguo Shixing Daguo Waijiao Zhanlüe Shizai Bixing," p. 7; see also Zalmay M. Khalilzad et al., *The United States and a Rising China: Strategic and Military Implications*, pp. xiii–xiv, 3–5.

[16] See Robert S. Ross, "The 1995–96 Taiwan Strait Confrontation: Coercion, Credibility, and the Use of Force," p. 113. For a Chinese overview of the evolving relationship, see Liu Xuecheng and Li Jidong, eds., *Zhongguo He Meiguo: Duishou Haishi Huoban* [China and the United States: Adversaries or partners].

ASEAN Regional Forum. In addition to broad discussions about joint efforts to improve relations, the meeting produced the announcement that President Jiang Zemin planned a state visit to the United States in fall 1997 that would be "of great significance to the establishment of a strategic partnership between the two countries oriented toward the 21st century."[17] Shortly afterward, the assistant secretary of state for East Asian and Pacific affairs, Stanley O. Roth, publicly confirmed the U.S. interest in recasting Sino-American ties along these lines, and planning for the summit moved into its final phase.[18]

When Presidents Clinton and Jiang met in Washington during October 1997, the PRC and the United States formally agreed to work toward a "constructive strategic partnership." This term for defining the Sino-American relationship had been chosen only after a good bit of haggling. The phrase "constructive strategic partnership" was crafted 1) to indicate that the countries would work together to solve problems threatening peace and stability (thus, a partnership); 2) to underscore the significance of this bilateral relationship for broader regional and international security (thus, strategic); and 3) to distinguish it from the closer ties already in place with Russia (thus, the need to work on making strained bilateral relations more constructive).[19] The announcement and subsequent explanations of the envisioned partnership emphasized the mutual economic benefits of exchange between the world's largest developed and largest developing countries, the advantages of close consultation on political and security issues (including establishing a Beijing-Washington hot line, regular meetings between cabinet level officials, exchange visits by military personnel, and joint efforts on counter-proliferation, environmental protection, and drug enforcement), and the importance of not permitting differences on any single issue (e.g., human rights, trade disputes) to obscure the big picture of common strategic interests.[20]

[17] Liu Huorong, Wu Dingbao, and Yang Zhongyi, "China: Qian Qichen Holds Talks with Albright"; "China: Further on Qian-Albright Comments after Talks."

[18] He Chong, "China and the United States Are Exploring the Possibility of Establishing a 'Strategic Partnership'—First in a Series on Prospects of Jiang Zemin's U.S. Visit."

[19] See the interview with China's Foreign Ministry spokesman, Shen Guofang: Guo Jian and Su Xiangxin, "China: Shen Guofang Hails Jiang Zemin's US Trip."

[20] On these broad purposes, see Gu Ping, "Sino-US Relations Are Facing Historic Opportunity." On the importance of mutual economic benefits, see He, "China and the United States Are Exploring the Possibility of Establishing a 'Strategic Partnership'"; also "Jiu Zhongmei Guanxi, Taiwan Wenti, Zhongguo Renda Zhidu Deng Wenti: Qiao Shi Jieshou Meiguo Jizhe Caifang"; He Chong, "China and the United States Declare Their Endeavor to Build a Constructive and Strategic Partnership Relationship"; "Interview with Song Baotian, Deputy Director of the China Institute for

Just as some observers had at first misinterpreted the Sino-Russian strategic partnership as a way station to an alliance, some mistakenly anticipated that the Sino-American strategic partnership was intended to herald an era of close cooperation that would preclude the sorts of conflicts that had plagued their relationship since the late 1980s. Diplomatic pleasantries and lofty rhetoric aside, however, the announced effort to build a Sino-American strategic partnership actually reflected an incomplete and still difficult search for a framework to manage the significant differences and conflicts of interest between the two major powers most active in Asia after the Cold War.

China had no intention of abandoning its aspiration for increased international influence, even if that conflicted with an American interest in preserving its primacy. Instead, strategic partnership with the United States was designed to better enable China to cope with the potentially dangerous constraints of American hegemony during China's rise to great power status. The envisioned partnership, after all, made cooperation conditional, linking it to American behavior that did not infringe on core Chinese security interests and clarifying the benefits a hostile United States might risk forfeiting. Implicit in the effort to build a Sino-American partnership was the threat that its collapse might lead Beijing to: 1) give other partners (Japan or Europe) preferential economic treatment; 2) complicate U.S. diplomacy by exercising China's veto in the UN Security Council; 3) be less circumspect in its export controls on sensitive military and dual-use technologies to states about which the United States has strong concerns; 4) delay its participation in agreements that comprise the nonproliferation regime, especially the Missile Technology Control Regime and the proposed agreement to cut off fissile material production; 5) limit its cooperation in the fight against international terrorism, especially in

---

International Relations." On the shared economic interest in a stable Middle East, see Wu Qiang and Qian Xuemei, "Zhongguo Yu Zhongdong De Nengyuan Hezuo" [Energy cooperation between China and the Middle East], p. 52. On common interests in Korea, see Zhou, "Xin Shiji De Guoji Anquan Yu Anquan Zhanlüe," p. 70. On measures to improve military-military relations as a way to avoid accidents and reduce dangerous misperceptions, see "China: Pact to Prevent Naval Accidents Initialed"; "China: Expanding Military Contacts Part of Diplomatic Strategy." China apparently believed military exchanges would make it "increasingly difficult for the 'China threat theory' spread by some people in the West to find a market" (Chi Haotian, "A Year of Our Army's Active Foreign Contacts," p. 7). The United States was eager to expand such exchanges not only to lessen the chance of inadvertent conflict, but also to counter an allegedly dangerous Chinese overestimation of American hostility and underestimation of the military capabilities that the United States could bring to bear in a war in Asia. See Jim Mannion, "Pentagon Study Sees Danger in Chinese View of US Power."

Central Asia; 6) be less helpful in containing regional tension in Korea or South Asia.[21] China, in short, saw partnership as a way to realize what amounted to a linkage strategy, focusing Washington's attention on the price the United States might incur if its actions reduced Beijing's willingness to play a constructive role on important economic, diplomatic, or military matters. It is also true, however, that China's own interests would make it reluctant to carry out these implicit threats. Moreover, even if they could make such threats to withhold cooperation credible, leaders in Beijing certainly understood that the consequences were unlikely to be a very tight constraint on American policy makers given the obvious material advantages of the United States. But they probably saw limited leverage as the best of a bad lot of options from which a relatively weak China could choose when trying to cope with life in the unipolar world the United States dominated.[22]

Troubled Ties

During Jiang Zemin's 1997 visit to Washington, Chinese and U.S. leaders publicly emphasized the hope that in working toward a constructive strategic partnership bilateral relations would evolve in a positive direction. In its relationship with the United States, however, unlike its quickly flowering partnership with Russia, China's first priority was avoiding renewed confrontation rather than making breakthroughs to resolve outstanding disagreements or promote ambitious cooperation.[23] Yet even with this modest aim, and de-

[21] Author's interviews, Beijing, June–July 1998, March 2000, October 2000. On China's role as a "balancing" force in the UN, see Teng Xiaodong, "Dialogue on 1996 International Situation: China in the United Nations," p. 5; Jin Xin, "Meiguo Yanfa TMD De Yitu Ji Dui Quanqiu He Woguo Anquan De Yingxiang" [U.S. plans for research and development of TMD and its influence on the security of the world and our country], p. 24. Since 1999, Beijing has occasionally indicated the link it sees between (and the hypocrisy of) U.S. decisions to share TMD technology with Asian states, especially Taiwan, and the efforts to institutionalize the Missile Technology Control Regime. China's view is that joint work on TMD amounts to the spread of missile technology to Japan and Taiwan. See Monte R. Bullard, "Undiscussed Linkages: Implications of Taiwan Strait Security Activity on Global Arms Control and Nonproliferation."

[22] Wise tactics can enhance the effectiveness of its linkage strategy. China's cultivation of ties to the U.S. business community, for example, helps it to maximize the political appeal of maintaining good Sino-American relations. See Michael D. Swaine and Ashley J. Tellis *Interpreting China's Grand Strategy: Past, Present, and Future*, p. 117.

[23] A point my interlocutors emphasized. See also "Jiang Zemin Zhuxi Huijian Ge'er Fuzongtong Shi Tichu Fazhan Zhongmei Guanxi" [While meeting with U.S. vice-president Gore, President Jiang Zemin raises developing Sino-American relations]; Gu Ping, "Zhongmei Guanxi Mianlin Lishi Jiyu" [Sino-American relations face

spite a successful follow-up return visit to China by President Clinton in June 1998, events soon began to pose a stiff test of the Sino-American strategic partnership still "under construction" that prompted both Beijing and Washington to reconsider its value.

In the United States, support for the partnership eroded dramatically beginning in late 1998. American disillusionment followed from disappointment with China's renewed clampdown on political and religious dissidents, emerging allegations of Chinese corporate and military espionage aimed at acquiring advanced American missile and nuclear warhead technologies, and the belief among some in Washington that China's Communist Party leaders had cynically fanned the flames of anti-Americanism after the accidental U.S. bombing of China's embassy in Belgrade, thereby contributing to violent demonstrations that targeted the U.S. embassy in Beijing. Although high-level American envoys to China continued to invoke the term "strategic partnership" during their private meetings with PRC leaders, in the United States it virtually disappeared as a way to refer to Sino-American relations in public, except when used pejoratively by critics of President Clinton's China policy.[24] Indeed, the phrase was increasingly seen as a symbol of the Clinton administration's naiveté in dealing with Beijing, much as conservative critics in the mid-1970s had associated the term "détente" with the alleged naiveté of U.S. policy toward Moscow. As with détente in the late 1970s, during the late 1990s the idea of building a strategic partnership with China quickly became a political liability in American politics. Early in the 2000 U.S. electoral cycle,

---

a historic opportunity], p. 1. In light of Taiwan president Lee Teng-hui's visit to the United States in May 1995 that had triggered renewed Sino-American tensions, Beijing was especially keen to get the United States to reiterate its "one-China" policy reflected in the three joint communiqués on which improved bilateral ties had been built since the Nixon visit in February 1972.

[24] One well-positioned Chinese interlocutor emphasized that in the tense period following the May 1999 Belgrade bombing, every high-level U.S. representative privately emphasized the American interest in continuing to work toward the constructive strategic partnership. In response, the Chinese side reportedly did not reject the idea, but also did not echo the American preference until Jiang Zemin's meeting with President Clinton during the fall 2000 UN session. Jiang's use of the term on that occasion was intended both to punctuate the end of the tensions that followed the Belgrade bombing and also to signal the U.S. public that China would remain interested in working toward a constructive strategic partnership after the Clinton administration left office. For China's press coverage that continued to use the term "strategic partnership" to describe the goal for Sino-American relations, see "Wrap-Up: Jiang Zemin Meets U.S. National Security Adviser"; "Tang, Albright Say Sino-U.S. Ties Can Move Forward; Discuss PNTR, Taiwan, NMD"; Erik Eckholm, "U.S. and Top Chinese Officials Try to Smooth over Differences," p. 7.

key advisers to the Republican Party's nominee, George W. Bush, seized on skepticism about the Democrats' China policy and began to argue that Beijing should be viewed as a strategic competitor rather than a strategic partner.[25]

In China, however, the upshot of the unexpected turbulence in Sino-American relations after 1998 was different and began to reveal the durability of Beijing's commitment to its grand strategy that had emerged in 1996. To be sure, trouble-plagued relations with the United States so soon after the two successful Jiang-Clinton summits did provoke a sharp internal debate. Yet, by late summer 1999, China's top-level leaders had reached a consensus that the strategic vision in which great power partnerships (especially one with the United States) were a central feature must remain in place.

From May through July 1999, China's mass media and foreign policy journals harshly criticized American recklessness and "hegemonic" aspirations. The tight, if imperfect, controls on publication in the PRC and the prominence of the think tanks whose journals produced these arguments both suggested that the views reflected the thinking of at least an important segment of the PRC's top leaders who evidently favored shifting to a more explicitly anti-American line in China's foreign policy.[26] These critics of the existing policy called for a serious reconsideration of Sino-American relations and warned against harboring unreasonable hopes for the widely touted constructive strategic partnership China and the United States claimed to be building. They pointed to a disquieting trend in the United States, where the right wing was said to be assuming dominant influence over American China policy. This trend increased the likelihood of growing tension in bilateral relations as the United States would place greater emphasis on the unacceptability of China's communist dictatorship and the need to prevent a rising China from challenging the United States' position as sole superpower.[27] The United States, it was argued, had actually combined containment and engagement when dealing with both China and Russia since the mid-1990s. At the turn of the century, having successfully enlarged NATO, revised the U.S.-Japan guidelines, and initiated plans for joint Japanese-American development of theater missile defense, the allegedly preferred U.S. strategy to encircle China and Russia was almost in place. Chinese critics of building a partnership with

[25] See Condoleezza Rice, "Campaign 2000—Promoting the National Interest"; "Commenting on Recent U.S. Policy toward China."

[26] On the debate's unusually wide range of views, see David M. Finkelstein, *China Reconsiders Its National Security: 'The Great Peace and Development Debate of 1999'*; Tao Wenzhao, "A Foreign Policy Debate in China after the Tragic Bombing of the Chinese Embassy in Belgrade."

[27] Lu, "Chongxin Shenshi Zhongguo De Anquan Huanjing," p. 60.

the United States asserted that Washington was seeking to ensure a weak China by encouraging its partial disintegration, following the pattern witnessed in the former Soviet Union and Yugoslavia. The United States not only hoped to promote China's internal decay but was also adopting policies toward Taiwan, the Nansha (Spratly) Islands, and Tibet that would hem China in and tie it down. Taiwan would be used to block China's avenues to the east, the Spratlys would be used to control China's access to the Indian Ocean through the Strait of Malacca, and a politically tense Tibet would limit China's ability to replace Russia as a key power in Central Asia.[28]

Defenders of President Jiang's policy rejected this portrayal of U.S. intentions as a caricature based on highlighting the views of only the most extreme American advocates of containing the PRC. Instead they asserted that U.S. foreign policy views were complex and diverse, that Sino-American relations were inherently "mixed" rather than exclusively those typical of friends or enemies, and that this realistic assumption, not naive optimism, had always been the basis for Jiang's effort to build a strategic partnership. Echoing a position put forth by American advocates of preserving constructive bilateral relations with China, Jiang's supporters also warned that a decision to treat the United States as an enemy would risk creating a self-fulfilling prophecy.[29] While they readily conceded that fundamental political differences with the United States and unexpected international events ensured there would be ups and downs in Sino-American relations, they insisted that China's interests would be best served by a strategic partnership that emphasized linkages and contingent cooperation. The confrontational alternative that critics of the partnership policy presented allegedly risked triggering a decisive shift by the United States toward a policy of Cold War–style containment. If this happened, then an outclassed China, like the Soviet Union, would face the prospect of "defeat without fighting."[30]

At the end of an extraordinary, if brief, period of semipublic debate about a central tenet of China's foreign policy, those advocating a shift to a new strategy of "resisting American hegemony" failed to carry the day. Instead, the conclusion that emerged was that the main theme of contemporary interna-

[28] Zhang Wenmu, "Kesuowo Zhanzheng Yu Zhongguo Xin Shiji Anquan Zhanlüe," pp. 3–4.

[29] Ye, "Zhongguo Shixing Daguo Waijiao Zhanlüe Shizai Bixing," p. 8.

[30] Chu Shulong and Wang Zaibang, "Guanyu Guoji Xingshi He Wo Duiwai Zhanlüe Ruogan Zhongda Wenti De Sikao" [Reflections on some important questions about the international situation and our external strategy], p. 21; Willy Wo Lap Lam, "Jiang to Pressure Clinton over Taiwan Stance," p. 1; Cheong Ching, "Cross-Strait Dispute: China Gives Peace a Chance," p. 40.

tional politics remained "peace and development," even if events such as the war in Kosovo and the embassy bombing in Belgrade had tempered the greater optimism that prevailed during the summer of 1998.[31] Therefore, barring a more dramatic shift in circumstances (such as an invasion of China or a bold Taiwanese attempt to declare independence), Beijing's basic foreign policy line would be maintained; economic development essential to China's rise, and efforts to foster the peaceful environment necessary for it, would remain the top national priority. Defenders of this approach had successfully argued that China's hope to increase its international influence required power that must be built on the foundation of a thoroughly modern economy and that such a foundation could be created only by ensuring continued access to trade and investment partners in the U.S.-led advanced industrial community. In short, China's leaders had concluded that it would be counterproductive to forsake their effort toward building the constructive strategic partnership announced at the October 1997 summit.

The different reactions in Beijing and Washington to the troubles that beset bilateral relations after late 1998 are partly explained by a key respect in which they revealed the two sides' different expectations about the partnership they set out to build. The American understanding of a "constructive" relationship included not only the anticipation of growing international cooperation, but also the expectation that in the interest of good relations China's leaders would at least moderate their domestic political practices in ways the United States would find more palatable. American expectations for a political reform payoff from engaging China rose when President Clinton's 1998 state visit included a relatively open discussion of sensitive political issues during an unprecedented live television broadcast of his joint news conference with Jiang Zemin, wide coverage for his speech at Beijing University, and then his participation in a free-wheeling talk radio forum in Shanghai.

---

[31] Finkelstein details the modification of China's view of its security environment, summarizing the position as "three important things had not changed, three had" (*sange bu bian, sange bianhua*). See Finkelstein, *China Reconsiders Its National Security*, pp. 21–23. This view acknowledged that events in the late 1990s served as a reminder of the need to remain on guard against challenges posed by "hegemony and power politics" (the U.S. effort to preserve its dominance, the West's neo-interventionist challenge to the basic principle of sovereignty, and the United States bucking the disarmament trend by increasing defense spending and building missile defenses). But its central conclusion was that the three main international trends on which China's foreign policy had been based had not changed: peace and development remained the main theme; the world was moving toward multipolarity; and the international situation was moving toward relaxation. See Zhou, "Xin Shiji De Guoji Anquan Yu Anquan Zhanlüe," pp. 69–70.

China's expectations were quite different, however. Partnership with the United States was a means for advancing China's own strategic interests, most importantly the national interest in development that would make China a wealthy and strong country. In this view, partnership facilitated cooperation on international issues where China's interests overlapped with or complemented those of the United States, but there was no presumption that international interests were identical, let alone that such cooperation implied a willingness to accommodate one another on domestic matters where differences in political values were acute. Parallel yet distinct interests, for example, led to coordinated efforts to restrain North Korea's missile program. Washington had a strong interest in limiting the capabilities of a "rogue" state; Beijing had a strong interest in eliminating the rationale that Pyongyang was providing for advocates of early U.S. deployment of ballistic missile defenses. Parallel interests also led to joint condemnation of India's nuclear tests in 1998. Washington had a general concern about the integrity of the international nonproliferation regime; Beijing had specific concerns about the potential dangers a rising India could pose, including 1) the possibility that a besieged Pakistan would become more vulnerable to Islamic extremism (with implications for stability in Xinjiang), 2) the possibility of India's strategic alignment with its Russian arms supplier or, more likely, with a politically sympathetic United States, and, most important, 3) the expectation of an enduring Sino-Indian nuclear rivalry fostered by New Delhi's invocation of the China threat justification for its decision to carry out the tests.[32]

But while parallel interests facilitated cooperation, remaining differences limited the steps each side was willing to take to sustain it. Since China's main motive for cultivating a partnership with the United States was to create the international conditions conducive to continued economic development, Beijing was simply not prepared to sacrifice what it saw as an equally essential domestic condition necessary for growth—the political stability it associated with one-party communist rule. Beijing's understanding of strategic partnership was a relationship both sides viewed as important enough to sustain de-

---

[32] Zhang Wenmu, "Heshihou Nanya Xingshi Ji Zouxiang" [The situation and trends in post–nuclear test South Asia], pp. 46–49. China was especially disturbed by the Indian claim that it needed a nuclear deterrent against China inasmuch as the tests came at a time of general improvement in Sino-Indian relations. Author's interviews, Beijing, June–July 1998. The Indian tests also triggered Chinese fears about a possible U.S.-India-China triangle in which the United States and India both seek leverage over China (Zhou, "Xin Shiji De Guoji Anquan Yu Anquan Zhanlüe," p. 70; Peng Shujie and Liu Yunfei, "News Analysis: Partnership Promotes China's All-around Diplomacy").

spite areas of deep disagreement. China's leaders, therefore, believed it would be possible to simultaneously cultivate closer diplomatic, economic, and military ties with the United States while rejecting Washington's criticisms about their suppression of democratic activists and independent religious groups that the CCP saw as a threat to the "unity and stability" essential during the country's controlled march along the developmental road to becoming a modern great power.[33]

With conflicting expectations about the nature of their embryonic strategic partnership, each side was disturbed by the other's failure to abide by what it believed were the basic ground rules. In the United States, few critics of the Clinton administration seriously questioned the importance of somehow remaining engaged with PRC. But as political changes that the United States hoped to see within China failed to materialize and Beijing instead seemed to defiantly tighten its political grip at home, American support for the idea of a "strategic partnership" that was being criticized as unrealistic, naive, and overblown eroded. By comparison, among the small group of relatively insulated Communist Party leaders who determine China's foreign policy, support for working toward a constructive strategic partnership with the United States remained strong despite the string of problems that rocked bilateral relations after the summer of 1998—renewed American criticism of China's human rights record: the release of the Cox Committee report leveling charges of extensive Chinese espionage in the United States; the double embarrassment for Premier Zhu Rongji of first having the proposed terms for China's accession to WTO that he carried with him to Washington in April 1999 rejected, and then having these major concessions to the United States leaked in the American media before he even returned to China; and, finally, the May 1999 American bombing of the Chinese embassy in Belgrade.[34]

---

[33] See Swaine and Tellis, *Interpreting China's Grand Strategy*, pp. 9–20, chapter 2. Some Chinese analysts noted, however, that post–Cold War cooperation lacked the strong incentive of a powerful common enemy that had tempered Sino-American disagreements rooted in ideology, culture, and domestic politics during the last two decades of the Cold War. See Ye, "Zhongguo Shixing Daguo Waijiao Zhanlüe Shizai Bixing," p. 7; Chen Demin, "90 Niandai Zhongmei Guanxi Tanxi" [A preliminary analysis of Sino-American relations in the 1990s], pp. 20–24; Jin Canrong, "Zhongmei Guanxi De Bian Yu Bubian" [What's changed and what hasn't changed in Sino-American relations], pp. 21–25.

[34] In China's view, other "harmful actions" the United States had undertaken even prior to the Belgrade bombing included: termination of Sino-American satellite launches and tightening of the limitations on technology transfers to China; continued U.S. arms sales to Taiwan; criticism of legitimate annual PLA exercises in the Taiwan Strait; and ratcheting up the demands for concessions before China would be permit-

To be sure, these troubling events (especially the embassy bombing) did spur the vigorous Chinese debate in mid-1999 that included calls for shifting to a new line emphasizing straightforward opposition to American hegemony, perhaps by uniting closely with Russia and the developing world.[35] By late summer 1999, however, a consensus had formed rejecting such a change in China's grand strategy. While China's leaders embraced the internal critics' more suspicious view of U.S. intentions, they also acknowledged that the other important lessons of its military action in Yugoslavia were that the American advantage in relative capabilities was proving remarkably robust, that not even the Russians could effectively stand in the way if Washington wanted to act, and, therefore, that the transition to a multipolar world would take even longer than previously anticipated.[36] Under such circumstances, China's own interests led them back to the seemingly inescapable conclusion that there was no feasible substitute for developing a positive working relationship with the United States.

At the August 1999 top-level party meeting at Beidaihe, Jiang Zemin "defended his two-year-old decision to seek a 'constructive strategic partnership' with the United States," though he wrapped the substance in a more defiant style that also "stressed China would never give up its principles for such a goal."[37] In part his reaffirmation of policy reflected the bracing realities of rela-

---

ted to accede to the WTO (Lu, "Chongxin Shenshi Zhongguo De Anquan Huanjing," p. 60). When the bombing of the Chinese embassy in Belgrade was piled on top of these problems, events "barely escaped spinning out of control" (Fang Hua, "Yatai Anquan Jiagou De Xianzhuang, Qushi Ji Zhongguo De Zuoyong" [The current Asia-Pacific security framework: Trends and China's role], p. 13).

[35] Author's interviews, Beijing, March–April 2000. For the argument that China should lose no time allying with Russia, see Zhou, "Xin Shiji De Guoji Anquan Yu Anquan Zhanlüe," p. 71; See also Pillsbury's reference to He Xin's call for a strong effort to form an anti-U.S. coalition (Pillsbury, *China Debates the Future Security Environment*, p. xl).

[36] This view began to emerge along with the recognition of the continued strength of the U.S. economy during the mid-1990s, but became widespread in the wake of the U.S. military performance in Kosovo, Afghanistan, and Iraq. Even so, Chinese analysts continued to argue that current trends represented only a temporary delay in the allegedly inevitable transition to multipolarity. The trend toward multipolarity had not been reversed, but the process is now seen as more complex, tortuous, and long-term. See Pillsbury, *China Debates the Future Security Environment*, pp. 13–15, 25, 27–28, 58; Xiao Feng, "Dui Guoji Xingshizhong Jige Redian Wenti De Kanfa" [Perspective on several hot issues in the international situation], p. 3; also Ni Jianmin, "Opportunities Are Greater Than Challenges in the Present International Environment"; Chu and Wang, "Guanyu Guoji Xingshi He Wo Duiwai Zhanlüe Ruogan Zhongda Wenti De Sikao," p. 17.

[37] "'Source' Says PRC to Pressure U.S. over Taiwan Issue"; author's interviews, Beijing, March–April, October 2000. China's modernization purportedly required

tive military power and the enduring economic importance of the United States for China's modernization. In part, however, it was a reaction to newly troublesome developments that occurred on the Taiwan front during the summer of 1999, even as the debate about the future of Sino-American relations raged in China. This new round of tension over Taiwan had served to underscore the continuing strategic importance of the United States for China's management of cross-strait relations, a matter that Beijing publicly and privately emphasized was one of its principal national security concerns.[38]

In July 1999 Taiwan's president, Lee Teng-hui, had publicly floated the idea that ties with the PRC should be characterized as "special state-to-state" relations, a new stance that ostensibly inched the island further in the direction of independence and that predictably elicited strong criticism from the mainland.[39] Cross-strait tension increased, and some worried that the militarized minicrisis of 1995–96 might be replayed. Occurring little more than a month after the U.S. bombing of the Chinese embassy in Belgrade, which strained ties between Beijing and Washington to the breaking point, the situation certainly seemed to have the potential to drive a final nail in the coffin of the Sino-American strategic partnership. In the event, the Clinton administration's carefully calculated reaction actually contributed to the PRC's decision to salvage it. President Clinton reiterated the long-standing U.S. preference for peace and stability in the Taiwan Strait. He also sent envoys to both Beijing and Taipei who urged Beijing to act with restraint and warned Taipei that there were limits to the conditions under which it could count on support from Washington. On balance the United States tacitly placed the onus for renewed tension on Lee Teng-hui, increased pressure on Taiwan to deny its intention to pursue independence, and created the opportunity for Beijing to appear responsible and moderate if only it limited itself to rhetorical salvos. With another presidential election on Taiwan looming in March 2000 and the

---

both resisting interference from and avoiding confrontation with the United States. The best way to accomplish both was to pursue a constructive strategic partnership that combined "struggle with cooperation" and helped limit the anti-China tendency in the United States that might otherwise lead it to engage in an all-out Cold War–style policy of containment aimed at China (Chu and Wang, "Guanyu Guoji Xingshi He Wo Duiwai Zhanlüe Ruogan Zhongda Wenti De Sikao," p. 21; Sun Jianshe, "Shiji Zhijiao Dui Woguo Anquan Huanjing De Sikao" [Reflections on our country's security environment at the turn of the century], pp. 21, 22).

[38] See "China's National Defence in 2000"; "Five-Year Draft Plan Depicts Further Development."

[39] See "President Lee's Deutsche Welle Interview." For the many interpretations, clarifications, and criticisms his statement provoked, see also the articles and papers collected in "Cross-Strait Tension: 'Special State-to-State.'"

possibility of an even more serious crisis if the election's winner were a candidate committed to independence, China could ill afford to sacrifice the sort of leverage its working relationship with the United States seemed to provide. In short, writing off the strategic partnership with the United States would not only complicate China's ability to enjoy the full fruits of participation in the international economy and clearly put China in the crosshair of an incomparably more powerful U.S. military. It would also free the United States to further upgrade its security ties with Taiwan (and Japan) since there would no longer be valued links with Beijing on matters such as proliferation or Korea that Washington would be putting at risk.

By the time the CCP's top leaders gathered for their annual policy review in August 1999, then, they had concluded that working toward a strategic partnership with the United States created linkages that still served a rising China's interests not only in economic development, but also in national unification. Cultivating an American partnership therefore would remain a central feature of the country's foreign policy.[40] Nevertheless, China's leaders had become more sensitive to the internal criticism that had surfaced in 1999 from those who worried about the potentially disruptive consequences of further exposing the country to the forces of globalization, as well as from those who preferred a more bluntly coercive Taiwan policy and a tougher line on the United States. Wary of charges that he was too willing to accommodate the United States, Jiang not only employed somewhat more fiery rhetoric, but he also moved very deliberately in repairing frayed relations with Washington.[41] Initiated in September 1999, the process dragged on for the better part of a year.

Halting Progress

Once they had decided not to forsake pursuit of the strategic partnership, in their subsequent meetings with top American officials China's leaders began to reaffirm that constructing such ties was the goal of bilateral relations. The first clear signals came at the informal Jiang-Clinton talks during the Auckland APEC meetings in September 1999.[42] Over the next nine months a succession

[40] On the CCP leaders' recognition of the need to clearly signal the United States that continued cooperation required Washington's help in trying to rein in Taiwan's Lee Teng-hui, see "'Source' Says PRC to Pressure U.S. over Taiwan Issue."

[41] On China's limited willingness to compromise in order to foster the strategic partnership, see Khalilzad et al., *The United States and a Rising China: Strategic and Military Implications*, pp. 5–9.

[42] See Xu Hongzhi and Huang Qing, "Advancing toward Multipolarization Amid Turbulence," p. 7. At the Auckland meeting between Clinton and Jiang, Clinton reportedly also invoked the term "constructive strategic partnership," but he paired this

of senior American leaders visited Beijing and conveyed the U.S. president's continuing commitment to building a constructive strategic partnership with China.[43] By early summer 2000, the effort to recast bilateral relations initiated in October 1997 seemed back on track, in part benefiting from a relaxation in tensions that followed the Clinton administration's quiet efforts to discourage Taiwan's new president Chen Shui-bian from acting on his party's independence platform after he won the March 2000 elections.[44]

In June, U.S. secretary of state Madeleine Albright met with China's foreign minister Qian Qichen and again endorsed the idea of working toward a "constructive strategic partnership." Qian responded by agreeing that the decision of both countries "to commit themselves to establishing a constructive strategic partnership is of vital importance for the maintenance of peace and stability in the Asia-Pacific region, and the world at large."[45] Albright's visit was followed in July 2000 by a visit from U.S. defense secretary William Cohen that advanced efforts to restore the military exchanges envisioned as a central feature of the partnership. And finally, after a year of such relatively quiet diplomacy aimed at getting Sino-American relations back on track, Jiang Zemin gave the clearest public signals that China would remain interested in working toward a constructive strategic partnership even after President Clinton left office. At Beidaihe in mid-August, President Jiang told the TV journalist Mike Wallace that he believed "whoever becomes the President of the United States [after the 2000 elections], he will try to improve Sino-U.S. relations, for this is in the strategic interest of the whole world," and that "as the new century approaches, it is imperative to 'build towards a constructive strategic partnership' between China and the United States."[46] Soon

---

with an insistence on the need to "pay attention to results" and to have "clarity about objectives," phrases that China saw as his attempt to cater to more conservative opinion in the United States that had become harshly critical of his China policy. See Ding Kuisong, "Zongjie Guoqu, Mianxiang Weilai—Ping Zhongmei Guanxi 50 Nian" [Summing up the past, facing that future—Evaluating 50 years of Sino-American relations], pp. 12–13.

[43] "PRC's Qian Qichen, Talbott Discuss Bilateral Ties, Taiwan"; "Xinhua 'Wrap-up': Jiang Zemin Meets U.S. Envoy Holbrooke"; "Comparison—PRC FM Holds Talks with Berger on Taiwan."

[44] Chapter 8 considers additional implications of the March 2000 election in Taiwan.

[45] "PRC Vice-Premier Qian Qichen Meets Albright on Sino-U.S. Ties, Taiwan Issue." See also Chen Jian, "Jiang Zemin Talks with Former U.S. President George Bush in Beijing on March 2 about Bilateral Ties, WTO"; Tong Ying, "PRC Expert Views U.S. Elections, Explains Why Beijing Feels Relieved"; "Sino-U.S. Military Exchanges Resume Gradually."

[46] "Jiang Zemin on Sino-U.S. Relations in CBS Interview."

thereafter, on the eve of the September 2000 Millennium Summit in New York, Jiang delivered a major speech to an American audience in which he asserted, "Both the Chinese and U.S. governments should . . . jointly dedicate ourselves to build a constructive strategic partnership between China and the United States that is oriented toward the 21st century."[47]

China's recommitment to a Sino-American partnership was soon tested again, however, following the election of George W. Bush as president of the United States. Beijing's initial anxiety about possible changes in China policy under the new American administration had been based on the Bush campaign's rhetoric about China as "a rival" or "competitor" rather than a "partner." This concern intensified when the newly elected president's key appointees included individuals believed to favor a U.S. security policy more explicitly hedging against a potential challenge from China. General unease about a possible shift in U.S. policy toward China soon gave way to specific tensions. During the first quarter of 2001, Beijing raised strong objections to reports that the Bush administration planned to authorize a robust package of arms sales to Taiwan, possibly including advanced destroyers that could become components of an integrated theater missile defense covering the Taiwan Strait.[48] Although the question of increased U.S. arms sales to Taiwan was an issue that both sides had already anticipated would cause friction between the new American administration and China, before that dispute was fully played out it was supplanted by an entirely unexpected and unusually sharp confrontation following the April 1 mid-air collision between a U.S. EP-3 reconnaissance aircraft and a Chinese fighter jet. The collision had resulted in the death of the Chinese pilot and the detention of the American crew on Hainan Island. Beijing and Washington then found themselves in a tense standoff about the fate of the plane and its crew that dragged on for twelve days while the two sides searched for a resolution that would allow both to save face.[49]

Cooler heads ultimately prevailed, and a carefully worded American apology was traded for the release of the crew and the promised return of the aircraft. But Sino-American relations seemed to be on a downward spiral. Shortly after the crew's return, the Bush administration formally announced the arms package it would approve for sale to Taiwan and the president publicly stated his personal interpretation of the U.S. obligation to do "whatever it took to

[47] See "Jiang Zemin on Sino-US Ties, Taiwan, WTO, Tibet."
[48] "PRC FM Tang Jiaxuan Warns U.S. Arms Sales to Taiwan Endanger Sino-U.S. Relations."
[49] See Cindy Sui, "More on U.S. Spy Plane Crew Leaves China after 12 Days in Captivity."

help Taiwan defend herself."[50] In reaction, some in China again argued that these inauspicious events during the first months of the new administration demonstrated that "struggle and opposing hegemony" rather than "peace and development" should become the central theme of China's foreign policy. By early summer, however, those who had resisted similar arguments in 1999 prevailed once more. As in late 1999, the United States and China began the process of working to get Sino-American relations back on track.

In June 2001, visiting U.S. trade representative Robert Zoellick indicated to his Chinese hosts that the Bush administration was interested in avoiding a further deterioration of the relationship. In July, Secretary of State Colin Powell visited Beijing and, along with China's premier, Zhu Rongji, expressed the hope that it would be possible "to develop" a relationship that is "constructive" and "cooperative."[51] If such surprisingly warm messages to China over the summer reflected a split on the future direction of China policy within the Bush administration (often portrayed as divided between the preferences of the Defense and State Departments), the terrorist strikes of September 11 and the reordering of American priorities that resulted resolved it in favor of the position that Secretary Powell had articulated. When Foreign Minister Tang Jiaxuan visited Washington in late September to discuss joint efforts in the struggle against terrorism, he returned to the rhetoric about "a constructive relationship of cooperation with the United States" that had been vetted in July.[52] And, most important, at the October 2001 APEC summit in

[50] Phil Chetwynd, "China Slams U.S. Arms Sales to Taiwan as Bush Talks Tough."

[51] My Chinese interlocutors insisted that Zoellick's visit was the turning point that put bilateral relations back on a positive trajectory (author's interviews, Shanghai, June 2001). See also "U.S., China Steer Clear of Collision"; Wang Yichao and Wang Jian, "U.S. Trade Representative Praises China's Economic Achievements." The clearest sign that China had decided the Zoellick visit opened a new chapter was Foreign Minister Tang's phone call to Secretary of State Powell shortly afterward in which he stated that "China attaches importance to its relations with the United States and hopes to forge constructive and cooperative relations [*jian she xing he zuo guan xi*] with the United States" ("Tang Jiaxuan Tells Powell PRC Wants 'Constructive,' 'Cooperative' Ties with U.S."). On Powell's July 2001 visit to Beijing, during which "constructive and cooperative relationship" became the new, politically acceptable phrase to describe the Sino-American partnership, see "Premier Zhu Rongji Meets Powell: Cooperation between China, U.S. Conducive to Both"; "China, U.S. Underline Constructive Ties."

[52] See "U.S. Vice President Meets with Visiting Chinese FM"; "PRC: Tang Jiaxuan Meets with Dick Cheney, Terrorism, Ties Discussed." While some analysts identify 9/11 as a turning point in U.S.-China relations that would otherwise have continued to deteriorate, this analysis suggests that the terrorist strikes on the United States catalyzed or accelerated, rather than triggered, a process of rapprochement that was already underway earlier in the summer of 2001.

Shanghai, Presidents Bush and Jiang both openly endorsed the new preferred formulation for describing Sino-American ties. President Jiang stated that "China stands ready to make joint efforts with the U.S. side to develop a constructive and cooperative relationship." President Bush indicated that the United States seeks "a relationship that is candid, constructive and cooperative," notably adding the third "c" word almost certainly to differentiate his present effort at recasting Sino-American relations from the attempt at building a strategic partnership associated with President Clinton. Bush's amended formulation was intended to alert American and Chinese audiences that although a constructive relationship facilitating cooperation on matters of common interest (terrorism, but also international trade and investment, nonproliferation, transnational crime, public health, and the global environment) was desirable, he would not refrain from forthrightly disagreeing with China about issues on which serious differences remain (especially human rights and the American relationship with Taiwan).[53]

Despite the frictions that had complicated ties with United States during the last years of the Clinton administration, and despite the tensions that seemed to confirm Beijing's concerns about the direction in which the new Bush team might take American China policy, by the end of 2001 the logic of a strategy that required nurturing relations with the United States remained compelling for China's leaders (even if American domestic politics precluded sticking with the term "strategic partnership"). A confrontational relationship with the United States would not only complicate the PRC's ability to enjoy the full fruits of participation in the international economy and forfeit the benefits Beijing derived from the linkages that partnership established. It would also unequivocally cast China as the adversary of an American military that was expected to remain incomparably more powerful than the PLA for the foreseeable future. Therefore, however difficult the process, China's leaders recommitted themselves to cultivating the sort of constructive and extensive bilateral ties with the United States that their grand strategy's emphasis on great power partnerships demanded.

China's Other Major Partners

As part of a strategy to establish linkages that reduce the likelihood it would confront a broad coalition united by hostility toward China, after April 1996

---

[53] Mike Allen and Philip P. Pan, "China Vows to Help in Terror Fight; in Shanghai, Jiang Offers Bush Support"; Gerard Baker, "Jiang and Bush Try for a Fresh Start"; "Wen Wei Po Views Results of Jiang Zemin-Bush Talks"; Avery Goldstein, "September 11, the Shanghai Summit, and the Shift in U.S. China Policy."

Beijing also intensified its efforts to build partnerships with other countries it expected to emerge as great powers and with regional organizations that it thought might become comparably influential actors in a future multipolar world.[54] The ties forged with key European states as well as the EU, Japan, India, and ASEAN were similar to the partnerships formed with Russia and the United States insofar as they entailed the lure of mutually beneficial economic arrangements and the promise of constructive efforts to address common international concerns. But, with the exception of the most recent links with ASEAN, Beijing did not initially label these "strategic" partnerships because their immediate effects on international security were expected to be less significant.[55] China instead chose distinct labels for each partnership: "long-term comprehensive partnership" for France, "comprehensive cooperative partnership" for Britain, "trustworthy partnership" for Germany, "long-term stable and constructive partnership" with the EU, "friendly and cooperative partnership" with Japan, and "long-term constructive and cooperative partnership" with India.[56]

China and Europe

Because China recognized that a united Europe with a common foreign policy remained a goal rather than a reality, it hedged its bets by simultaneously cultivating separate partnerships with Europe's three leading states (France, Britain, and Germany) as well as with the supranational institutions of the

[54] China established partnerships with a few countries in addition to those described below, but these were not as widely touted and are less relevant to Beijing's strategic interest in using such partnerships to court what it sees as the most influential actors in a future multipolar world. Indeed, China first used the term "strategic partnership" in 1993 in discussions with Brazil, though the words did not yet carry the connotation they acquired after 1996. See "Tang Jiaxuan Meets with Brazilian Foreign Minister"; "China, Brazil Issue Joint Communiqué." On the use of partnership to describe other bilateral ties, see "Jiang Zemin Sees 'Rich Fruit' from Sino-Pakistani Relations"; "China, Pakistan Highlight Cooperation in Beijing"; "ROK's Kim: Partnership with PRC Helps Peace, Stability"; "PRC, ROK Issue Joint Statement on Building 'All-Round' Cooperative Partnership"; Luo Qinwen, "Hu Jintao Meets with Canadian Prime Minister Jean Chrétien."

[55] In some cases (France, Britain, and the EU), however, and without the formal declarations that accompanied their initiation, Beijing has begun to emphasize the strategic nature of these partnerships as well. See note 58 below.

[56] See Xue Longgen, "Zhengzai Shenhua Fazhan De Zhongfa Quanmian Huoban Guanxi" [The deepening and developing Sino-French comprehensive partnership], p. 26; Zhang Zhenan, "British Vice Prime Minister Meets Chi Haotian"; Tan Guoqi, "Li Peng Meets French Delegation"; Qian Tong and Li Mingjiang, "Jiang Zemin Meets German Vice Chancellor in Beijing."

EU.[57] The lure of upgrading bilateral relations with China and especially an interest in improving economic relations induced first France (1997) and then each of the other key European powers to adopt a more accommodating posture toward the PRC on human rights policy, on the Taiwan dispute, and on the conditions for China's trade with Europe.[58] While China established these partnerships with France, Britain, and Germany, the tempo of China's efforts to build links with the EU also accelerated.

With great fanfare the first China-EU summit was held in April 1998 (labeled the beginning of "a new era" in relations with China). Premier Zhu Rongji made a highly publicized tour of Europe that ended with the announcement that "Beijing agreed to give the EU privileged partner status in

[57] "Prospects of China's Diplomatic Activities in 1998." Chinese analysts, like their foreign counterparts, seem to have a wide variety of views about Europe's political future, specifically the likelihood that the EU will ever develop a common foreign and security policy. In the interim, France and Germany are usually viewed as important international powers in their own right. Britain, though arguably the most militarily capable of the three major European nation-states, is often viewed as simply following the American lead (author's interviews, Beijing, June–July 1998).

[58] At what was arguably the peak of optimism about the prospective payoff from the great power partnerships, one Chinese analysis asserted that the Europeans' wooing of China reflected the growing realization of its central international role and economic attractiveness. See Wang Xingqiao, "A Positive Step Taken by the European Union to Promote Relations with China"; also Peng and Liu, "News Analysis: Partnership Promotes China's All-around Diplomacy"; Han Hua, "Four Keys in 1998 Chinese Diplomacy"; "Editorial: Great Success in China's Big-Nation Diplomacy"; "China's International Status Is in the Ascendance"; "Diplomatic News Highlights for 23–29 Oct." On China's partnership with France, see "Presidents Jiang and Chirac Agree to Build 'Comprehensive Partnership'"; Xue, "Zhengzai Shenhua Fazhan De Zhongfa Quanmian Huoban Guanxi," p. 26; "French Support Needed on Taiwan Issue: Official"; "'Full Text' of Joint Declaration of China and France—Deepen the Comprehensive Strategic Partnership (Quan Mian Zhan Lue Huo Ban Guan Xi) between China and France and Build a World That Is Safer, More Respectful of Diversity, and More United"; "China, France Vow to Boost Partnership." On the Sino-British partnership, see Huang Xingwei, "Roundup: Sino-British Relations Develop Steadily"; "Text of China-UK Joint Statement on Strategic Partnership." Relations with Germany, in particular, fulfilled Beijing's expectations for its great power partnerships, eliciting German praise for "the positive role that China is playing in world affairs" and encouraging Berlin's deference to Beijing's sensitivity about governmental ties with or arms sales to Taiwan. Yet Beijing has been slow to label Sino-German ties strategic, instead linking them closely with the strategic partnership emerging with the EU. See Si Jiuyue and Huang Yong, "Zhu Rongji Meets German Chancellor, Addresses Industry-Trade Council"; "China, Germany to Establish Partnership of Global Responsibility"; "Premier Wen Jiabao Holds Talks with German Chancellor Gerhard Schroeder."

line with the United States."[59] And on April 28, 1998, the EU reciprocated by announcing that it had "adopted a proposal to remove the label of 'non–market economy' previously applying to Chinese products in its antidumping policy," which should result in "much fairer treatment" for "enterprises oper-ating in China."[60] On June 29, 1998, the EU announced plans "to intensify high-level contacts, including possible annual summits," and ratified a new China policy. This approval of a new China policy "establishing a com-prehensive partnership with China" originally submitted by the EU Council in March 1998 occurred just as the United States and China were firming up their bilateral ties during President Clinton's June 1998 state visit. The Chi-nese media, conveying confidence in the wisdom of the new approach to dealing with major powers, portrayed the timing not as coincidental but rather as evidence that the United States and EU were competing for in-fluence with an increasingly indispensable China.[61] During a follow-up visit to China in October 1998, European Commission president Jacques Santer fully embraced the Chinese locution and emphasized the need "to design and give full importance to a Sino-European partnership into the next millen-nium."[62]

The regular flow of visits to Europe by China's top three leaders (Jiang Zemin, Li Peng, and Zhu Rongji) at the end of the 1990s suggested that Bei-jing anticipated treating the Europeans as a virtual strategic partner, limited only by doubts about the EU's ability to speak with a weighty single voice in international affairs.[63] Such reservations notwithstanding, in the opening years

[59] "Chinese Premier's First European Trip Crowned with Glory."

[60] "EU Adopts New Anti-Dumping Rules for China." See also "China and EU to Step up Dialogue, May Hold Annual Summits." Comments at the second Asia-Europe Meetings (ASEM) in April 1998 indicated substantial progress in developing Sino-European ties in the two years since Premier Li Peng's general discussion of an Asian-European partnership at the first ASEM in March 1996 in Bangkok, Thailand. See Ren Xin, "1996: A Year of Diplomatic Feats for China."

[61] "China's International Status Is in the Ascendance."

[62] "European Union Calls for New Partnership with China." See also "President Jiang Zemin to Tour Italy, Switzerland, Austria Next March"; Wang, "A Positive Step Taken by the European Union to Promote Relations with China."

[63] Some in China envisioned the blossoming Sino-European partnership as a potential counterbalance to U.S. dominance, particularly on economic affairs, as multi-polarity emerged. See Huang Qing, "Ya'ou Huiyi He Duojihua" [ASEM and multi-polarization]. Michael Pillsbury notes that some Chinese analysts saw the effort to ele-vate the EU's role on the international stage as a way in which China, rather than remaining passive, could "assist the trend toward multipolarity and increase its pace." See Pillsbury, *China Debates the Future Security Environment*, p. 54.

of the twenty-first century China's EU partnership deepened, and by the Sixth China-EU Summit in 2003, the two sides issued a joint statement citing its "growing strategic nature" and commended one another for issuing policy papers that "promote the development of an overall strategic partnership between China and the EU."[64] Shortly thereafter, France took the lead in encouraging the EU to lift its embargo on arms sales to China imposed after the 1989 crackdown in Beijing. Continuing European objections to China's record on human rights, as well as American concerns that China might one day use European arms against either Taiwan or U.S. forces deployed to the Taiwan Strait, limited the prospects for a true end to the embargo. But with France, Germany, and finally Britain endorsing a change in the EU's arms policy, the debate symbolized the rising European interest in sustaining a healthy relationship with Beijing, precisely the sort of change China envisions from its partnerships.[65]

China and Japan

In comparison to its ties with Europe, China's relationship with Japan advanced more slowly under the new strategy. The lag certainly did not reflect a lower priority accorded relations with Japan. On the contrary, Japan loomed much larger than Europe on China's strategic radar screen. But Japan did not yet play an international role commensurate with its capabilities, and China remained nervous about taking steps that might encourage Japan to depart from its familiar role as a limited, constrained junior ally of the United States. As a result, Beijing's approach to a partnership with Japan remained distinctly ambivalent. In 1997, even as China was celebrating smooth cooperation with Britain in the reversion of Hong Kong to Chinese rule and was issuing joint statements with President Chirac of France about shared interests in building a multipolar world, Beijing was still expressing displeasure with what it saw as signs of an anti-China undercurrent in Japan—including renewed controversy

---

[64] "Sixth China-EU Summit Issues Joint Press Statement." See also "China's EU Policy Paper"; Wu Liming, "Hu Jintao Meets with EU Leaders"; "China-EU Partnership Is of Great Significance, Premier Wen Says"; "China, EU Developing 'Mature Partnership'"; "China Calls for Deepening of Strategic Partnership with EU."

[65] See Judy Dempsey, "Chirac Urges EU Leaders to Lift Arms Embargo Imposed on Beijing in 1989"; Raphael Minder, "Rebuff for French Call on China Embargo"; David Shambaugh, "Lifting the China Arms Ban Is Only Symbolic"; Josephine Ma, "Wen Heads Home after Charm Offensive; Visit Helps Cement Sino-EU Trade Ties, but Premier Fails to Get Arms Embargo Lifted or to Secure Market-Economy Status"; Philip Webster, Roland Watson, and Charles Bremner, "Britain Aims to Lift Arms Ban on China."

about the disputed Diaoyu (Senkaku) Islands, thinly veiled China threat references inserted in Tokyo's Defense White Papers, and especially the revised
guidelines for the U.S.-Japan security relationship.[66] At the same time, however, Beijing was also suggesting that Tokyo's self-interest would best be
served by fostering better bilateral relations with China. In particular, Japan
faced an increasingly competitive global economy, with the spreading Asian
financial crisis after summer 1997 compounding the challenges already confronting a stagnant Japan.[67] Under these circumstances, Beijing anticipated that
its partnership strategy could provide it with substantial leverage; Japan would
seek to improve bilateral ties or it would run the risk of losing out as the
Europeans and Americans seized opportunities in the China market.[68]

In 1998, as the twentieth anniversary of the Sino-Japanese Peace and
Friendship Treaty loomed, Beijing predicted that "the two sides will construct
from the high plane of orienting to the 21st Century a new framework of relations of the two big neighboring nations."[69] Yet, because of the historical
legacy of Sino-Japanese animosity and because China believed that Japan either could not or should not play a leadership role on most international-
strategic matters, in the late 1990s Beijing reportedly resisted Tokyo's suggestions that a joint statement be issued labeling their increasingly extensive bilateral ties a strategic partnership.[70] Given China's long-standing conviction that

[66] Zhang Guocheng, "Riben De Daguo Waijiao" [Japan's great power diplomacy].
These objections to the Defense White Papers dated to 1996: "This year, Japan has
trumpeted more flagrantly than ever the so-called 'China threat,' and claimed for the
first time that 'attention must be paid to trends in the Chinese military.' Its 1996 Defense White Paper said China has been 'modernizing its nuclear strike capability as well
as its naval and air forces, expanding activities at sea, and conducted military exercises
in the Taiwan Strait which has heightened tensions there'" (Da Jun, "True Threat
Comes from Those Trumpeting 'China Threat.'")

[67] See Avery Goldstein, "The Political Implications of a Slowdown."

[68] See Liu Di, "Deng Xiaoping's Thinking on Diplomatic Work—Interview with
Liang Shoude, Dean for College of International Relations for Beijing University."
See also "Editorial: Great Success in China's Big-Nation Diplomacy."

[69] "Prospects of China's Diplomatic Activities in 1998"; also Shi Nangen, "1997: A
Fruitful Year in China's Multi-Dimensional Diplomacy," pp. 6–8.

[70] Most of my interlocutors continue to insist on the importance of increasingly
distant historical events that bred a lack of trust limiting the improvement in Sino-
Japanese relations. One expert, well informed about the Sino-Japanese negotiations,
indicated that, at least during the late 1990s, China preferred some alternative to the
term "strategic" to describe a Sino-Japanese partnership. China and Japan ultimately
agreed to use the term "friendly and cooperative partnership" (author's interviews,
Beijing, June–July 1998). On the historical legacy of Sino-Japanese tensions, see also

Japan's aggressive behavior in the past is a reliable guide to its future inclinations, as well as the high priority Beijing assigns to the Taiwan issue, in 1998 China's asking price for establishing a Sino-Japanese partnership was apparently a more convincing display of contrition for Japan's actions in China during World War II and ironclad assurances that Tokyo would not become involved in any future Taiwan Strait crisis. China's leaders may have thought that an economically troubled Japan, needing a viable partner in the region, would so covet improved ties that it would be willing to accommodate Beijing's desire for an unvarnished apology for its aggression against China during World War II and for clear limitations (excluding Taiwan contingencies) on possible Japanese support for future U.S. military operations in the "peripheral areas of the Far East" under the terms of the revised U.S.-Japan security guidelines. Japan's leaders, however, resisted.

As the two sides prepared for a November 1998 Sino-Japanese summit in Tokyo, Prime Minister Obuchi indicated he would not agree to issue a formal written apology for Imperial Japan's aggression against China. In his meetings with President Jiang Zemin, Obuchi refused to go beyond previous public expressions of regret for Japan's wartime role in China.[71] Japanese interlocutors familiar with the internal and bilateral negotiations prior to Jiang's visit gave two reasons for the prime minister's somewhat surprising decision not to offer China's president the sort of explicit public apology he had just given South Korea's president Kim Dae-jung. First, on several different occasions Japanese leaders had expressed remorse to the Chinese about Japan's behavior during World War II, something that they had not yet done for their Korean neighbors. Second, and arguably more important, Korea's Kim had promised in advance that an appropriately worded apology would be accepted as finally closing the book on that chapter of history. By contrast, the Chinese were unwilling to offer such a promise, convincing leaders in Tokyo that no matter how explicit and sincere the apology, their Chinese counterparts would never be satisfied and consider the matter resolved. Instead, it would be reintroduced whenever Beijing found it convenient.[72]

On the matter of revised security guidelines with the United States, Japan's leaders also refused to go beyond their existing Taiwan policy that recognized Beijing as the sole government of China or to offer promises about actions

---

Thomas J. Christensen, "China, the U.S.-Japan Alliance, and the Security Dilemma in East Asia."

[71] "RMRB Article Warns Japan against 'Hurting' China, Ties with History, Taiwan."

[72] Author's interviews, Tokyo, March 1999.

they might decide to take in unforeseeable future circumstances. Prior to President Jiang's trip to Tokyo, the Japanese Foreign Ministry clearly indicated that there would be no strengthening of Japan's noninterventionist commitments regarding Taiwan, or even any endorsement of the "three noes" regarding limits on support for Taiwan that President Clinton had articulated during his summer 1998 visit to China.[73]

The upshot of the tough bargaining that characterized the run-up to the talks was that the summit ended with no ceremony to sign a communiqué. Instead, in a postsummit speech Jiang simply announced that the two countries had "agreed that we should establish a friendly and cooperative partnership in which we make efforts together for peace and development."[74] Observers immediately characterized the Chinese president's visit to Japan a disappointment that stood in sharp contrast with Jiang's highly publicized successes on recent state visits to other countries.[75]

Yet what appeared at the time to be a potentially significant setback in Sino-Japanese relations turned out to be small and temporary. Indeed, in substance if not in name, bilateral ties continued to develop most of the characteristics of a strategic partnership: extensive economic ties, regular summit meetings (including reciprocal visits by top government officials), and even military-to-military exchanges. Chinese premier Zhu Rongji's visit to Japan in October 2000 seemed to represent a renewed effort to boost the partnership and to mute some of the problems that had marred Jiang's 1998 trip. As one commentary previewing the trip noted, "If we say that President Jiang's visit to Japan two years ago has charted the direction for Sino-Japanese relations in the 21st century, then Premier Zhu's upcoming visit to Japan will certainly be injecting new vitality into bilateral economic and trade cooperation and will

[73] Willy Wo-Lap Lam, "China, Japan Struggle on Accord; Leaders Fail to Sign Joint Statement after Disagreement over Apology for War Atrocities"; "Japan Rejects Any Chinese Pressure Over Taiwan." For the continuing tension in China's approach to Japan, compare "Japan, China Agree on Mutual Visits by Warships: Report" and "China Wary of U.S.-Japan Military Pact."

[74] Yumiko Miyai and Mami Tsukahara, "Jiang Hails New Era in Japan-China Ties; 3 Hecklers Held for Interrupting Waseda Speech"; Lam, "China, Japan Struggle on Accord." Press reports also suggested that Jiang Zemin's visit to Japan originally set for September 1998 had been delayed not because of the flood emergency in China (the official explanation), but rather because the two sides were unable to agree on a joint statement about Taiwan. See "Chinese President Jiang's Visit to Japan May Be Delayed to Next Year"; Michael Zielenziger, "Talks Fall Short for China, Japan."

[75] Following the summit, China's Foreign Ministry summarized the ambivalent state of bilateral relations and emphasized the lingering disagreements about World War II and Taiwan. See "Japan: Bilateral Political Relations."

remove obstacles to the development of the friendly and cooperative partnership between the two countries."[76] While in Japan, Zhu Rongji gave a press conference at which he clearly tried to establish a different tone than Jiang had when he noted, "*Demanding an apology is not our aim. Our aim is to 'learn from history, look forward to the future,'* and create a future when the two peoples can be friends for generations to come. The principle of 'learning from history, and looking forward to the future' not only is applicable to the Japanese people, but also to the Chinese people as well."[77]

To the extent the two sides were able to prevent their differences with respect to addressing the historical legacy of Japan's aggression in the mid-twentieth century from sidetracking relations, it became easier to establish the sorts of linkages that China hoped would temper Japan's readiness to cooperate with American efforts in Asia to promote policies deemed "anti-China."[78] Though the events of 1998 suggest that economic leverage cannot easily be translated into political clout, the increased importance of trade with and investment in China as an engine of Japan's economic recovery after 2002 provides strong incentives for Tokyo to carefully consider Beijing's views. Of course, Beijing recognizes that even a robust Sino-Japanese partnership will not enable it to shape debates in Tokyo about matters such as missile defenses as effectively as Japan's long-standing ally in Washington. And, as emphasized in the next chapter, Beijing remains suspicious about Japan's ultimate intentions. But if China succeeds in cultivating a sound working relationship with Japan on important regional security concerns and offers attractive economic opportunities to vested Japanese interests, Beijing expects this will at least alter the cost-benefit calculations underlying Tokyo's foreign policy. Japan's initially quite cautious embrace of U.S. plans for cooperation in deploying missile defenses as quickly as possible was perhaps an example of the sort of re-

[76] Ho Chung, "Prospects of Zhu Rongji's Trip to Japan."

[77] Tao Guangxiong, Liu Jingshi, and Wang Xiaohui, "Further on Zhu Rongji News Conference at Tokyo Press Club" (emphasis added). On the less strident exchanges between Chinese and Japanese leaders during Zhu's October 2000 visit, when the emphasis was on "looking to the future, while not forgetting the past," see "PRC Zhu Rongji Urges Drawing History Lessons from Sino-Japanese Ties"; Wang Dajun, Zhang Haibo, and Wang Yan, "Zhu, Mori Stress Friendly Cooperation at Banquet in Honor of Zhu Rongji."

[78] One Chinese interlocutor familiar with the deliberations at China's Foreign Ministry insisted that Premier Zhu's visit represented a victory for those advisers who believed that China should emphasize the importance of Japan's integration within a regional economic community, and that this meant deemphasizing, though not forgetting, disputes over issues "left over from history" on which Jiang had focused attention in 1998 (author's interviews, Beijing, October 2000).

luctance to ignore China's clearly stated strong objections that Beijing hoped to encourage. Japan's wariness after 2002 about the toughest American proposals (to which Beijing objected) for coercing North Korea to abandon its nuclear ambitions may be yet another.[79]

China and India

India occupied a distinctive if ambiguous position in China's grand strategic vision during the 1990s. Several considerations account for the circuitous path followed toward the partnership that Beijing finally established with New Delhi in 2003, and for the apparent difficulty in cementing that relationship. First, border disputes and disagreements about China's rule in Tibet that erupted in a brief war in October 1962 had resulted in a humiliating defeat for India that left a legacy of mutual suspicion. The war was followed by a Cold War pattern of Soviet support for India and Chinese support for Pakistan in their ongoing conflict that reinforced and sustained Sino-Indian tensions over the ensuing decades. Intermittent attempts to repair bilateral relations began in the last years of the Cold War and continued afterward, but they failed to resolve the most sensitive territorial and political disputes that led each side to view the other as a potential adversary. Second, as post-Mao economic reforms began to bear fruit, especially in the 1990s, many Chinese were skeptical that they should view India as either a peer competitor or a prospective great power in the multipolar world they expected to emerge sometime in the twenty-first century. Bluntly stated, Beijing was not convinced that relations with India would be as strategically significant for China as the relations it was cultivating with other major powers.[80]

[79] See Doug Struck, "Asian Allies See Hazards Ahead; Bush Plan Raises Sensitive Defense Issues for Japan, S. Korea." For China's criticisms of Japan's rationale for developing theater missile defenses, see Gu Ping, "A New Pretext for Joining the TMD System." See Scheherazade Daneshku and Barney Jopson, "Trade with China Boosts Japan Surplus"; Brendan Pearson, "Japanese Exports Hit Record"; Brendan Pearson, "Exuberance Reigns in Japan"; Todd Zaun, "Japan Almost Doubles Forecast for Economic Growth."

[80] My Chinese interlocutors (Beijing, June–July 1998 and March–April and October 2000) often expressed rather skeptical, even dismissive, views of India's prospects. Some claimed that inherent problems with Indian culture were the basis for their gloomy forecasts of India's future; others pointed to domestic politics in India's complex democratic, federal system as a complication that would inhibit the shedding of antimarket policies, a complication that China did not face. Regardless, most argued that it was pointless to analyze China's relations with India in the same way that they analyzed relations with the other major powers. They saw the notion that India was a country about to emerge as a major economic, military, and political actor on the

Third, and perhaps most important, India's decision to conduct nuclear tests in May 1998 and openly declare itself a nuclear weapons state unexpectedly stalled a more substantial improvement in bilateral relations that finally seemed to be afoot in 1996–97. Although Beijing in a sense benefited by joining in the international condemnation of the Indian (and Pakistani) nuclear tests because it provided an opportunity to burnish China's reputation as a responsible member of the nonproliferation regime and to demonstrate common interests with the United States, the tests were a sharp, if brief, setback for Sino-Indian relations. China's objection to India's tests was rooted less in a sense of outrage that New Delhi had violated the international nonproliferation norm than anger that India had invoked concerns about China as a principal reason it needed a full-fledged nuclear deterrent. This claim echoed India's original rationale for its nuclear weapons program initiated during the mid-1960s—that it was a reaction to China's emerging capability. Yet after conducting a "peaceful nuclear explosion" in 1974, New Delhi had apparently been satisfied with remaining an "opaque nuclear weapons state" until the late 1990s. Its demonstrated nuclear potential seemed to suffice in dealing with the similarly opaque nuclear capability rival Pakistan had developed in response to India's program.[81]

Therefore, Beijing was incensed in May 1998 when India not very subtly let it be known that a major reason for its dramatic decision to abandon opacity and test nuclear weapons was the need to prepare for an uncertain future in which a rapidly rising China might pose new challenges. It saw New Delhi's claim as a flimsy pretext created to divert attention from the true motive—to boost the status of an India that resented China's growing international prominence. India's assertion that a possible China contingency was a major reason for its nuclear test was especially galling to Beijing because Sino-Indian relations had been improving rather than deteriorating since the 1980s and hardly warranted Delhi's momentous decision to change policy, buck world opinion, and go nuclear. Beijing, in short, saw India's claims about hedging against the uncertainties a more powerful China would create not as a justifiable reason to test, but rather as a handy excuse used to explain a step the am-

---

world stage as a theme that had reappeared periodically since the 1950s and one that they expected would fade when India once again failed to fulfill its promise. See also Pillsbury, *China Debates the Future Security Environment*, chapter 3.

[81] See Devin T. Hagerty, *The Consequences of Nuclear Proliferation: Lessons from South Asia*; Sumit Ganguly, "India's Pathway to Pokhran II: The Prospects and Sources of New Delhi's Nuclear Weapons Program"; George Perkovich, *India's Nuclear Bomb: The Impact on Global Proliferation*; Ashley J. Tellis, *India's Emerging Nuclear Posture: Between Recessed Deterrent and Ready Arsenal*.

bitious new Bharatiya Janata Party (BJP) government of Prime Minister Vajpayee wanted to take for other reasons. But perhaps more troubling than the
sense that the Indians were being disingenuous was the belief that by pointing
to a rising China and suggesting the dangers it might pose, India was adding
its voice to the chorus of those who had been heralding a looming China
threat that needed to be countered.

The immediate effect of India's nuclear weapons tests was a temporary halt
to the ongoing rapprochement with China. The tensions caused by the nuclear issue then became intermingled with Beijing's anxiety about the possibility that Indian-American relations, decidedly frosty during the last decades
of the Cold War, were beginning to warm. Despite Washington's sharp criticism of New Delhi's nuclear ambitions and its imposition of sanctions in response to the tests, India and the United States soon began a push not just to
restore but to strengthen their bilateral relations. Some urging closer ties had
begun to reemphasize the two countries' shared democratic values, while others suggested their shared strategic interest in creating centers of power in Asia
other than the one emerging in Beijing. The clearest sign of improving Indian-American relations was President Clinton's state visit in March 2000.
Prominent conservative voices in the United States, including many who
were critical of the Clinton administration's China policy, welcomed the
move but viewed it as only a first step. They called for India to become part of
a reorientation of American strategic policy in Asia that would emphasize
closer ties with the region's democracies and a more robust hedge against potential Chinese challenges. When the Bush administration took office in 2001,
this view began to be translated into planning and policy.[82] As a result of these
changes in play after the May 1998 nuclear tests, Jiang Zemin's hopeful an-

---

[82] The Bush team included several advisers who argued for shifting the emphasis in
U.S. Asian policy from China to Asian allies (especially Japan) and friendly democra-
cies in the region, especially India. This perspective was reflected in a bipartisan re-
port coordinated by Joseph Nye and Richard Armitage in October 2000. See "The
United States and Japan: Advancing toward a Mature Partnership"; Lee Siew Hua,
"Time to Put Japan Firmly Back on U.S. Radar Screen"; Ren Yujun, "U.S., Indian
Relations Warm up Further"; Jian Hua, "The United States, Japan Want to Rope in
India Which Cherishes the Dream of Becoming a Major Country"; K. K. Katyal,
"Perceptions & Prescriptions"; Jairam Ramesh, "Author Sees China as Motive for
Pentagon's 'India-Friendly' Leanings, Policies"; Sumit Ganguly, "The Start of a
Beautiful Friendship? The United States and India"; Jane Perlez, "U.S. Ready to End
Sanctions on India to Build Alliance." China's concern about a tilt toward India in
U.S. Asia policy was alleviated after the terrorist attacks of September 11, 2001, al-
tered American priorities. See Martin Sieff, "Commentary: Bush's India-China
Switch."

nouncement made during his November 1996 visit to New Delhi that China and India would "seek to forge a 21st century oriented, constructive and co-operative partnership" looked like a false start.[83]

Yet in the end, the nuclear issue and its aftermath may have helped to catalyze a transformation in China's view of the importance of its bilateral relations with India that ultimately reenergized the effort to build a partnership. By 2001, when the two sides sought to restore the momentum of 1996–97, Beijing's skepticism about the strategic significance of an economically vibrant, internationally active, militarily modernizing India and the need to include it in China's great power diplomacy had faded. Chinese statements about bilateral relations began to invoke the themes used in reference to its ties with other major powers. In January 2001, China's second-ranking party leader, Li Peng, spoke to an audience in India and told his hosts "reality requires us to push the Sino-Indian relations into a new phase in the 21st century" and called on his hosts to carry forward the agreement from 1996 to establish "a constructive cooperative partnership oriented toward the 21st century" and help to accelerate the transition to a multipolar world.[84]

The resumption of efforts to build the partnership culminated in the June 2003 visit to China by Indian premier Vajpayee. On this visit the new generation of leaders in Beijing led by President and Party Chairman Hu Jintao and Premier Wen Jiabao not only adopted the language that Jiang Zemin had used in 1996 to describe the goal for Sino-Indian relations, but also inked a series of agreements typical of those China had reached with other great power partners.[85] These identified the multiple arenas in which exchanges would be expanded as well as international issues of common interest on which Beijing and New Delhi would foster cooperation. While acknowledging areas of disagreement, Vajpayee insisted that India did not see China as a foe and urged both countries to learn from history rather than allow themselves to be trapped by it.[86] The "Declaration on Bilateral Ties" that resulted from the visit announced that both countries were determined to build a "long-term constructive and cooperative partnership" and create a "quali-

[83] "China, India to Seek to Build 21-Century-Oriented Partnership"; "Jiang Zemin Says Sino-Indian Ties 'Lifted One Level'"; "India, China Agree to Develop Cooperative Ties."

[84] Li Peng, "Promote Understanding, Develop Friendship, Enhance Cooperation." See also comments on Premier Zhu Rongji's January 2002 visit to India in "Sun Yuxi Says, the Momentum of Development of Sino-Indian Relations Is Good."

[85] See the "nine documents on cooperation in economy, law and justice, science and technology, and culture" in "China, India Sign Declaration on Bilateral Ties."

[86] "India PM: India, China Can Build Partnership."

tatively new relationship." In addition to outlining principles on which the partnership would rest, the declaration reprised the familiar themes of material benefits it would yield for both countries as well as the partnership's usefulness for building a peaceful multipolar world in which economic globalization could play a positive role.[87] And, while there was no guarantee that renewed efforts to seek a fair resolution of their outstanding border disputes would prove more fruitful than those that had failed in the past, both sides committed themselves to give it a try. Perhaps to get these negotiations off on the right foot, India's Vajpayee used the Beijing trip to reiterate India's stance that Tibet is part of China, and China reciprocated with an economic agreement that tacitly recognized India's absorption of Sikkim.[88]

Neither the spectacular success of the 2003 Vajpayee visit to China nor the Sino-Indian partnership it yielded eliminates the underlying reasons for mutual mistrust between these neighboring Asian giants. Diplomacy cannot foreclose the possibility that their rivalry may intensify in coming decades as each draws on growing capabilities to pursue its regional interests. The budding partnership nevertheless fits with China's current grand strategic emphasis on cultivating relations with the world's major powers that fall somewhere between those of traditional allies or adversaries; the partnership gives New Delhi a larger stake in keeping ties with Beijing on an even keel. Underscoring the potential benefits of good relations, as well as the costs of taking steps that put them at risk, serves China's strategic interest in trying to head off what at the dawn of the twenty-first century looked like an increasingly prominent role for India as an American ally if the United States ever got serious about containing China through a strategy of encirclement.

China and ASEAN

As noted in chapter 5, during the mid-1990s, China's determination to expand its military power-projection capabilities in defense of increasingly strident sovereignty claims to maritime territories in the South China Sea had inspired some of the first warnings about the dangerous implications of China's rise. It had also prompted nervous ASEAN neighbors to respond by hedging their bets against the need to counter the threat a more powerful China might pose. Yet what once appeared to be the opening chapter of a familiar balance-of-power story has since then taken an unexpected turn. The

[87] See "China, India Agree to Address Differences Peacefully"; "China, India Sign Declaration on Bilateral Ties (Full Text)."

[88] See "Chinese Experts Applaud China-India Declaration on Bilateral Ties"; "Triumph of Pragmatism"; Happymon Jacob, "Enter the Dragon."

surprising course of events in large measure resulted from the grand strategy China embraced in the second half of the decade. Most importantly, as described in chapter 6, Beijing backed away from its relatively assertive posture on territorial disputes that emphasized bilateral negotiations with individual Southeast Asian states and began to embrace the possibilities of exploring areas for cooperation within the burgeoning network of multilateral forums growing on the ASEAN organizational trellis.[89] But in addition, by the opening years of the twenty-first century, Beijing had apparently concluded that its interests could be even better served by complementing multilateral cooperation with a bilateral partnership between China and ASEAN.

Having clearly shed its fear that ASEAN might simply be a front for American influence that could threaten China, early in the twenty-first century Beijing was beginning to view ASEAN as an entity that might actually help China maximize the opportunities and minimize the risks it faced in Southeast Asia. The resulting change in China's approach to ASEAN during 2002–2003 went well beyond the stylistic shift widely described as a "charm offensive," though the deft personal touch of a new generation of Chinese leaders visiting the region undoubtedly helped underscore the new emphasis in policy. The more important substantive change was a deepening commitment to the goal of establishing a China-ASEAN Free Trade Area and especially the October 2003 joint declaration of a China-ASEAN "strategic partnership for peace and prosperity."[90]

While this was "China's first time in establishing a strategic partnership

[89] For China, these most importantly include meetings under the auspices of the ASEAN Regional Forum and ASEAN+3 (China, Japan, and the Republic of Korea). For the growing variety of meetings and organizations tied to ASEAN, see http://www.aseansec.org/home.htm.

[90] *Joint Declaration of the Heads of State/Government of the Association of Southeast Asian Nations and the People's Republic of China on Strategic Partnership for Peace and Prosperity.* On the "charm offensive," see Philip Pan, "China's Improving Image Challenges U.S. in Asia"; "Premier's Bali Trip Raises China-ASEAN Ties to New Level: FM." On the economic commitments in which China offered early, favorable treatment for some ASEAN products under the "early harvest" program, see *Framework Agreement on Comprehensive Economic Co-operation between the Association of South East Asian Nations and the People's Republic of China; Protocol to Amend the Framework Agreement on Comprehensive Economic Co-operation between the Association of South East Asian Nations and the People's Republic of China; Agreement on Trade in Goods of the Framework Agreement on Comprehensive Economic Co-operation between the Association of Southeast Asian Nations and the People's Republic of China; Agreement on Dispute Settlement Mechanism of the Framework Agreement on Comprehensive Economic Co-Operation Between the Association of Southeast Asian Nations and the People's Republic of China*

with a regional organization," this partnership, like all those it had promoted since 1996, was designed to encourage others to remain attuned to Beijing's regional concerns by increasing the anticipation of growing mutual benefits (especially economic) if sound bilateral ties were sustained.[91] To be sure, as with China's Japanese partnership, this linkage arguably gives Beijing no more than a limited ability to shape the foreign policy choices of the ASEAN states since several have long-standing military ties to Washington and most harbor nagging uncertainties about the prospect of a regionally dominant China. But for decision makers in each of the capitals of the diverse ASEAN member states, this strategic partnership at least underscores the costs of ignoring China's interests and may well make it more difficult for the United States should it try to rally regional support behind initiatives to which Beijing expresses strong opposition.[92] In the near term, the China–ASEAN partnership already seems to be facilitating Beijing's campaign to firm up regional support for its Taiwan policy and to be winning ASEAN praise for China's role in sustaining the negotiations to discover a diplomatic solution to the Korean nuclear standoff.[93]

*   *   *

Beijing's grand strategy that emerged after the mid-1990s aimed not only to ensure the country's security in a narrow sense, but also to facilitate China's rise to great power status. The central challenge was to craft an approach that would make this possible during an era of American dominance in which the both the United States and some of its Asian allies have the capability to complicate, if not completely frustrate, China's efforts. For Beijing success re-

---

[91] "China's Peaceful Rise—A PLA General's View."

[92] China's concerns about U.S. efforts to bolster military ties in Southeast Asia, perhaps under the guise of countering terrorism, are reflected in "A Drunkard Means Otherwise Than in Wine." In 2003, Western media reported on the speculation about redeployment of some U.S. forces from Northeast to Southeast Asia. See Esther Schrader, "U.S. to Realign Troops in Asia."

[93] See *ASEAN China Foreign Ministers' Informal Meeting Joint Press Release*; also Larry Teo, "ASEAN Doesn't Want Taipei to Destabilise Region." Beijing's proactive ASEAN policy also reduces the risk that either Japan or (less likely) India might preempt a significant Chinese role in the region. Tokyo and New Delhi each followed China in announcing their intention to accede to ASEAN's Treaty of Amity and Cooperation. On these competitive dynamics, see Kwan Weng Kin, "Japan 'to Remain Top ASEAN Partner for Next 20 Years'; but It Will Have to Jostle with China for the Position in 50 Years, Says PM Goh in Press Interview"; Brendan Pearson, "Japan Resists China's Influence"; Kwan Weng Kin, "Japan's PM Upbeat on China's Growth; China's Economic Growth Is Not a Threat and Would Benefit Both ASEAN and Japan, Says Koizumi."

quired a foreign policy that maintained a peaceful international environment in which China could proceed with the arduous task of domestic economic development on which national prosperity and strength ultimately depend. How do the political, economic, and military means Beijing has embraced serve its grand strategic ends? China's increased participation in multilateral forums, restrained currency policy, and active cultivation of major power partnerships are designed to mute perceptions of a "China threat," to build China's reputation as a responsible actor, and to convince others of the benefits of engagement with China as well as the counterproductive consequences of attempting to threaten, isolate, or contain it. Expanding relations with a diverse array of trade partners and sources of foreign investment are designed to weave a network of beneficial economic relations and limit the leverage of any single power over the terms of China's international involvement.[94] Dip-

---

[94] Since December 2003, China has increased the number of partnerships it is prepared to designate "strategic." In some cases (France and Britain) the change simply redefines existing major power partnerships. In other cases, however, the new wave of strategic partnerships reflects a broad effort to strengthen China's bilateral ties with key countries in each of the world's regions. By the end of 2004, China had announced strategic partnerships with Mexico, Algeria, Brazil (as mentioned in note 54 above, reviving the term first used in different circumstances during the early 1990s), Argentina, and Italy. Following the pattern that has emerged since 1996, the official announcements of these strategic partnerships refer to mutual economic benefits and common strategic interests. They also typically pay homage to Beijing's "one-China" position with respect to Taiwan, suggesting the link between cultivating this array of partnerships and Beijing's effort to limit the likelihood China would face international isolation if it were to use military force to deal with Taiwan.

Beijing's recent partnerships may also reflect an attempt to diversify and strengthen ties to countries with natural resources (especially petroleum) essential for China's booming economy. In addition, the new wrinkle in China's partnership diplomacy has included an emphasis on South-South relations as a way to build a more equitable international order. This theme resonates both with the more egalitarian domestic development strategy the CCP's leaders have promoted since 2002, and also with China's preference to hasten the demise of U.S.-led unipolarity. Notably, at the same time China announced its intention to establish a strategic partnership with Indonesia, it endorsed plans for Jakarta to host the fiftieth anniversary of the 1955 Bandung Asian-African summit in April 2005, celebrating a landmark event in the annals of the Cold War's nonaligned movement. See "Chinese, French Leaders Reach Broad Consensus"; "China, UK Vow to Develop Strategic Partnership: Joint Statement"; "Sino-British Ties Grow Healthy: FM"; "China, Mexico Establish Strategic Partnership"; "Algeria, China Pledge to Boost Overall Ties"; "Full Text of China-Algeria Joint Communiqué Signed on 4 February 2004"; "China, Argentina To Establish Strategic Partnership"; "China, Italy to Establish Stable, Long-term, Comprehensive Strategic Partnership"; "Chinese, Italian Presidents Hail Strong Bilateral Relations"; "Chinese

lomatic efforts to contain political tensions while fostering integration with the global economy in turn complement the role of China's military forces, an essential consideration in any state's grand strategy. To the extent Beijing is able to create conditions for its peaceful rise during the era of American unipolarity, the strategy 1) reduces the likelihood that the PLA will need to fight a battle for which it is far from ready (especially in the Taiwan Strait);[95] 2) creates some breathing space for the daunting long-term task of comprehensive force modernization; 3) mutes the security dilemma dynamic that encourages prospective rivals to respond quickly to offset even measured improvement in the quantity and quality of the PLA's capabilities; and 4) increases access to advanced technologies that are essential if China hopes to move beyond the stopgap, second-best solution of importing Russian equipment (most of which falls short of the best available) and attempting to reverse engineer their own versions.[96]

President Begins State Visit to Brazil"; "Indonesia, China to Build Strategic Partnership: Officials." See also Ye Zicheng, "Carrying Forward, Developing and Pondering Deng Xiaoping's Foreign Policy Thinking in the New Situation."

[95] See Michael O'Hanlon, "Why China Cannot Conquer Taiwan."

[96] The controversy about how much the Chinese learned about rocket guidance from working with the U.S. company Loral in investigating a failed satellite launch reflects the recognition of potentially fruitful connection between the economic and military aspects of China's grand strategy. See Jeff Gerth, "Congress Investigating Sales of Satellite Technology to China"; "The Sanctity of Missile Secrets"; also Michael Hirsch, "The Great Technology Giveaway?" China has not demonstrated an ability to gain much production expertise from the extensive opportunities it has had to engage in reverse engineering using the many Soviet and Russian fighter aircraft it has in its inventory. On the contrary, China continues to have problems with the simpler problems of aircraft engine maintenance. See "U.S. Report Discusses China Weapons Upgrades."

8

Will the Current Grand Strategy Endure?

The basic political, economic, and military components of China's grand strategy that aims for a peaceful transition as it rises to become a true great power during the era of American unipolarity seem logically coherent and reflect a pragmatic response to the country's circumstances. Yet the consensus on this vision guiding China's foreign policy has only been evident for a relatively short period. Is it likely to last?

As noted in the previous chapter, China's current approach has already survived the tough tests of unexpected events in 1999 and 2001 that produced serious Sino-American friction challenging one of its central features (great power partnerships). Ultimately, however, the durability of Beijing's grand strategy will depend on more general internal and external political conditions as much as unpredictable specific events. At the opening of the twenty-first century, there are two reasons to believe it should have staying power: 1) the strategy's demonstrated usefulness has solidified its broad appeal among China's foreign policy elite, and 2) the strategy is robust with respect to changes in China's international circumstances.

Political Viability

First, the current grand strategy seems politically sustainable among the elite that shapes China's foreign policy. The approach has demonstrated its worth as an effective compromise between more exclusively "soft" and "hard" lines, each of which were partly discredited by the events of the mid-1990s generally, and the Taiwan Strait crisis of 1995–96 in particular.

Those associated with a more accommodating soft line, sometimes identified with the Ministry of Foreign Affairs, were embarrassed during the spring of 1995 in what many Chinese perceived to be a double cross by the United States. Since President Clinton's announcement on May 26, 1994, that he had decided "to delink human rights from the annual extension of Most Favored Nation trading status for China," Sino-American relations had been improving.[1] Beijing saw Washington shifting toward a forthright policy of engagement and took the Clinton administration at its word when it offered assurances that it would not grant a visa for Taiwan's president Lee Teng-hui to visit the United States. Despite these assurances, the U.S. Congress soon forced the Clinton administration to reverse its position and the door was opened for Lee's landmark visit to his alma mater, Cornell University, in May 1995. In Ithaca, Lee advanced his policy to elevate Taiwan's international profile, challenging Beijing's "one China" principle that set strict limits on the roles Taiwan should be permitted to play on the world stage. When he did, there was no face-saving fallback for those in China who had been supportive not only of improving relations with the United States, but also of a moderating reunification line on Taiwan clearly articulated by President Jiang Zemin just three months before Lee's trip to Cornell.[2] As a predictable backlash unfolded in China, more assertive hard-line views easily prevailed in Beijing, and the leadership quickly agreed on the wisdom of forceful action to stem what it deemed a dangerous trend that could eventually lead to the final loss of Taiwan, a prospect unacceptable to all within China's foreign policy elite.[3]

But however strong the consensus behind the PRC's decision to apply military pressure from July 1995 to March 1996 as a warning necessary to halt Taiwan's drift toward independence, the ramifications of this decision for China's broader international position proved troubling. As emphasized in previous chapters, military exercises that included missiles launched across the Taiwan Strait aggravated the already growing sense of alarm within the region about China's increasing capabilities and nurtured what Beijing termed the "China threat theory." Perhaps most worrisome for Beijing, the missile firings

[1] "Text of President Clinton's Address about China."

[2] "President's Speech on Taiwan Reunification." See also Michael D. Swaine, "Chinese Decision-Making Regarding Taiwan, 1979–2000," pp. 313–19; author's interviews, Beijing, June–July 1998.

[3] Paul Heer cautions against the assumption of deep divisions among the top leaders on the core security questions such as Taiwan ("A House United"). Michael Swaine concurs with this view in the context of the 1995–96 decisions to take a firm stance on the Taiwan crisis. See Swaine, "Chinese Decision-Making Regarding Taiwan, 1979–2000," pp. 321–27. For an alarmist assessment that justified using all available means to ensure Taiwan's reunification with the mainland because it is seen as a litmus test of Beijing's ability to ensure China's sovereignty in an Asia-Pacific region the United States dominates, see Wang Yiwei, "Dui Tai Junshi Douzheng Dui Shijie Zhanlüe Geju De Yingxiang Chutan" [A preliminary exploration of the effects on the international strategic situation of military action against Taiwan], p. 29.

eventually prompted the United States to respond by maneuvering two air-craft carriers near the Taiwan Strait. The Clinton administration's signal emphasized the continuing likelihood of an American response if the mainland ever decided to use military force against Taiwan, altered the context for the announcement the following month about revision of the U.S.-Japan alliance that was already in the pipeline, and underscored the significance of a cautionary note about China that was inserted into Japan's 1996 Defense White Paper issued in July.[4]

In short, "soft" diplomacy and "hard" coercion had each revealed their limited usefulness as the Taiwan crisis of 1995–96 played itself out. Against this background, China's subsequent, more nuanced foreign policy line had obvious attractions. It included both the threat of noncooperation if great power partners infringed on China's core interests as well as the cultivation of cooperative bilateral relations that maintain an international economic and security environment conducive to China's modernization. The current strategy thus appeals to those within the Chinese elite who mainly worry that their government may be too willing to compromise in the face of foreign, especially American, pressure but who also recognize the difficulties their country faces in developing a capability to offset potentially threatening U.S. power. And it appeals to others within the elite who mainly worry about the implications of leaning too heavily on coercive power as a tool to ensure China's interests because they believe the early post–Cold War experience demonstrated that this was sure to trigger a counterproductive international reaction.[5] This

---

[4] For the text of the Tokyo declaration that appeared in April 1996 and called for a review of U.S.-Japan security guidelines, see "Japan-U.S. Joint Declaration on Security Alliance for the 21st Century." For the September 1997 announcement of the planned revisions, see *Joint Statement, U.S.-Japan Security Consultative Committee, Completion of the Review of the Guidelines for U.S.-Japan Defense Cooperation.* For the text of the white paper, see *Defense of Japan, 1996.* For Chinese reaction to the white paper, see Da Jun, "The Threat Comes From Those Trumpeting 'Threat Theory.'" See also "White Paper Airs Concern on China Military Buildup."

[5] Although Chinese institutions have individuals holding both "hard" and "soft" views, foreign analysts have noted distinct modal views associated with the elite in particular organizations. The current strategy's emphasis on more active diplomacy, including multilateralism, arguably makes it especially appealing to younger civilian elites in the Foreign Ministry and some of the think tanks that advise it. The tough side of the strategy, coercion held in reserve should diplomacy fail, may appeal to those, especially PLA officers and civilians working in the think tanks that advise the military, many of whom express disdain for Foreign Ministry officials. See Thomas J. Christensen, "Realism with Chinese Characteristics: Beijing's Perceptions of Japan, the United States, and the Future of East Asian Security," p. 16. For recent reviews of the changing role of China's community of analysts, see David Shambaugh, "China's In-

lesson learned from the 1995–96 Taiwan Strait crisis that helped forge a broad base of support for the current strategy was reinforced in 1999 during the "two-states" controversy when, as explained in chapter 5, the United States quietly helped contain the potentially explosive consequences of Lee Teng-hui's proposal for redefining Taiwan's status. When cross-strait tensions rose again in 2000, the strategy's usefulness and the reason for its broad appeal among China's foreign policy elite were once more apparent.

A Second Taiwan Test

In the month before the March 2000 elections on Taiwan, China's intelligence sources warned Beijing that Chen Shui-bian, candidate of the traditionally pro-independence Democratic Progressive Party, looked increasingly like the winner in a three-way race for president.[6] China's response to the worrisome prospect of a leader on Taiwan who, China feared, might be even more enthusiastic than Lee Teng-hui about seeking separate statehood was in line with its new strategy: stake out a contingent position that was neither as soft as the diplomacy of early 1995, nor as hard as the coercive tactics adopted after May of that year. While China's leaders prepared for the possibility of a Taiwan crisis whose gravity exceeded that of 1995–96, a delegation of top-level U.S. national security officials visited Beijing to urge restraint. Given their experience in the spring of 1995, when they felt the United States had reneged on its promises about Lee Teng-hui's visa, however, China's leaders this time were not going to bank too heavily on the Clinton administration's assurances about its pro–status quo stance on cross-strait relations. Instead, although it welcomed the official U.S. position, the Chinese government simultaneously prepared the release of a new white paper on Taiwan more strongly reaffirming Beijing's long-standing position that it reserved the right to use force against an island it considers its sovereign territory.[7] Specifically, the new statement broadened the circumstances under which force might be used, for the first time indicating that the Taiwan authorities' indefinite refusal to negotiate (and not just an explicit declaration of independence or foreign intervention) could prompt China to take military action.[8]

But the white paper also carefully avoided increasing the urgency for rely-

---

ternational Relations Think Tanks: Evolving Structure and Process"; Bonnie S. Glaser and Phillip C. Saunders, "Chinese Civilian Foreign Policy Research Institutes: Evolving Roles and Increasing Influence"; Bates Gill and James Mulvenon, "Chinese Military-Related Think Tanks and Research Institutions."

[6] Author's interviews, Beijing, March–April 2000.

[7] See Jane Perlez, "Warning by China to Taiwan Poses Challenge to U.S."

[8] See "The One-China Principle and the Taiwan Issue."

ing on coercion inasmuch as it did not provide a real deadline for progress on reunification. As some on the mainland began to put it, this was "a deadline without a date"—a concession to the hard-line position that ultimately force might have to be used, but in the form of a policy that granted leaders on both sides of the Strait time (and provided them with stronger incentives) to discover a negotiated solution. Coercive ambiguity served multiple purposes. By suggesting that Beijing's patience had its limits, the policy signaled the United States that there were risks to an American policy of increasing support for Taiwan (especially the sale of military equipment), which China saw as a key reason for Taipei's growing intransigence. By leaving open the question of the time frame for Beijing's patience, however, the policy allowed China's leaders to avoid putting their international reputation on the line, as they would if they set a true deadline for resolution and failed to act or acted and failed to accomplish their objectives (a likely outcome for the immediate future). And by indicating that the regime retained the option to use force, the policy also enabled Beijing's leaders to save face domestically, since it did not require acknowledging that the exercise of restraint on Taiwan reflected fear of the likely U.S. response.[9]

When Chen Shui-bian did in fact win the presidential election on Taiwan, China stood its conditional middle ground. In the opening months of Chen's administration, Beijing alternately rattled its still-sheathed saber, excoriating those it viewed as ardent advocates of Taiwan independence (especially Chen's vice president, Annette Lu), and expressed its preference for resuming a dialogue with Taipei, but only on terms it deemed acceptable.[10] China's Russian strategic partner offered unwavering support for Beijing's hard sovereignty position on Taiwan (a stance Beijing continued to reciprocate on Chechnya). China's European and Japanese partners nervously stood aloof lest they jeopardize growing economic ties to the mainland (whose potential at-

---

[9] Beijing's coercive diplomacy thus reflects a sensitivity to the difficulties and risks of compellence (as opposed to deterrence). Unlike deterrence, which aims to preserve the status quo and which does not require the target of one's threats to engage in visibly embarrassing compliance for its effectiveness, compellence demands a change in the status quo that will entail a costly loss of face—for the victim if it complies, for the party attempting to compel a change if change is not forthcoming. See Thomas C. Schelling, *Arms and Influence*; Avery Goldstein, *Deterrence and Security in the 21st Century*, esp. pp. 31–32; 279–85. For consideration of some of the strategic complications in the Taiwan context, see Robert R. Ross, "Navigating the Taiwan Strait."

[10] See "Spokesmen for CPC Central Committee's Taiwan Work Office and State Council's Taiwan Affairs Office Issue Statement on Annette Lu's 'Taiwan Independent' Remarks"; "Renmin Ribao Says Taiwan's Annette Lu 'Lunatic Advocate'"; "AFP: PRC Spokesman Suggests Flexibility on One-China."

tractiveness soared with its anticipated accession to the WTO). And China's American partner, wary of undoing the progress achieved in getting bilateral relations back on track after mid-1999, quietly cautioned Taiwan's president-elect against indulging his party's most provocative independence policies and tacitly signaled Beijing that the United States was not interested in aggravating a delicate situation.[11] As a result, it soon became clear that China had successfully limited the opportunity for Taiwan's new leader to take steps that Beijing viewed as unacceptable.[12]

Beijing's approach to the spring 2000 incarnation of its Taiwan problem, then, underscored the combination of determination, flexibility, and growing sophistication that characterizes China's current grand strategy. It also highlighted why it is incorrect to label China's post-1996 grand strategy as representing the views of either soft-liners or hard-liners, and thus why it is unlikely that factional realignments in Beijing would result in a fundamental shift in foreign policy. The festering Taiwan issue instead has demonstrated that China's current grand strategy includes both "hard" and "soft" options in the service of a broadly supported agenda that enables Beijing to pursue its goals by relying on the sort of conditional cooperation associated with linkage. This flexibility increases the likelihood that the approach will survive all but the most extreme shifts in the leadership's composition, a judgment seemingly confirmed in 2003–2004 as a new generation of leaders in Beijing confronted escalating concerns about a renewed push toward independence associated with the run-up to the island's 2004 presidential election, as will be detailed below.

[11] Shortly after Chen Shui-bian's election, the Clinton administration limited the types of advanced military equipment proposed for sale to Taiwan. Part of the explanation for the limitations was a desire not to undermine the prospects for successful cross-strait dialogue at a clearly delicate moment. See Ted Plafker, "Chinese Protest U.S. Sale of Weapons, Radar to Taiwan." On U.S. contacts with President-elect Chen, see Sofia Wu, "Taiwan President-Elect Meets U.S. Delegation"; Cary Huang, "U.S. Role in Taipei-Beijing Relations Viewed."

[12] In his inaugural address, President Chen stated, "as long as the CCP regime has no intention to use military force against Taiwan, I pledge that during my term in office, I will not declare independence, I will not change the national title, I will not push forth the inclusion of the so-called 'state-to-state' description in the Constitution, and I will not promote a referendum to change the status quo in regards to the question of independence or unification. Furthermore, the abolition of the National Reunification Council or the National Reunification Guidelines will not be an issue" (Chen Shui-bian, "Full Text of President Chen Shui-bian's Inaugural Speech [I]"). See also Tetsuya Suetsugu, "Taiwan's Chen Sworn in; President Vows Not to Declare Independence."

The Bush Test

The strategy's usefulness, which sustains its appeal among the elite in Beijing, was also evident in the way it encouraged a surprisingly quick tempering of President George W. Bush's China policy during his first year in office and the improvement of Sino-American relations thereafter. As noted in chapter 7, after January 2001 the new U.S. administration began to flesh out a foreign policy more explicitly hedging against the potential for conflict with a rising China by emphasizing closer cooperation with America's Asian allies and increasing support for Taiwan. But within six months, the Bush team backed away from this approach as the costs of a decisive break with the broad contours of the Clinton administration's China policy became clear. When actually confronting the prospect of a sharp downturn in Sino-American relations during the EP-3 spy plane incident in April 2001, the United States decided instead to begin a process of fence mending that was underway by early summer. The terrorist attacks of 9/11 altered American strategic priorities and served as a catalyst that accelerated the rethinking about China already underway. Because Washington valued the benefits of a sound working relationship with Beijing in the unfolding war on international terrorism and was not prepared to forfeit the usefulness of China's cooperation on matters that the United States wanted to assign a lower priority (including tensions over Taiwan's future, but also potential problems on the Korean peninsula), it was imperative to avoid the sort of deterioration in bilateral relations that had seemed likely when the president first came to office. This was, of course, precisely the sort of leverage that Beijing expected from its grand strategy.

As the Bush Doctrine took shape after 9/11, Washington placed top priority on fighting terrorism and preventing states hostile to American interests from acquiring weapons of mass destruction. In this new context, the "constructive and cooperative Sino-American relationship" forged during the summer and explicitly endorsed by President Bush in October 2001, like the Clinton administration's "strategic partnership," provided Beijing the opportunity to play a helpful, if not decisive, role in addressing major American foreign policy concerns.[13] Although Chinese analysts had always professed confidence that the Bush administration, like its Democratic predecessor, would eventually abandon its harsh campaign rhetoric and seek to mend fences, Sino-American relations were being put back on a sound footing much

[13] On the Bush administration's strategic shift from confrontation to cooperation with China, see the comments of Liu Jianfei, analyst at China's Communist Party School (Liu Jianfei, "'The Period of Strategic Opportunity' and Sino-U.S. Ties," pp. 56–57).

sooner than most expected. Unpredictable events (the EP-3 incident and especially 9/11) had certainly accelerated the process by which the United States
concluded that containing tensions with China served American interests. But
this was a conclusion that China's grand strategy had been designed to encourage. Beijing's foreign policy choices after mid-2001 continued the effort
to reinforce Washington's belief in the value, if not indispensability, of having
China as a partner rather than an adversary.

After 9/11, China supported the broadening U.S. campaign against international terrorism, even moderating its expressions of concern about American military deployments in Central Asia during the war against Al Qaeda and
its Taliban state sponsors in Afghanistan. In the run-up to the Iraq war, too,
China muted its criticism of the United States, voted in favor of the first UN
Security Council resolution demanding Baghdad's compliance with all disarmament requests, and then carefully maintained a low profile during the protracted debate about a second resolution to authorize the use of force in early
2003. Unlike France and Russia, China did not publicly signal an intention to
veto the U.S.-sponsored resolution. By all accounts, Beijing's representative
would have abstained had it been brought to a vote. The belief in China was
that its restraint would further cement relations with the United States and
thereby serve the PRC's national interests.[14]

China had also stepped up cooperation with the United States after September 2002 in response to the apparent North Korean acknowledgment of a
clandestine program to develop a nuclear weapons capability. While Beijing
disagreed with Washington about the specific steps it could take to facilitate a
diplomatic resolution of the simmering Korean nuclear crisis (in some respects

---

[14] This was the clear message I heard from interlocutors during interviews conducted in early March 2003 with Chinese military officers, government officials, and
academic analysts whose views about U.S. foreign policy otherwise varied substantially.
The reasoning most often articulated was telling: Iraq was far from China and, although China did have an economic stake there, it was not a vital interest for China;
relations with the United States were too important and, unlike France's or Russia's
ties with the United States, were too fragile to be put in jeopardy simply to stand on
principle in symbolic resistance to American unilateralism; and China preferred to
score points with the United States that it hoped would follow from Washington's appreciation of Beijing's restraint, again underscoring the value of sustaining good bilateral relations. Rumors also circulated that some in China believed that restraint on Iraq
and cooperation in solving the Korean nuclear problems would lead the United States
to adopt a Taiwan policy that was more sympathetic to Beijing's views. On Taiwan's
concerns about the possible payoff from China's Iraq policy, see Lin Cheng-yi, "War
in Iraq Is Shaking up Strategic Calculations"; also Sofia Wu, "Foreign Minister Says
Prolonged War in Iraq Could Affect Taiwan's Interests."

expressing reservations about the usefulness of coercive threats that America's Asian allies were also voicing), by early 2003 China's leaders began to play the more active and constructive role in prodding Pyongyang that the Bush administration had sought. A key sign of Beijing's changing role was its temporary suspension in April of the flow of vital energy supplies to economically dependent North Korea, a tacit signal to Pyongyang about the cards China held. By the end of the month, Beijing had succeeded in bringing the United States and North Korea together for trilateral talks, breaking the communications impasse that existed because Pyongyang demanded direct bilateral talks with the United States, while the United States insisted the forum be multilateral.[15] When North Korea's intransigence at the first round of talks apparently angered both Beijing and Washington, optimism about finding a diplomatic solution faded. Again, however, China took steps that not only served its own interest in a peaceful resolution of the Korean crisis, but also demonstrated to Washington the helpful role Beijing could play. In July 2003 President Hu Jintao had a letter hand-delivered to Kim Jong-il in Pyongyang bluntly pressing him to accept the U.S. demand for multilateral talks about ending North Korea's nuclear weapons program. On July 30, Hu telephoned President Bush with the news that North Korea was officially agreeing to the U.S. demand. Afterward, President Bush praised Hu and emphasized the usefulness of China's role in bringing North Korea around.[16] As the difficult negotiations staggered ahead in 2004, Beijing continued to play its strategically vital intermediary role.

In sum, following an initially rocky start, Sino-American relations during the Bush administration witnessed an improvement that was swift, significant, and sustained. Although this trend partly resulted from events and choices beyond Beijing's control, the strategic approach China had fully embraced dur-

---

[15] See Gady A. Epstein, "From Beijing, Stern Words for an Uneasy Ally; China Seen Toughening Stance against N. Korea Nuclear Development"; Howard W. French, "North Korea's Reaction on Iraq Is Subdued So Far"; Karen DeYoung and Doug Struck, "Beijing's Help Led to Talks; U.S. Cuts Demands on North Korea"; John Pomfret and Glenn Kessler, "China Puts North Korea Talks in Brighter Light; Unusual Briefing Suggests Beijing Is Eager to Keep Talks between Washington, Pyongyang on Track." For a frank discussion that includes reconsideration of China's and Korea's interests both in the 2003 crisis and at the time of the Korean War in the 1950s, see "PRC Scholar Shi Yinhong on Gains, Losses, Winners, Losers in Korean War."

[16] See Catherine Armitage, "Beijing Wades into Korea Crisis"; Steven R. Weisman, "North Korea Seen as Ready to Agree to Wider Meetings"; James Brooke, "U.S. And North Korea Announce Accord on Wider Atom Talks."

ing the late 1990s made it easier to seize opportunities as they arose.[17] Following a brief June 2003 meeting between Presidents Hu and Bush, the spokesman for China's embassy in the United States singled out what he saw as evidence of the solid foundation put in place for the future development of "constructive and cooperative relations": the pattern of regular high-level meetings of political leaders, the restoration of military exchanges, booming bilateral trade, cooperation in fighting terrorism and drug-trafficking, and coordination in the search for a peaceful solution to the Korean nuclear issue. The benefits of such cooperation, he noted, would remain available to both sides as long as they continued to manage the "natural differences" that exist on matters such as human rights and religion while avoiding missteps on handling the Taiwan issue.[18]

U.S. domestic politics might have required a change in labels, but Sino-American relations were following the path Beijing originally envisioned for the "constructive strategic partnership" it set out to build in 1997. Demonstrated success in managing China's most important, and perhaps most problematic, bilateral relationship reinforces support in Beijing for the present strategy in which major power partnerships are a central feature. In particular, its emphasis on a sound working relationship with Washington had helped China limit the challenge it saw from pro-independence forces on Taiwan in 1999 and 2000. It proved useful again in late 2003–2004 as the unfolding presidential campaign on the island raised the possibility of a renewed cross-strait crisis.

A Third Taiwan Test

Unhappy with Chen Shui-bian's narrow election as president of Taiwan in 2000, Beijing became increasingly alarmed at his efforts to advance Taiwan's independence once in office. Chinese leaders hoped—and were convinced—he would be defeated at the polls in March 2004. Their conviction rested on a belief that Taiwan's voters not only were dissatisfied with the incumbent's management of the island's affairs, but also increasingly valued the growing economic benefits of good relations with the mainland and, therefore, would more likely opt for Chen's challengers on the "pan-blue" ticket known to be

[17] According to one leading Chinese analyst, the rationale for a strategy emphasizing contingent cooperation with major powers, especially the United States, seemed more compelling that ever. See Ni Jianmin, "Opportunities Are Greater Than Challenges in the Present International Environment."

[18] Yu Donghui, "The Spokesman of the Chinese Embassy in the United States Says Sino-U.S. Relations Further Developed in the First Half of This Year."

less objectionable to Beijing.[19] The PRC's desire to see Chen removed from office intensified during the last two years of his first term. In August 2002, Chen had added his own personal wrinkle to Lee Teng-hui's 1999 "state-to-state" description of cross-strait relations. He argued that there was not "one China," as Beijing insisted, but rather "one country on each side of the Strait," and he coupled this claim with calls for legislation that would ultimately make possible a referendum on Taiwan independence even though he had promised in his May 2000 inaugural address not to hold such a referendum unless the PRC threatened Taiwan.[20] Despite resistance to his proposal from Taiwan's legislature (which may have been influenced by China's harsh criticism), Chen boldly stated he would nevertheless push ahead and demonstrate the right to hold referendums by scheduling one on a major policy matter no later than the 2004 presidential election.[21]

By late summer 2003, cross-strait tensions escalated as Chen's push to establish the right of referendum became inextricably intertwined with his suggestion that once the precedent were set, Taiwan should use it to adopt a new constitution through a vote to be held on World Human Rights day in December 2006.[22] Beijing viewed the linking of referendums, the presidential election in 2004, and a new constitution as especially worrisome. Taiwan's

[19] The "pan-blue" coalition brought together the Kuomintang's Lien Chan and the People First Party's James Soong, the two candidates Chen had defeated in March 2000. It faced the "pan-green" coalition combining Chen's Democratic Progressive Party (DPP) with elements of the Kuomintang sympathetic to the DPP's independence agenda.

[20] See John Pomfret, "Taiwan's Chen Backs Vote on Independence"; Monique Chu, "Analysts Mull the Results of Chen's Pronouncement." For collected materials discussing the controversy over Chen's claim, see "'One Country on Each Side' Statement."

[21] "Chen Determined to Call Popular Vote by Next Presidential Poll"; "Chen Hints Referendum Will Be Held with Election." At the time, it seemed likely the referendums would address controversial nuclear energy policy, the size of the legislature, and Taiwan's quest for observer status in the World Health Assembly; in the end, two items (one about responding to China's missile deployments, the other about dialogue with the PRC) appeared on the ballot. For collected materials covering the referendum controversy, see "Referendum Issue." See also Michael D. Swaine, "Trouble in Taiwan."

[22] Chen contended that Taiwan needed a new constitution because the existing one was hopelessly obsolete, having originally been drafted in 1946 for a Republic of China that encompassed both the mainland and offshore islands including Taiwan. See Kathrin Hille, "Taiwan President Calls for New Constitution"; "Interview with Taiwanese President Chen Shui-bian"; Laurence Chung, "Chen Wants New Taiwan Constitution by 2008."

voters might well see any referendum in March 2004 as a precursor to a direct vote on independence that was itself still too risky to attempt. If so, the referendum might not only mobilize Chen's supporters, increasing his chances of reelection, but it could also be a decisive step toward a new constitution representing the claim that political sovereignty in the Republic of China ultimately derived from the people on Taiwan rather than the people of all China, the basis for sovereignty in the existing ROC Constitution Chen hoped to replace. The regime on Taiwan would then have a clear legal statement of separate statehood, whether or not its leaders chose to take any of the most provocative steps—renaming the country, adopting a new flag, or publicly declaring independence from the mainland—that were likely to trigger a Chinese military attack.

Beijing predictably responded to Chen's referendum plans with increasingly grave reminders that it reserved the right to use force to prevent Taiwan's permanent political separation.[23] The stern signals intended to persuade the island's leaders to change course at first seemed effective. In November 2003, Taiwan's legislature strictly limited the right of referendum that Chen sought, stipulating narrow circumstances for any vote on the sensitive matter of sovereignty.[24] Chen, however, was not persuaded; surprising many, including those in his own party, he announced plans to establish the principle of a right to hold referendums by scheduling a vote coinciding with the presidential election in March 2004 on a topic that (he argued) conformed to the new law's guidelines. His determination quickly prompted a further escalation of the military threats from Beijing.[25] As cross-strait tensions rose, China's premier Wen Jiabao visited the United States.

While generally boosting Sino-American ties that had been on the upswing since the summer of 2001, Wen's visit in December 2003 also provided an opportunity for Beijing to bring pressure to bear on Taiwan by once again tapping its American partner's interest in sustaining healthy bilateral relations. The United States had tried to walk a fine line on the referendum issue, supporting democracy on Taiwan but cautioning against referendums that touched on sovereignty or cross-strait issues, yet the Bush administration believed that Chen Shui-bian had rebuffed its warnings. Seated next to Premier Wen, President Bush, therefore, more bluntly stated U.S. opposition to any

[23] Philip P. Pan, "China Warns Taiwan Again on Issue of Independence: Official Vows 'Strong Reaction' If Referendum Law Is Passed."

[24] Keith Bradsher, "Taiwan Puts Limits in Referendum Bill."

[25] "Taiwan's Chen Promises to Hold 'Security' Referendum on Election Day"; John Pomfret, "China's Military Warns Taiwan."

unilateral efforts to alter the status quo in the Taiwan Strait, and specifically his unhappiness with Chen's planned referendum. Although there was no way for the United States to prevent Chen from holding the vote, Wen's success in getting President Bush to warn Taiwan apparently did alleviate Beijing's concerns, at least for a time.[26] The U.S. president's comments and subsequent messages American envoys delivered to Taiwan before the election also effectively undercut support for the two referendums put to a vote on March 20. Although Chen won a hotly contested reelection with a razor-thin majority, too few voters cast ballots on the referendums for either to pass. Moreover, after the election, the Bush administration, like the Clinton administration in spring 2000, immediately began to outline its concerns about future steps Chen might envision and provided strong suggestions that his inaugural address in May 2004 avoid language likely to provoke Beijing.[27]

In sum, China's grand strategy had once more helped Beijing manage the Taiwan challenge by leveraging ties with an American partner who saw its own interests served by sustaining a constructive relationship with the PRC—especially useful for Washington in 2003–2004 as it sought a regional response to the North Korean nuclear program while the United States was preoccupied with a difficult situation in Iraq. To be sure, these events also confirmed that the American interest in cooperation with China that Beijing's strategy seeks to foster provides only limited leverage for China in addressing its Taiwan problem. As noted above, China does not yet have capabilities sufficient for it to promise to make a major contribution in addressing many international problems outside its immediate neighborhood, and China's self-interest in addressing many of the problems on which it is most useful for the United States (such as regional terrorism, proliferation, and tension in Korea) reduces the credibility of implicit threats to withhold cooperation if it is not satisfied with American policy toward Taiwan. But if China's current strategy provides only limited leverage, the major alternatives for coping with the Taiwan challenge are not much more appealing today than they were in 1996.

The "hard," exclusively military alternative emphasizing the use of force to

---

[26] Dana Milbank and Glenn Kessler, "President Warns Taiwan on Independence Efforts: Bush Says Referendum on China Should Not Be Held"; Philip P. Pan, "China Thanks Bush for Taiwan Stance: Beijing Issues New Warning against Move toward Independence." Chen did not cancel the referendum, but he did alter the topics in an attempt to allay American concerns about their original wording.

[27] See especially James A. Kelly, "Overview of U.S. Policy toward Taiwan"; also Sofia Wu, "DPP Whip Says Chen Aide's Washington Visit to Help Boost Taiwan-US Ties"; Charles Snyder, "Today's Speech Will Keep the US Satisfied: Diplomat"; Melody Chen, "Chen's Speech Was Constructive: Leach."

block independence and ultimately to realize reunification remains unattractive because China's PLA still does not have the capabilities necessary for high confidence in military success, certainly not if the United States intervenes on Taiwan's behalf, a prudent assumption ever since the 1996 crisis. Bluntly threatening or resorting to the use of force would also badly damage the improved international reputation China has carefully cultivated since the mid-1990s and deal a major blow to the country's development drive if it led to the rupture of economic ties with not just the United States but also its advanced industrial allies in Europe and Asia. A "soft," exclusively diplomatic alternative according to which Beijing offers Taiwan terms for reunification even more generous than those outlined between 1979 and 1995 remains unattractive because these concessions (on the political, economic, and military arrangements that would follow unification) cannot address the unwillingness of a growing segment of Taiwan's population to forsake their increasingly separate identity. Although this approach would enable Beijing to avoid the risks of defeat in battle and international political and economic isolation, it would put at risk the internal "stability and unity" that the regime insists is essential to China's continued development. If, as experience suggests is likely, the soft approach failed to entice Taiwan to agree to a plan for unification, there could well be a domestic backlash not only from erstwhile hard-liners within the leadership, but also from a general public who for more than fifty years have been told that reunification with Taiwan is the sacred duty of all Chinese nationalists. To them, a policy of patient and unrequited generosity that permits Taiwan's leaders to inch toward establishing their separate sovereignty would appear at best feckless and at worst treasonous. Because China's Communist Party leaders understand that their regime's legitimacy now rests on its nationalist credentials rather than a discredited, irrelevant Marxist ideology, they fear that failing the Taiwan test would trigger a major challenge to their rule. Passing that test requires, at minimum, defending the principle of China's claim to sovereignty and preventing Taiwan's independence. The PRC's current strategy arguably serves these twin purposes better than the more extreme alternatives.

In contrast with approaches that more exclusively emphasize force or diplomacy, China's current strategy keeps both options in play, provides incentives for others to help Beijing avoid worst-case outcomes (fighting and losing a war, or having to accept Taiwan's peaceful march toward independence), and at least creates the possibility that China can hold down the costs of conflict if it proves unavoidable. While it remains unlikely that any of Beijing's partners would side with it against Taiwan in a military conflict, their growing self-interest in China's economic health and its willingness to play a constructive international role could well limit the support they offer Taiwan or the United States during the conflict and, perhaps as important, their willingness to support policies aimed at isolating and containing China afterward.

The recurrent challenge of managing cross-strait relations, then, illustrates the usefulness as well as the limits of the grand strategy Beijing has embraced since 1996. It retains broad appeal among China's foreign policy elite because they recognize its advantages compared with the alternatives. Nevertheless, supporters of the strategy as well as its critics occasionally vent frustration with its limits, as they did in 2004. Although partnership with the United States had again helped Beijing avoid a disastrous confrontation across the Taiwan Strait, it had not helped move the matter toward any final resolution. Indeed, concerned that the United States either failed to understand Chen Shui-bian's ambitions or was inclined to encourage them, by late spring 2004 China's leaders were again angrily voicing their dissatisfaction with Chen (whom they expected would continue his quest for independence) as well as with enduring American security ties to his regime.[28] Domestic critics of Beijing's foreign policy seized upon developments in the Taiwan Strait to articulate objections that became part of their broader questioning of the use of the label "peaceful rise" that party and government leaders had been attaching to China's grand strategy since November 2003. These critics suggested that the importance of a strong military to defend national interests was being given short shrift and specifically argued that a one-sided emphasis on a "peaceful" foreign policy dangerously emboldened separatists on Taiwan who already doubted Beijing would ever dare carry out its threat to use force.[29] If so, the new lingo would

---

[28] For China's reaction to Chen's inaugural address, see Edward Cody, "Relationship with Taiwan Remains Tense, China Warns"; Cheong Ching, "Cause of Cross-Strait Instability Still There, Warns Beijing"; "Taiwanese Leader 'Man of Bad Faith'"; Sui Noi Goh, "China Ready to Sacrifice Games to Block Chen." China issued unusually strong expressions of concern about the continuing dangers in the Taiwan Strait and warnings about U.S. support for Taiwan during the July 2004 visit of U.S. national security adviser Condoleezza Rice. See "Jiang Zemin Huijian Meiguo Zongtong Guojia Anquan Shiwu Zhuli Laisi" [Jiang Zemin meets the U.S. president's national security adviser Rice]; "China Will Never Tolerate Taiwan Independence: Jiang Zemin"; "China 'Gravely Concerned' over US Arms to Taiwan."

[29] See Evan S. Medeiros, "China Debates Its 'Peaceful Rise Strategy'"; Robert Sutter, "China's Peaceful Rise and U.S. Interests in Asia – Status and Outlook." On the link to Taiwan, see Shi Yinhong. "Beijing's Lack of Sufficient Deterrence to Taiwan Leaves a Major Danger"; Wang Wei and Cai Yifeng, "'Heping Jueqi' Yu 'Heping Tongyi'" ["Peaceful rise" and "peaceful unification"]; Tao Deyan and Zhang Binyang, "Zhuanjia Zonglun Zhongguo Heping Jueqi Jinglüe" [Experts discuss China's peaceful rise strategy]; "China's New Path of Development and Peaceful Rise."

only weaken deterrence and increase the likelihood China would have to use force against Taiwan. Moreover, if conflict occurred, others would cite the contrast between "peaceful" rhetoric and actual behavior as evidence that China could never be taken at its word, a gratuitous addition to the already long list of costs for war in the Taiwan Strait.

Either the persuasiveness of these criticisms or support for them from China's partially retired elder statesman, Jiang Zemin, soon prompted a change in the language China's leaders used to describe their foreign policy.[30] By April 2004, "peaceful development" (safely rooted in Deng Xiaoping's claim that "peace and development" were the main trend of the current era) began to replace "peaceful rise" in the public discourse.[31] Yet even though the "peaceful rise" label diminished in prominence, Beijing continued to embrace the central argument its advocates had presented—that China's strategy would facilitate the country's rise as a great power through a protracted program of ambitious economic development requiring a relaxed international environment. "Peaceful rise," after all, had essentially been no more than a restatement of the core logic of the broadly supported grand strategy in place since the mid-1990s—a strategy emphasizing conditional cooperation that reflected a preference for, and emphasized the possibility of, China's peaceful rise to the

[30] Some claim that Jiang Zemin, who retained informal influence as well as his formal position as chairman of the Central Military Commission, objected less to the substance of the "peaceful rise" thesis than to its presentation as a major policy innovation by his successor Hu Jintao, whom he saw as too eager to build his own political stature and reduce Jiang's remaining clout. See Joseph Kahn, "Former Leader Is Still a Power in China's Life."

[31] See Hu Jintao, "China's Development Is an Opportunity for Asia (Speech by President Hu Jintao of China at the Opening Ceremony of the Boao Forum for Asia 2004 Annual Conference)." While repeating the central themes of the "peaceful rise" argument, Hu eschewed the label. See "Peaceful Rise: Strategic Choice for China." For the prominence accorded "peaceful rise" between its introduction at the November 2003 Boao Forum until Hu's April 2004 speech, see Zhan Xinhui, Zhou Hongyang, and Dian Zhehan, "Premier Wen Jiabao Delivers Keynote Speech at the Boao Forum"; "China's Road of Peaceful Rise"; Wen Jiabao, "Turning Your Eyes to China"; Gu Ping, "China's 'Peaceful Rise,' Which Emphasizes Achieving Modernization through Self-Reliance, Will Benefit Mankind"; "China's Peaceful Rise: A Road Chosen for Rejuvenation of a Great Nation." Elaboration on the argument by its original advocate can be found in Zheng Bijian, "New Path for China's Peaceful Rise and the Future of Asia"; "Strategic Opportunities: This Is the Fourth Opportunity in Modern History"; Zheng Bijian, "The Path of Peaceful Rise—The Multiplication and Division Method of 1.3 Billion"; Zheng Bijian, "China's Peaceful Rise and Opportunities for the Asia-Pacific Region." An extensive collection of documents can be found at *Zhongguo de Heping Jueqi zhi Lu* [China's road of peaceful rise].

ranks of the great powers during the era of American-led unipolarity by rely-ing on a combination of globally engaged economic development, prudent military modernization, and deft diplomacy. Events in the Taiwan Strait had once again revealed this strategy's enduring usefulness. Critics could identify its shortcomings; they could not, however, come up with a more appealing alternative.

Robustness with Respect to International Change

China's current grand strategy is likely to prove durable not only because of its domestic political viability, but also because it offers a prudent hedge against changes in China's international political circumstances. The approach enables China to deal with its immediate security problems without sacrificing future flexibility. At present, unmatched American capabilities and those of its allies in East Asia make the United States the chief constraint on China's abil-ity to pursue its international interests; if provoked, the United States also poses the most serious military threat. A central feature of Beijing's strategy at present, therefore, is the effort to mute tensions with the United States while also reducing the incentives for other major powers and regional actors to align with Washington against China. But the interests that lead the United States as a geographical outsider to adopt the sorts of measures in East Asia that most worry China are derivative of Washington's global interests and mainly reflect diffuse American concerns—about the economic spillovers from regional instability, about the importance of its general reputation as a reliable ally, about its principled stand against the use of force to change the international status quo, and most importantly about ensuring that it remains the sole superpower in a unipolar system.[32] Although Chinese analysts expect the massive American advantage in terms of overall capabilities to continue for at least several decades, there is less certainty about the durability of its interest in a major physical presence in East Asia.[33] For China's current strategy to re-

---

[32] My American interlocutors in Washington, D.C., cited these as the principal American concerns about events in East Asia, especially in their comments about the U.S. stake in the Taiwan dispute (author's interviews, Washington, D.C., February–March 2000). See also Zbigniew Brzezinski, *The Grand Chessboard: American Primacy and Its Geostrategic Imperatives*, pp. 188–89.

[33] The Clinton administration's proclamation that the United States would maintain its presence in East Asia, including 100,000 troops, spoke as much to the issue of inter-ests and commitments as military capabilities. When China's military analysts have sug-gested that the United States would be unwilling to absorb heavy losses in a confronta-tion over Taiwan, their argument often rests in part on a belief that the United States does not have the sort of vital interest at stake that is necessary to underpin resolve. See

main viable, therefore, it must not only help manage the immediate risk of confrontation with the preponderant United States, but also provide a hedge against the possibility of new risks emerging.

Changing Threats

Among the many possible new risks China might face (e.g., a resurgent Russia, a rising India), the one that has most often animated Beijing's thinking is the prospect of a more independent and assertive Japan. While the United States is in East Asia by choice and its interests are derivative, Japan is in East Asia of necessity, could relatively quickly fill out its presently incomplete portfolio of great power attributes, and has intrinsic interests (economic and territorial) in the region that ensure it will remain a highly motivated actor.

China's reintensified concern about Japan's changing role in East Asia following the Taiwan Strait crisis of 1995–96, discussed above, was one of the key triggers for the adjustment in Beijing's foreign policy that I label its grand strategy. Uncertainty and doubts about Tokyo's intentions and growing military capabilities in part reflect concerns that arise as a consequence of the security dilemma many states confront. They are exacerbated in this specific case, however, by the historical legacy of Japanese aggression.[34] While the reflexive alarmism of China's older generation that directly experienced the events of the mid-twentieth century fades in importance, the legacy of that experience refracted through historical lessons conveyed to new generations infuses contemporary analysis and feeds a belief that if Japan were to reemerge as a truly independent player in East Asia, it would likely be a key rival for China. The end of the Cold War did not make this prospect inevitable, but for some it increased the plausibility. Since the urgency of the Soviet threat that had led Tokyo to remain tightly tethered to its American protector has disappeared, the U.S.-Japan alliance might weaken: either the Americans could tire of a free-riding

---

Chas. W. Freeman, "Preventing War in the Taiwan Strait; Restraining Taiwan—and Beijing." One of China's senior military analysts also argued that the humanistic tradition in U.S. strategic culture leads American planners to emphasize sophisticated weapons because they facilitate quick wars that minimize casualties. This American concern allegedly grants leverage to weaker countries, including China, with more vital interests at stake and with the will to endure a bloody struggle in which they inflict heavy losses on the United States (Fu Liqun, "Several Basic Ideas in U.S. Strategic Thinking"). See also Thomas J. Christensen, "Posing Problems without Catching Up: China's Rise and Challenges for U.S. Security Policy," esp. pp. 17–20.

[34] Author's interviews, Beijing, June–July 1998. See also Thomas J. Christensen, "China, the U.S.-Japan Alliance, and the Security Dilemma in East Asia"; Thomas J. Christensen, "Chinese Realpolitik."

ally, or the Japanese could tire of playing second fiddle. Regardless, the result could be a new, potentially serious, challenge for China.

During the late 1980s, the concern that Japan might reemerge as a militarily potent great power had reflected the belief that this result was likely to be a byproduct of its growing economic wealth. But even when Japan's economy faltered after 1990, Beijing's concerns about Tokyo's future role did not fade much. Instead, during the 1990s, the disruptive political consequences of economic stagnation, the weakening of forty years of predictable LDP leadership in Tokyo, signs that the pacifism of the immediate postwar period was eroding with generational change, and more frequent expressions of Japanese apprehension about the policies China might adopt in the future continued to feed the uncertainty against which Beijing believed it needed to hedge.[35] Such worries help explain China's ambivalence about the U.S.-Japan alliance after the mid-1990s: China both feared its reorientation in ways that would threaten China's regional interests and appreciated its function as an anchor on Tokyo.[36] The former concern, as noted in previous chapters, was prominent in the late 1990s because China's leaders believed they saw a link between changes in the U.S.-Japan security relationship and the sensitive issues of Taiwan and ballistic missile defenses. Beijing's concern about missile defenses, in particular, was not merely their potential to reduce the usefulness of China's ballistic missiles in Asia, especially in the Taiwan theater. Beijing also worried that technology transfers resulting from joint Japanese-American re-

[35] See Liu Changmin, "Shixi Dangjin Riben Zhengzhi De Youqinghua" [A tentative analysis of the right-wing drift in contemporary Japanese politics], pp. 23, 25–26; also Fang Hua, "Yatai Anquan Jiagou De Xianzhuang, Qushi Ji Zhongguo De Zuoyong" [The current Asia-Pacific security framework: Trends and China's role], p. 14. On China's need for a flexible hedge against the uncertainty of Japan's future role, see Ye Zicheng, "Zhongguo Shixing Daguo Waijiao Zhanlüe Shizai Bixing" [The imperative for China to implement a great power diplomatic strategy], p. 9. On Japan's strong economic interest in Southeast Asia and its alleged role in generating China threat arguments in that region to minimize China's prospects there, see Lu Jianren, "Yatai Daguo Zai Dongnan Yazhou Diqu De Liyi" [Asia-Pacific great powers' interests in Southeast Asia], pp. 42–43, 45. For the argument that Japan now seeks to create a "theory of China as an economic threat" to divert attention from Tokyo's inability to solve its own economic problems, see "PRC Academics Discuss Japan's Economic Problems, 'China Threat Theory.'" See also Liu Di, "Deng Xiaoping's Thinking on Diplomatic Work—Interview with Liang Shoude, Dean for College of International Relations for Beijing University"; Christensen, "Realism with Chinese Characteristics"; Christensen, "Chinese Realpolitik."

[36] For an unusually frank analysis of the positive role of the U.S.-Japan alliance, see Ni Feng, "Meiri Tongmeng Yu Diqu Anquan" [The U.S.-Japan alliance and regional security], pp. 71–72.

search and development together with Japan's sophisticated nuclear expertise, plentiful supply of fissile materials, and already-advancing missile capabilities would move Tokyo ever closer to becoming a nuclear weapons state and full-fledged great power.[37]

Anxiety about the prospect of confronting a hostile and assertive Japan did diminish somewhat when bilateral relations improved after Zhu Rongji's visit in 2000 and as Beijing grew more skeptical that an aging and resource-poor Japan would be able to compete with China in the long run.[38] Yet even as this mellowing trend appeared, suspicion about Japan's intentions remained a prominent theme in the mass media and among many Chinese foreign policy analysts.[39] The continuing argument has been that Japan seizes every available pretext to inch toward its goal of becoming a "normal country" and a major military power, with obvious implications for future rivalry with China. In this view, the revision of U.S.-Japan security guidelines that had been justified by invoking the pretext of Korean contingencies was simply one key step in an ongoing process of Japan grasping opportunities to break free of the constraints on its international role. Since 1996, analysts making this argument

[37] On the worries about strengthened U.S.-Japan security cooperation since 1996, especially on TMD, see Lu Youzhi, "Chongxin Shenshi Zhongguo De Anquan Huanjing" [A fresh examination of China's security environment], p. 59; Chen Ying, "Zhanqu Daodan Fangyu Xitong Yu Dongya Anquan Xingshi" [Theater missile defense and East Asia's security situation], p. 29; Jin Xin, "Meiguo Yanfa TMD De Yitu Ji Dui Quanqiu He Woguo Anquan De Yingxiang" [US plans for research and development of TMD and its influence on the security of the world and our country], p. 25; Fang, "Yatai Anquan Jiagou De Xianzhuang," p. 14; Lu, "Yatai Daguo Zai Dongnan Yazhou Diqu De Liyi," pp. 42–43. As Japan began to expand its role in peacekeeping operations and debated contingency plans for dealing with the North Korean nuclear threat, Chinese concerns about Japan's international role again increased. See Gao Yijun, "Will Japanese Militarism 'Revive' Taking Advantage of DPRK Nuclear Issue?"; Sun Dongmin, "'Emergencies Legislation' Is Legislation That Serves War Preparation"; Gao Hong, "Behind the 'Legislation for Emergencies.'"

[38] See, for example, Jin Xide et al., "Reorienting Sino-Japanese Relations."

[39] David Shambaugh notes in particular that the "anti-Japanese sentiment one encounters among the PLA at all levels is palpable." See David Shambaugh, *Modernizing China's Military*, p. 301. There is, however, a recent countercurrent in the public debate about Sino-Japanese relations that calls for moving beyond the problems of the past and avoiding the caricatures and exaggeration that often mark discussion of the relationship. For an overview of the sometimes heated debate prompted by the unorthodox call for "new thinking" about Japan in articles by Ma Licheng, a commentator with *Renmin Ribao*, and Shi Yinhong, a professor at People's University, both published in the prestigious journal *Strategy and Management*, see Liu Xiaobiao, "Where Are Sino-Japanese Relations Heading—A Commentary on Observations by Scholars and Concerns among the People."

have criticized Japan's annual Defense White Papers for invoking the pretext of growing Chinese capabilities (especially missile deployments) to build support for increased investment in the military. They have also criticized leaders in Tokyo for invoking the pretext of participation in the American-led global war on terrorism after 9/11 (including limited roles in Afghanistan and Iraq) and then the dangers posed by North Korea's resurfaced nuclear weapons program after 2002 to gradually whittle away at the legal restrictions on the role of the Self-Defense Forces and to encourage a steady expansion of Japan's power-projection and intelligence-gathering capabilities.[40]

Is China's current grand strategy robust enough to offer a hedge against chronic concerns about Japan's future role? In the short term, Beijing's strategy has mainly emphasized the cultivation of a partnership with Japan to increase Tokyo's stake in avoiding a sharp deterioration in Sino-Japanese relations. If such a deterioration were nevertheless to set in, the linkages that have recently been cultivated not only would provide Tokyo with incentives to exercise some restraint, but Beijing's partnerships with other major powers would also be expected to provide them with incentives to refrain from lining up with Japan against China. In this way, the logic of the strategy that currently informs China's efforts to cope with the risks a hostile United States might pose provides for flexibility should new risks, such as a hostile Japan, emerge in the future.

Changing Power

Change in the identity of rivals is just one of the possible international challenges to the robustness of China's current grand strategy. Significant changes in the international balance of power could also lead Beijing to reconsider its

[40] For China's strongly negative reaction to Japan's ten-year defense program announced in December 2004, see "China Expresses 'Deep Concern' With Japan's New Defense Guidelines"; "Bizarre Indication of 'China threat' in Japanese Defense Program." For an example of the especially strident criticism of the Japan Defense White Paper submitted in August 2003, see Zhang Baiyu, "Analysis of Japan's New Defense White Paper." See also Lu Zhongwei, "What Is the Purpose of the 'New Guidelines'?"; Gu, "A New Pretext for Joining the TMD System"; "Article Slams Japan's 2001 Defense White Paper for Spreading New 'China Threat Theory'"; Yu Shuang, "A Look at Japan's Military Expansion from Its Attempt to Upgrade Self Defense Agency"; Liang Ming, "'Defense White Paper' Reveals Japan's Military Intentions"; "Riben Zhanji Yao Feiyue Taipingyang Canjia Meiguo Junshi Yanxi" [Japanese warplanes to fly across the Pacific to participate in U.S. military exercises]; Wang Xiaomei, "Japan Is Advancing Step by Step to Becoming a Military Power"; Li Heng, "Is Japan Advancing toward a 'Normal Country'"; "Japan Has an Axe to Grind: News Analysis."

strategy's suitability. To the extent that the relative capabilities of states typically shift slowly, however, power considerations are arguably yet another reason to expect China's current grand strategy to endure.

As others have noted, China's contemporary leaders, like their predecessors in Imperial China, prize the practice of realpolitik. Beijing's keen sensitivity to the importance of relative capabilities, a sensitivity that Iain Johnston attributes to China's *parabellum* strategic culture, underpins its current approach designed to facilitate China's rise in an era when it remains relatively weak.[41] Indeed, today's grand strategy reflects one of the bedrock principles that Johnston's work highlights—minimize others' perception of one's strength even as one's strength grows. Deng Xiaoping's frequently cited admonition for China to "bide our time and conceal our capabilities" (*tao guang yang hui*) seemingly echoed this precept, as did Jiang Zemin's similar counsel that China, while it is at a material disadvantage, must "enhance confidence, decrease troubles, promote cooperation, and avoid confrontation."[42] Because China's ability to improve its international power position is sharply limited both by the burden of a still-developing economy and by the long head start of its advanced industrial rivals, this emphasis on a cautious foreign policy line is likely to continue well into the twenty-first century.[43]

The central consideration of relative power suggests the sorts of dramatic changes in China's circumstances that would probably have to occur for Beijing to fundamentally revise its present grand strategy. China might forsake its

---

[41] See Alastair Iain Johnston, *Cultural Realism: Strategic Culture and Grand Strategy in Chinese History*; Alastair Iain Johnston, "Cultural Realism and Strategy in Maoist China," pp. 219–20, 247; Christensen, "Chinese Realpolitik"; Michael Pillsbury, *China Debates the Future Security Environment*, pp. xxxv, xxxix; Michael D. Swaine and Ashley J. Tellis, *Interpreting China's Grand Strategy: Past, Present, and Future*, pp. xii, 231, 233, 236.

[42] Pillsbury, *China Debates the Future Security Environment*, p. xxxix n.13. In contemporary thinking about how to cope with the dominant United States, Pillsbury detects the influence of traditional Chinese strategic notions dating to the Warring States period that explains "how to survive destruction at the hands of a predator hegemon" (ibid., xxxv). See also Swaine and Tellis, *Interpreting China's Grand Strategy*, especially chapter 3.

[43] Swaine and Tellis predicted that China's cautious "calculative strategy" rooted in China's material disadvantages is likely to last at least through "2015–2020" and probably even longer because of the daunting challenges China faces in terms of economic, military, and political development (Swaine and Tellis, *Interpreting China's Grand Strategy*, pp. 155–81). For a Chinese view of naval modernization that similarly anticipates at least three decades of arduous effort before China can hope to become a strong regional maritime power with advanced long-range capabilities, see Liu Yijian, "Zhongguo Weilai De Haijun Jianshe Yu Haijun Zhanlüe" [The future of China's navy building and naval strategy], pp. 99, 100.

current approach under two scenarios—one in which external constraints became much tighter, and one in which they became much looser.[44]

If a still weak China found itself facing dire threats from one or more great powers whose might it could not match—a situation similar to that which the PRC faced during much of the Cold War—core survival concerns would probably lead Beijing to attempt to reprise that era's approach of straightforward counterbalancing. China would most likely rely on its nuclear deterrent as the ultimate security guarantee while also attempting to win the backing of a powerful ally, perhaps transforming one or more of its strategic partnerships into a traditional military alliance.[45] Alternatively, if China's relative capabilities were to increase dramatically, or if Beijing concluded that the system's most capable actors lacked the interest or resolve to resist Chinese initiatives, it might believe that it no longer needed to reassure others or forestall their collaboration. China might then shift to a strategy that more assertively attempted to reshape the international system according to its own preferences. Such a relaxation of the external constraints on China's foreign policy could result from an improbably rapid process of economic and military modernization that quickly elevated the PRC to superpower status or if China's strongest competitors proved unable or unwilling to remain internationally engaged. Under such circumstances, Beijing would not be free to do as it pleased on the world scene, but it would have greater latitude than it now does to follow preference rather than necessity.[46]

---

[44] For other possible, though less plausible, scenarios that might lead to a change in grand strategy, see Swaine and Tellis, *Interpreting China's Grand Strategy*, pp. 152, 153–79; 183–97.

[45] The alleged need to respond to an intense threat, of course, was the justification cited by those who argued for a change in China's foreign policy during the 1999 debate discussed in chapter 7. See also Swaine and Tellis, *Interpreting China's Grand Strategy*, p. 236; Yan Xuetong, "Dui Zhongguo Anquan Huanjing De Fenxi Yu Sikao" [Analysis of and reflections on China's security environment], pp. 7, 8, 10; Zhou Guiyin, "Xin Shiji De Guoji Anquan Yu Anquan Zhanlüe" [International security and security strategy in the new century], pp. 69–70; Lu, "Chongxin Shenshi Zhongguo De Anquan Huanjing," pp. 56, 57; Chu Shulong and Wang Zaibang, "Guanyu Guoji Xingshi He Wo Duiwai Zhanlüe Ruogan Zhongda Wenti De Sikao" [Reflections on some important questions about the international situation and our external strategy], 18–19.

[46] See Johnston, "Cultural Realism and Strategy in Maoist China," p. 247; Pillsbury, *China Debates the Future Security Environment*, p. xxxv. Swaine and Tellis similarly expect that a future, stronger China would "pursue most, if not all, of the core elements of those assertive grand strategies pursued by major powers in the past." Their forecast rests on not just realist reasoning but also a recognition of China's past experience with regional primacy, its humiliation while weak, and resentment of U.S. efforts to preserve its own hegemony that China sees as an attempt to limit its influence (Swaine and

For the foreseeable future, however, neither of these more extreme alternatives seems as plausible as a slow but steady increase in China's economic and military power within an East Asia where potential rivals remain vigilant.[47] Indeed, China's own strategic analysts forecast a protracted and multifaceted struggle caused by American efforts to prolong the present era of unipolarity and the efforts of other countries (especially China, Russia, and France) that hope to hasten the transition to a multipolar world. As noted above, by the turn of the century China's leaders reluctantly embraced what had previously been a heterodox view—that United States dominance was likely to endure for decades longer than they anticipated when the Cold War ended. Some Chinese analysts even began to assert that the U.S. advantage might actually increase for a while before the onset of an allegedly inevitable American decline. In this respect, the 1999 Kosovo War was seen as further evidence of the inability of a weak Russia and China to affect U.S. war plans and also as evidence that there was as yet not any European entity on the horizon that might challenge U.S. supremacy and prefigure the transition to multipolarity.[48] Subsequently, the Bush doctrine, U.S. prosecution of the war on terrorism, and the initial assessment of the Iraq war of 2003 only reinforced this sobering view of a protracted unipolar era for which a rising China's current grand strategy is designed.[49]

Tellis, *Interpreting China's Grand Strategy*, pp. xii; 153–54, 231, 233, 236). For a view questioning realist predictions about a more powerful China's regional role, see David C. Kang, "Getting Asia Wrong: The Need for New Analytical Frameworks."

[47] For a summary of the consensus of expert opinion, along with dissenting views, see "Chinese Military Power, Report of an Independent Task Force." This early twenty-first-century forecast generally comports with the less alarmist assessments from the 1990s. See also Brzezinski, *The Grand Chessboard*, pp. 164, 165–67. For Chinese discussion of the power trajectories of various countries, including discussions of "comprehensive national power," see Yan Xuetong, *Zhongguo Guojia Liyi Fenxi* [Analysis of China's national interest], pp. 87–95; Gao Heng, ed., *2020 Daguo Zhanlüe* [Great power strategy in 2020]; Pillsbury, *China Debates the Future Security Environment*, p. 203, chapter 5.

[48] See Ye, "Zhongguo Shixing Daguo Waijiao Zhanlüe Shizai Bixing," pp. 6, 7

[49] See Dong Guozheng, "Multipolarization: Irresistible Tide of History—Interview with National Defense University Associate Professor Jin Yinan"; Zhu Yanhua, "China's Military Affairs Expert Says That Iraqi War Has Hindered the Trend Towards Multipolarization in the World." Still, China's analysts stuck with the position that had emerged in the late 1990s—the evident strengthening of the United States was only a "setback in the transition to a new [i.e., multipolar] world structure"; its arrival might be slow, but it was inevitable (Pillsbury, *China Debates the Future Security Environment*, pp. 13, 15, 25, 28, 58, 65–72, 73–76; Xiao Feng, "Dui Guoji Xingshizhong Jige Redian Wenti De Kanfa" [Perspective on several hot issues in the international situation],

China's leaders, then, have reconciled themselves to the reality that unipolarity will endure for at least several decades. They similarly accept that their country's military capabilities will lag significantly behind those of the United States. Despite strides in military modernization, China's strategic weapons remain outclassed by the U.S. nuclear arsenal, both in terms of quantity and quality, China's improving air force remains overmatched, and China's navy remains unable to project power far beyond the mainland if it faces serious opposition. Even as the PLA has made strides in some areas, it has fallen further behind in others (especially computerization and missile defenses).[50] Because the regime has made its top priority economic modernization, both to ensure domestic political stability and as an investment in the foundation needed for future military strength, China's strategists must assume that for the foreseeable future the PLA will have little choice but to continue to upgrade only selected forces and to adopt clever varieties of asymmetric warfare in the event it is called upon to fight the superior adversary.[51]

---

pp. 1–3; Chu and Wang, "Guanyu Guoji Xingshi He Wo Duiwai Zhanlüe Ruogan Zhongda Wenti De Sikao," p. 17; Lu, "Chongxin Shenshi Zhongguo De Anquan Huanjing," pp. 57–58; Sun Jianshe, "Shiji Zhijiao Dui Woguo Anquan Huanjing De Sikao" [Reflections on our country's security environment at the turn of the century], p. 19).

[50] See Yan, "Dui Zhongguo Anquan Huanjing De Fenxi Yu Sikao," pp. 7, 9. See "Chinese Military Power, Report of an Independent Task Force." On the priority that China attaches to overcoming its deficiencies in the rapidly advancing "revolution in military affairs," see "Jiang Zemin Hu Jintao Deng Huijian Di Shisici Wuguang Gongzuo Huiyi Daibiao" [Jiang Zemin, Hu Jintao, and others meet with representatives to the Fourteenth Work Conference of Military Officers].

[51] To offset U.S. advantages, for example, some have called for identifying and exploiting distinctive American military vulnerabilities (especially critical nodes of its high-technology systems), the long supply lines that a distant United States must maintain, and a purported American aversion to casualties. See Mark Burles and Abram N. Shulsky, *Patterns in China's Use of Force: Evidence from History and Doctrinal Writings.* Some have argued that China may be able to exploit selected technologies associated with the "revolution in military affairs" more effectively than the allegedly hidebound United States and therefore acquire at least a limited capability to paralyze superior American forces. See Pillsbury, *China Debates the Future Security Environment,* pp. 65–72, 73–76, chapter 6. See also Qiao Liang and Wang Xiangsui, *Unrestricted Warfare;* Zhang Wenmu, "Kesuowo Zhanzheng Yu Zhongguo Xin Shiji Anquan Zhanlüe" [The Kosovo War and China's security strategy in the new century], p. 4; Chu Shulong, "Lengzhanhou Zhongguo Anquan Zhanlüe Sixiang De Fazhan" [The development of China's thinking about security strategy after the Cold War], p. 13; Zalmay M. Khalilzad et al., *The United States and a Rising China: Strategic and Military Implications,* pp. 39–44, 48–59. In August 2000, China's president, Jiang Zemin, was reported to have called for a focus on strategically decisive weapons, especially those

Moreover, while China's leaders recognize the distance they must travel to field a great power military in the twenty-first century, the experience of the early 1990s has also taught them that even the modest improvement in PLA's capabilities they now seek may trigger concerns in Washington as well as among neighboring countries that the United States can try to exploit if it wants to hem China in.[52] Beijing's interest in minimizing the risk of provoking such a dangerous deterioration in its international environment as it gradually builds its strength within the constraints of a unipolar world is an important reason why it is likely to adhere to its present approach—a grand strategy that aims to increase China's influence, but without relying on methods, such as rapid armament, that would alarm potential military rivals and alienate valued economic partners.[53]

If anything, confidence in the suitability of the grand strategy Beijing embraced by the late 1990s has grown stronger in the opening years of the twenty-first century. The surprisingly quick and sharp improvement of Sino-American relations after the summer of 2001, noted above, has apparently

---

that may be secretly developed or may be unexpectedly decisive in battle (*mimi shashou wuqi*). See "Chuanwen Jiang Zemin Zhishi Gaibian Zhonggong De Guofang Zhengce" [Jiang Zemin said to indicate a change in CCP national defense policy]; also Cary Huang, "Jiang Zemin Reportedly Urges Development of Strategic Weapons." Jiang's suggestion mirrors the call made by some of China's strategic analysts to develop the "assassin's mace" (*shashoujian*), which seems to mean an innovative counter to an ostensibly more powerful adversary's military strength. A closer English synonym for such a weapon might be "magic bullet." See also Yan, "Dui Zhongguo Anquan Huanjing De Fenxi Yu Sikao," p. 10. For a more traditional military assessment that calls for substantial investment in technologically advanced air and naval forces to offset the threat a superior United States allegedly poses to China's disputed and restive regions (Taiwan, the Spratly Islands, Tibet, Xinjiang), see Zhang, "Kesuowo Zhanzheng Yu Zhongguo Xin Shiji Anquan Zhanlüe," p. 4. On the daunting (and growing) challenges that even a weaker and less sophisticated China poses for U.S. forces, see Khalilzad et al., *The United States and a Rising China: Strategic and Military Implications,* pp. 39–44, 48–59; also Swaine and Tellis, *Interpreting China's Grand Strategy,* p. 4.

[52] See Chu and Wang, "Guanyu Guoji Xingshi He Wo Duiwai Zhanlüe Ruogan Zhongda Wenti De Sikao," p. 20; Yan, "Dui Zhongguo Anquan Huanjing De Fenxi Yu Sikao," pp. 6ff.

[53] See Wang Sheng, "'Taoguang Yanghui' Bu Shi Quan Yi Zhi Ji" ['Concealing one's strength and biding one's time' is not a stopgap]. See also Pillsbury, *China Debates the Future Security Environment,* p. xxxix; Guo Shuyong, "21 Shiji Qianye Zhongguo Waijiao Dazhanlüe Chuyi" [A modest proposal for China's diplomatic grand strategy on the eve of the twenty-first century], pp. 92–93, 94. For a view that frankly endorses a more ambitious Chinese agenda, see Ye, "Zhongguo Shixing Daguo Waijiao Zhanlüe Shizai Bixing." On the argument for a "preventive" but not "confrontational" strategy, see Yan, "Dui Zhongguo Anquan Huanjing De Fenxi Yu Sikao," p. 9.

been taken as further evidence that the current approach best serves China's national interest. By late 2002, Chinese analysts were asserting that the PRC's foreign policy line had made it possible to capitalize on the shift in American priorities after September 11, 2001, and usher in a period in Sino-American relations better than at any time in the post–Cold War era. As a result, a two-decade window of "strategic opportunity" was allegedly opened during which Beijing would be able to safely continue emphasizing domestic development. This idea of a period of strategic opportunity was officially articulated by President Jiang Zemin at the 16th CCP Congress in October 2002, and it quickly became a prominent theme in China's commentary on world affairs.[54] Although China's grand strategy was well suited to making the most of this opportunity, analysts did not argue that currently favorable circumstances were sure to last indefinitely. On the contrary, they acknowledged the possibility that in the more distant and uncertain future changed circumstances might require China to adopt a new grand strategy. But even if that happened, the optimal way to prepare for the day when China would be one of several great powers in a multipolar world was to seize the opportunity to pursue steady development over at least the next twenty years.[55] For the duration of the current era, in other words, the grand strategy of fostering contingent cooperation with the major powers while seeking to reassure nervous neighbors would continue to serve the country's national interest in a peaceful context for its continued rise.

[54] See "Strategic Opportunities: This Is the Fourth Opportunity in Modern History." At the 10th National People's Congress in March 2003, newly selected president Hu Jintao reprised the theme ("Released with Authorization from the 'Two Sessions': President Hu Jintao's Speech at the First Session of the 10th National People's Congress"). See also Ren Zhongping, "Zaigan Yige Ershi Nian! Lun Woguo Gaige Fazhan De Guanjian Shiqi" [Work hard for another 20 years! On a critical period in our country's reform and development]. Dissenting voices in China continue to worry about U.S. intentions in the near term. See Wang Weixing, "The United States and China Start a Quasi-Military Alliance," pp. 10–12; "Commentary: U.S. Dreams of Asian NATO."

[55] See "Promoting Rapid Development of Military Modernization—Ninth Commentary on Study, Implementation of Spirit of 16th CPC National Congress"; Liu, "'The Period of Strategic Opportunity' and Sino-U.S. Ties." For a view that also emphasizes the need for China to take advantage of the "period of strategic opportunity" to democratize, thereby reducing a major irritant in Sino-American relations, see Liu Jianfei, "The Building of Democratic Politics in China and Sino-US Relations."

The Rising Challenge

If Beijing does adhere to its current approach, what are the likely consequences for international security? As explained in chapter 3, international relations theory provides no definitive answers, but it does provide multiple reasons to worry about the disruptive effects of a rising great power. In addition to such theoretical concerns, some have offered troubling forecasts that are inspired by historical analogies between China today and other rising powers in the past. The truly disturbing parallels are those invoking some of the twentieth century's most disruptive actors—Wilhelmine or Nazi Germany, Imperial Japan, and the Soviet Union.[1] For reasons set forth below, however, such analogies seem inappropriate. Instead, I suggest that if there is a helpful historical analogy (and even this one cannot be pushed too far), it may be a somewhat less troubling one—Germany in the era of Otto von Bismarck. I begin this chapter by considering this analogy's relevance. I then briefly address the uncertainties that are inherent in any attempt to forecast the implications for international security of China's rise in the opening decades of the twenty-first century and conclude by discussing the challenges its rise presents for policy makers.

Clues from the Past?

Like China, Bismarck's Germany was a geopolitically central rising power whose current and projected future capabilities naturally drew the attention of

---

[1] See Arthur Waldron, "Statement of Dr. Arthur Waldron." See also Edward Friedman, "The Challenge of a Rising China: Another Germany?" China's analysts have begun to respond to the claim that their country will follow the path that history's revisionist and aggressive rising powers have followed. See "China's New Path of Development and Peaceful Rise."

the system's other major actors. Though this broad similarity in the countries' international circumstances accounts for a rough similarity in grand strategic design, important substantive differences between the two cases, even aside from the obvious cultural and historical differences, account for important differences in strategic content. The historical analogy, in short, is only a loose one and must be heavily qualified.[2] Given the trajectory Germany followed in the years after Bismarck and today's concerns about China's future behavior, this imperfect comparison is worth exploring briefly, but four qualifications that identify key similarities and differences must be kept in mind.

Strategic Motivation

Bismarck's era was long, and the chancellor's concerns evolved over time. Although the fundamental logic of his grand strategy endured (his goal was to maximize Germany's flexibility in unfavorable geopolitical circumstances that precluded English-style aloofness), between the 1850s and 1880s Bismarck's focus changed. In the 1850s and 1860s, his chief goal was to preserve Prussia's leadership of Germany. Having succeeded in this task, Bismarck by the 1870s established as his chief, though not sole, goal for a Germany unified under Prussia's leadership ensuring that its newfound strength did not provoke foreign powers to combine against it. China's struggle for national unification basically ended with the CCP's victory in 1949, and the period in which it was focused on preserving the fruits of its revolution basically ended along with the Cold War. China's current grand strategic challenge is closer to that of Germany during the last two decades of Bismarck's leadership. As such, Kissinger's characterization of Germany's concern after the Franco-Prussian War might well be applied to China's concern about strategic encirclement after the Cold War: "Once Germany was transformed from a potential victim

[2] I thank Walter McDougall and Marc Trachtenberg for their criticisms that helped me refine my thinking about the China-Bismarck analogy. On the usefulness of historical analogies applied to China, see Richard Baum and Alexei Shevchenko, "Will China Join an Encompassing Coalition with Other Great Powers?" For a less sanguine view that invokes the Bismarck analogy, see the comments of U.S. admiral Dennis C. Blair, commander in chief of the U.S. Pacific Command (Blair, "The Role of Armed Forces in Regional Security Cooperation"). Josef Joffe employed a Bismarckian analogy in his assessment of U.S. strategic options shortly after the Cold War ("'Bismarck or Britain'? Toward an American Grand Strategy after Bipolarity"). China is arguably a more apt analogue than the United States for two reasons. First, like Germany, China lacks the distinctive geographical separation from other major powers that the United States enjoys. Second, like Bismarck's Germany, China is a rising, rather than a dominant, great power.

of aggression to a threat to the European equilibrium, the remote contingency of the other states of Europe uniting against Germany became a real possibility."[3]

Military Risk

Like Bismarck's Germany, a rising China today is eyed with suspicion. And like Bismarck's Germany, China deploys capabilities that lag behind those of the world's premier power (then Britain, now the United States). Unlike Bismarck's Germany, however, China today has deep concerns about the capabilities and intentions of the system's leading state. Britain, though the leading military power, was not Germany's principal strategic problem in Bismarck's day. Britain was mainly a naval power and did not tap its larger economy to deploy ground forces of a size and type that would allow it to dominate on the continent. Bismarck's strategy was designed to avoid giving Britain any strong reason to shoulder the additional burden that would be required if it wanted to offset land-power Germany's growing strength. The United States, however, *is* China's principal strategic problem today. Washington has already tapped the world's premier economy to deploy military forces of a size and type that give it unparalleled power projection capabilities throughout East Asia. In particular, the range and sophistication of U.S. air and naval forces give it the clout not only to threaten China's core security interests, but also to offset Beijing's ability to exert influence over continental and maritime developments in the region beyond the PRC's borders. In this respect, early twenty-first century China is more tightly constrained by the system's leading military power than was late nineteenth century Germany and faces clearer incentives to tread cautiously.

Available Allies

Unlike Germany in Bismarck's era of multipolarity, China in today's era of unipolarity must forge its grand strategy without the availability of allies that could effectively tip the balance of power. Bismarck could develop an exquisitely complex network of crosscutting alliances designed to check potential enemies while Germany grew from one among several European great powers to become the dominant actor on the continent. With an eye to coalition dy-

---

[3] Henry Kissinger, *Diplomacy*, p. 134; see also ibid., pp. 122–23, 125, 134, 158. For histories of Bismarck's diplomacy, see W. N. Medlicott and Dorothy K. Covney, eds., *Bismarck and Europe*; Theodore S. Hamerow, *Otto Von Bismarck: A Historical Assessment*; George O. Kent, *Bismarck and His Times*; D. G. Williamson, *Bismarck and Germany, 1862–1890*.

namics (and a keen sense of what we now label the security dilemma), after 1871 Bismarck insisted that his country was a "saturated power" and he steadfastly eschewed expansionism that might have encouraged rivals to ally against Germany:

> We ought to do all we can to weaken the bad feeling which has been called out through our growth to the position of a real Great power. . . . It has always been my ideal aim, after we had established our unity within the possible limits, to win the confidence not only of the smaller European states, but also of the Great Powers, and to convince them that German policy will be just and peaceful, now that it has repaired the *injuria temporum*, the disintegration of the nation. In order to produce this confidence it is above everything necessary that we should be honourable, open, and easily reconciled in case of friction or untoward events.[4]

Bismarck's strategy was strikingly successful during the latter decades of the nineteenth century. It subsequently broke down, however, as the complex alliances that he had managed with much difficulty proved too difficult for his less capable and more ambitious successors to sustain.[5]

China's leaders have similarly sought to convince prospective rivals that it harbors no hegemonic ambitions and, like Bismarck, have been trying to prevent the hardening of a hostile alliance network while they focus on developing China's own capabilities. In the era of unipolarity, however, Beijing has not had the option of reprising the sort of alliance building Bismarck undertook. Instead of formal alliances, it has sought to establish a set of bilateral relations with the other major powers, the partnerships described in chapter 7. Although Beijing's approach is clearly different from Bismarck's, the array of partnerships China has nurtured, like Bismarck's complex web of alliances, demands a level of sophisticated management that promises to test the talents of Beijing's present and future leaders.

This begs an important question: If China's current strategy, like Bismarck's, proves unsustainable, will China in the early twenty-first century, like Germany in the half century after Bismarck, become a disruptor of international security? Although it is possible that China would follow a similarly

[4] In Medlicott and Covney, *Bismarck and Europe*, pp. 178–79. As Williamson noted, "The implications of France's defeat in 1871 were far reaching. . . . Yet the new Germany was still a 'delicate compromise' which could be destroyed by a hostile European coalition. Consequently, Bismarck attempted to do 'everything to stave off the consequences of his own work' by assuring the great powers that Germany was 'saturated' and had no further territorial ambitions." See Williamson, *Bismarck and Germany*, p. 65; see also Hamerow, *Otto Von Bismarck*, p. xv; Kent, *Bismarck and His Times*, p. 104.

[5] Near the end of his time in power the strategy may have been proving unsustainable even for Bismarck. See Kissinger, *Diplomacy*, pp. 127–28, 136, 146, 160–61, 166.

worrisome trajectory, a fourth qualification of the analogy with Bismarck's Germany tempers such concerns.

The Role of Military Force

Important military-strategic differences distinguish the late nineteenth and early twentieth centuries from the contemporary era. Foreign policy in Bismarck's age was made in circumstances where leaders expected that it was a question of when, not whether, great power war would occur.[6] Expectations today are much different. A role for military force endures, a reflection of the permissive environment of international anarchy, but its use is now more tightly constrained than it was in Bismarck's time. Most importantly, the advent of nuclear weapons has clarified the consequences of general war among the great powers and provides strong incentives for managing those crises and conflicts that cannot be avoided, as explained in chapter 4.[7] The presence of nuclear weapons has also diminished the plausibility of dominating another state by achieving military superiority (even outgunned nuclear adversaries can dissuade potential aggressors by posing a risk of horrifying retaliation).

In addition, and only partly related to the consequences of the "nuclear revolution," grave doubts about the costs and benefits of military force to achieve political objectives are stronger today than in Bismarck's era.[8] Although such beliefs are no guarantee that states will refrain from using force, among the great powers the brutal lessons of twentieth-century war fighting, including the unhappy experience of great powers attempting to shape political outcomes in weak, developing countries, have reduced the attractiveness of the military option. Concerns about the effectiveness of relying on military means are reinforced by concerns about its appropriateness, specifically a norm against using force to resolve disputes if it can be avoided. At a minimum, this consideration encourages leaders to provide extensive justification to both domestic and international audiences before embarking on military missions.[9]

[6] See George F. Kennan, *The Decline of Bismarck's European Order: Franco-Russian Relations, 1875–1890*, p. 423.

[7] In rhetoric, at least, China was late to grasp this point. One of the major changes in China's military thought after Mao Zedong's 1976 death was the abandonment of his argument that general war, including the use of nuclear weapons, was inevitable and perhaps imminent.

[8] For the view that great power war became obsolete after the mid-twentieth century mainly because of political and social changes that had little to do with the "nuclear revolution," see John E. Mueller, *Retreat from Doomsday: The Obsolescence of Major War*.

[9] The domestic constraints on the use of force that might entail American casualties

While a norm against the use of force except as a last resort cannot prevent the powerful from taking actions to which others object, even the ostensibly unconstrained sole superpower in the unipolar era has not ignored it. U.S. efforts to cultivate support from the international community prior to undertaking military operations in the Persian Gulf, the Balkans, Central Asia, Iraq, and Korea simultaneously reflected concern for this norm and revealed its ultimate weakness as a constraint on the actions of a powerful and determined state.

Altered expectations about the role of force in the contemporary era have also changed the relative emphasis placed on the military and economic aspects of grand strategy. Military competition continues, but there is an increased focus on international economic rivalry. Economic strength, of course, has always been one of the foundations of great power. But by the end of the twentieth century the increased significance of science and rapidly changing technology as determinants of relative power, including military clout, has meant that security is usually better served by a strategy that facilitates economic development than by one that seeks to increase immediately available military assets or to acquire foreign territory, resources, and population. This consideration, as well, is a reason that the costs and benefits of the use of force to advance national interests are much different in the present era than they were in Bismarck's.[10]

These last two qualifications suggest not only important limits to an otherwise intriguing comparison with Bismarck's Germany; they also suggest reasons to be wary about the relevance of most historical analogies for understanding international relations in the early twenty-first century, which are characterized by unipolarity and a dramatically changed role for the use of

---

have been important considerations for all U.S. foreign policy makers since President Reagan's defense secretary Caspar Weinberger identified this as a key lesson of the Vietnam War. Although the September 11, 2001, terrorist strikes on New York and Washington may have relaxed concerns about a casualty-averse U.S. public, the absence of effective military opposition to major U.S. interventions thus far makes firm conclusions impossible.

[10] For the strong form of this argument, see Richard N. Rosecrance, *The Rise of the Trading State: Commerce and Conquest in the Modern World*; see also Steven Van Evera, "Why Europe Matters, Why the Third World Doesn't: American Grand Strategy after the Cold War"; Stephen G. Brooks, "The Globalization of Production and the Changing Benefits of Conquest"; cf. Peter Liberman, "The Spoils of Conquest." The collapse of the Soviet Union may provide the clearest evidence of the importance of economic competitiveness rather than control of resources in the contemporary era. Despite its large population and great natural resources, the Soviet regime's inability to satisfy either civilian or military demands eroded its political base of support and opened the door to the systemic failure that unfolded after 1989.

force. The analogy between contemporary China and Bismarck's Germany is, then, imperfect at best, and it is invoked only to identify a few broad similarities in the two countries' circumstances that may account for some equally broad similarities in their strategic choices. The comparison does, however, seem more apt than the alarming ones noted above that others have suggested. Unlike Wilhelmine Germany, China is not eagerly pursuing imperialist glory; unlike Imperial Japan, China is not bereft of resources to the point that it is driven to minimize its dependence through expansion; unlike Nazi Germany, China does not have an ideology of racial superiority and a lust for *Lebensraum* that would motivate it to conquer neighbors; unlike the Soviet Union, China no longer sees itself as the champion of a universally relevant way of life whose dissemination justifies an unremitting effort to erode that championed by its rival.[11] In these respects, China is instead more like Bismarck's Germany, a nationalist rising power whose interests sometimes conflict with others', but one that so far lacks a thirst for expansion, let alone domination, strategic purposes that would pose a serious threat to international peace.

But what if China's rise to power results in newfound ambitions or intensifies conflicts with suspicious rivals that lead it to abandon its present moderate strategy?[12] After all, for a time Bismarck's complex and subtle approach for managing Germany's rise to power served Berlin's interests without increasing the risks of a major European war. In the end, however, Bismarck's strategy came unraveled with disastrous consequences.[13] That experience serves as a reminder that even a currently benign foreign policy line that benefits both China and its neighbors may contain hidden dangers. What might they be?

The chief danger is not likely to be an echo of the sort of aggressive nationalism that reared its head in twentieth-century Germany or in Imperial Japan. Chinese nationalism may be a potent force to which the country's legitimacy-challenged leaders must attend, but it is a nationalism focused on

---

[11] Indeed, some of my Chinese interlocutors have noted, and lamented, the lack of universal appeal of their country's current pragmatic, eclectic socioeconomic program that is tailored to its own particular problems. They explicitly contrast this with the revolutionary socialist paradigms of the Soviet Union and Maoist China, as well as with the universality of political and economic principles that underpin what Joseph Nye labels contemporary America's "soft power." See Joseph S. Nye and William A. Owens, "America's Information Edge"; see also Samuel P. Huntington, "The U.S.-Decline or Renewal."

[12] Though not offering determinate predictions, the strategic culture argument cited above at least suggests that China's changing capabilities might result in a shift to a more assertive strategy, even absent an external trigger.

[13] See Kent, *Bismarck and His Times*, p. 104.

protecting the territorial and political integrity of the country as delimited at the close of World War II and ensuring international respect for China as a great power.[14] While bitterness may linger about the ravages of imperialism (including territorial losses) China suffered during the late Qing dynasty, there is little indication of a serious interest in redressing such historically distant grievances. Nor are there indications of an interest in incorporating foreign territories in which large populations of ethnic Chinese now reside. China's principal claims to territory currently beyond its control in the East and South China Seas (Taiwan, the Diaoyus, the Spratlys) do not in themselves reveal a revisionist, expansionist mentality, but rather Beijing's determination to restore what it believes are the outlines of the de jure status quo.

There is, then, scant evidence at present on which to base predictions that China is likely to abandon its current, relatively conservative, approach and instead adopt a grand strategy that would seek to overturn, rather than adjust to or attempt to reform, the international order it faces.[15] Instead, the more realistic concern is the danger of unintended consequences that might follow even as Beijing pursues its interests within the framework of its present, more circumspect grand strategy.[16] And in this respect, the historical experience of

---

[14] A satisfactory treatment of the question of nationalism in contemporary China falls outside the scope of this project. In many ways it is an area where research has hardly kept up with a changing reality. Early indications are that ongoing empirical work will reveal a more complex and nuanced set of beliefs among the Chinese public than the strident caricature that many presume is representative of nationalism in China today. See Alastair Iain Johnston, "The Correlates of Nationalism in Beijing Public Opinion." On contemporary Chinese nationalism, see also Michel Oksenberg, "China's Confident Nationalism"; Allen S. Whiting, "Chinese Nationalism and Foreign Policy after Deng"; Zheng Yongnian, *Discovering Chinese Nationalism in China: Modernization, Identity, and International Relations*; Richard Baum and Alexei Shevchenko, "Bringing China In: A Cautionary Note"; Suisheng Zhao, "Chinese Nationalism and Its International Orientations."

[15] On the contrary, a review of China's foreign policy since the end of the Cold War suggests it is more plausibly defined as a "status quo" rather than a "revisionist" power. See Alastair Iain Johnston, "Is China a Status Quo Power?"

[16] As the literature about the security dilemma indicates, even policies aiming only to preserve the status quo and protect existing national interests can contribute to adversarial relations (especially when the unavoidable consequences of anarchy are compounded by historically grounded mutual suspicion, as in the Sino-Japanese relationship). The grand strategy that China's leaders have embraced since the mid-1990s, however, suggests that they are gradually becoming more aware of the sort of worried reaction that myopic, self-interested behavior can trigger. In this respect, China's strategy works to reduce rather than exacerbate the potentially dangerous consequences of a security dilemma rooted in the uncertainties of life in an anarchic international realm.

Bismarck's Germany may be worth keeping in mind. Like Germany in the last decades of the nineteenth century, China at the dawn of the twenty-first century embraces a grand strategy that calls for establishing extensive and intensive linkages with states that have overlapping, competing, and common interests. As long as relations are more cooperative than conflictive, fostering tight interdependence may be attractive. But the risk in this sort of arrangement, as Bismarck's successors discovered, is that when problems emerge they tend to ripple through the system in unpredictable ways that complicate efforts at management. Should China's relations with any of the major powers significantly deteriorate, especially if this happens in an international system that edges closer to genuine multipolarity, others may be inclined to reinterpret Beijing's remaining strategic partnerships as de facto alliances.[17] States intimately entangled, unable to remain aloof, might feel compelled to choose sides. Thus, the largely benign consequences of a prudently self-interested China's adherence to a conservative grand strategy in the present era of low tension should not obscure the complexity and challenges such an approach poses for all drawn into its orbit. Because international norms, economic self-interest, and the advent of nuclear weapons have dramatically altered the role of force for resolving interstate disputes, a disastrous "fail deadly" scenario—a twenty-first-century reprise of July 1914—seems implausible. An era of renewed international division into rival economic and military blocs would be unfortunate enough.

The Challenge Ahead

Even the most apt historical analogy is a poor substitute for an explanation that identifies causes and the effects they are likely to produce. While China's current situation shares some similarities with the one that confronted a rising Germany in the latter decades of the nineteenth century, the significant differences in context and content mitigate against pushing the comparison too far. More important than such situational parallels are the domestic and international political reasons outlined above that explain why China is, and for at least several decades is likely to remain, a state interested primarily in ensuring its own interests rather than infringing on others'.

In the end, however, the assessment offered here ultimately leaves open the important question about China's strategic intentions in the more distant fu-

[17] For the view that China's partnerships, like the one with Russia, may turn out to be "quasi-alliances" that serve as a hedge against a deterioration in Sino-American relations, see Ye Zicheng, "Zhongguo Shixing Daguo Waijiao Zhanlüe Shizai Bixing," pp. 9, 10.

ture. Once its capabilities have expanded and it is less tightly constrained, as its transitional grand strategy runs its course, will China still be a status quo state? Or will a China at last free to indulge now unseen preferences turn out to be a dissatisfied, "revisionist" state so determined to remake the international system to suit its interests that it is willing to run higher risks of great power war? Answers are elusive not only because the future is inherently unpredictable, but also because the evidence on which to build a forecast remains both skimpy and ambiguous. One can discern a bit of each of these orientations in China's foreign policy since the mid-1990s. Beijing's rhetoric sometimes condemning American hegemony and power politics suggests the possibility of a latent revisionist agenda—a long-term interest in challenging an international order that the United States has created and leads. Yet, in practice, China's foreign policy behavior continues to conform closely to that typical of a status quo state, especially as Beijing works hard to be welcomed as a responsible member of the existing international community whose acceptance is crucial to China's continued modernization.[18] At present there is simply no way to know whether this approach reflects an unhappy accommodation to reality that will be forsaken if a more prosperous and powerful China has the chance to choose more freely, whether this approach is sincerely preferred and not just accepted as necessary, or whether this approach, today embraced out of necessity, might eventually become China's preferred choice as protracted participation in the existing international order has a socializing effect on those responsible for the country's foreign policy.[19]

The most reasonable conclusion at present, therefore, may be that both labels—"status quo" and "revisionist"—constitute unwise oversimplifications that obscure the mix of interests and goals reflected in China's current grand strategy designed to sustain a peaceful setting for the country's rise to the ranks of the great powers.[20] And, as indicated in the book's opening chapter, it is

[18] See Johnston, "Is China a Status Quo Power?"

[19] Chu Shulong, one of China's most respected analysts, observed, "As China rises, there is a sense that we are now insiders in the international system. We benefit from it. It's in our interest to maintain it" (John Pomfret, "A New Direction for Chinese Diplomacy; Nuclear Threat in North Korea Prompts Ambitious Moves toward Multilateralism"). For intimations of China's "socialization," see Thomas G. Moore and Dixia Yang, "Empowered and Restrained: Chinese Foreign Policy in the Age of Economic Interdependence"; Elizabeth Economy, "The Impact of International Regimes on Chinese Foreign Policy-Making: Broadening Perspectives and Policies . . . But Only to a Point."

[20] The labels "revisionist power" and "status quo power" are often difficult to apply, especially if one ignores the distinction between near- and long-term preferences. In the long term, China seeks change, not the indefinite continuation of a U.S.-

likely that the role China ultimately plays will be shaped by interdependent choices that leaders in Beijing and elsewhere, especially Washington, make during the coming decades. The contingency of choice, moreover, suggests on the one hand that the apocalyptic clash between a dominant hegemon and a rising challenger that some realists anticipate is not inevitable, but on the other hand that the risk of such serious conflict will persist. Neither the United States nor China has yet firmly decided that the other is an unquestionably trustworthy friend or an unremittingly hostile enemy; uncertainty about how the other may use its capabilities instead leads each to hedge its bets. The United States views a more capable China's assertion of its interests as possible harbingers of a boldness that it worries may grow along with Beijing's power—even if its current actions may themselves be modest and ostensibly directed only to achieving finite goals (e.g., with respect to Taiwan, disputes in the South China Sea, modernization of its small nuclear arsenal). And Beijing, in turn, has been quick to view such American concerns about an allegedly more assertive and more powerful PRC as revealing a degree of unprovoked antagonism that requires it to prepare for the possibility that the world's sole superpower is ultimately determined to block China from realizing its great power aspirations.[21]

---

dominated unipolar system. In the near term, however, China prefers the status quo to some of the changes that would be likely under present circumstances: it prefers the status quo in the Taiwan Strait to any change that increases the likelihood of permanent separation; it prefers the continuation of a U.S.-Japan security alliance with Washington in charge to shifts that would give Japan a larger, more independent role; and it prefers the continuation of international economic arrangements (e.g., the WTO) essential for its modernization program to alternatives that might result in neomercantilist competition. On China's ability to free ride on the benefits of the status quo the United States maintains, see Johnston, "Is China a Status Quo Power?" p. 32. By contrast, the United States may have a long-term preference to maintain the status quo in which it wields unmatched global influence, but it also has demonstrated a near-term preference for changing the status quo (e.g., NATO expansion that enhances American leadership in Europe and perhaps beyond; preventive war against state and nonstate actors who may be acquiring weapons of mass destruction; regime change to enlarge the community of democracies; and deployment of missile defenses that some interpret as challenging the status quo condition of mutual vulnerability among the nuclear powers).

[21] For Beijing's claims that the U.S. Defense Department's 2004 *Annual Report on the Military Power of the People's Republic of China* demonstrated a revival of China threat arguments, see "Foreign Ministry Spokesman Refutes Pentagon's 2004 Edition of 'Annual Report on China's Military Forces'"; Liu Aicheng, "When Will the Cold War Mentality Find It's [sic] Resting Place?"; Zhao Feng, "US Dept. of Defense 'Report on the Military Power of the People's Republic of China' Is a Replay of the Old 'China

Given the enduring level of mutual suspicion between China and the United States, intense disagreements about the international order that some realists anticipate are, then, not unthinkable. They do, however, seem unlikely to arise in the near future. Instead, the existing and foreseeable disputes between China and the United States appear to be the sort amenable to compromises that both would find acceptable or, for the most serious ones like Taiwan, at least preferable to the outcomes they might obtain after first relying on the use of force. Nevertheless, as the rich theoretical literature on prewar crisis bargaining and the history of war fighting both indicate, even when acceptable compromises exist, the ability to recognize and agree on them each time disputes develop is not assured.[22] In each instance, the information on which bargaining is based will be incomplete and the potential for misperception or misunderstanding will be present. Moreover, as time passes, rivals repeatedly face the difficult task of updating their beliefs about the other side's capabilities and intentions as well as their estimate about its resolve to stand firm if pushed.[23] This complex dynamic suggests an important reason to worry that Sino-American compromises may become progressively harder to achieve. An increasingly alarmed United States, worried that its concessions granting China a greater voice in shaping regional and international affairs was facilitating the emergence of dangerous peer competitor, might decide to dig in its heels and become more willing to run higher risks of military confrontation. Or, an increasingly confident China might eventually grow impatient

---

Threat Theory'"; "Misrepresenting China's Might"; Ding Gang, "Anti-China Undercurrent Exposes Cold War Posture"; "Why America Always Picks at China?" Exaggeration of the U.S. views notwithstanding, American wariness about China's military modernization was reflected in Washington's efforts during 2004 to discourage the European Union from lifting its embargo on arms sales to China, to block Czech plans to sell China a militarily useful advanced radar system, and (after convincing Israel to cancel the sale of Phalcon AWACS) to discourage Israel's continuing interest in cultivating China's military as a client. See Philip Webster, Roland Watson, and Charles Bremner, "Britain Aims to Lift Arms Ban on China"; Justin Sparks, "US Fear over Czech Radar"; Jiri Kom and David Mulholland, "Czech Republic Shelves Sale of Vera-E Radar to China"; Bill Gertz, "Radar Sale to China Stopped; U.S. May Buy Czech System"; Adam Sharon, "US Panel Slams Israeli Weapons Sales to China"; Richard McGregor, "China Is Priority for Trade Boost, Says Israeli Minister."

[22] On the links between the process of prewar bargaining and the decision to resort to force, see Geoffrey Blainey, *The Causes of War.*

[23] See especially James D. Fearon, "Rationalist Explanations for War"; Robert Powell, "Uncertainty, Shifting Power, and Appeasement." See also James D. Fearon, "Domestic Political Audiences and the Escalation of International Disputes" and "Bargaining, Enforcement, and International Cooperation"; Robert Powell, *In the Shadow of Power.*

with the sorts of concessions a still dominant United States was prepared to make and decide that it is willing to run higher risks to increase its influence over international matters in which it has important economic, political, and military interests. However unlikely such a recipe for disastrous conflict seems in current circumstances, the specter looms over and complicates the future of Sino-American relations, the relationship that seems most likely to determine whether the peace among great powers that has prevailed since 1945 will endure. A crucial question for international security in the twenty-first century, then, may not be whether a rising China is intent on challenging the United States for leadership in Asia and beyond, but rather whether both China and the United States are able to rise to the challenge of managing their inevitable disagreements in a world where China plays a more prominent and active role.

Finally, in the book's introduction I claimed that grasping China's grand strategy would help clarify the consequences of U.S. policies for Sino-American relations. What does Beijing's current strategy suggest about the choices available to American policy makers?

First, China's grand strategy undermines the feasibility and desirability of a U.S. policy of containment. Beijing has forged solid working relations with its smaller neighbors and other major powers while also becoming more active in regional and global multilateral organizations. This achievement makes it more difficult for Washington to rally the sort of broad international support that made containment of the Soviet empire feasible. In addition, China's strategy gives precedence to a protracted process of domestic economic development as the key to building a solid foundation for future international influence; it eschews a Soviet-style emphasis on maximizing military capabilities. This economic focus makes it harder for Washington to portray a militarily lagging China's capabilities as the sort of clear and present threat to U.S. interests necessary to mobilize domestic (and international) political support for the sustained diversion of resources from other purposes that the logic of containment would require.

Moreover, as noted above, Beijing's strategy does not feature a revisionist international agenda (beyond sharing with many other major countries a preference for reducing the U.S. advantage that characterizes the current era of unipolarity). Absent a clear and distinctively Chinese intention to challenge the status quo, it is then more difficult to mobilize support for a policy of containment by arguing that even a weak but determined China poses a serious threat to U.S. interests. Without obviously troublesome Chinese aims, it is difficult for the United States to suggest that China is a potential adversary meriting higher priority than other, more readily apparent proximate threats the United States and its allies face—especially from the nexus of religious-fundamentalist terrorists, weapons of mass destruction, and rogue states. On the contrary, current priorities actually magnify the opportunity costs that would flow from a policy of containment aimed at China. It would trigger a cold war–style rivalry with Beijing in which China contingencies would become a huge sponge absorbing military resources needed elsewhere. The resulting deterioration in bilateral relations would also mean forfeiting China's help, not only in the struggle against terrorism and proliferation, but also in addressing other issues important to the United States (including environmental degradation, stability of the international economy, public health, and transnational crime) whose management increasingly requires Beijing's cooperation.

Yet while Beijing's current strategy undermines the feasibility and desirability of a U.S. policy of containment based on viewing China as a prospective adversary, the alternative of engagement that views China as a prospective friend or ally has its own shortcomings. Because China's strategy is ultimately designed to serve China's interests, not those of the United States, there are limits to the prospects for Sino-American cooperation; a policy of engagement seems unlikely to eliminate them.

Advocates of engagement have argued that more extensive ties with China will inexorably nudge it along a path toward capitalist democracy and that this will gradually eliminate clashing values as an irritant plaguing Sino-American relations. But the authoritarian rulers in Beijing are determined to resist domestic and especially foreign pressures for the sorts of liberalizing social and political changes that threaten their grip on power. Indeed, their current grand strategy is partly aimed at demonstrating that the Communist Party merits its exclusive claim to continue leading a Chinese renaissance. At a minimum, the CCP's predictable resistance to change and the likely best-case scenario of a glacial process of political evolution will make engagement a hard sell for years to come. Beijing's human rights, labor, and minority policies that Americans find objectionable will continue to limit the closeness of bilateral ties that the U.S. public and their government representatives will find acceptable.

As important, even if engagement one day yields a China that is a liberal democracy, it would still have its own distinctive national interests. It would not be surprising if such national interests engendered disagreements with the United States (and others) about international priorities and problems, as well as about the distribution of burdens and benefits associated with joint efforts at addressing them. After all, America's long-standing friends and allies among contemporary Europe's democracies often refuse to follow Washington's lead.

Because an internationally preponderant United States after the Cold War has been both able and willing to pay the premium for unilateralism, their objections have had relatively little impact. If, however, China not only evolves into a liberal democracy (as engagement advocates hope), but also rises to the ranks of the great powers (as China's leaders expect), it will have the clout to complicate the U.S. exercise of international leadership far more profoundly than have France, Germany, and Russia in the early twenty-first century. Thus, it is not obvious that engagement is desirable if it simply facilitates the rise of a Chinese great power, even a democratic one, without also considering the unpleasant constraints it would impose on U.S. foreign policy.

Containment and engagement each have substantial shortcomings. By comparison, the hybrid policy of congagement mentioned in the introduction better serves U.S. interests in dealing with China as it adheres to its current grand strategy.[24] The logic of congagement provides the basis for U.S. policies toward China that are both feasible and desirable, realistically linking current means with future goals. Its broad aim is to increase the likelihood that a Chinese great power that emerges if Beijing's transitional strategy succeeds will be one with whom the United States can peacefully coexist without jeopardizing American interests. This purpose is served by responding to Beijing's present grand strategy with an American strategy of contingent cooperation. Tapping the vast means (both hard and soft power) the United States possesses in the era of American preponderance during which China must rise, such an approach encourages Beijing to sustain its current emphasis on responsible international behavior beyond the transitional era for which its strategy was originally devised.

Rather than basing policy on premature projections about China's future capabilities or assumptions about China's future intentions, the United States in following a strategy of contingent cooperation treats the coming decades of China's attempted rise as the time for a necessary process of learning through experience. Indeed, both Beijing and Washington have questions about one another whose answers simply cannot be known in advance. Time and experience will enable Beijing, for example, to assess American assurances that it is not determined to "hold China down" (as alarmists in China fear) but instead welcomes its growing role on the world stage (as the architects of peaceful rise

---

[24] Others have suggested variations of the engagement and containment themes. David Shambaugh recommends a policy of wary engagement, not because it is likely to be fully satisfactory, but because of the clearer shortcomings of containment ("Containment or Engagement of China: Calculating Beijing's Responses"). Gerald Segal recommends "constrainment," essentially a softened containment strategy ("East Asia and the 'Constrainment' of China").

hope). Time and experience will also enable Washington to assess Chinese assurances that it is not the sort of dangerous challenger the United States needs to confront (as American advocates of containment warn), but instead the sort of state whose interests and ambitions the United States can safely accommodate and with whom it can peacefully coexist (as advocates of engagement assert). Moreover, such a China policy carries reasonably low risks for the United States. America enjoys a substantial power advantage that provides plenty of cushion should it become necessary to change course because China's behavior suggests it is a rival determined to exploit U.S. cooperation rather than a partner willing to reciprocate it.[25] Beijing's current grand strategy reflects China's attempt to play its "weak hand" well. Holding so many of the high cards, Washington needs only to ensure the United States does not play its "strong hand" poorly.

The opening decades of the twenty-first century will be, as the Chinese have argued, a period of strategic opportunity—not just for China to pursue its rise in a peaceful setting, but also for the United States to figure out what sort of Chinese great power it is facing. An American policy during this period that rewards the positive aspects of China's present approach, especially its constructive participation in international organizations and cooperative partnerships with other major powers, while clarifying the costs to China of more obstructionist or narrowly self-interested international behavior, can shape, though it cannot determine, the course a rising China chooses. Even if both China and the United States strive for cooperation, missteps by either or conflicts provoked by third parties that neither controls (such as North Korea or Taiwan) may ultimately foil the attempt to nurture a Sino-American modus vivendi for the twenty-first century. But a U.S. policy that reciprocates China's grand strategy at least creates the opportunity to cultivate cooperation while hedging against the dangers of possible conflict, without presuming that either outcome is inevitable.

[25] For arguments that identify both the power advantages of the United States and the geopolitical constraints on China as reasons to doubt Beijing will pose a serious challenge for at least several decades, see William C. Wohlforth, "The Stability of a Unipolar World"; William C. Wohlforth and Stephen G. Brooks, "American Primacy in Perspective"; and Robert S. Ross, "The Geography of the Peace."

Works Cited

The following abbreviations are used in the Works Cited:

FBIS   Foreign Broadcast Information Service

WNC   World News Connection Document Number. WNC is provided to the National Technical Information Service (NTIS) by the Foreign Broadcast Information Service and made available by Dialog, A Thomson Business

LexisNexis   LexisNexis, Reed Elsevier, Inc.

CNC   ClariNet Communications Corporation

"AFP: PRC Spokesman Suggests Flexibility on One-China." *Agence France-Presse*, April 11, 2000, FBIS-CHI-2000-0411, WNC: 0FSWMMU0162RR3.

Agreement on Dispute Settlement Mechanism of the Framework Agreement on Comprehensive Economic Co-Operation Between the Association of Southeast Asian Nations and the People's Republic of China, November 29, 2004, http://www.aseansec.org/16635.htm.

Agreement on Trade in Goods of the Framework Agreement on Comprehensive Economic Co-operation between the Association of Southeast Asian Nations and the People's Republic of China, November 29, 2004, http://www.aseansec.org/16646.htm.

"Air Forces of the World—China." *Flight International*, July 5, 1995, LexisNexis.

Alcorn, Gay. "China 'Real Reason' for Missile Shield." *Sydney Morning Herald*, July 28, 2000, http://www.smh.com.au/news/0007/28/text/world03.html.

"Algeria, China Pledge to Boost Overall Ties." *People's Daily Online*, October 15, 2004, http://english.people.com.cn/20041015/eng.20041015_160332.html.

Allen, Mike, and Philip P. Pan. "China Vows to Help in Terror Fight; in Shanghai, Jiang Offers Bush Support." *Washington Post*, October 19, 2001, p. A1, LexisNexis.

"'American Interests and the U.S.-China Relationship': Address by Warren Christopher." In *Federal Department and Agency Documents*, May 17, 1996, Federal Document Clearing House, LexisNexis.

"Analyst Interviewed on APEC's Prospects." *Chuon Koron*, December 4, 1995, pp. 30–44, FBIS-EAS-95-232.

Annual Report on the Military Power of the People's Republic of China, July 28, 2003. U.S. Department of Defense, http://www.defenselink.mil/pubs/20030730chinaex.pdf.

Annual Report on the Military Power of the People's Republic of China, May 28, 2004. U.S. Department of Defense, http://www.defenselink.mil/pubs/d20040528PRC.pdf.

Anselmo, Joseph C. "China's Military Seeks Great Leap Forward." *Aviation Week and Space Technology* 146, no. 20 (May 12, 1997): 68, LexisNexis.

"Anti-Terrorist Exercises of SCO to Be Held in Kazakhstan, China." *Itar-Tass (Moscow)* , May 30, 2003, FBIS-SOV-2003-0530, WNC: ohfusqhoox9bck.

Antweiler, Werner. "Purchasing Power Parity." *Pacific Exchange Rate Service*, The University of British Columbia, Sauder School of Business, 2003, http://fx.sauder.ubc.ca/PPP.html.

"ARF Support Group Meeting Ends in Beijing." *Xinhua*, March 8, 1997, FBIS-CHI-97-067.

Armitage, Catherine. "Beijing Wades into Korea Crisis." *The Australian*, July 16, 2003, p. 7, LexisNexis.

"Arms Exports to China Assessed."*Itar-Tass (Moscow)*, April 22, 1997, FBIS-TAC-97-112.

Arnett, Eric. "Military Technology: The Case of China." *SIPRI Yearbook 1995: Armaments, Disarmament and International Security*, 359–86. New York: Oxford University Press, 1995.

Arreguin-Toft, Ivan. "How the Weak Win Wars: A Theory of Asymmetric Conflict." *International Security* 26, no. 1 (Summer 2001): 93–128.

Art, Robert J. "A Defensible Defense: America's Grand Strategy after the Cold War." *International Security* 15, no. 4 (Spring 1991):5–53.

———. "Geopolitics Updated: The Strategy of Selective Engagement." *International Security* 23, no. 3 (Winter 1998–99): 79–113.

———. *A Grand Strategy for America*. Ithaca, NY: Cornell University Press, 2003.

———. "To What Ends Military Power?" *International Security* 4, no. 4 (Spring 1980): 3–35.

"Article Slams Japan's 2001 Defense White Paper for Spreading New 'China Threat Theory.'" *Jiefangjun Bao*, July 10, 2001, p. 5, FBIS-CHI-2001-0710, WNC: oGGO9E702S4DP9.

Asa-El, Amotz, and Robert Daniel. "Bulls in a China Shop." *Jerusalem Post*, February 22, 2002, p. 3, LexisNexis.

"ASEAN China Foreign Ministers' Informal Meeting Joint Press Release," June 21, 2004, http://www.aseansec.org/16167.htm.

"ASEAN, China Hope to Sign South China Sea Code of Conduct This Year." *Agence France-Presse*, July 28, 2000, CNC.

"ASEAN Declaration On The South China Sea Manila, Philippines," July 22, 1992, http://www.aseansec.org/1196.htm.

"Asian Reaction Swift to China's Maritime Expansion." *Reuters*, May 17, 1996, CNC.

"Australia Denies Proposed Asian Security Alliance with U.S. Aimed at China." *Agence France-Presse*, July 31, 2001, FBIS-CHI-2001-0731, WNC: oGHE4PB038UT34.

"Australia, Japan: Hashimoto, Howard Discuss Security Issues, Environment." *Kyodo (Tokyo)*, April 29, 1997, FBIS-EAS-97-119.

"Australia: PRC Criticism over Security Pact with U.S. Noted." *Melbourne Radio Australia*, August 7, 1996, FBIS-EAS-96-153.

"AWACs for China." *Defense & Foreign Affairs Strategic Policy*, March 1997, p. 19, LexisNexis.

Works Cited 223

Axelrod, Robert M. *The Evolution of Cooperation*. New York: Basic Books, 1984.

Baker, Gerard. "Jiang and Bush Try for a Fresh Start." *Financial Times*, October 20, 2001, p. 5, LexisNexis.

Baldwin, David A., ed., *Neorealism and Neoliberalism: The Contemporary Debate*. New York: Columbia University Press, 1993.

Ball, Desmond. "Arms and Affluence: Military Acquisitions in the Asia-Pacific Region." *International Security* 18, no. 3 (Winter 1993): 78–112.

Barnett, A. Doak. *The Making of Foreign Policy in China: Structure and Process*. Boulder, CO: Westview Press, 1985.

Basken, Paul. "Clinton: U.S. Wants 'Peaceful' One-China." *UPI*, July 23, 1996, CNC.

Baum, Richard. "China after Deng: Ten Scenarios in Search of Reality." *China Quarterly*, no. 145 (March 1996): 153–75.

Baum, Richard, and Alexei Shevchenko. "Bringing China In: A Cautionary Note." In *The New Great Power Coalition: Toward a World Concert of Nations*, ed. Richard N. Rosecrance, 327–44. Boulder, CO: Rowman and Littlefield, 2001.

———. "Will China Join an Encompassing Coalition with Other Great Powers?" In *Creating an Encompassing Coalition to Prevent International Conflict*, ed. Richard N. Rosecrance, 298–314. Lanham, MD: Rowman and Littlefield, 2001.

Beaufre, André. *An Introduction to Strategy*. Translated by Major-General R. H. Barry. London: Faber and Faber, 1965.

"Beijing Has Fulfilled GATT Terms." *Straits Times (Singapore)*, February 28, 1994, p. 7, LexisNexis.

"Beijing Urged to Keep Regional Power Focus." *South China Morning Post*, September 29, 1998, http://www.taiwansecurity.org/SCMP-980929.htm.

"The Beijing-Washington Back-Channel and Henry Kissinger's Secret Trip to China, September 1970–July 1971." In *Briefing Book No. 66*, ed. William Burr. Washington, DC: National Security Archive, February 27, 2002, http://www.gwu.edu/~nsarchiv/NSAEBB/NSAEBB66/.

Benson, Brett V., and Emerson M. S. Niou. "Comprehending Strategic Ambiguity: US Policy toward Taiwan Security." *Taiwan Security Research* (2000), http://taiwansecurity.org/IS/IS-Niou-0400.htm.

Bernstein, Richard, and Ross H. Munro. *The Coming Conflict with China*. New York: Alfred A. Knopf, 1997.

Betts, Richard K. *Nuclear Blackmail and Nuclear Balance*. Washington, DC: Brookings Institution, 1987.

———. "Wealth, Power, and Instability: East Asia and the United States after the Cold War." *International Security* 18, no. 3 (Winter 1993–94): 34–77.

Bianco, Lucien. *Origins of the Chinese Revolution, 1915–1949*. Translated by Muriel Bell. Stanford, CA: Stanford University Press, 1971.

"Bizarre Indication of 'China Threat' in Japanese Defense Program." *People's Daily Online*, December 12, 2004, http://english.peopledaily.com.cn/200412/12/eng20041212_166991.html.

Blainey, Geoffrey. *The Causes of War*. New York: Free Press, 1973.

"Blair Looks to Profit in Beijing." *South China Morning Post*, October 6, 1998, LexisNexis.

Blair, Bruce G. *The Logic of Accidental Nuclear War*. Washington, DC: Brookings Institution, 1993.

Blair, Dennis C. "The Role of Armed Forces in Regional Security Cooperation." *Pacific Forum, CSIS, PacNet 34,* August 25, 2000, http://taiwansecurity.org/IS/PacNet-082500.htm.

Blasko, Dennis J. "Better Late Than Never: Non-Equipment Aspects of PLA Ground Force Modernization." In *Chinese Military Modernization,* ed. C. Dennison Lane, Mark Weisenbloom, and Dimon Liu, 125–43. New York: Kegan Paul International, 1996.

Blasko, Dennis J., Philip T. Klapakis, and John F. Corbett Jr. "Training Tomorrow's PLA: A Mixed Bag of Tricks." *China Quarterly,* no. 146 (June 1996): 488–524.

Bluth, Christopher. "Beijing's Attitude to Arms Control." *Jane's Intelligence Review* 8, no. 7 (July 1996): 328–29.

Bowen, Wyn Q., and Stanley Shephard. "Living under the Red Missile Threat." *Jane's Intelligence Review* 8, no. 12 (December 1996): 560ff., LexisNexis.

Bradsher, Keith. "Taiwan Puts Limits in Referendum Bill." *New York Times,* November 27, 2003, http://www.taiwansecurity.org/NYT/2003/NYT-271103.htm.

Brodie, Bernard. *War and Politics.* New York: Macmillan, 1973.

Brooke, James. "U.S. and North Korea Announce Accord on Wider Atom Talks." *New York Times,* August 2, 2003, p. A2, LexisNexis.

Brookes, Peter. "The Case for Missile Defense." *Far Eastern Economic Review,* September 7, 2000, http://www.feer.com/_0009_07/p33fcol.html.

Brooks, Stephen G. "The Globalization of Production and the Changing Benefits of Conquest." *Journal of Conflict Resolution* 43, no. 5 (Oct. 1999): 646–70.

Brown, Michael E., Owen R. Cote Jr., Sean M. Lynn-Jones, and Steven E. Miller, eds. *The Rise of China.* Cambridge, MA: MIT Press, 2000.

Brown, Michael E., Sean M. Lynn-Jones, and Steven E. Miller, eds. *East Asian Security.* Cambridge, MA: MIT Press, 1996.

Brzezinski, Zbigniew. *The Grand Chessboard: American Primacy and Its Geostrategic Imperatives.* New York: Basic Books, 1997.

Bullard, Monte R. "Undiscussed Linkages: Implications of Taiwan Straits Security Activity on Global Arms Control and Nonproliferation." *CNS Reports,* October 11, 2000, http://cns.miis.edu/pubs/reports/illinois.htm.

Burles, Mark, and Abram N. Shulsky. *Patterns in China's Use of Force: Evidence from History and Doctrinal Writings.* Santa Monica, CA: RAND, 2000.

Buruma, Ian, Seth Faison, and Fareed Zakaria. "The 21st Century Starts Here: China Booms. The World Holds Its Breath." *New York Times,* February 18, 1996.

"Catching Up." *Flight International,* September 27, 1995, LexisNexis.

Chan, Christine. "Time Not Ripe for Yuan Float." *South China Morning Post,* June 28, 2000, p. 6, LexisNexis.

Chandra, Rajiv. "China: European, U.S. Aircraft Producers Compete for Boom Market." *Inter Press Service,* July 19, 1996, LexisNexis.

Chen Demin. "90 Niandai Zhongmei Guanxi Tanxi" [A preliminary analysis of Sino-American relations in the 1990s]. *Xiandai Guoji Guanxi,* no. 9 (1999). Reprinted in *Zhongguo Waijiao,* no. 1 (2000): 20–24.

"Chen Determined to Call Popular Vote by Next Presidential Poll." *Taiwan News,* July 16, 2003, http://www.taiwansecurity.org/TN/2003/TN-071603.htm.

"Chen Hints Referendum Will Be Held with Election." *Taiwan News,* September 28, 2003, http://taiwansecurity.org/TN/2003/TN-092803.htm.

Chen Jian. "Jiang Zemin Talks with Former U.S. President George Bush in Beijing on

March 2 about Bilateral Ties, WTO." *Zhongguo Xinwen She*, March 2, 2000, FBIS-CHI-2000-0302.

Chen Lineng. "The Japanese Self Defense Forces Are Marching toward the 21st Century." *Guoji Zhanwang* [World outlook], no. 2 (February 8, 1996), FBIS CHI-96-085.

Chen Qimao. "New Approaches in China's Foreign Policy: The Post–Cold War Era." *Asian Survey* 33, no. 3 (March 1993): 237–51.

Chen Shui-bian. "Full Text of President Chen Shui-bian's Inaugural Speech (I)," May 20, 2000, http://www.fas.org/news/taiwan/2000/e-05-20-00-8.htm.

Chen Xiaoqin. "Buru 21 Shiji De Zhong'e Guanxi" [Sino-Russian relations entering the 21st century]. *Zhongguo Waijiao*, no. 3 (2000): 31–35.

Chen Ying. "Zhanqu Daodan Fangyu Xitong Yu Dongya Anquan Xingshi" [Theater missile defense and East Asia's security situation]. *Shijie Jingji yu Zhengzhi Luntan*, no. 4 (1999): 28–30.

Chen, Melody. "Chen's Speech Was Constructive: Leach." *Taipei Times*, May 21, 2004, FBIS-CHI-2004-0521, WNC: ohy8ogao2tapls.

Chetwynd, Phil. "China Slams U.S. Arms Sales to Taiwan as Bush Talks Tough." *AFP*, April 25, 2001, FBIS-CHI-2001-0425, WNC: 0GCEH6No1RoJQD.

Cheung, Tai Ming. "China's Entrepreneurial Army: The Structure, Activities and Economic Returns of the Military Business Complex." In *Chinese Military Modernization*, ed. C. Dennison Lane, Mark Weisenbloom, and Dimon Liu, 168–97. New York: Kegan Paul International, 1996.

———. "The People's Armed Police: First Line of Defence." *China Quarterly*, no. 146 (June 1996): 525–47.

"Chi Haotian Yu Riben Fangweiting Zhangguan Huitan, Huijian Riben Zimindang Ganshizhang He Zhengtiaohuizhang" [Chi Haotian holds consultations with the director of Japan's Defense Agency, meets with Japan's LDP secretary general and the head of the LDP Policy Research Council]. *Renmin Ribao*, February 5, 1998.

"Chi Haotian Zai Riben Fabiao Yanjiang, Zhuozhong Chanshu Zhongguo Guofang Zhengce" [Chi Haotian's lecture in Japan setting forth China's national defense policy]. *Renmin Ribao*, February 5, 1998, http://www.snweb.com/gb/people_daily/gbrm.htm.

Chi Haotian. "A Year of Our Army's Active Foreign Contacts." *Renmin Ribao*, December 26, 1997, p. 7, FBIS-CHI-98-0047.

———. "Zou Fuhe Woguo Guoqing Bing Fanying Shidai Tezheng De Guofang Xiandaihua Jianshe Daolu" [Follow the path of modernizing national defense suited to our national conditions and the characteristics of our times]. *Qiushi* 188, no. 8 (April 1996).

"China Aims to Change Perception as 'Potential Aggressor,' Says Malaysia." *Agence France-Presse*, November 27, 2000, CNC.

"China and EU to Step up Dialogue, May Hold Annual Summits." *Agence France-Presse*, April 2, 1998, CNC.

"China and WTO." *Financial Times*, December 29, 1994, p. 9, LexisNexis.

"China Bucks G-7 Membership, Wants WTO." *UPI*, July 2, 1996, CNC.

"China Building up for Spratlys—U.S. Official." *Reuters*, January 23, 1996, CNC.

"China Calls for Deepening of Strategic Partnership with EU." *People's Daily Online*, December 10, 2004, http://english.people.com.cn/200412/10/eng20041210_166818.html.

"China Cautious on Primakov Plan." *The Hindu*, December 23, 1998, LexisNexis.

"China Claims Readiness for 'Future War.'" *UPI*, March 18, 1996, CNC.

"China Confident in Fulfilling Foreign Trade Target for This Year." *Xinhua News Agency*, July 9, 1996, LexisNexis.

"China Could Float the Yuan This Year: Prominent Economist." *Agence France-Presse*, May 11, 2000, LexisNexis.

"China Defense Minister Says Threat Theory Absurd." *Reuters*, June 27, 1996, CNC.

"China Denies Selling of USD Assets." *People's Daily Online*, December 10, 2004, http://english.people.com.cn/200412/10/eng20041210_166882.html.

"China Develops Stealthy Multi-Role Fighter." *Jane's Defence Weekly* 27, no. 9 (March 5, 1997): 3, LexisNexis.

"China Expresses "Deep Concern" With Japan's New Defense Guidelines." *People's Daily Online*, December 11, 2004, http://english.peopledaily.com.cn/200412/11/eng20041211_166930.html.

"China 'Gravely Concerned' over US Arms to Taiwan." *People's Daily Online*, July 14, 2004, http://english.peopledaily.com.cn/200407/14/eng20040714_149562.html.

"China Growth Seen at 9.8 Pct, Reserves at $140 Bln." *Reuters*, June 3, 1997, CNC.

"China Pushes Peace but Ignores Spratlys Code." *Agence France-Presse*, November 24, 2000, CNC.

"China Says Future U.S. Ties Hinge on Taiwan." *Reuters*, February 8, 1996, CNC.

"China Slams U.S. Demands for WTO Entry." *UPI*, July 21, 1996, CNC.

"'China Threat' Fallacy Refuted. (Western Allegations)." *Beijing Review* 38, no. 40 (October 2, 1995): 6.

"China to Take Missile Shield Opposition to ASEAN." *Reuters*, July 21, 2000.

"China Wary of US-Japan Military Pact." *Agence France-Presse*, April 28, 1998, CNC.

"China Will Never Seek Hegemony, Said Chinese Premier." *People's Daily Online*, June 28, 2004, http://english.peopledaily.com.cn/200406/28/eng20040628_147806.html.

"China Will Never Tolerate Taiwan Independence: Jiang Zemin." *People's Daily Online*, July 9, 2004, http://english.people.com.cn/200407/08/eng20040708_148956.html.

"China, Argentina to Establish Strategic Partnership." *People's Daily Online*, November 17, 2004, http://english.people.com.cn/200411/17/eng20041117_164230.html.

"China, ASEAN Sign Declaration on Code of Conduct in South China Sea." *Xinhua*, November 4, 2002, FBIS-CHI-2002-1104, WNC: 0H53VRIo2LM5M2.

"China, Brazil Issue Joint Communiqué." *Xinhua*, May 24, 2004, FBIS-LAT-2004-052, WNC: 0hy9ufao149mng.

"China, EU Developing 'Mature Partnership.'" Embassy of the People's Republic of China in the United States of America, May 5, 2004, at China, http://www.china-embassy.org/eng/xw/t94811.htm.

"China, France Vow to Boost Partnership." *People's Daily Online*, July 5, 2004, http://english.peopledaily.com.cn/200407/05/print20040705_148438.html.

"China, Germany to Establish Partnership of Global Responsibility." *Xinhua*, May 4, 2004, http://news.xinhuanet.com/english/2004–05/04/content_1452391.htm.

"China, India Agree to Address Differences Peacefully." *People's Daily Online*, June 24, 2003, http://english.peopledaily.com.cn/200306/24/eng20030624_118821.shtml.

"China, India Sign Declaration on Bilateral Ties." *People's Daily Online*, June 24, 2003, http://english.peopledaily.com.cn/200306/24/eng20030624_118770.shtml.

"China, India Sign Declaration on Bilateral Ties (Full Text)." *People's Daily Online*, June 25, 2003, http://english.peopledaily.com.cn/200306/25/eng20030625_118823.shtml.

"China, India to Seek to Build 21-Century-Oriented Partnership." *Xinhua*, November 29, 1996, FBIS-CHI-96-231, WNC: 0E1T59403Y4522.

"China, Italy to Establish Stable, Long-term, Comprehensive Strategic Partnership." *Xinhua*, May 8, 2004, http://service.china.org.cn/link/wcm/Show_Text?info_id=94723&p_qry =italy%20and%20strategic.

"China, Mexico Establish Strategic Partnership." December 13, 2003, http://www.chinaembassy.ee/eng/dtxw/t111998.htm.

"China, Pakistan Highlight Cooperation in Beijing." *Xinhua*, November 3, 2003, FBIS-CHI-2003-1103, WNC: 0hntylm03q3ufq.

"China, Russia Issue Beijing Declaration." *Xinhua*, July 18, 2000, LexisNexis.

"China, UK Vow to Develop Strategic Partnership: Joint Statement." *People's Daily Online*, May 11, 2004, http://english.peopledaily.com.cn/200405/11/eng20040511_142893.html.

"China, U.S. Underline Constructive Ties." *People's Daily Online*, July 29, 2001, http://fpeng.peopledaily.com.cn/200107/29/eng20010729_76012.html.

"China: Expanding Military Contacts Part of Diplomatic Strategy." *Xinhua*, February 20, 1998, FBIS-CHI-98-051.

"China: Further on Qian-Albright Comments after Talks." *Xinhua*, July 26, 1997, FBIS-CHI-97-207, WNC: 0EE3OHJ023W2VV.

"China: Pact to Prevent Naval Accidents Initialed." *Xinhua*, December 12, 1997, FBIS-CHI-97-347.

"China: Qian Qichen on 'Constructive' Strategic Partnerships." *Xinhua*, November 3, 1997, FBIS-CHI-97-307.

"China's EU Policy Paper." *Ministry of Foreign Affairs of the People's Republic of China*, October 13, 2003, http://www.fmprc.gov.cn/eng/wjb/zzjg/xos/dqzzywt/t27708.htm.

"China's Forex Reserves Not Too High—Official." *Reuters*, November 30, 1996, CNC.

"China's International Status Is in the Ascendance." *Ta Kung Pao*, July 6, 1998, FBIS-CHI-98-187.

"China's Jiang Zemin Warns against Japan Militarism." *Reuters*, November 13, 1995, CNC.

"China's Military Expenditure." In *Military Balance 1995–1996*, 270–75. London: IISS and Oxford University Press, 1995.

"China's National Defence in 2000." *China Daily*, October 17, 2000, pp. 5–8.

"China's New Path of Development and Peaceful Rise." *Beijing Xuexi Shibao (Online)*, November 23, 2004, FBIS document CPP20041123000205.

"China's New Premier Takes Centre Stage but Avoids Limelight." *Agence France-Presse*, April 4, 1998, CNC.

"China's Peaceful Rise—A PLA General's View." *Straits Times (Singapore)*, June 29,2004, LexisNexis. Adapted by the *Straits Times* from a speech delivered by Cai Bingkui, a major general in the People's Liberation Army and vice chairman of the China Institute for International Strategic Studies, at the ASEAN-China Forum organized by the Institute of South-east Asian Studies in Singapore on June 23–24.

"China's Peaceful Rise: A Road Chosen for Rejuvenation of a Great Nation." *Xinhuanet*,

February 19, 2004, http://news.xinhuanet.com/english/2004-02/19/content_1321769. htm.

"China's Road of Peaceful Rise." *Xinhua*, April 23, 2004, FBIS-CHI-2004-0423, WNC: ohws5wm046iiof.

"China-ASEAN Foreign Ministers' Informal Meeting Held in Qingdao." *Ministry of Foreign Affairs of the People's Republic of China*, June 21, 2004, http://www.fmprc. gov.cn/eng/topics/3rdministermeetingofacd/t140504.htm.

"China-EU Partnership Is of Great Significance, Premier Wen Says." *Xinhua*, April 29, 2004, FBIS-CHI-2004-0429, WNC: ohwzjpvooeq3ot.

"Chinese Experts Applaud China-India Declaration on Bilateral Ties." *Xinhua*, June 26, 2003, FBIS-CHI- 2003-0626, WNC: ohh534e015h6ao.

"Chinese Military Power, Report of an Independent Task Force." *Council on Foreign Relations*, June 12, 2003, http://www.cfr.org/pdf/China_TF.pdf.

"Chinese Premier's First European Trip Crowned with Glory." *Agence France-Presse*, April 8, 1998, CNC.

"Chinese President Begins State Visit to Brazil." *People's Daily Online*, November 12, 2004, http://english.people.com.cn/200411/12/eng20041112_163648.html.

"Chinese President Jiang's Visit to Japan May Be Delayed to Next Year." *Agence France-Presse*, September 10, 1998, CNC.

"Chinese President Tells ASEAN Summit of Hopes for 'Good-Neighbourly Partner-ship.'" *Xinhua*, December 18, 1997, BBC Summary of World Broadcasts, Lexis-Nexis.

"Chinese, French Leaders Reach Broad Consensus." *People's Daily Online*, October 11, 2004, http://english.people.com.cn/200410/11/eng20041011_159653.html.

"Chinese, Italian Presidents Hail Strong Bilateral Relations." *People's Daily Online*, December 7, 2004, http://english.people.com.cn/200412/07/eng20041207_166358.html.

Ching, Cheong. "Cause of Cross-Strait Instability Still There, Warns Beijing." *Straits Times (Singapore)*, May 25, 2004, LexisNexis.

Ching, Cheong. "Cross-Strait Dispute: China Gives Peace a Chance." *Straits Times (Singapore)*, August 25, 1999, p. 40, LexisNexis.

Christensen, Thomas J. "China, the U.S.-Japan Alliance, and the Security Dilemma in East Asia." *International Security* 23, no. 4 (Spring 1999): 49–80.

———. "Chinese Realpolitik." *Foreign Affairs* 75, no. 5 (September–October 1996): 37–52.

———. "The Contemporary Security Dilemma: Deterring a Taiwan Conflict." *Washington Quarterly* 25, no. 4 (Autumn 2002): 7–21.

———. "New Challenges and Opportunities in the Taiwan Strait: Defining America's Role. *An Executive Summary of the Report of the National Committee on United States–China Relations Conference on U.S. Policy Toward Relations Across the Taiwan Strait, Pocantico Conference Center*, August 8–10, November, 2003, http://www. ncuscr.org/taiwan%20report.pdf.

———. "Parsimony Is No Simple Matter: International Relations Theory, Area Studies, and the Rise of China," February 26, 1998, unpublished ms.

———. "Perceptions and Alliances in Europe, 1865–1940." *International Organization* 51, no. 1 (Winter 1997): 65–98.

———. "Posing Problems without Catching Up: China's Rise and Challenges for U.S. Security Policy." *International Security* 25, no. 4 (2001): 5–40.

———. "Realism with Chinese Characteristics: Beijing's Perceptions of Japan, the United States, and the Future of East Asian Security." Research report submitted to the Asia Security Project, Olin Institute for Strategic Studies, Harvard University, typescript, November 28, 1996.

———. "Theater Missile Defense and Taiwan's Security." *Orbis* 44, no. 1 (Winter 2000): 79–90.

———. *Useful Adversaries: Grand Strategy, Domestic Mobilization, and Sino-American Conflict, 1947–1958.* Princeton, NJ: Princeton University Press, 1996.

Christensen, Thomas J., and Jack Snyder. "Chain Gangs and Passed Bucks: Predicting Alliance Patterns in Multipolarity." *International Organization* 44, no. 2 (Spring 1990): 137–68.

Chu Shulong. "Lengzhanhou Zhongguo Anquan Zhanlüe Sixiang De Fazhan" [The development of China's thinking about security strategy after the Cold War]. *Shijie Jingji yu Zhengzhi*, no. 9 (1999): 11–15.

Chu Shulong and Wang Zaibang. "Guanyu Guoji Xingshi He Wo Duiwai Zhanlüe Ruogan Zhongda Wenti De Sikao" [Reflections on some important questions about the international situation and our external strategy]. *Xiandai Guoji Guanxi*, no. 8 (1999): 16–21.

Chu, Monique. "Analysts Mull the Results of Chen's Pronouncement." *Taipei Times*, August 4, 2002, http://taiwansecurity.org/TT/2002/TT-080402.htm.

"Chuanwen Jiang Zemin Zhishi Gaibian Zhonggong De Guofang Zhengce" [Jiang Zemin said to indicate a change in CCP national defense policy]. *Xinwen Zhongxin*, August 5, 2000, http://dailynews.sina.com/focusReport/1603/1514817-1.html.

Chung, Laurence. "Chen Wants New Taiwan Constitution by 2008." *Straits Times (Singapore)*, November 12, 2003, http://www.taiwansecurity.org/ST/2003/ST-121103-1.htm.

Chuter, Andy. "China's Fighter Skips Generation." *Flight International*, March 27, 2001, p. 22, LexisNexis.

"Clinton: Japan, U.S. Must Continue to Be Partners." *Daily Yomiuri*, April 19, 1996, LexisNexis.

Cody, Edward. "Relationship with Taiwan Remains Tense, China Warns." *Washington Post*, May 24, 2004, p. A10, LexisNexis.

Cohen, Eliot A. "Defending America in the Twenty-First Century." *Foreign Affairs* 79, no. 6 (November–December 2000): 40–56.

"Commentary: China for the G-8." *Straits Times (Singapore)*, June 14, 2004, Lexis-Nexis.

"Commentary: U.S. Dreams of Asian NATO." *People's Daily Online*, July 18, 2003, http://english.peopledaily.com.cn/200307/18/print20030718_120535.html.

"Commenting on Recent US Policy toward China." *Hong Kong Wen Wei Pao*, July 27, 2000, FBIS-CHI-200-0727, WNC: 0FYEYZ602VGB1U.

"Comparison—PRC FM Holds Talks with Berger on Taiwan." *Xinhua*, March 29, 2000, FBIS-CHI-2000-0329, WNC: 0FS8L1V01DDYSG.

"Containing China." *The Economist*, July 29, 1995, pp. 11–12.

Copeland, Dale C. *The Origins of Major War.* Ithaca, NY: Cornell University Press, 2000.

"Cross-Strait Tension: 'Special State-to-State.'" *Taiwan Security Research*, http://taiwansecurity.org/TSR-State-to-State.htm.

Crothall, Geoffrey. "Beijing Threatens GATT Talks Boycott If 'Final Offer' Rejected." *South China Morning Post*, July 11, 1994, p. 1, LexisNexis.

Curtis, Gerald. "Japan: Kato on Domestic, International Politics." *Tokyo Chuo Koron*, September 1997, pp. 28–43, FBIS-EAS-97-238.

Da Jun. "True Threat Comes from Those Trumpeting 'China Threat.'" *Xinhua*, October 16, 1996, FBIS-CHI-96-202, WNC: 0DZHS2604CI3VT.

Daneshku, Scheherazade, and Barney Jopson. "Trade with China Boosts Japan Surplus." *Financial Times*, February 24, 2004, p. 8, LexisNexis.

De Jonquieres, Guy. "China Pressed over WTO Entry: EU and U.S. Say Beijing Must Accept World Trade Body's Rules." *Financial Times*, April 14, 1994, p. 5, LexisNexis.

Declaration on the Conduct of Parties in the South China Sea, Phnom Penh. November 4, 2002, http://www.aseansec.org/13163.htm.

Defense of Japan, 1996, http://www.jda.go.jp/e/index_.htm.

Dempsey, Judy. "Chirac Urges EU Leaders to Lift Arms Embargo Imposed on Beijing in 1989." *Financial Times*, December 13, 2003, p. 7, LexisNexis.

Deng Xiaoping. "An Idea for the Peaceful Reunification of the Chinese Mainland and Taiwan, June 26, 1983." *Selected Works of Deng Xiaoping*, 1983, http://english.peopledaily.com.cn/dengxp/vol3/text/c1120.html.

———. "We Must Safeguard World Peace and Ensure Domestic Development, May 29, 1984." *Selected Works of Deng Xiaoping*, 1984, http://english.peopledaily.com.cn/dengxp/vol3/text/c1200.html.

Deutsch, Karl W., and J. David Singer. "Multipolar Power Systems and International Stability." In *International Politics and Foreign Policy*, ed. James N. Rosenau, 315–24. New York: Free Press, 1969.

DeYoung, Karen, and Doug Struck. "Beijing's Help Led to Talks; U.S. Cuts Demands on North Korea." *Washington Post*, April 17, 2003, p. A01, LexisNexis.

Ding Gang. "Anti-China Undercurrent Exposes Cold War Posture." *Renmin Ribao*, April 30, 2004, FBIS-CHI-2004-0430, WNC: 0hx54ac015tapi.

Ding Kuisong. "Zongjie Guoqu, Mianxiang Weilai—Ping Zhongmei Guanxi 50 Nian" [Summing up the past, facing that future—Evaluating 50 years of Sino-American relations]. *Xiandai Guoji Guanxi*, no. 10 (1999). Reprinted in *Zhongguo Waijiao* no. 2 (2000): 9–13.

Ding Shichuan and Li Qiang. "Chaoxian Bandao Heping Jizhi Ji Qi Qianjing" [A peace mechanism for the Korean peninsula and its prospects]. *Xiandai Guoji Guanxi* 4 (1999): 42–44.

Ding, Arthur S. "China's Defence Finance: Content, Process and Administration." *China Quarterly*, no. 146 (June 1996): 428–42.

"Diplomatic News Highlights for 23–29 Oct." *Xinhua*, October 30, 1999, FBIS-CHI-1999-1101.

"Diversifying Consumer Purchases in China." *COMLINE Daily News Electronics*, June 18, 1996, LexisNexis.

Dong Guozheng. "Multipolarization: Irresistible Tide of History—Interview with National Defense University Associate Professor Jin Yinan." *Jiefangjun Bao*, July 2, 2002, FBIS-CHI-2002-0702, WNC: 0GYS33401V0PLX.

Dong, Li, and Alec M. Gallup. "In Search of the Chinese Consumer." *China Business Review* 22, no. 5 (September 1995): 19, LexisNexis.

Downing, John. "China's Evolving Maritime Strategy, Part I." *Jane's Intelligence Review* 8, no. 2 (March 1996): 129–33, LexisNexis.

———. "China's Evolving Maritime Strategy, Part II." *Jane's Intelligence Review* 8, no. 4 (April 1996): 186–91, LexisNexis.

Doyle, Michael W. "Kant, Liberal Legacies, and Foreign Affairs." *Philosophy and Public Affairs* 12 (Fall 1983): 323–53.

"A Drunkard Means Otherwise Than in Wine." *People's Daily Online*, June 16, 2004, http://english.peopledaily.com.cn/200406/16/eng20040616_146546.html.

Eckholm, Erik. "U.S. And Top Chinese Officials Try to Smooth over Differences." *New York Times*, July 14, 2000, p. 7.

Economy, Elizabeth. "The Impact of International Regimes on Chinese Foreign Policy-Making: Broadening Perspectives and Policies . . . But Only to a Point." In *The Making of Chinese Foreign and Security Policy in the Era of Reform*, ed. David M. Lampton, 230–53. Stanford, CA: Stanford University Press, 2001.

"Editorial: Great Success in China's Big-Nation Diplomacy." *Ta Kung Pao*, April 2, 1998, FBIS-CHI-98–092.

Elman, Colin. "Cause, Effect and Consistency: A Response to Kenneth N. Waltz." *Security Studies* 6, no. 1 (Fall 1996): 58–61.

———. "Horses for Courses: Why Not Neorealist Theories of Foreign Policy?" *Security Studies* 6, no. 1 (Autumn 1996): 7–53.

Epstein, Gady A. "From Beijing, Stern Words for an Uneasy Ally; China Seen Toughening Stance against N. Korea Nuclear Development." *Baltimore Sun*, March 28, 2003, p. 12A, LexisNexis.

"EU Adopts New Anti-Dumping Rules for China." *Agence France-Presse*, April 28, 1998, CNC.

"EU Chief Congratulates China as Pillar of Asian Economy." *Agence France-Presse*, October 26, 1998, CNC.

"European Union Calls for New Partnership with China." *Agence France-Presse*, October 28, 1998, CNC.

Fang Hua. "Yatai Anquan Jiagou De Xianzhuang, Qushi Ji Zhongguo De Zuoyong" [The current Asia-Pacific security framework: Trends and China's role]. *Shijie Jingji yu Zhengzhi*, no. 2 (2000): 11–15.

Fang Yinwan and Yang Guojun. "Beneficial Enlightenment for Large Countries to Build a New Type of Relationship." *Xinhua*, April 25, 1996, FBIS-CHI96–082.

Farber, Henry S., and Joanne Gowa. "Polities and Peace." *International Security* 20, no. 2 (Fall 1995): 123–46.

Fearon, James D. "Bargaining, Enforcement, and International Cooperation." *International Organization* 52, no. 2 (Spring 1998): 269–305.

———. "Domestic Political Audiences and the Escalation of International Disputes." *American Political Science Review* 88, no. 3 (September 1994): 577–92.

———. "Rationalist Explanations for War." *International Organization* 49, no. 3 (Summer 1995): 379–414.

Feis, Herbert. *The China Tangle*. Princeton, NJ: Princeton University Press, 1972.

Fewsmith, Joseph. *China since Tiananmen: The Politics of Transition*. New York: Cambridge University Press, 2001.

———. *Elite Politics in Contemporary China*. Armonk, NY: M.E. Sharpe, 2001.

Fewsmith, Joseph, and Stanley Rosen. "The Domestic Context of Chinese Foreign

Policy: Does 'Public Opinion' Matter?" In *The Making of Chinese Foreign and Security Policy in the Era of Reform, 1978–2000*, ed. David M. Lampton, 151–87. Stanford, CA: Stanford University Press, 2001.

Finkelstein, David M. *China Reconsiders Its National Security: 'The Great Peace and Development Debate of 1999.'* Alexandria, VA: CNA Corporation, 2000.

Fisher, Richard D. "The Accelerating Modernization of China's Military." *Heritage Foundation Reports*, June 2, 1997, LexisNexis.

————. "China's Purchase of Russian Fighters: A Challenge to the U.S." *Heritage Foundation Reports*, July 31, 1996, LexisNexis.

"Five-Nation Agreement Provides Model in Peaceful Conflict Resolution." *Jiefang Ribao*, April 27, 1996, p. 4, FBIS-CHI-96-145.

"Five-Year Draft Plan Depicts Further Development." Fifth Plenary Session of the 15th Congress of the Communist Party of China, October 18, 2000, http://chinadaily.com.cn.net/highlights/plan/index.html.

"Foreign Ministry Spokesman Refutes Pentagon's 2004 Edition of 'Annual Report on China's Military Forces.'" *Xinhua*, June 1, 2004, FBIS-CHI-2004-0601, WNC: ohyonok03qzmkj.

"Former Vice-Premier Calls for New Dimensions to Five Principles of Peaceful Coexistence." *People's Daily Online*, June 14, 2004, http://english1.people.com.cn/200406/14/eng20040614_146297.html.

Framework Agreement on Comprehensive Economic Co-operation between the Association of South East Asian Nations and the People's Republic of China, November 4, 2002, http://www.aseansec.org/13196.htm.

Francis, David R. "How to Make the G-8 'Club' a Little Less Cozy." *Christian Science Monitor*, June 10, 2004, p. 17, LexisNexis.

Frankenstein, John, and Bates Gill. "Current and Future Challenges Facing Chinese Defence Industries." *China Quarterly*, no. 146 (June 1996): 394–427.

Fravel, M. Taylor, and Evan S. Medeiros. "China's New Diplomacy." *Foreign Affairs* 82, no. 6 (November–December 2003): 22–35.

Freeman, Chas. "China's Changing Nuclear Posture," *Proliferation Brief* 2, no. 10 (May 11, 1999), Carnegie Endowment for International Peace.

————. "Preventing War in the Taiwan Strait: Restraining Taiwan—and Beijing." *Foreign Affairs* 77, no. 4 (July–August 1998): 6–11.

"French Support Needed on Taiwan Issue: Official." *Xinhua*, January 19, 2004, FBIS-CHI-2004-0119, WNC: ohrsoe703bk3vs.

French, Howard W. "North Korea's Reaction on Iraq Is Subdued So Far." *New York Times*, April 2, 2003, p. A6, LexisNexis.

French, Sara. "U.S. Rates and Yuan to Weigh on Growth." *South China Morning Post*, June 17, 2000, p. 3, LexisNexis.

Friedberg, Aaron. "Ripe for Rivalry: Prospects for Peace in a Multipolar Asia." *International Security* 18, no. 3 (Winter 1993–94): 5–33.

Friedman, Edward. "The Challenge of a Rising China: Another Germany?" In *Eagle Adrift: American Foreign Policy at the End of the Century*, ed. Robert J. Lieber, 215–45. New York: Addison Wesley Longman, 1997.

Friedman, Thomas L. "Maids vs. Occupiers." *New York Times*, June 17, 2004, p. 29, LexisNexis.

Fu Fuyuan. "Zhiyi Shidai De Qiwen" [Questioning *Time's* weird story]. *Renmin Ri-bao*, September 9, 1997.

Fu Liqun. "Several Basic Ideas in U.S. Strategic Thinking." *Zhongguo Junshi Kexue*, February 20, 1997, pp. 28–37, FBIS-CHI-97-108.

"Full Text of China-Algeria Joint Communiqué Signed on 4 February 2004." *Xinhua*, February 4, 2004, WNC: ohstneo0ob8qpr.

"'Full Text' of Joint Declaration of China and France—Deepen the Comprehensive Strategic Partnership (Quan Mian Zhan Lue Huo Ban Guan Xi) between China and France and Build a World That Is Safer, More Respectful of Diversity, and More United." *Xinhua*, January 27, 2004, FBIS-CHI-2004-0127, WNC: ohs7h7t02ftdz9.

Gaddis, John Lewis. *Strategies of Containment: A Critical Appraisal of Postwar American National Security Policy*. New York: Oxford University Press, 1982.

Gallagher, Michael G. "China's Illusory Threat to the South China Sea." *International Security* 19, no. 1 (Summer 1994): 169–94.

Ganguly, Sumit. "India's Pathway to Pokhran II: The Prospects and Sources of New Delhi's Nuclear Weapons Program." *International Security* 23, no. 4 (Spring 1999): 148–77.

———. "The Start of a Beautiful Friendship? The United States and India." *World Policy Journal* 20, no. 1 (Spring 2003): 25–30.

Gao Heng, ed. *2020 Daguo Zhanlüe* [Great power strategy in 2020]. Shijiazhuang: Hebei Renmin Chubanshe, 2000.

Gao Hong. "Behind the 'Legislation for Emergencies.'" *Renmin Ribao*, May 27, 2003, FBIS-CHI-2003-0527, WNC: ohfneau02ldq54.

Gao Yijun. "Will Japanese Militarism 'Revive' Taking Advantage of DPRK Nuclear Issue?" *Renmin Wang*, February 11, 2003, FBIS-CHI-2003-0211, WNC: 0HAAWT500SVGR4.

Garrett , Banning N., and Bonnie S. Glaser. "Chinese Perspectives on Nuclear Arms Control." *International Security* 20, no. 3 (Winter 1995–96): 43–78.

———. "Looking across the Yalu: Chinese Assessments of North Korea." *Asian Survey* 35, no. 6 (June 1995): 528–45.

Garver, John W. "The Chinese Communist Party and the Collapse of Soviet Communism." *China Quarterly*, no. 133 (March 1993): 1–26.

———. "The PLA as an Interest Group in Chinese Foreign Policy." In *Chinese Military Modernization*, ed. C. Dennison Lane, Mark Weisenbloom, and Dimon Liu, 246–81. New York: Kegan Paul International, 1996.

Gerth, Jeff. "Congress Investigating Sales of Satellite Technology to China." *New York Times*, April 16, 1998, p. A5, LexisNexis.

Gertz, Bill. "Radar Sale to China Stopped; U.S. May Buy Czech System." *Washington Times*, May 26, 2004, p. A8, LexisNexis.

Gill, Bates. "The Impact of Economic Reform Upon Chinese Defense Production." In *Chinese Military Modernization*, ed. C. Dennison Lane, Mark Weisenbloom, and Dimon Liu, 144–67. New York: Kegan Paul International, 1996.

Gill, Bates, and James Mulvenon. "Chinese Military-Related Think Tanks and Research Institutions." *China Quarterly*, no. 171 (September 2002): 617–24.

Gilpin, Robert. *War and Change in World Politics*. New York: Cambridge University Press, 1981.

Glaser, Bonnie S. "China's Security Perceptions: Interests and Ambitions." *Asian Survey* 33, no. 3 (March 1993): 252–71.

Glaser, Bonnie S., and Phillip C. Saunders. "Chinese Civilian Foreign Policy Research Institutes: Evolving Roles and Increasing Influence." *China Quarterly*, no. 171 (September 2002): 597–616.

Glosny, Michael A. "Strangulation from the Sea? A PRC Submarine Blockade of Taiwan." *International Security* 28, no. 4 (Spring 2004): 125–60.

Godwin, Paul H. B. *The Chinese Defense Establishment: Continuity and Change in the 1980s*. Boulder, CO: Westview Press, 1983.

———. "The Chinese Defense Establishment in Transition: The Passing of a Revolutionary Army?" In *Modernizing China*, ed. A. Doak Barnett and Ralph N. Clough, 63–80. Boulder, CO: Westview Press, 1986.

———. "Force Projection and China's National Military Strategy." In *Chinese Military Modernization*, ed. C. Dennison Lane, Mark Weisenbloom, and Dimon Liu, 69–99. New York: Kegan Paul International, 1996.

———. "From Continent to Periphery: PLA Doctrine, Strategy and Capabilities Towards 2000." *China Quarterly*, no. 146 (June 1996): 464–87.

Goh, Sui Noi. "China Ready to Sacrifice Games to Block Chen." *Straits Times (Singapore)*, May 25, 2004, LexisNexis.

Goldstein, Avery. "Across the Yalu: China's Interests and the Korean Peninsula in a Changing World." Paper presented at New Directions in Chinese Foreign Policy: A Conference in Honor of Allen S. Whiting, Fairbank Center for East Asian Research, Harvard University, November 8–9, 2002.

———. "Balance-of-Power Politics: Consequences for Asian Security Order." In *Asian Security Order: Instrumental and Normative Features*, ed. Muthiah Alagappa, 171–209. Stanford, CA: Stanford University Press, 2003.

———. *Deterrence and Security in the 21st Century: China, Britain, France, and the Enduring Legacy of the Nuclear Revolution*. Stanford, CA: Stanford University Press, 2000.

———. "Discounting the Free Ride: Alliances and Security in the Postwar World." *International Organization* 49, no. 1 (Winter 1995): 39–72.

———. *From Bandwagon to Balance-of-Power Politics: Structural Constraints and Politics in China, 1949–1978*. Stanford, CA: Stanford University Press, 1991.

———. "The Political Implications of a Slowdown." *Orbis* 43, no. 2 (Spring 1999): 203–21.

———. "Robust and Affordable Security: Some Lessons from the Second-Ranking Powers During the Cold War." *Journal of Strategic Studies* 15, no. 4 (December 1992): 476–527.

———. "September 11, the Shanghai Summit, and the Shift in U.S. China Policy." *Foreign Policy Research Institute, E-Notes*, November 2001, http://fpri.org/enotes/americawar.20011109.goldstein.sept11china.html.

———. "Structural Realism and China's Foreign Policy: Much (but Never All) of the Story." In *Perspectives on Structural Realism*, ed. Andrew Hanami, 119–54. New York: Palgrave Macmillan, 2003.

Goldstein, Lyle, and William Murray. "Undersea Dragons: China's Maturing Submarine Force." *International Security* 38, no. 4 (Spring 2004): 161–96.

Gong, Gerrit, Robert Kapp, Nicholas Lardy, Greg Mastel, Dwight Perkins, and Edward Steinfeld. "China into the Abyss?" *Washington Quarterly* 22, no. 2 (Spring 1999): 27–85.

Gordon, Michael R. "U.S. Nuclear Plan Sees New Weapons and New Targets." *New York Times*, March 10, 2002, LexisNexis.

"Gouzhu Xin Shiji De Xinxing Guoji Guanxi" [Building a new type of international relations for the new century]. *Renmin Ribao*, December 8, 1997, p. 6.

Graham, Bradley, and Walter Pincus. "Nuclear Targeting Draft Shifts Focus from Russia; More Emphasis Given to China, N. Korea, Mideast." *Washington Post*, March 10, 2002, p. A27.

Greenhouse, Steven. "New Tally of World's Economies Catapults China into Third Place." *New York Times*, May 20, 1993, p. A1, LexisNexis.

Gu Ping. "China's 'Peaceful Rise,' Which Emphasizes Achieving Modernization through Self-Reliance, Will Benefit Mankind." *Renmin Ribao*, February 17, 2004, FBIS-CHI-2004-0217, WNC: 0hxi30803nbrsl.

———. "A New Pretext for Joining the TMD System." *Renmin Ribao*, August 4, 2000, FBIS-CHI-2000-0804, WNC: 0FYXADC03I5ZQL.

———. "Sino-US Relations Are Facing Historic Opportunity." *Renmin Ribao*, October 19, 1997, FBIS-CHI-97-292, WNC: 0EIH70S01RYY90.

———. "Zhongmei Guanxi Mianlin Lishi Jiyu" [Sino-American relations face a historic opportunity]. *Renmin Ribao*, November 5, 1997, p. 1.

"The Guidelines for Japan-U.S. Defense Cooperation." *Ministry of Foreign Affairs of Japan*, September 23, 1997, http://www.mofa.go.jp/region/n-america/us/security/guideline2.html.

Guo Jian and Su Xiangxin. "China: Shen Guofang Hails Jiang Zemin's US Trip." *Zhongguo Xinwenshe*, November 2, 1997, FBIS-CHI-97-306.

Guo Shuyong. "21 Shiji Qianye Zhongguo Waijiao Dazhanlüe Chuyi" [A modest proposal for China's diplomatic grand strategy on the eve of the twenty-first century]. *Taipingyang Xuebao*, no. 2 (1999): 91–96.

Hagerty, Devin T. *The Consequences of Nuclear Proliferation: Lessons from South Asia.* Cambridge, MA: MIT Press, 1998.

Hamerow, Theodore S. *Otto Von Bismarck: A Historical Assessment.* 2nd ed. Lexington, MA: D.C. Heath and Company, 1972.

Hamrin, Carol Lee. "Elite Politics and the Development of China's Foreign Relations." In *Chinese Foreign Policy: Theory and Practice*, ed. Thomas W. Robinson and David Shambaugh, 70–112. Oxford: Oxford University Press, 1994.

Han Hua. "Four Keys in 1998 Chinese Diplomacy." *Wen Wei Po*, March 4, 1998, FBIS-CHI-98-063.

———. "Jiang Zemin to Go to Kuala Lumpur in Mid-December to Attend East Asia–ASEAN Summit, China to Establish Partnership with ASEAN." *Wen Wei Po*, December 3, 1997, p. A1, FBIS-CHI-97-337.

———. "Zhang Yishan [Chinese Foreign Ministry Official] on China's Multilateral Diplomacy." *Wen Wei Po*, January 7, 1997, p. A2, FBIS-CHI-97-009.

Harding, Harry. "China's Cooperative Behaviour." In *Chinese Foreign Policy: Theory and Practice*, ed. Thomas W. Robinson and David Shambaugh, 375–400. Oxford: Oxford University Press, 1994.

———. *China's Second Revolution: Reform after Mao.* Washington, DC: Brookings Institution, 1987.

Harsanyi, John C. "Game Theory and the Analysis of International Conflict." In *International Politics and Foreign Policy*, ed. James N. Rosenau, 370–79. New York: Free Press, 1969.

He Chong. "China and the United States Are Exploring the Possibility of Establishing a 'Strategic Partnership'—First in a Series on Prospects of Jiang Zemin's U.S. Visit." *Zhongguo Tongxunshe*, October 24, 1997, FBIS-CHI-97-297, WNC: 0EIQGZD03INWSQ.

———. "China and the United States Declare Their Endeavor to Build a Constructive and Strategic Partnership Relationship." *Zhongguo Tongxunshe*, November 3, 1997, FBIS-CHI-97-307, WNC: 0EJ7BIW010JZV7.

———. "The International Plot Behind the Diaoyu Islands Dispute Provoked by Japan." *Zhongguo Tongxunshe*, September 9, 1996, FBIS-CHI-96-176, WNC: 0DXL7GG00LIBL.

Heer, Paul. "A House United." *Foreign Affairs* 79, no. 4 (July–August 2000): 18–25.

Herz, John H. "Idealist Internationalism and the Security Dilemma." *World Politics* 2, no. 2 (January 1950): 157–80.

Hille, Kathrin. "Taiwan President Calls for New Constitution." *Financial Times*, September 29, 2003, http://taiwansecurity.org/News/2003/FT-092903.htm.

Hirsch, Michael. "The Great Technology Giveaway?" *Foreign Affairs* 77, no. 5 (September–October 1998): 2–9.

Ho Chung. "Prospects of Zhu Rongji's Trip to Japan." *Zhongguo Tongxun She*, October 11, 2000, FBIS-CHI-2000-1011, WNC: 0G2DEY001WO7ZM.

House National Security Committee. *Testimony of Floyd D. Spence: National Security, Security Challenges, China*, March 20 1996, LexisNexis.

Hu Jintao. "China's Development Is an Opportunity for Asia (Speech by President Hu Jintao of China at the Opening Ceremony of the Boao Forum for Asia 2004 Annual Conference)." *People's Daily Online*, April 24, 2004, http://english.peopledaily.com.cn/200404/24/eng20040424_141419.shtml.

Hu, Weixing. "Beijing's Defense Strategy and the Korean Peninsula." *Journal of Northeast Asian Studies* 14, no. 3 (Fall 1995): 50–67.

Huai Chengbo. "Behind the Fear of a 'China Threat.'" *Beijing Review* 36, no. 9 (March 1, 1993): 10.

Huang Qing. "Ya'ou Huiyi He Duojihua" [ASEM and multipolarization.] *Renmin Ribao*, April 9, 1998, http://www.snweb.com/gb/people_daily/gbrm.htm.

Huang Xingwei. "Roundup: Sino-British Relations Develop Steadily." *Xinhua*, October 18, 1999, FBIS-CHI-1999-1018, WNC: 0FJVALB00ET3BU.

Huang Zongliang. "Miandui Beiyue Xin Zhanlüe Chonggu Zhong'e Guanxi" [Reassessing Sino-Russian relations in the face of NATO's New Strategy]. *Xin Shiye* [New vision], no. 5 (1999): 25–28. Reprinted in *Zhongguo Waijiao* [China's diplomacy], no. 1 (2000).

Huang, Cary. "Jiang Zemin Reportedly Urges Development of Strategic Weapons." *Hong Kong Mail*, August 5, 2000, FBIS-CHI-2000-0805, WNC: 0FYXT0S00W4QXV.

———. "US Role in Taipei-Beijing Relations Viewed." *The Hong Kong Standard*, May 23, 2000, p. 8, FBIS-CHI-2000-0524, WNC: 0FV4EME04E8SWC.

Huntington, Samuel P. *The Clash of Civilizations and the Remaking of World Order*. New York: Simon and Schuster, 1996.

———. "The Clash of Civilizations?" *Foreign Affairs* 72, no. 3 (Summer 1993): 22–49.

———. "The U.S.—Decline or Renewal." *Foreign Affairs* 67, no. 2 (Winter 1988): 76–96.

"India PM: India, China Can Build Partnership." *People's Daily Online*, June 22, 2003, http://english.peopledaily.com.cn/200306/22/eng20030622_118700.shtml.

"India, China Agree to Develop Cooperative Ties." *Xinhua*, August 5, 1997, FBIS-CHI-97-217, WNC: 0EEIH08051997000680.

"Indonesia, China to Build Strategic Partnership: Officials." *People's Daily Online*, November 6, 2004, http://english.people.com.cn/200411/06/eng20041106_162985.html.

Instrument of Accession to the Treaty of Amity and Cooperation in Southeast Asia, October 8, 2003, http://www.aseansec.org/15271.htm.

"Interview with Song Baotian, Deputy Director of the China Institute for International Relations." *News Report and Current Events, Beijing China Radio International*, November 13, 1997, FBIS-CHI-97-317.

"Interview with Taiwanese President Chen Shui-bian." *Washington Post*, October 10, 2003, http://taiwansecurity.org/WP/2003/WP-101003.htm.

"Iraq Crisis Revealed Collapse of US Global Authority: Chinese Analysts." *Agence France-Presse*, March 9, 1998, CNC.

Ito, Nobuyuki. "Reading the World: The Strategic Environment in the 21st Century." *Tokyo Asagumo*, January 8, 1998, p. 1, FBIS-EAS-98-048.

Jacob, Happymon. "Enter the Dragon." *The Pioneer*, June 25, 2003, FBIS-NES-2003-0625, WNC: 0hh39w000aifht.

"Japan Has an Axe to Grind: News Analysis." *People's Daily Online*, August 7, 2003, http://english.peopledaily.com.cn/200308/07/eng20030807_121870.shtml.

"Japan Rejects Any Chinese Pressure over Taiwan." *Agence France-Presse*, October 28, 1998, CNC.

"Japan, China Agree on Mutual Visits by Warships: Report." *Agence France-Presse*, April 28, 1998, CNC.

"Japan: Bilateral Political Relations." *Foreign Ministry of the People's Republic of China*, November 15, 2000, http://www.fmprc.gov.cn/eng/wjb/zzjg/yzs/gjlb/2721/2722/t15969.htm.

"Japan: Kato on Domestic, International Politics." *Tokyo Chuo Koron*, September 1997, pp. 28–43.

"Japan-U.S. Joint Declaration on Security Alliance for the 21st Century." *Ministry of Foreign Affairs of Japan*, April 17, 1996, http://www.mofa.go.jp/region/n-america/us/security/security.html.

Jencks, Harlan. "'People's War under Modern Conditions': Wishful Thinking, National Suicide, or Effective Deterrent?" *China Quarterly*, no. 98 (June 1984), 305–19.

Jervis, Robert. "Cooperation under the Security Dilemma." *World Politics*, 30, no. 2 (January 1978): 167–214.

———. "Hypotheses on Misperception." *World Politics* 20, no. 3 (April 1968): 454–79.

———. *The Illogic of American Nuclear Strategy*. Ithaca, NY: Cornell University Press, 1986.

———. *The Meaning of the Nuclear Revolution: Statecraft and the Prospect of Armageddon*. Ithaca, NY: Cornell University Press, 1989.

Jia Bei. "Gorbachev's Policy toward the Asian Pacific Region." *Guoji Wenti Yanjiu*, April 13, 1987, FBIS, China Daily Report, May 14, 1987, pp. C8–C14.

Jian Hua. "The United States, Japan Want to Rope in India Which Cherishes the Dream of Becoming a Major Country." *Ta Kung Pao*, June 4, 2001, FBIS-CHI-2001-0604, WNC: 0GETK07017N4KA.

"Jiang Zemin Hu Jintao Deng Huijian Di Shisici Wuguang Gongzuo Huiyi Daibiao" [Jiang Zemin, Hu Jintao, and others meet with representatives to the Fourteenth Work Conference of Military Officers]. *Renminwang*, July 20, 2003, http://peopledaily.com.cn/GB/shizheng/1024/1975937.html.

"Jiang Zemin Huijian Meiguo Zongtong Guojia Anquan Shiwu Zhuli Laisi" [Jiang Zemin meets the U.S. president's national security advisor Rice]. *Renminwang*, July 9, 2004, http://www1.people.com.cn/GB/paper464/12420/1117085.html.

"Jiang Zemin on Sino-US Relations in CBS Interview." *Xinhua*, September 4, 2000, FBIS-CHI-2000-0904, WNC: 0G0F5N800F4IOB.

"Jiang Zemin on Sino-US Ties, Taiwan, WTO, Tibet." *Xinhua*, September 8, 2000, FBIS-CHI-2000-0909, WNC: 0G0SF5E03MA75Z.

"Jiang Zemin Says Sino-Indian Ties 'Lifted One Level.'" *Xinhua*, November 30, 1996, FBIS-CHI-96-232, WNC: 0E1UZGH023OIVO.

"Jiang Zemin Sees 'Rich Fruit' from Sino-Pakistani Relations." *Xinhua*, December 1, 1996, FBIS-CHI-96-232, WNC: 0E1UZGM03N5FHE.

"Jiang Zemin Zhuxi Huijian Ge'er Fuzontong Shi Tichu Fazhan Zhongmei Guanxi" [While meeting with U.S. vice president Gore, President Jiang Zemin raises developing Sino-American relations]. *Renmin Ribao*, March 27, 1997, http://www.snweb.com/gb/people_daily/gbrm.htm.

"Jieshou Meiguo Youxian Xinwen Dianshiwang Jizhe Caifang, Jiang Zemin Changtan Zhongmei Guanxi Ji Taiwan Deng Wenti" [Giving an interview to an American CNN reporter, Jiang Zemin speaks freely about Sino-American relations, Taiwan, and other questions]. *Renmin Ribao*, May 10, 1997, http://www.snweb.com/gb/peopledaily/gbrm.htm.

Jin Canrong. "Zhongmei Guanxi De Bian Yu Bubian" [What's changed and what hasn't changed in Sino-American relations]. *Guoji Jingji Pinglun* [International economics review], no. 11/12 (1999). Reprinted in *Zhongguo Waijiao*, no. 3 (2000): 21–25.

Jin Xide, Cui Shiguang, Lin Xiaoguang, Wan Xinsheng, and Jiang Ruiping. "Reorienting Sino-Japanese Relations." *Shijie Zhishi*, no. 15 (August 1, 2003): 46–48, FBIS Document ID: CPP20030807000174.

Jin Xin. "Meiguo Yanfa TMD De Yitu Ji Dui Quanqiu He Woguo Anquan De Yingxiang" [US plans for research and development of TMD and its influence on the security of the world and our country]. *Guoji Guancha* [International observer], no. 4 (1999): 22–25.

"Jiu Zhong'e Liangguo Zui Gaoji Huiwu, Shuangbian Guanxi Deng Wenti, Jiang Zhuxi Jieshou Eluosi Jizhe Caifang" [President Jiang's interview with Moscow reporters about the Sino-Russian Summit Meeting, bilateral relations, etc.]. *Renmin Ribao*, April 18, 1997, http://www.snweb.com/gb/people_daily/gbrm.htm.

"Jiu Zhongmei Guanxi, Taiwan Wenti, Zhongguo Renda Zhidu Deng Wenti: Qiao Shi Jieshou Meiguo Jizhe Caifang" [Qiao Shi takes questions from American reporters on Sino-American relations, the Taiwan problem, the National People's Congress system, etc.]. *Renmin Ribao*, January 17, 1997, http://www.snweb.com/gb/people_daily/gbrm.htm.

Joffe, Ellis. *The Chinese Army after Mao.* Cambridge, MA: Harvard University Press, 1987.

———. "Party-Army Relations in China: Retrospect and Prospect." *China Quarterly,* no. 146 (June 1996): 299–314.

Joffe, Joseph. "'Bismarck or Britain'? Toward an American Grand Strategy after Bipolarity." *International Security* 19, no. 4 (Spring 1995): 94–117.

Johnson, Chalmers A. *Peasant Nationalism and Communist Power: The Emergence of Revolutionary China, 1937–1945.* Stanford, CA: Stanford University Press, 1962.

Johnston, Alastair Iain. "China's New 'Old Thinking': The Concept of Limited Deterrence." *International Security* 20, no. 3 (Winter 1995–96): 5–42.

———. "The Correlates of Nationalism in Beijing Public Opinion." Working paper for the Institute of Defence and Strategic Studies, Singapore, 2003.

———. "Cultural Realism and Strategy in Maoist China." In *The Culture of National Security: Norms and Identity in World Politics,* ed. Peter J. Katzenstein, 216–70. New York: Columbia University Press, 1996.

———. *Cultural Realism: Strategic Culture and Grand Strategy in Chinese History.* Princeton, NJ: Princeton University Press, 1995.

———. "Is China a Status Quo Power?" *International Security* 27, no. 4 (Spring 2003): 5–56.

———. "Prospects for Chinese Nuclear Force Modernization: Limited Deterrence versus Multilateral Arms Control." *China Quarterly,* no. 146 (June 1996): 548–76.

Johnston, Alastair Iain, and Paul Evans. "China's Engagement with Multilateral Security Institutions." In *Engaging China,* ed. Alastair Iain Johnston and Robert S. Ross, 235–72. London: Routledge, 1999.

Johnston, Alastair Iain, W. K. H. Panofsky, Marco DiCapua, and Lewis R. Franklin. *The Cox Committee Report: An Assessment Center for International Security and Cooperation,* Stanford University, December 1999, http://www.ceip.org/files/projects/npp/pdf/coxfinal3.pdf.

"Joint Communiqué between the People's Republic of China and the United States of America (China-U.S. August 17 Communiqué)," August 17, 1982, http://hongkong.usconsulate.gov/uscn/docs/jc/790101.htm.

"Joint Communiqué of the United States of America and the People's Republic of China (Shanghai Communiqué)," February 28, 1972, http://hongkong.usconsulate.gov/uscn/docs/jc/720227.htm.

"Joint Communiqué on the Establishment of Diplomatic Relations between the People's Republic of China and the United States of America," January 1, 1979, http://hongkong.usconsulate.gov/uscn/docs/jc/790101.htm.

Joint Declaration of the Heads of State/Government of the Association of Southeast Asian Nations and the People's Republic of China on Strategic Partnership for Peace and Prosperity, October 8, 2003, http://www.aseansec.org/15265.htm.

"Joint Statement by the PRC President and the Russian Federation President on the Antimissile Issue." *Xinhua,* July 18, 2000, FBIS-CHI-2000-0718, WNC: 0FXY4TI01WVMI5.

Joint Statement, U.S.-Japan Security Consultative Committee, Completion of the Review of the Guidelines for U.S.-Japan Defense Cooperation, http://www-mofa.mofa.go.jp/region/n-america/us/security/defense.html.

"Jundui Yao Shiying Gaige He Fazhan De Xin Xingshi, Gengjia Zijue Fucong Fuwu

Dang He Guojia Da Ju" [The army must adapt to the new situation of reform and development, be even more aware of complying with and serving the Party's and country's overall situation]. *Renmin Ribao*, March 11, 1998, http://www.snweb.com/gb/people_daily/gbrm.htm.

Kahn, Joseph. "Former Leader Is Still a Power in China's Life." *New York Times*, July 16, 2004, http://www.nytimes.com/2004/07/16/international/asia/16chin.html.

Kang, David C. "Getting Asia Wrong: The Need for New Analytical Frameworks." *International Security* 27, no. 4 (Spring 2003): 57–85.

Karmel, Solomon M. "The Chinese Military's Hunt for Profits." *Foreign Policy*, no. 107 (Summer 1997): 102–13.

Karniol, Robert. "China Is Poised to Buy Third Batch of Su-27s." *Jane's Defence Weekly* 25, no. 17 (April 24, 1996): 10, LexisNexis.

Katsumata, Hidemichi. "Dream of Domestic Jet Fighter Realized." *Daily Yomiuri*, August 10, 2001, p. 3, LexisNexis.

Katyal, K. K. "Perceptions & Prescriptions." *The Hindu*, May 21, 2001, FBIS-CHI-2001-0521, WNC: 0GDQNG5031765U.

Kaufmann, William W. *Assessing the Base Force: How Much Is Too Much?* Washington, DC: Brookings Institution, 1992.

Kaufmann, William W., and John D. Steinbruner. *Decisions for Defense: Prospects for a New Order*. Washington, DC: Brookings Institution, 1991.

Kelly, James A. "Overview of U.S. Policy toward Taiwan." In *Testimony of Assistant Secretary of State for East Asian and Pacific Affairs James A. Kelly at a hearing on Taiwan, House International Relations Committee*, April 21, 2004, http://www.state.gov/p/eap/rls/rm/2004/31649pf.htm.

Kennan, George F. *The Decline of Bismarck's European Order: Franco-Russian Relations, 1875–1890*. Princeton, NJ: Princeton University Press, 1979.

Kennedy, Paul. "Grand Strategy in War and Peace: Toward a Broader Definition." In *Grand Strategies in War and Peace*, ed. Paul Kennedy, 1–7. New Haven, CT: Yale University Press, 1991.

———. *The Rise and Fall of the Great Powers*. New York: Vintage, 1987.

Kent, George O. *Bismarck and His Times*. Carbondale: Southern Illinois University Press, 1978.

Keohane, Robert O. *After Hegemony: Cooperation and Discord in the World Political Economy*. Princeton, NJ: Princeton University Press, 1984.

Keohane, Robert O., and Joseph S. Nye. *Power and Interdependence*. 2nd ed. Boston: Scott, Foresman and Co., 1989.

Khalilzad, Zalmay M., Abram N. Shulsky, Daniel L. Byman, Roger Cliff, David Orletsky, David Shlapak, and Ashley J. Tellis. *The United States and a Rising China: Strategic and Military Implications*. Santa Monica, CA: RAND, 1999.

Kin, Kwan Weng. "Japan 'to Remain Top ASEAN Partner for Next 20 Years'; but It Will Have to Jostle with China for the Position in 50 Years, Says PM Goh in Press Interview." *Straits Times (Singapore)*, December 3, 2003, LexisNexis.

———. "Japan's PM Upbeat on China's Growth; China's Economic Growth Is Not a Threat and Would Benefit Both ASEAN and Japan, Says Koizumi." *Straits Times (Singapore)*, December 13, 2003, LexisNexis.

Kindleberger, Charles P. *The World in Depression, 1929–1939*. Berkeley: University of California Press, 1975.

Kissinger, Henry. *Diplomacy*. New York: Touchstone, 1994.

Klare, Michael. "East Asia's Militaries Muscle Up: East Asia's New-Found Riches Are Purchasing the Latest High-Tech Weapons." *Bulletin of the Atomic Scientists* 53, no. 1 (January 11, 1997), 56–61, LexisNexis.

Kom, Jiri, and David Mulholland. "Czech Republic Shelves Sale of Vera-E Radar to China." *Jane's Defence Weekly*, June 2, 2004, LexisNexis.

Krasner, Stephen D., ed. *International Regimes*. Ithaca, NY: Cornell University Press, 1983.

Kristof, Nicholas. "The Rise of China." *Foreign Affairs* 72, no. 5 (November–December 1993): 59–74.

———. "Tension with Japan Rises Alongside China's Star." *New York Times*, June 16, 1996, p. E3.

Kupchan, Charles A., and Clifford A. Kupchan. "Concerts, Collective Security, and the Future of Europe." *International Security* 16, no. 1 (1991): 114–61.

Kwan, Daniel. "Beijing Urged to Keep Regional Power Focus." *South China Morning Post*, September 29, 1998, p. 10, LexisNexis.

Kydd, Andrew. "Trust Building, Trust Breaking: The Dilemma of NATO Enlargement." *International Organization* 54, no. 2 (Autumn 2001): 801–28.

Lam, Willy Wo-Lap. "China, Japan Struggle on Accord; Leaders Fail to Sign Joint Statement after Disagreement over Apology for War Atrocities." *South China Morning Post*, November 27, 1998, LexisNexis.

———. "Jiang to Pressure Clinton over Taiwan Stance." *South China Morning Post*, August 14, 1999, p. 1, LexisNexis.

———. "Singing a Different Tune to the US." *South China Morning Post*, July 26, 2000, 2000, http://taiwansecurity.org/SCMP/SCMP-072600.htm.

Lamson, James A., and Wyn Q. Bowen. "'One Arrow, Three Stars': China's MIRV Programme, Part I." *Jane's Intelligence Review* 9, no. 5 (May 1997): 216–18, LexisNexis.

———. "'One Arrow, Three Stars': China's MIRV Programme, Part II." *Jane's Intelligence Review* 9, no. 6 (June 1997): 266–69, LexisNexis.

Lane, Charles. "TRB from Washington: Re-Orient." *New Republic*, May 20, 1996, p. 6.

Lardy, Nicholas R. *China in the World Economy*. Washington, DC: Institute for International Economics, 1994.

———. "The Future of China: China's Growing Economic Role in Asia." *NBR Analysis* 3, no. 3 (August 1992): 5–12.

———. *Integrating China into the Global Economy*. Washington, DC: Brookings Institution, 2002.

"Law on the Territorial Sea and the Contiguous Zone of the People's Republic of China, February 25, 1992, http://www.un.org/Depts/los/LEGISLATIONANDTREATIES/ PDFFILES/CHN_1992_Law.pdf.

Layne, Christopher. "Kant or Cant: The Myth of the Democratic Peace." *International Security* 19, no. 2 (Fall 1994): 5–49.

Lee Kim Chew. "China Agrees to an ASEAN N-Arms Ban." *Straits Times (Singapore)*, July 28, 1999, p. 1, LexisNexis.

Lee Siew Hua. "Time to Put Japan Firmly Back on US Radar Screen." *Straits Times (Singapore)*, October 13, 2000, p. 66, LexisNexis.

Leifer, Michael. *The ASEAN Regional Forum*, Adelphi Paper 302. London: International Institute for Strategic Studies, July 1996.

Lewis, John Wilson, and Hua Di. "China's Ballistic Missile Programs: Technologies, Strategies, Goals." *International Security* 17, no. 2 (Fall 1992): 5–40.

Lewis, John W., and Xue Litai. *China Builds the Bomb*. Stanford, CA: Stanford University Press, 1988.

———. *China's Strategic Seapower*. Stanford, CA: Stanford University Press, 1994.

Li Heng. "Is Japan Advancing toward a 'Normal Country?'" *People's Daily Online*, July 3, 2003, http://english.peopledaily.com.cn/200307/03/eng20030703_119391.shtml.

Li Jijun. "On Strategic Culture." *Zhongguo Junshi Kexue* 38, no. 1 (February 1997): 8–15, FBIS-CHI-97-092.

"Li Peng Zai Mosike Jishou Jizhe Fangwen" [Li Peng's interview with reporters in Moscow]. *Renmin Ribao*, February 19, 1998, http://www.snweb.com/gb/people_daily/gbrm.htm.

Li Peng. "Promote Understanding, Develop Friendship, Enhance Cooperation." *Xinhua*, January 13, 2001, FBIS-CHI-2001-0113, WNC: 0G7D2V002CY5EH.

Li Xuejiang. "The 'Two Anchors' of the United States." *Renmin Ribao*, August 6, 1996, FBIS-CHI-96-156.

Li, Cheng. *China's Leaders: The New Generation*. Lanham, MD: Rowman and Littlefield, 2001.

Li, Hongshan. "China Talks Back: Anti-Americanism or Nationalism? A Review of Recent 'Anti-American' Books in China." *Journal of Contemporary China* 6, no. 14 (March 1997): 153–60.

Li, Nan. "The PLA's Evolving Warfighting Doctrine, Strategy and Tactics, 1985–1995: A Chinese Perspective." *China Quarterly*, no. 146 (June 1996): 443–63.

Liang Ming. "'Defense White Paper' Reveals Japan's Military Intentions." *Liaowang*, August 26, 2002, pp. 55–56, FBIS-CHI-2002-0905, WNC: 0H285F900P1ZCZ.

Liberman, Peter. "The Spoils of Conquest." *International Security* 18, no. 2 (Fall 1993): 125–53.

Lieberthal, Kenneth. *Governing China*. New York: W. W. Norton, 1995.

Lim, Benjamin Kang. "Beijing Slams West for Playing up China Threat." *Reuters*, November 3, 1995, CNC.

Lin Cheng-yi. "War in Iraq Is Shaking up Strategic Calculations." *Taipei Times*, March 28, 2003, FBIS-CHI-2003-0328, WNC: 0hcmvmr0015ta9.

Lin, Chong-pin. "The Military Balance in the Taiwan Straits." *China Quarterly*, no. 146 (June 1996): 577–95.

———. "The Power Projection Capabilities of the People's Liberation Army." In *Chinese Military Modernization*, ed. C. Dennison Lane, Mark Weisenbloom, and Dimon Liu, 100–125. New York: Kegan Paul International, 1996.

Liu Aicheng. "When Will the Cold War Mentality Find It's [*sic*] Resting Place?" *Renmin Ribao*, June 8, 2004, p. 3, FBIS-CHI-2004-0608, WNC: 0hz1n4hoojvpg1.

Liu Changmin. "Shixi Dangjin Riben Zhengzhi De Youqinghua" [A tentative analysis of the right-wing drift in contemporary Japanese politics]. *Shijie Jingji yu Zhengzhi Luntan*, no. 6 (1999): 23–26.

Liu Di. "Deng Xiaoping's Thinking on Diplomatic Work—Interview with Liang Shoude, Dean for College of International Relations for Beijing University." *Ta Kung Pao*, November 2, 1997, p. A6, FBIS-CHI-97-310.

Liu Huaqiu. "China's Diplomatic Achievements in 1992." *Beijing Review*, 35, no. 52 (December 28, 1992): 8–11.

———. "Strive for a Peaceful International Environment." *Jiefang Ribao*, November 17, 1997, FBIS-CHI-97–321.

Liu Huorong, Wu Dingbao, and Yang Zhongyi. "China: Qian Qichen Holds Talks with Albright." *Xinhua*, July 26, 1997, FBIS-CHI-97-207, WNC: 0EE3OHL03Y2KDD.

Liu Jianfei. "The Building of Democratic Politics in China and Sino-US Relations." *Zhanlüe Yu Guanli* [Strategy and management], March 1, 2003, pp. 76–82. FBIS Document ID: CPP-2003-0506-000226

———. "'The Period of Strategic Opportunity' and Sino-US Ties." *Liaowang*, no. 3 (January 20, 2003): 56–57, FBIS-CHI-2003-0207, WNC: 0HA44OT006JU2N.

Liu Xiaobiao. "Where Are Sino-Japanese Relations Heading—A Commentary on Observations by Scholars and Concerns among the People." *Renmin Ribao*, August 13, 2003, FBIS-CHI-2003-0814, WNC: ohjtfc303c8bfa.

Liu Xuecheng and Li Jidong, eds. *Zhongguo He Meiguo: Duishou Haishi Huoban* [China and the United States: Adversaries or partners]. Beijing: Jingji Kexue Chubanshe, 2001.

Liu Yijian. "Zhongguo Weilai De Haijun Jianshe Yu Haijun Zhanlüe" [The future of China's navy building and naval strategy.] *Zhanlüe yu Guanli* [Strategy and management], no. 5 (1999): 96–100.

Lovejoy, Charles D., and Bruce W. Watson, eds. *China's Military Reforms*. Boulder, CO: Westview Press, 1986.

Lu Jianren. "Yatai Daguo Zai Dongnan Yazhou Diqu De Liyi" [Asia-Pacific great powers' interests in Southeast Asia]. *Shijie Jingji yu Zhengzhi*, no. 2 (2000): 41–45.

Lu Jin and Liu Yunfei. "New Analysis: From Beijing to Washington and from Moscow to Beijing—A Revelation of New-Type Relations between Major Powers." *Xinhua*, November 9, 1997, FBIS-CHI-97-313, WNC: 0EJK2JM027ZWZ4.

Lu Ning. *The Dynamics of Foreign-Policy Decisionmaking in China*. 2nd ed. Boulder, CO: Westview Press, 2000.

Lu Youzhi. "Chongxin Shenshi Zhongguo De Anquan Huanjing" [A fresh examination of China's security environment]. *Shijie Jingji yu Zhengzhi*, no. 1 (2000): 56–61.

Lu Zhongwei. "What Is the Purpose of the 'New Guidelines'?" *Renmin Ribao*, April 30, 1999, p. 7, FBIS-CHI-1999-0430, WNC: 0FB6D603GNDO3.

Luo Qinwen. "Hu Jintao Meets with Canadian Prime Minister Jean Chrétien." *Zhongguo Xinwen She*, October 19, 2003, FBIS-LAT-2003-1019, WNC: ohn3zr804ehyax.

Luttwak, Edward N. *The Grand Strategy of the Roman Empire: From the First Century A.D. to the Third*. Baltimore, MD: Johns Hopkins University Press, 1976.

———. *The Grand Strategy of the Soviet Union*. New York: St. Martin's Press, 1983.

———. *Strategy: The Logic of War and Peace*. Cambridge, MA: Belknap Press of Harvard University Press, 1987.

Ma Junwei. "Political Trends in Japan Following the General Election." *Xiandai Guoji Guanxi*, no. 2 (February 20, 1997), FBIS-CHI-97-089.

Ma, Josephine. "Wen Heads Home after Charm Offensive; Visit Helps Cement Sino-EU Trade Ties, but Premier Fails to Get Arms Embargo Lifted or to Secure Market-Economy Status." *South China Morning Post*, May 14, 2004, p. 6, LexisNexis.

Macartney, Jane. "China Army Wants Nuclear Arms Destruction, Test End." *Reuters*, June 13, 1996, CNC.

Mack, Andrew. "Why Big Nations Lose Small Wars: The Politics of Asymmetric Conflict." *World Politics* 27, no. 2 (January 1975): 175–200.

Mandelbaum, Michael. *The Nuclear Revolution: International Politics before and after Hiroshima.* New York: Cambridge University Press, 1981.

Mann, James H. *About Face: A History of America's Curious Relationship with China, from Nixon to Clinton.* New York: Alfred A. Knopf, 1998.

Mannion, Jim. "Pentagon Study Sees Danger in Chinese View of US Power." *Agence France-Presse,* March 7, 1998, CNC.

Mansfield, Edward D., and Jack Snyder. "Democratic Transitions, Institutional Strength, and War." *International Organization* 56, no. 2 (Spring 2002): 297–337.

———. "Democratization and the Danger of War." *International Security* 20, no. 1 (Summer 1995): 5–38.

Mao Xuncheng. "Chaoxian Bandao Jushi De Fanfu Ji Qi Yuanyin" [The causes of the recurrent situation on the Korean peninsula]. *Shanghai Shifan Daxue Xuebao,* March 1996, pp. 100–102.

McDougall, Walter A. *Promised Land, Crusader State: The American Encounter with the World since 1776.* Boston: Houghton Mifflin, 1997.

McGregor, Richard. "China Is Priority for Trade Boost, Says Israeli Minister,. *Financial Times,* June 25, 2004, p. 10, LexisNexis.

Mead, Walter Russell. *Power, Terror, Peace, and War: America's Grand Strategy in a World at Risk.* New York: Alfred A. Knopf, 2004.

Mearsheimer, John J. "Back to the Future: Instability in Europe after the Cold War." *International Security* 15, no. 1 (Summer 1990): 5–56.

———. "The False Promise of International Institutions." *International Security* 19, no. 3 (Winter 1994–95): 5–49.

Medeiros, Evan S. "China Debates Its 'Peaceful Rise Strategy.'" *Yale Global Online,* June 22, 2004, http://yaleglobal.yale.edu/display.article?id=4118.

Medlicott, W. N., and Dorothy K. Covney, eds. *Bismarck and Europe.* New York: St. Martin's Press, 1972.

Mi Ligong and Lei Bosong. "Premier Zhu Rongji Attends Sixth China-ASEAN Summit." *Xinhua,* November 4, 2002, FBIS-EAS-2002-1104, WNC: 0H53VRD044ICB4.

Milbank, Dana, and Glenn Kessler. "President Warns Taiwan on Independence Efforts: Bush Says Referendum on China Should Not Be Held." *Washington Post,* December 10, 2003, p. A1, http://taiwansecurity.org/WP/2003/WP-101203.htm.

Minder, Raphael. "Rebuff for French Call on China Embargo." *Financial Times,* December 18, 2003, p. 15, LexisNexis.

"Misrepresenting China's Might." *People's Daily Online,* June 30, 2004, http://english.peopledaily.com.cn/200406/30/eng20040630_148042.html.

Miyai, Yumiko, and Mami Tsukahara. "Jiang Hails New Era in Japan-China Ties; 3 Hecklers Held for Interrupting Waseda Speech." *Yomiuri Shimbun,* November 29, 1998, p. 1, LexisNexis.

Moeller, Kay. "China and Korea: The Godfather Part Three." *Journal of Northeast Asian Studies* 15, no. 4 (Winter 1996): 35–48.

Moore, Thomas G., and Dixia Yang. "Empowered and Restrained: Chinese Foreign Policy in the Age of Economic Interdependence." In *The Making of Chinese Foreign and Security Policy in the Era of Reform,* ed. David M. Lampton, 191–229. Stanford, CA: Stanford University Press, 2001.

Morada, Noel M., and Christopher Collier. "The Philippines: State Versus Society?" In *Asian Security Practice: Material and Ideational Influence*, ed. Muthiah Alagappa, 549–78. Stanford, CA: Stanford University Press, 1998.

Morgan, David. "Gingrich Calls for U.S. Defense against Nuclear Attack." *Reuters*, January 27, 1996, CNC.

Morgenthau, Hans. *Politics among Nations*. 5th ed. New York: Knopf, 1973.

Mueller, John E. *Retreat from Doomsday: The Obsolescence of Major War*. New York: Basic Books, 1989.

Nathan, Andrew J. "What's Wrong with American Taiwan Policy." *Washington Quarterly* 23, no. 2 (Spring 2000): 93–106.

Nathan, Andrew J., and Perry Link, eds. *The Tiananmen Papers*. New York: Public Affairs, 2001.

Nathan, Andrew J., and Robert S. Ross. *The Great Wall and the Empty Fortress: China's Search for Security*. New York: W. W. Norton, 1997.

The National Security Implications of the Economic Relationship Between the United States and China: Report To Congress Of The U.S.-China Security Review Commission, July, 2002, http://www.uscc.gov/researchreports/2000_2003/reports/anrpo2.htm.

"The National Security Strategy of the United States of America." The White House, Office of the President of the United States, September 17, 2002, http://www.whitehouse.gov/nsc/nss.pdf.

Naughton, Barry. "The Third Front: Defence Industrialization in the Chinese Interior." *China Quarterly*, no. 115 (September 1988): 351–86.

Nelsen, Harvey W. *Power and Insecurity: Beijing, Moscow, and Washington, 1949–1988*. Boulder, CO: Lynne Rienner, 1989.

"New Zealand: Spying Capacity Upgrade in New Zealand Linked to China." *Agence France-Presse*, July 30, 1997, FBIS-EAS-97-211.

"News Agency Interviews Russian President on Visit to China," July 18, 2000, BBC Summary of World Broadcasts, LexisNexis.

Ni Feng. "Meiri Tongmeng Yu Diqu Anquan" [The U.S.-Japan alliance and regional security]. *Taipingyang Xuebao* [Pacific journal], no. 2 (1999): 65–76.

Ni Jianmin. "Opportunities Are Greater Than Challenges in the Present International Environment." *Liaowang*, March 11, 2002, FBIS-CHI-2002-0315, WNC: 0GTDO1NooYTOB7.

Nishihara, Masashi. "Aiming at New Order for Regional Security—Current State of ARF." *Gaiko Forum*, November 1997, pp. 35–40, FBIS-EAS-97-321.

Nordlinger, Eric A. *Isolationism Reconfigured: American Foreign Policy for a New Century*. Princeton, NJ: Princeton University Press, 1995.

Nye, Joseph S., and William A. Owens. "America's Information Edge." *Foreign Affairs* 75, no. 3 (March–April 1996): 20–36.

O'Hanlon, Michael. *Defense Planning for the Late 1990s*. Washington, DC: Brookings Institution, 1995.

———. "Why China Cannot Conquer Taiwan." *International Security* 25, no. 2 (Fall 2000): 51–86.

Oksenberg, Michel. "China's Confident Nationalism." *Foreign Affairs* 65 (Winter 1987): 501–23.

"The One-China Principle and the Taiwan Issue." Released by the Taiwan Affairs

Office and the Information Office of the State Council, February 21, 2000, http://taiwansecurity.org/IS/White-Paper-022100.htm.

"'One Country on Each Side' Statement." *Taiwan Security Research,* http://www.taiwansecurity.org/TSR-OneSide.htm.

Opall, Barbara. "China Boosts Air Combat Capabilities." *Defense News,* September 2, 1996, p. 3, LexisNexis.

———. "Skeptics Doubt Value of PLA White Paper." *Defense News,* December 9, 1996, p. 3, LexisNexis.

Organski, A. F. K., and Jacek Kugler. *The War Ledger.* Chicago: University of Chicago Press, 1980.

Overholt, William H. *The Rise of China.* New York: W. W. Norton, 1993.

Pan, Philip P. "China Thanks Bush for Taiwan Stance: Beijing Issues New Warning against Move toward Independence." *Washington Post,* December 22, 2003, p. A22, http://www.taiwansecurity.org/WP/2003/WP-221203.htm.

———. "China Warns Taiwan Again on Issue of Independence: Official Vows 'Strong Reaction' If Referendum Law Is Passed." *Washington Post,* November 27, 2003, p. A14, http://www.taiwansecurity.org/WP/2003/WP-271103-1.htm.

———. "China's Improving Image Challenges U.S. in Asia." *Washington Post,* November 15, 2003, p. A1.

Parker, Jeffrey. "China Taiwan Drills 'Proof' of PLA Modernization." *Reuters,* March 19, 1996, CNC.

"Peaceful Rise: Strategic Choice for China." *Xinhua,* April 24, 2004, FBIS-CHI-2004-0424, WNC: ohws5xp00tn1ub.

Pearson, Brendan. "Exuberance Reigns in Japan." *Australian Financial Review,* July 2, 2004, p. 31, LexisNexis.

———. "Japan Resists China's Influence." *Australian Financial Review,* December 11, 2003, p. 10, LexisNexis.

———. "Japanese Exports Hit Record." *Australian Financial Review,* June 24, 2004, p. 12, LexisNexis.

Peng Shujie and Liu Yunfei. "News Analysis: Partnership Promotes China's All-around Diplomacy." *Xinhua,* February 28, 1999, FBIS-CHI-1999-0228, WNC: 0F7XOVK045Z03B.

Pepper, Suzanne. *Civil War in China: The Political Struggle, 1945–1949.* Berkeley: University of California Press, 1978.

Perkovich, George. *India's Nuclear Bomb: The Impact on Global Proliferation.* Berkeley: University of California Press, 1999.

Perlez, Jane. "U.S. Ready to End Sanctions on India to Build Alliance." *New York Times,* August 27, 2001, p. A6, LexisNexis.

———. "Warning by China to Taiwan Poses Challenge to U.S." *New York Times,* February 27, 2000, http://taiwansecurity.org/NYT/NYT-022700-Challenge-to-US.htm.

"Perry Criticized on Taiwan." *Associated Press,* February 28, 1996, Clari.china.

"Philippines Studying Russian Offer of Mig-29s." *Reuters,* March 7, 1997, LexisNexis.

"Philippines to Seek Revision of Defense Pact with U.S." *Japan Economic Newswire,* May 14, 1997, LexisNexis.

Pillsbury, Michael. *China Debates the Future Security Environment.* Washington, DC: National Defense University Press, 2000.

Pincus, Walter. "Hill Report on Chinese Spying Faulted, Five Experts Cite Errors, 'Unwarranted' Conclusions by Cox Panel." *Washington Post*, December 15, 1999, p. A16.

Plafker, Ted. "Chinese Protest U.S. Sale of Weapons, Radar to Taiwan." *Washington Post*, April 19, 2000, http://taiwansecurity.org/WP/WP-041900.htm.

Plan of Action to Implement the Joint Declaration on ASEAN-China Strategic Partnership for Peace and Prosperity, November 29, 2004, http://www.aseansec.org/16805.htm.

"Plans for the Predictable Future." *Jane's Intelligence Review* 3, no. 5 (May 1996): 6, LexisNexis.

"Political Scientist Criticizes Planned Reform of Russian Missile Forces." *Interfax News Agency*, July 26, 2000, LexisNexis.

Pomfret, John. "China's Military Warns Taiwan." *Washington Post*, December 4, 2003, p. A25, http://www.taiwansecurity.org/WP/2003/WP-041203.htm.

———. "A New Direction for Chinese Diplomacy; Nuclear Threat in North Korea Prompts Ambitious Moves toward Multilateralism." *Washington Post*, August 16, 2003, p. A17, LexisNexis.

———. "Taiwan's Chen Backs Vote on Independence." *Washington Post*, August 4, 2002, p. A21, http://taiwansecurity.org/WP/2002/WP-080402.htm.

Pomfret, John, and Glenn Kessler. "China Puts North Korea Talks in Brighter Light; Unusual Briefing Suggests Beijing Is Eager to Keep Talks between Washington, Pyongyang on Track." *Washington Post*, April 29, 2003, p. A20, LexisNexis.

Porteous, Holly. "China's View of Strategic Weapons." *Jane's Intelligence Review* 8, no. 2 (March 1996): 134–37.

Posen, Barry R. *The Sources of Military Doctrine: France, Britain, and Germany between the World Wars*. Ithaca, NY: Cornell University Press, 1984.

Posen, Barry R., and Andrew L. Ross. "Competing Visions for U.S. Grand Strategy." *International Security* 21, no. 3 (Winter 1996–97): 5–54.

Powell, Robert. "Guns, Butter, and Anarchy." *American Political Science Review* 87, no. 1 (March 1993): 115–32.

———. *In the Shadow of Power: States and Strategies in International Politics*. Princeton, NJ: Princeton University Press, 1999.

———. "Uncertainty, Shifting Power, and Appeasement." *American Political Science Review* 90, no. 4 (December 1996): 749–64.

"PRC Academics Discuss Japan's Economic Problems, 'China Threat Theory.'" *Ta Kung Pao*, February 11, 2002, FBIS-CHI-2002-0211, WNC: 0GRJ7HK033L01K.

"PRC Academics Interviewed on Putin's Visit to China." *Hong Kong Ming Pao*, July 19, 2000, p. A15, FBIS-CHI-2000-0719, WNC: 0FY29DZ03ZW26H.

"PRC FM Tang Jiaxuan Warns U.S. Arms Sales to Taiwan Endanger Sino-US Relations." *Xinhua*, March 6, 2001, FBIS-CHI-2001-0306, WNC: 0G9U3D102ELBCV.

"PRC Outlines 5 Principles to Reduce Tension in Koreas." *Xinhua*, January 22, 1999, FBIS-CHI-99-022, WNC: OF66PDK02EOTEP.

"PRC Scholar Shi Yinhong on Gains, Losses, Winners, Losers in Korean War." *Qianlong Wang*, July 28, 2003. FBIS Document ID: CPP20030730000190.

"PRC Spokesman: Beijing Hopes for Negotiations on Korea." *Agence France-Presse*, April 18, 1996, FBIS-CHI-96-076, WNC: 0DQ4PPO047NXHJ.

"PRC Vice-Premier Qian Qichen Meets Albright on Sino-US Ties, Taiwan Issue." *Xinhua*, June 22, 2000, FBIS-CHI-2000-0622, WNC: 0FWTVPC00EX55I.

"PRC Zhu Rongji Urges Drawing History Lessons from Sino-Japanese Ties." *Xinhua*, October 13, 2000, FBIS-CHI-2000-1013, WNC: oG2IY8Go2GIBWC.

"PRC, ROK Issue Joint Statement on Building 'All-Round' Cooperative Partnership." *Xinhua*, July 8, 2003, FBIS-CHI-2003-0708, WNC: ohhrbhzo3pn635.

"PRC: Li Peng Meets Boeing's Board Members." *Xinhua*, June 24, 1996, FBIS-CHI-96-123, WNC: oDTMM9LoILMV7N.

"PRC: More on Sino-Russian Strategic Partnership." *Xinhua*, April 25, 1996, FBIS-CHI-96-081.

"PRC: Qian Qichen, Primakov Hold Breakfast Meeting." *Xinhua*, April 25, 1996, WNC: oDQHOZPoITAVSL.

"PRC: Tang Jiaxuan Meets with Dick Cheney, Terrorism, Ties Discussed." *Xinhua*, September 21, 2001, FBIS-CHI-2001-0921, WNC: oGK816GooQ5BLi.

"PRC's Qian Qichen, Talbott Discuss Bilateral Ties, Taiwan." *Zhongguo Xinwen She*, February 18, 2000, FBIS-CHI-2000-0218, WNC: oFQCFXMo3PR7AX.

"Premier Wen Jiabao Holds Talks with German Chancellor Gerhard Schroeder." *Foreign Ministry of the People's Republic of China*, May 4, 2004, http://www.fmprc.gov.cn/eng/topics/pwjbve/t94864.htm.

"Premier Zhu Rongji Meets Powell: Cooperation between China, U.S. Conducive to Both." *Xinhua*, July 28, 2001, FBIS-CHI-2001-0728, WNC: oGHAF4EooRZIOW.

"Premier's Bali Trip Raises China-ASEAN Ties to New Level: FM." *Xinhua*, October 8, 2003, FBIS-CHI-2003-1008, WNC: ohmjjkxo2hbn4q.

"President Jiang Zemin to Tour Italy, Switzerland, Austria Next March." *Agence France-Presse*, October 28, 1998, CNC.

"President Lee's Deutsche Welle Interview," July 9, 1999, http://taiwansecurity.org/TS/SS-990709-Deutsche-Welle-Interview.htm.

"President's Speech on Taiwan Reunification." *New China News Agency*, January 31, 1995, BBC Summary of World Broadcasts, LexisNexis.

"Presidents Jiang and Chirac Agree to Build 'Comprehensive Partnership.'" *Xinhua*, May 17, 1997, BBC Summary of World Broadcasts, LexisNexis.

"Promoting Rapid Development of Military Modernization—Ninth Commentary on Study, Implementation of Spirit of 16th CPC National Congress." *Jiefangjun Bao*, February 8, 2003, FBIS-CHI-2003-0211, WNC: oHA79NGo2OR2oC.

"Prospects of China's Diplomatic Activities in 1998." *Beijing Central People's Radio*, January 25, 1998, FBIS-CHI-98-028.

Protocol to Amend the Framework Agreement on Comprehensive Economic Co-operation between the Association of South East Asian Nations and the People's Republic of China, October 6, 2003, http://www.aseansec.org/15157.htm.

Qi Deliang and Tang Shuifu. "Li, Yi Yong-Tok Discuss Economic Ties." *Xinhua*, November 1, 1994, FBIS-CHI-94-212, Article Id: drchi212_d_94007.

Qian Qichen. "Adhering to Independent Foreign Policy." *Beijing Review* 34, no. 52 (December 30, 1991): 7–10.

———. "An Independent Foreign Policy of Peace: Excerpts from Chinese Foreign Minister Qian Qichen's March 12, 1992, Speech." *Beijing Review* 35, no. 13 (March 30, 1992): 13–15.

Qian Tong and Li Mingjiang. "Jiang Zemin Meets German Vice Chancellor in Beijing." *Xinhua*, December 12, 2000, FBIS-CHI-2000-1212, WNC: oG5KEH4o2oJZI8.

Qiang Zhai. "Mao Zedong and Dulles's 'Peaceful Evolution' Strategy: Revelations from Bo Yibo's Memoirs." *Cold War International History Project Bulletin*, no. 6–7 (Winter 1995–96), http://www.gwu.edu/~nsarchiv/CWIHP/BULLETINS/b6-7a19.htm.

Qiao Liang and Wang Xiangsui. *Unrestricted Warfare.* Beijing: PLA Literature and Arts Publishing House, 1999. Reprint, FBIS translation, available http://www.terrorism.com/infowar/index.shtml.

"Quadrennial Defense Review Report." United States Department of Defense, September 30, 2001, http://www.defenselink.mil/pubs/qdr2001.pdf.

Quak, Hiang Whai. "Flexible Yuan Won't Hurt Hk£ Money Chief." *Business Times (Singapore)*, September 5, 2000, pp. 1, 2, LexisNexis.

"Quanmian Kaichuang Jiushi Niandai Waijiao Xin Jumian—Dang De Shisida Yilai Woguo Waijiao Gongzuo Shuping" [Comprehensively initiating the new situation in 1990s diplomacy—A review of our country's diplomatic work since the Fourteenth Party Congress]. *Renmin Ribao*, September 6, 1997.

Ramesh, Jairam. "Author Sees China as Motive for Pentagon's 'India-Friendly' Leanings, Policies." *Telegraph (Calcutta)*, April 17, 2003, FBIS-NES-2003-0417, WNC: 0hdji2301ajzhd.

"Referendum Issue." In *Taiwan Security Research*, http://taiwansecurity.org/TSR-Referendum.htm.

"Released with Authorization from the 'Two Sessions': President Hu Jintao's Speech at the First Session of the 10th National People's Congress." *Xinhua*, March 18, 2003, FBIS-CHI-2003-0318, WNC: 0hc1xdn03h48va.

Ren Xin. "1996: A Year of Diplomatic Feats for China." *Beijing Review* (January 6–12, 1997): 9–13.

———. "'China Threat': Theory Untenable." *Beijing Review* 39, no. 6 (February 5, 1996): 10–11.

Ren Yujun. "US, Indian Relations Warm up Further." *Renmin Ribao*, May 21, 2001, FBIS-CHI-2001-0521, WNC: 0GDSGXI00AH5ZF.

Ren Zhongping. "Zaigan Yige Ershi Nian! Lun Woguo Gaige Fazhan De Guanjian Shiqi" [Work hard for another twenty years! On a critical period in our country's reform and development]. *Renmin Ribao*, July 12, 2004, p. 1, http://www.people.com.cn/GB/paper464/12439/1118713.html.

"Renmin Ribao Says Taiwan's Annette Lu 'Lunatic Advocate.'" *Xinhua*, April 9, 2000, FBIS-CHI-2000-0409, WNC: 0FSUUCI008K6DB.

Report to Congress of the U.S.-China Economic and Security Review Commission, June 2004, http://www.uscc.gov/researchreports/2004/04annual_report.PDF.

"Revised Weights for the World Economic Outlook; Annex IV." *World Economic Outlook*, May 1993, LexisNexis.

"Riben Zhanji Yao Feiyue Taipingyang Canjia Meiguo Junshi Yanxi" [Japanese warplanes to fly across the Pacific to participate in U.S. military exercises]. *Guofang Bao*, May 13, 2003, p. 1, http://www.pladaily.com.cn/gb/defence/2003/05/13/20030513017009_gjjs.html.

Rice, Condoleezza. "Campaign 2000—Promoting the National Interest." *Foreign Affairs* 79, no. 1 (January–February 2000): 45–62.

Richardson, Michael. "China's Push for Sea Control Angers ASEAN." *The Australian*, July 23 1996, p. 6.

Ripsman, Norrin M., and Jean-Marc F. Blanchard. "Commercial Liberalism under

Fire: Evidence from 1914 and 1936." *Security Studies* 6, no. 2 (Winter 1996–97): 4–50.

"RMRB Article Warns Japan against 'Hurting' China, Ties with History, Taiwan." *Renmin Ribao*, September 7, 2001, FBIS-CHI-2001-0910, WNC: 0GJJW1M03D7YVW.

Roach, Stephen. "The Hypocrisy of Bashing China." *Financial Times*, August 6, 2003, p. 17.

Robinson, Thomas W. "Chinese Foreign Policy from the 1940s to the 1990s." In *Chinese Foreign Policy: Theory and Practice*, ed. Thomas W. Robinson and David Shambaugh, 555–602. Oxford: Oxford University Press, 1994.

Rohwer, Jim. "Rapid Growth Could Make China World's Largest Economy by 2012." *South China Morning Post*, November 28, 1992, p. 1, LexisNexis.

"ROK's Kim: Partnership with PRC Helps Peace, Stability." *Xinhua*, November 12, 1998, FBIS-CHI-98-316, WNC: 0F2DQAO03YOV4W.

Romberg, Alan D. *Rein in at the Brink of the Precipice: American Policy toward Taiwan and U.S.-PRC Relations*. Washington, DC: Henry L. Stimson Center, 2003.

Rosecrance, Richard N. "Bipolarity, Multipolarity, and the Future." In *International Politics and Foreign Policy*, ed. James N. Rosenau, 325–35. New York: Free Press, 1969.

———. *The Rise of the Trading State: Commerce and Conquest in the Modern World*. New York: Basic Books, 1985.

Rosecrance, Richard, and Arthur A. Stein, eds. *The Domestic Bases of Grand Strategy*. Ithaca, NY: Cornell University Press, 1993.

Ross, Robert S. "The 1995–96 Taiwan Strait Confrontation: Coercion, Credibility, and the Use of Force." *International Security* 25, no. 2 (Fall 2000): 87–123.

———. "The Geography of the Peace." *International Security* 23, no. 81 (Spring 1999): 81–118.

———. "Navigating the Taiwan Strait: Deterrence, Escalation Dominance, and U.S.-China Relations." *International Security* 27, no. 2 (Fall 2002): 48–85.

———. *Negotiating Cooperation: The United States and China, 1969–1989*. Stanford, CA: Stanford University Press, 1995.

"Roundup: China Becoming Active Force in Multilateral Cooperation." *Xinhua*, January 2, 1997, FBIS-CHI-97-001.

Roy, Denny. "Hegemon on the Horizon? China's Threat to East Asian Security." *International Security* 19, no. 1 (Summer 1994): 149–68.

Rozman, Gilbert. "Sino-Russian Relations in the 1990s: A Balance Sheet." *Post-Soviet Affairs* 14, no. 2 (April–June 1998): 93–113.

Ruan Zongze. "Through Diplomatic Efforts, China Is Now Putting up a Platform for Its Own Peaceful Rise." *Liaowang*, no. 50 (December 15, 2003): 14–16, FBIS-CHI-2004-0203, WNC: ohso8udo1i4a6u.

Ruggie, John Gerard. "Multilateralism: The Anatomy of an Institution." In *Multilateralism Matters*, ed. John Gerard Ruggie, 3–36. New York: Columbia University Press, 1993.

"Russia and Israel to Supply Airborne Radar to China." *BBC Summary of World Broadcasts*, May 20, 1997, LexisNexis.

"Russia Offers Its Jetfighters to Indonesia." *UPI*, June 9, 1997, CNC.

"Russian-Chinese Military-Technical Cooperation Background." *Itar-Tass (Moscow)*, April 22, 1997, LexisNexis.

Sa Benwang. "Woguo Anquan De Bianhua Ji Xin De Pubian Anquanguan De Zhu-yao Tezheng" [The change in our country's security and the main features of the new concept of universal security]. *Shijie Jingji yu Zhengzhi Luntan*, no. 1 (2000): 50–52.

Schelling, Thomas C. *Arms and Influence.* New Haven, CT: Yale University Press, 1966.

———. *The Strategy of Conflict.* New York: Oxford University Press, 1960.

Schrader, Esther. "U.S. to Realign Troops in Asia." *Los Angeles Times*, May 30, 2003, p. A2.

Schwartz, Benjamin I. *Chinese Communism and the Rise of Mao.* New York: Harper and Row, 1967.

Schweller, Randall L. "Bandwagoning for Profit: Bringing the Revisionist State Back In." *International Security* 19, no. 1 (Summer 1994): 72–107.

"SDF to Deploy F-2 Fighter Jets by 2000." *Daily Yomiuri*, May 30, 1998, p. 2, Lexis-Nexis.

"SE Asians Arming up to Protect Their Resources." *Reuters*, January 29, 1996, CNC.

Segal, Gerald. "China Takes on Pacific Asia." In *Jane's Defence '96 The World in Conflict*, ed. Mark Stenhouse, 67–68. Alexandria, Va: Jane's Information Group, 1996.

———. "East Asia and the 'Constrainment' of China." *International Security* 20, no. 4 (Spring 1996): 107–35.

———. "The Taiwanese Crisis: What Next?" *Jane's Intelligence Review* 8, no. 6 (June 1996): 269–70.

"Select Committee on U.S. National Security and Military/Commercial Concerns with the People's Republic of China." House Report 105–851, Submitted by Mr. Cox of California, Chairman, June 14, 1999, http://www.gpo.gov/congress/house/hr105851-html/index.html.

Shambaugh, David. "China's Commander-in-Chief: Jiang Zemin and the PLA." In *Chinese Military Modernization*, ed. C. Dennison Lane, Mark Weisenbloom, and Dimon Liu, 209–45. New York: Kegan Paul International, 1996.

———. "China's International Relations Think Tanks: Evolving Structure and Process," *China Quarterly*, no. 171 (September 2002), pp. 575–96.

———. "China's Military in Transition: Politics, Professionalism, Procurement and Power Projection." *China Quarterly*, no. 146 (June 1996): 265–98.

———. "Containment or Engagement of China: Calculating Beijing's Responses." *International Security* 20, no. 4 (Fall 1996): 180–209.

———. "Growing Strong: China's Challenge to Asian Security." *Survival* 36, no. 2 (Summer 1994): 43–59.

———. "Lifting the China Arms Ban Is Only Symbolic." *Financial Times*, March 5, 2004, p. 19, LexisNexis.

———. *Modernizing China's Military: Progress, Problems, and Prospects.* Berkeley: University of California Press, 2002.

———. "The United States and China: A New Cold War?" *Current History* 94, no. 593 (September 1995): 241–47.

Sharon, Adam. "US Panel Slams Israeli Weapons Sales to China." *Jerusalem Post*, June 16, 2004, p. 4, LexisNexis.

Shi Nangen. "1997: A Fruitful Year in China's Multi-Dimensional Diplomacy." *Beijing Review* 41, no. 7 (February 16–22, 1998): 6–8, FBIS-CHI-98-053.

Shi Yinhong. "Beijing's Lack of Sufficient Deterrence to Taiwan Leaves a Major Danger." *Ta Kung Pao*, June 23, 2004, p. A19, FBIS-CHI-2004-0623, WNC: ohzv8zoo4otrvv.

Si Jiuyue and Huang Yong. "Zhu Rongji Meets German Chancellor, Addresses Industry-Trade Council." *Xinhua*, June 30, 2000, FBIS-CHI-2000-0630, WNC: oFX4UV4ooHYC1S.

Sieff, Martin. "Commentary: Bush's India-China Switch." *United Press International*, October 20, 2001.

"Singapore's Lee Warns of Growing Power of China." *Reuters*, February 24, 1996, CNC.

"Sino-British Ties Grow Healthy: FM." *People's Daily Online*, October 28, 2004, http://english.peopledaily.com.cn/200410/28/eng20041028_161848.html.

"Sino-U.S. Military Exchanges Resume Gradually." *Hong Kong Wen Wei Po*, November 4, 2000, FBIS-CHI-2000-1104, WNC: oG3LYEXo15SLHX.

Sisci, Francesco. "Neighbours Push for Better Ties with Russia—China: Military Transfers Get Boost after Talks." *Straits Times (Singapore)*, November 4, 2000, LexisNexis.

"Sixth China-EU Summit Issues Joint Press Statement." *Xinhua*, October 30, 2003, FBIS-CHI-2003-1030, WNC: ohnmiv6oos2hxc.

Slevin, Peer. "China Could Not Easily Overwhelm Taiwan, Analysts Agree." *Philadelphia Inquirer*, February 16, 1996, p. A4.

Snyder, Charles. "Today's Speech Will Keep the US Satisfied: Diplomat." *Taipei Times*, May 20, 2004, FBIS-CHI-2004-0520, WNC: ohy2k55o11s9di.

Snyder, Glenn. "The Security Dilemma in Alliance Politics." *World Politics* 36, no. 4 (July 1984): 461–95.

Soh, Felix. "US Warns against Restrictions in South China Sea, Block Press Tour to Spratlys." *Straits Times (Singapore)*, May 12, 1995, p. 1.

"'Source' Says PRC to Pressure US over Taiwan Issue." *Agence France-Presse*, August 14, 1999, FBIS-CHI-1999-0814.

"Southeast Asia Nuclear-Weapon-Free Zone Treaty (Treaty of Bangkok)." Inventory of International Nonproliferation Organizations and Regimes, September 10, 2003, Center for Nonproliferation Studies, Monterey Institute of International Studies, http://cns.miis.edu/pubs/inven/pdfs/seanwfz.pdf.

Sparks, Justin. "US Fear over Czech Radar." *Sunday Times (London)*, May 16, 2004, LexisNexis.

"Spokesmen for CPC Central Committee's Taiwan Work Office and State Council's Taiwan Affairs Office Issue Statement on Annette Lu's 'Taiwan Independent' Remarks." *Xinhua*, April 7, 2000, FBIS-CHI-2000-0407, WNC: oFSUUC3ooRZ654.

"Stable RMB Exchange Rate Benefits World Economy: Premier Wen." *People's Daily Online*, August 7, 2003, http://english.peopledaily.com.cn/200308/05/eng20030805_121752.shtml.

Starr, Barbara. "China Could 'Overwhelm' Regional Missile Shield." *Jane's Defence Weekly* 27, no. 16 (April 23, 1997): 16, LexisNexis.

"Strategic Opportunities: This Is the Fourth Opportunity in Modern History." *Wen Wei Po*, March 13, 2003, FBIS-CHI-2003-0313, WNC: ohbwldyo201wth.

Struck, Doug. "Asian Allies See Hazards Ahead; Bush Plan Raises Sensitive Defense Issues for Japan, S. Korea." *Washington Post*, May 3, 2001, p. A16.

Su Huimin. "View of a 'China Threat' Groundless." *Beijing Review* 36, no. 21 (May 24, 1993): 10–11.

Suetsugu, Tetsuya. "Taiwan's Chen Sworn in President Vows Not to Declare Independence." *Yomiuri Shimbun*, May 21, 2000, p. 1, LexisNexis.

Sui, Cindy. "More on US Spy Plane Crew Leaves China after 12 Days in Captivity." *AFP*, April 12, 2001, FBIS-CHI-2001-0412, WNC: 0GBQE5F0066AUP.

Sun Baoshan. "Shilun Lengzhanhou Guoji Guanxizhong De Huoban Guanxi" [Preliminary discussion of partnerships in post–Cold War international relations]. *Taipingyang Xuebao*, no. 2 (1999): 84–90.

Sun Dongmin. "'Emergencies Legislation' Is Legislation That Serves War Preparation." *Renmin Ribao*, May 20, 2003, FBIS-CHI-2003-0520, WNC: 0hfjrt002n3q5c.

Sun Jianshe. "Shiji Zhijiao Dui Woguo Anquan Huanjing De Sikao" [Reflections on our country's security environment at the turn of the century]. *Shijie Jingji yu Zhengzhi Luntan*, no. 6 (1999): 19–22.

"Sun Yuxi Says, the Momentum of Development of Sino-Indian Relations Is Good." *Xinwenshe*, January 10, 2002, FBIS-CHI-2002-0110, WNC: 0GPS12W02NXK0W.

Sutter, Robert. "China's Peaceful Rise and U.S. Interests in Asia—Status and Outlook." *PacNet*, June 24, 2004, http://www.csis.org/pacfor/pac0427.pdf.

Swaine, Michael D. "Chinese Decision-Making Regarding Taiwan, 1979–2000." In *The Making of Chinese Foreign and Security Policy in the Era of Reform*, ed. David M. Lampton, 289–336. Stanford, CA: Stanford University Press, 2001.

———. "Don't Demonize China; Rhetoric about Its Military Might Doesn't Reflect Reality." *Washington Post*, May 18, 1997, p. C1, LexisNexis.

———. "The PLA in China's National Security Policy: Leaderships, Structures, Processes." *China Quarterly*, no. 146 (June 1996): 360–93.

———. "Trouble in Taiwan." *Foreign Affairs* 83, no. 2 (March–April 2004): 39–49.

Swaine, Michael D., and Ashley J. Tellis. *Interpreting China's Grand Strategy: Past, Present, and Future.* Santa Monica, CA: RAND, 2000.

"Taiwan to Take Delivery of Five More U.S. F-16s." *Deutsche Presse-Agentur*, May 15, 1997, LexisNexis.

"Taiwan's Chen Promises to Hold 'Security' Referendum on Election Day." *Agence France-Presse*, November 29, 2003, http://www.taiwansecurity.org/AFP/2003/AFP-291103.htm.

"Taiwanese Leader 'Man of Bad Faith.'" *South China Morning Post*, May 25, 2004, p.1, LexisNexis.

Tan Guoqi. "Li Peng Meets French Delegation." *Xinhua*, December 18, 2000, FBIS-CHI-2000-1218, WNC: 0G5X7IL00G5W7I.

Tang Guanghui. "Behind the Warming of Australian-U.S. Relations." *Beijing Shijie Zhishi*, October 16, 1996, pp. 19–21, FBIS-CHI-97-021.

"Tang Jiaxuan Attends and Speaks at China-ASEAN Foreign Ministerial Dialog Meeting." *Xinhua Domestic Service*, August 1, 2002, FBIS-EAS-2002-0801, WNC: 0H07T6C04EN0Z4.

"Tang Jiaxuan Meets with Brazilian Foreign Minister." *Xinhua*, September 21, 1998, FBIS-CHI-98-264, WNC: 0EZUPWA00O315E.

"Tang Jiaxuan Supports Nuclear-Free Southeast Asia." *Agence France-Presse*, July 28, 1999, FBIS-CHI-1999-0728, WNC: 0FFNE2V03XJLMP.

"Tang Jiaxuan Tells Powell PRC Wants 'Constructive,' 'Cooperative' Ties with U.S." *Xinhua*, June 28, 2001, FBIS-CHI-2001-0628, WNC: 0GFPD6K010MN52.

Tang Tianri. "Relations between Major Powers Are Being Readjusted." *Xinhua*, December 15, 1997, FBIS-CHI-97-351, WNC: 0ELGR5E04DSN21.

"Tang, Albright Say Sino-US Ties Can Move Forward; Discuss PNTR, Taiwan, NMD." *Xinhua*, June 22, 2000, FBIS-CHI-2000-0622, WNC: 0FWTVOP0441OIA.

Tao Deyan and Zhang Binyang. "Zhuanjia Zonglun Zhongguo Heping Jueqi Jinglue" [Experts discuss China's peaceful rise strategy]. *Xinhuanet*, April 7, 2004, http://news.xinhuanet.com/herald/2004-04/07/content_1406137.htm.

Tao Guangxiong, Liu Jingshi, and Wang Xiaohui. "Further on Zhu Rongji News Conference at Tokyo Press Club." *Zhongguo Xinwen She*, October 16, 2000, FBIS-CHI-2000-1016, WNC: 0G2KWI0040IW1U.

Tao Wenzhao. "China's Position Towards the Korean Peninsula." Paper presented at the ASEM 2000 People's Forum, Seoul, Korea, October 17–20, 2000.

———. "A Foreign Policy Debate in China after the Tragic Bombing of the Chinese Embassy in Belgrade." Institute of American Studies, Chinese Academy of Social Sciences, Beijing, China, n.d.

Tellis, Ashley J. *India's Emerging Nuclear Posture: Between Recessed Deterrent and Ready Arsenal*. Santa Monica, CA: Rand, 2001.

Teng Xiaodong. "Dialogue on 1996 International Situation: China in the United Nations." *Jiefangjun Bao*, December 26, 1996, p. 5, FBIS.

Teo, Larry. "ASEAN Doesn't Want Taipei to Destabilise Region." *Straits Times (Singapore)*, June 22, 2004, LexisNexis.

"Testimony before the House International Relations Committee Subcommittee on Asia and the Pacific, by Admiral Richard C. Macke, U.S. Navy Commander in Chief, United States Pacific Command." *Federal News Service*, June 27, 1995, Federal Information Systems Corporation, LexisNexis.

"Text of China-UK Joint Statement on Strategic Partnership." *BBC Monitoring Asia Pacific*, May 10, 2004, http://health.mappibiz.com/mpelembe/China-UK.html.

"Text of Chinese Foreign Minister's Speech to ASEAN," July 31, 2000, BBC Summary of World Broadcasts, LexisNexis.

"Text of President Clinton's Address about China." CNN transcript 406-2, May 26, 1994, LexisNexis.

"The Sanctity of Missile Secrets." *New York Times*, April 15, 1998, p. A24, LexisNexis.

Tong Ying. "PRC Expert Views U.S. Elections, Explains Why Beijing Feels Relieved." *Hong Kong Wen Wei Po*, November 10, 2000, FBIS-CHI-2000-1109, WNC: 0G3YXSZ01ROSQY.

Torode, Greg. "Philippines Offered US Jets; Manila Warns over Continued Chinese Construction Work on Mischief Reef." *South China Morning Post*, August 2, 1995.

Tow, William T. "China and the International Strategic System." In *Chinese Foreign Policy: Theory and Practice*, ed. Thomas W. Robinson and David Shambaugh, 115–57. Oxford: Oxford University Press, 1994.

"Triumph of Pragmatism." *The Hindu*, June 25, 2003, FBIS-CHI-2003-0625, WNC: 0hh39who1sgwjd.

"Tulao De Wudao" [Futile misdirection]. *Renmin Ribao*, January 22, 1997, http://www.snweb.com/gb/people_daily/gbrm.htm.

Tyler, Patrick E. "As China Threatens Taiwan, It Makes Sure U.S. Listens." *New York Times*, January 24, 1996, p. A3.

————. "Beijing Steps up Military Pressure on Taiwan Leader." *New York Times,* March 7, 1996, pp. A1, A10.

————. *A Great Wall: Six Presidents and China—an Investigative History.* New York: Public Affairs, 1999.

————. "In China's Outlands, Poorest Grow Poorer." *New York Times,* October 26, 1996, p. A1, LexisNexis.

————. "Shadow over Asia: A Special Report; China's Military Stumbles Even as Its Power Grows." *New York Times,* December 3, 1996, p. A1.

Unger, Jonathan, ed. *Chinese Nationalism.* Armonk, NY: M. E. Sharpe,1996.

"The United States and Japan: Advancing toward a Mature Partnership." In *Institute for National Strategic Studies: Special Report.* Washington, DC: National Defense University, 2000.

The United States Security Strategy for the East Asia-Pacific Region. Washington, DC: Office of International Security Affairs, 1995.

The United States Security Strategy for the East Asia-Pacific Region. Washington, DC: Office of International Security Affairs, 1998. Reprinted at http://www.defenselink. mil/pubs/easr98/easr98.pdf.

"United States to Retain Strong Presence in Pacific: Christopher." *Agence France-Presse,* July 23, 1996, LexisNexis.

"U.S. Forces Welcome in South China Sea." *UPI,* May 20, 1997, CNC.

"U.S. Report Discusses China Weapons Upgrades." *Reuters,* October 11, 2000.

"U.S. Report Projects China's Economic Rise in 2010." *Xinhua,* January 12, 1988, LexisNexis.

"US Vice President Meets with Visiting Chinese FM." *People's Daily Online,* September 21, 2001, http://english.peopledaily.com.cn/200109/21/eng20010921_80740. html.

"U.S., China Steer Clear of Collision." *Australian Financial Review,* June 6, 2001, p. 8, LexisNexis.

Valencia, Mark J. *China and the South China Sea Disputes,* Adelphi Paper 298. London: International Institute for Strategic Studies, October 1995.

Van Evera, Steven. "Primed for Peace: Europe after the Cold War." *International Security* 15, no. 3 (Winter 1990–91): 7–57.

————. "Why Europe Matters, Why the Third World Doesn't: American Grand Strategy after the Cold War." *Journal of Strategic Studies* 13, no. 2 (June 1990): 1–51.

"Vietnam, China in Dispute over Offshore Drilling." *Reuters,* March 17, 1997, CNC.

Waldron, Arthur. "Statement of Dr. Arthur Waldron." *House Armed Services Committee,* June 21, 2000, http://www.house.gov/hasc/testimony/106thcongress/00-06-21waldron.html.

Walt, Stephen M. "Alliance Formation and the Balance of World Power." *International Security* 9, no. 4 (Spring 1985): 3–43.

————. *The Origins of Alliances.* Ithaca, NY: Cornell University Press, 1988.

Waltz, Kenneth N. "The Emerging Structure of International Politics." *International Security* 18, no. 2 (Fall 1993): 44–79.

————. "International Politics Is Not Foreign Policy." *Security Studies* 6, no. 1 (Autumn 1996): 54–57.

————. "International Structure, National Force, and the Balance of World Power."

In *International Politics and Foreign Policy*, ed. James N. Rosenau, 304–14. New York: Free Press, 1969.

———. *Man, the State, and War: A Theoretical Analysis*. New York: Columbia University Press, 1959.

———. "The Myth of National Interdependence." In *The International Corporation*, ed. Charles P. Kindleberger, 205–23. Cambridge, MA: MIT Press, 1970.

———. "Nuclear Myths and Political Realities." *American Political Science Review* 84, no. 3 (September 1990): 731–45.

———. *Theory of International Politics*. Menlo Park, CA: Addison-Wesley, 1979.

Wang Dajun, Zhang Haibo, and Wang Yan. "Zhu, Mori Stress Friendly Cooperation at Banquet in Honor of Zhu Rongji." *Xinhua*, October 13, 2000, FBIS-CHI-2000-1013, WNC: 0G2IY8H036KGXS.

Wang Jianwei. "China's Policy Towards Territorial Disputes in the South China Sea." Paper presented at the 94th Annual Meeting of American Political Science Association, Boston, September 3–6, 1998.

Wang Jisi. "Shiji Zhi Jiao De Zhongmei Guanxi" [Sino-American relations at the turn of the century]. *Renmin Ribao*, March 1, 1997, http://www.snweb.com/gb/people_daily/gbrm.htm.

Wang Sheng. "'Taoguang Yanghui' Bu Shi Quan Yi Zhi Ji" ["Concealing one's strength and biding one's time" is not a stopgap]. *Huanqiu Shibao* [Global times], August 17, 2001, http://www.peopledaily.com.cn/GB/paper68/4027/31430/index.html.

Wang Wei and Cai Yifeng. "'Heping Jueqi' Yu 'Heping Tongyi'" ["Peaceful rise" and "peaceful unification"]. *Haixia Shengwang*, April 8, 2004.

Wang Weixing. "The United States and China Start a Quasi-Military Alliance." *Shijie Zhishi*, July 1, 2002, pp. 10–12.

Wang Xiaomei. "Japan Is Advancing Step by Step to Becoming a Military Power." *Guofang Bao*, July 1, 2003, p. 2, FBIS Document ID: CPP20030701000056.

Wang Xingqiao. "A Positive Step Taken by the European Union to Promote Relations with China." *Xinhua*, July 10, 1998, FBIS-CHI-98-191, WNC: 0EW1NOH01FUZ64.

Wang Yichao and Wang Jian. "U.S. Trade Representative Praises China's Economic Achievements." *Zhongguo Xinwen She*, June 7, 2001, FBIS-CHI-2001-0607, WNC: 0GEVDOK0200BGY.

Wang Yiwei. "The Dimensions of China's Peaceful Rise." *Asia Times*, May 14, 2004, http://taiwansecurity.org/News/2004/AT-140504.htm.

———. "Dui Tai Junshi Douzheng Dui Shijie Zhanlüe Geju De Yingxiang Chutan" [A preliminary exploration of the effects on the international strategic situation of military action against Taiwan]. *Shijie Jingji yu Zhengzhi Luntan*, no. 6 (1999): 27–29.

Wang, Fei-ling. "Ignorance, Arrogance, and Radical Nationalism: A Review of China Can Say No." *Journal of Contemporary China* 6, no. 14 (March 1997): 161–65.

Wang, Shaoguang. "Estimating China's Defence Expenditure: Some Evidence from Chinese Sources." *China Quarterly*, no. 147 (September 1996): 889–911.

Webster, Philip, Roland Watson, and Charles Bremner. "Britain Aims to Lift Arms Ban on China." *Times (London)*, June 1, 2004, LexisNexis.

Wei Zhengyan. "China's Diplomacy in 1993." *Beijing Review* 37, no. 3 (January 17, 1994): 10–15.

Weir, Fred. "Putin Tries Big Shift in Military Strategy." *Christian Science Monitor*, August 2, 2000, p. 1.

Weisman, Steven R. "North Korea Seen as Ready to Agree to Wider Meetings." *New York Times*, August 1, 2003, p. A1, LexisNexis.

Wen Jiabao. "Turning Your Eyes to China." Speech by premier of the PRC's State Council delivered at Harvard University, December 12, 2003, http://www.chinaembassy.se/eng/60242.html.

"Wen Wei Po Views Results of Jiang Zemin-Bush Talks." *Wen Wei Po*, October 20, 2001, FBIS-CHI-2001-1020, WNC: 0GLM6UC03FNL38.

"White Paper Airs Concern on China Military Buildup." *Daily Yomiuri*, July 20, 1996, p. 1, LexisNexis.

"White Paper—China: Arms Control and Disarmament." *Xinhua News Agency*, November 16, 1995, LexisNexis.

Whiting, Allen S. "ASEAN Eyes China: The Security Dimension." *Asian Survey* 37, no. 4 (April 1997): 299–322.

———. "Chinese Nationalism and Foreign Policy after Deng." *China Quarterly*, no. 142 (June 1995): 295–316.

"Why America Always Picks at China?" *People's Daily Online*, July 26, 2004, http://english.peopledaily.com.cn/200407/26/eng20040726_150777.html.

Williams, Brian. "Japan Sees China as Growing Military Challenge." *Reuters*, July 19, 1996, CNC.

Williamson, D. G. *Bismarck and Germany, 1862–1890*. New York: Longman, 1986.

"Wo Caijun Dashi Zai Lianda Yiwei Qiangdiao, Ying Fangzhi Ba Caijun Mubiao Yinxiang Fazhanzhong Guojia" [Our disarmament ambassador at the General Assembly's first session emphasizes, [we] should guard against making the developing countries the target of disarmament]. *Renmin Ribao*, October 16, 1997, http://www.snweb.com/gb/people_daily/gbrm.htm.

"Wo Daibiao Tan Junshi Touming Wenti, Chanshu Kongzhi Xiao Wuqi Wenti Lichang" [Our representative discusses the question of military transparency, sets forth our stance on controlling small arms]. *Renmin Ribao*, November 18, 1997, http://www.snweb.com/gb/people_daily/gbrm.htm.

"Wo Dashi Zai Lianheguo Caijun Weiyuanhui Zhichu, Jianli Wuhequ Youli Heping" [Our ambassador at the UN Conference on Disarmament points out, establishing nuclear-free zones is good for peace]. *Renmin Ribao*, April 10, 1998, http://www.snweb.com/gb/people_daily/gbrm.htm.

Wohlforth, William C. *The Elusive Balance*. Ithaca, NY: Cornell University Press, 1993.

———. "The Perception of Power: Russia in the Pre-1914 Balance." *World Politics* 39, no. 3 (April 1987): 353–81.

———. "The Stability of a Unipolar World." *International Security* 24, no. 1 (Summer 1999): 5–41.

Wohlforth, William C., and Stephen G. Brooks. "American Primacy in Perspective." *Foreign Affairs* 81, no. 4 (July–August 2002): 20–26.

Wolf, Jim. "China Aides Gave U.S. Nuclear Warning, Official Says." *Reuters*, March 17, 1996, CNC.

———. "U.S. Navy Says China Rehearsed Taiwan Invasion." *Reuters*, November 11, 1996, CNC.

Wortzell, Larry M., ed. *China's Military Modernization*. New York: Greenwood Press, 1988.

"Wrap-Up: Jiang Zemin Meets US National Security Adviser." *Xinhua*, March 30, 2000, FBIS-CHI-2000-0330, WNC: 0FSAFBY03AQ1ZF.

Wu Liming. "Hu Jintao Meets with EU Leaders." *Xinhua*, October 30, 2003, FBIS-CHI-2003-1030, WNC: 0hns38a03jitci.

Wu Qiang and Qian Xuemei. "Zhongguo Yu Zhongdong De Nengyuan Hezuo" [Energy cooperation between China and the Middle East]. *Zhanlüe yu Guanli*, no. 2 (1999): 49–52.

Wu Songzhi and Yi Shuguang. "Gongzhu Mulin Youhao Hezuo Guanxi" [Building together cooperative good neighborly relations]. *Renmin Ribao*, April 22, 1997.

Wu, Sofia. "DPP Whip Says Chen Aide's Washington Visit to Help Boost Taiwan–US Ties." *Central News Agency*, April 26, 2004, FBIS-CHI-2004-0426, WNC: 0hwtzu600yd6ci.

———. "Foreign Minister Says Prolonged War in Iraq Could Affect Taiwan's Interests." *Central News Agency*, March 24, 2003, FBIS-CHI-2003-0324, WNC: 0hcb67z008m9xu.

———. "Taiwan President-Elect Meets U.S. Delegation." *Central News Agency*, May 19, 2000, FBIS-CHI-2000-0519, WNC: 0FUYQ6E0388IJB.

Wu Xinbo. "The Promise and Limitations of a Sino-U.S. Partnership." *The Washington Quarterly* 27, no. 4 (Autumn 2004): 115–26.

WuDunn, Sheryl. "Japanese Move to Broaden Military Links to the U.S." *New York Times*, April 29, 1998, p. A6, LexisNexis.

Xia Liping. "Some Views on Multilateral Security Cooperation in Northeast Asia." *Xiandai Guoji Guanxi*, December 20, 1996, 12–15, FBIS-CHI-97-074.

Xiao Feng. "Dui Guoji Xingshizhong Jige Redian Wenti De Kanfa" [Perspective on several hot issues in the international situation]. *Xiandai Guoji Guanxi*, no. 12 (1999): 1–3.

Xie Meihua. "PRC Ambassador for Disarmament Speaks at UN Session." *Xinhua*, April 14, 1999, FBIS-CHI-1999-0414, WNC: 0FA961G00OLAT4.

Xie Wenqing. "U.S.-Soviet Military Contention in the Asia–Pacific Region." *Shijie Zhishi*, March 16, 1987, FBIS China Daily Report, March 31, 1987, p. A2.

Xing Hua. "China's Successful Diplomacy." *Beijing Review* 35, no. 19 (May 11, 1992): 12–16.

"Xinhua 'Wrap-up': Jiang Zemin Meets US Envoy Holbrooke." *Xinhua*, March 21, 2000, FBIS-CHI-2000-0321, WNC: 0FRTWJ202C4U02.

Xu Hongzhi and Huang Qing. "Advancing toward Multipolarization amid Turbulence." *Renmin Ribao*, December 16, 1999, p. 7, FBIS-CHI-2000-0116, WNC: 0FOL4SS00VVGBV.

Xue Longgen. "Zhengzai Shenhua Fazhan De Zhongfa Quanmian Huoban Guanxi" [The deepening and developing Sino-French comprehensive partnership.] *Shijie Jingji yu Zhengzhi Luntan*, no. 5 (1999): 25–27.

Yan Xuetong. "Dui Zhongguo Anquan Huanjing De Fenxi Yu Sikao" [Analysis of and reflections on China's security environment]. *Shijie Jingji yu Zhengzhi*, no. 2 (2000): 5–10.

———. *Zhongguo Guojia Liyi Fenxi* [Analysis of China's national interest]. Tianjin: Tianjin Renmin Chubanshe, 1997.

Yang Ge. "China's Rise: Threat or Not? (International Community's Fears of Chinese Supremacy." *Beijing Review* 38, no. 5 (January 30, 1995): 23–25.

Ye Zicheng. "Carrying Forward, Developing and Pondering Deng Xiaoping's Foreign Policy Thinking in the New Situation." *Shijie Jingji yu Zhengzhi,* 11 (November 2004): 8–14, FBIS document CPP20041124000200.

———. "Zhongguo Shixing Daguo Waijiao Zhanlüe Shizai Bixing" [The imperative for China to implement a great power diplomatic strategy]. *Shijie Jingji yu Zhengzhi* [World economics and politics], no. 1 (2000): 5–10.

"Yici Yiyi Zhongda Yingxiang Shenyuan De Fangwen–Zhuhe Jiang Zhuxi Fang E Yuanman Chenggong" [A trip of great significance and far-reaching influence—Congratulations on President Jiang's completely successful Russian visit]. *Renmin Ribao,* April 27, 1997.

Yu Donghui. "The Spokesman of the Chinese Embassy in the United States Says Sino–US Relations Further Developed in the First Half of This Year." *Zhongguo Xinwen She,* July 23, 2003, FBIS-CHI-2003-0723, WNC: 0hij3tx047t1cx.

Yu Shuang. "A Look at Japan's Military Expansion from Its Attempt to Upgrade Self Defense Agency." *Jiefangjun Bao,* August 25, 2002, p. 4, FBIS-CHI-2002-0826, WNC: 0H20PZP03K2AN5.

"Yuan Must Remain Stable, Says China's Central Bank Governor." *Agence France-Presse,* October 30, 1998, CNC.

Zaun, Todd. "Japan Almost Doubles Forecast for Economic Growth." *New York Times,* July 22, 2004, http://www.nytimes.com/2004/07/22/business/worldbusiness/22yen.html?pagewanted=all.

Zhan Xinhui, Zhou Hongyang, and Dian Zhehan. "Premier Wen Jiabao Delivers Keynote Speech at the Boao Forum." *Renminwang,* November 2, 2003, FBIS-CHI-2003-1102, WNC: 0hns39c01g4nre.

Zhang Baiyu. "Analysis of Japan's New Defense White Paper." *Renmin Ribao,* August 14, 2003, p. 3, FBIS-CHI-2003-0814, WNC: 0hjnuyjo3je2da.

Zhang Dezhen. "Qianghua Junshi Tongmeng Buhe Shidai Chaoliu" [Strengthening military alliance does not conform with trend of the times)." *Renmin Ribao,* January 31, 1997, p. 6.

Zhang Guocheng. "Hewei 'Zhoubian You Shi'?—Xie Zai Xin 'Rimei Fangwei Hezuo Fangzhen' Qiaoding Zhi Shi" [What's the meaning of "situations arising on the periphery"?—Written in the new "Japan-U.S. Joint Defense Guidelines"]. *Renmin Ribao,* September 25, 1997, p. 6.

———. "Ling Ren Guanzhu De Xin Dongxiang—Rimei Xiugai Fangwei Hezuo Fangzhen Chuxi" [A new trend catching people's attention—The emerging Japan-U.S. Revised Guidelines for Defense Cooperation]. *Renmin Ribao,* June 14, 1997.

———. "Quadripartite Talks Enter Substantive Stage." *Renmin Ribao,* January 29, 1999, p. 6, FBIS-CHI-99-030, WNC: 0F6JMO503HYFPI.

———. "Riben De Daguo Waijiao" [Japan's great power diplomacy]. *Renmin Ribao,* December 19, 1997.

Zhang Shuo. "The Shanghai Cooperation Organization Holds Its Third Summit, Issues 'Moscow Declaration.'" *Zhongguo Xinwen She,* May 29, 2003, FBIS-CHI-2003-0529, WNC: 0hfp91k01ksi69.

Zhang Wenmu. "Heshihou Nanya Xingshi Ji Zouxiang" [The situation and trends in post–nuclear test South Asia]. *Zhanlüe yu Guanli,* no. 2 (1999): 46–49.

————. "Kesuowo Zhanzheng Yu Zhongguo Xin Shiji Anquan Zhanlüe" [The Kosovo War and China's security strategy in the new century]. *Zhanlüe yu Guanli*, no. 3 (1999): 1–10.

Zhang Yifan. "From 'Playing Card' to Establishing Strategic Partnership: Special Interview with Yang Chengxu, Director of the China Institute of International Studies." *Hsin Pao*, December 25, 1997, p. 5, FBIS-CHI-97-364.

Zhang Zhenan. "British Vice Prime Minister Meets Chi Haotian." *Xinhua*, January 13, 2000, FBIS-CHI-2000-0113, WNC: 0FOJN4W01OIMXM.

Zhao Feng. "US Dept. of Defense 'Report on the Military Power of the People's Republic of China' Is a Replay of the Old 'China Threat Theory.'" *Jiefangjun Bao*, June 15, 2004, p. 5, FBIS-CHI-2004-0615, WNC: 0hzel803g7247.

Zhao Gangzhen. "Daguo Guanxi, 'Huoban Re'" [Big power relations: "Partnership fever"]. *Renmin Ribao*, April 21, 1998.

Zhao Longgeng. "Zhong'e Zhanlüe Xiezuo Huoban Guanxi Maixiang Jianshi Zhi Lu" [Strides towards strengthening the Sino-Russian strategic cooperative partnership]. *Xiandai Guoji Guanxi*, no. 5 (1999): 30–34.

Zhao, Suisheng. "Chinese Nationalism and Its International Orientations." *Political Science Quarterly* 115, no. 1 (Spring 2000): 1–33.

————. "Deng Xiaoping's Southern Tour: Elite Politics in Post-Tiananmen China." *Asian Survey* 33, no. 8 (August 1993): 739–56.

Zheng Bijian. "China's Peaceful Rise and Opportunities for the Asia-Pacific Region." Speech by Chairman Zheng Bijian of China Reform Forum at the Roundtable Meeting between Bo'ao Forum for Asia and China Reform Forum, April 24, 2004, http://www.crf.org.cn/peacefulrise/zbjspeech2.htm.

————. "New Path for China's Peaceful Rise and the Future of Asia." Speech delivered at Bo'ao Forum for Asia, November 3, 2003, http://history.boaoforum.org/english/E2003nh/dhwj/t20031103_184101.btk.

————. "The Path of Peaceful Rise—The Multiplication and Division Method of 1.3 Billion." *Ming Pao*, March 3, 2004, FBIS-CHI-2004-0303, WNC: 0hw2896007bkla.

Zheng Yongnian. *Discovering Chinese Nationalism in China: Modernization, Identity, and International Relations*. New York: Cambridge University Press, 1999.

"Zhong'e Zui Gaoji Huiwu" [Sino-Russian summit meeting]. *Renmin Ribao*, November 7, 1997.

Zhongguo de Heping Jueqi zhi Lu [China's road of peaceful rise], http://www1.china.com.cn/chinese/zhuanti/hp/530363.htm.

"Zhonghua Renmin Gongheguo He Meilijian Hezhongguo Guanyu Jianli Waijiao Guanxi De Lianhe Gongbao" [Joint communiqué on the establishment of diplomatic relations between the People's Republic of China and the United States of America]. *Ministry of Foreign Affairs of the People's Republic of China*, January 1, 1979, http://www.fmprc.gov.cn/chn/ziliao/wzzt/2350/2353/t11073.htm.

"Zhonghua Renmin Gongheguo He Meilijian Hezhongguo Lianhe Gongbao" [Joint communiqué of the United States of America and the People's Republic of China]. *China Internet Information Center*, February 28, 1972, http://www1.china.org.cn/chinese/HIAW/107316.htm.

Zhou Guiyin. "Xin Shiji De Guoji Anquan Yu Anquan Zhanlüe" [International security and security strategy in the new century]. *Shijie Jingji yu Zhengzhi Luntan*, no. 1 (2000): 69–71.

Zhu Feng. "TMD Yu Dangqian Zhongmei Guanxi" [TMD and current Sino-American relations]. *Shijie Jingji yu Zhengzhi*, no. 5 (1999): 10–16.

Zhu Qizhen. "China's Foreign Policy: Independent Policy of Peace." *Beijing Review* 34, no. 17 (April 29, 1991): 35–39.

Zhu Tingchang. "Xin Shiji Zhongguo Anquan Zhanlüe Gouxiang" [China's security concept for the new century]. *Shijie Jingji yu Zhengzhi*, no. 1 (2000): 11–15.

Zhu Yanhua. "China's Military Affairs Expert Says That Iraqi War Has Hindered the Trend Towards Multipolarization in the World." *Zhongguo Xinwen She*, March 22, 2003, FBIS-CHI-2003-0322, WNC: ohc9tds029ngq7.

Zielenziger, Michael. "Talks Fall Short for China, Japan." *Philadelphia Inquirer*, November 27, 1998, pp. A1, A4.

Index

In this index an "f" after a number indicates a separate reference on the next page, and an "ff" indicates separate references on the next two pages. A continuous discussion over two or more pages is indicated by a span of page numbers, e.g., "57–59." *Passim* is used for a cluster of references in close but not consecutive sequence.

Taiwan Strait Crises (1950s), 41n, 78

Taiwan Strait Crisis (1995–96), 7, 47, 61, 67, 73–74, 75, 79, 139n, 154, 177–80; and U.S.-Japan alliance, 108, 194; and China threat, 178–79; and Taiwan's 2000 presidential election, 180

Taiwan's military: arms purchases from U.S., 7, 66, 92; modernization of, 66; purchases from France, 66

Taliban, 184

Tang Jiaxuan, 123, 158

Tellis, Ashley J., 23n, 25n, 45n, 113n, 117n, 198n, 199n

Theater missile defense (TMD), 105, 140, 148, and Taiwan dispute, 139, 141, 146n, 157, 195; and Japan, 141, 167f, 196

Tiananmen Square incident (1989), 3, 43f, 71, 97; and sanctions imposed on China, 44–47 *passim*, 97, 116, 163

Tibet, 29, 149, 168, 172, 202n

Trachtenberg, Marc, 205n

Transitional strategy, *see* China's grand strategy after the Cold War

Treaty of Amity and Cooperation in Southeast Asia, 124, 174n

Truman, Harry S., 4

Unipolarity, 209; and China's grand strategy, 12, 22–28, *passim*, 34–40 *passim*, 77, 89, 117, 127, 131, 133, 175n, 176, 193, 200ff, 206f; and power-balancing, 88f; and Sino-American relations, 89; and missile defense, 105, 141

United Nations, 46n, 146n, 147n; Security Council, 50n, 70, 145, 184

U.S. China policy: containment, 11, 75n, 90, 104, 106n, 111, 148f, 216–19 *passim*; engagement, 11, 47, 75n, 148, 178, 217–18, 219; congagement, 11f, 218; and most-favored-nation trade status, 47, 178; and Nixon opening, 70, 79; and human rights, 76, 85, 127, 152, 159, 178, 186, 217; and George W. Bush, 148, 157, 159, 186; and China's grand strategy, 216; and con-

tingent cooperation, 218–19; and U.S. preponderance, 218f; and China's rise, 219

U.S. grand strategy: and Cold War containment, 4, 10, 19, 40n, 45n; post-Cold War-revision of, 8–11, 127, 209n; and China, 9ff, 85, 102; and military transformation, 9; and Russia, 9; and weapons of mass destruction, 9f, 214n; and Asian alliances, 102–3, 109

U.S. preponderance: China's view of, 7, 12, 127, 133, 153–54, 159, 174n, 200–201; and U.S. China policy, 8, 218f; and missile defense, 141; and U.S. military performance, 153n

U.S. Taiwan policy, 4, 5–6, 33, 76, 147n, 154, 193n; and democracy, 6–7; arms sales, 7, 92, 152n, 157f, 181, 182n; and crisis intervention, 66, 79; and Taiwan's 2000 presidential election, 156; and Taiwan's 2004 presidential election, 188–89

U.S.-Australia alliance: post-Cold War revision of, 103–5; China's concerns about, 103–5, 134; and missile defense, 104

U.S.-Japan alliance: post-Cold War revision of, 103, 105; China's concerns about, 105–9, 134, 138, 148, 164f, 214n; and guidelines for defense cooperation, 105–9, 148, 164f, 179n, 196; and Korea, 106; and China threat, 106n; and South China Sea disputes, 108

Vajpayee, Atal Bihari, 170ff

Van Evera, Steven, 89n

Vietnam, 64; U.S. war in, 41n, 78, 209; China's war in 78, 209n

Wallace, Mike, 156

Walt, Stephen M., 19n, 31n, 86n, 113n

Waltz, Kenneth N., 24n, 31n, 78n, 86n

War on terrorism, 1, 10, 121n, 197; and Sino-American relations, 145, 183f;